A CULTURAL HISTORY
OF SEXUALITY

VOLUME 2

A Cultural History of Sexuality

General Editor: Julie Peakman

Volume 1

A Cultural History of Sexuality in the Classical World
Edited by Mark Golden and Peter Toohey

Volume 2

A Cultural History of Sexuality in the Middle Ages
Edited by Ruth Evans

Volume 3

A Cultural History of Sexuality in the Renaissance
Edited by Bette Talvacchia

Volume 4

A Cultural History of Sexuality in the Enlightenment
Edited by Julie Peakman

Volume 5

A Cultural History of Sexuality in the Age of Empire
Edited by Chiara Beccalossi and Ivan Crozier

Volume 6

A Cultural History of Sexuality in the Modern Age
Edited by Gert Hekma

A CULTURAL HISTORY
OF SEXUALITY

IN THE
MIDDLE AGES

Edited by Ruth Evans

B L O O M S B U R Y
LONDON · NEW DELHI · NEW YORK · SYDNEY

Bloomsbury Academic

An imprint of Bloomsbury Publishing Plc

50 Bedford Square
London
WC1B 3DP
UK

1385 Broadway
New York
NY 10018
USA

www.bloomsbury.com

Hardback edition first published in 2011 by Berg Publishers, an imprint of
Bloomsbury Academic
Paperback edition first published by Bloomsbury Academic 2014

British Library Cataloguing-in-Publication Data
A catalogue record for this book is available from the British Library.

ISBN: HB: 978-1-84788-801-3
PB: 978-1-4725-5477-2
HB Set: 978-1-84520-702-1
PB Set: 978-1-4725-5480-2

Library of Congress Cataloging-in-Publication Data
A catalog record for this book is available from the Library of Congress.

Typeset by Apex CoVantage, LLC, Madison, WI, USA
Printed and bound in Great Britain

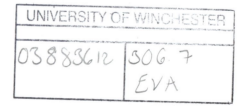

CONTENTS

PREFACE

A Cultural History of Sexuality is a six-volume series reviewing changes in sexual attitudes and behavior throughout history. Each volume follows the same basic structure and begins with an outline account of sexuality in the period under consideration. Academic experts examine major aspects of sex and sexuality under seven key headings: heterosexuality, homosexuality, sexual variations, religion and the law, medicine and disease, popular beliefs and culture, prostitution, and erotica. Readers can choose a synchronic or a diachronic approach to the material—a single volume can be read to obtain a thorough knowledge of the body in a given period, or one of the seven themes can be followed through time by reading the relevant chapters of all six volumes, providing a thematic understanding of changes and developments over the long term. The six volumes divide the history of sexuality as follows:

Volume 1: A Cultural History of Sexuality in the Classical World (800 B.C.E. to 350 C.E.)

Volume 2: A Cultural History of Sexuality in the Middle Ages (350 C.E. to 1450)

Volume 3: A Cultural History of Sexuality in the Renaissance (1450 to 1650)

Volume 4: A Cultural History of Sexuality in the Enlightenment (1650 to 1820)

Volume 5: A Cultural History of Sexuality in the Age of Empire (1820 to 1920)

Volume 6: A Cultural History of Sexuality in the Modern Age (1920 to 2000)

Julie Peakman, General Editor

SERIES ACKNOWLEDGMENTS

This series has been a long time in the making, mainly because it is not an easy task to bring together fifty-four international scholars, even when we were all willing and eager. Every one of us had other commitments—to our universities, other books, and/or to our families. I therefore appreciate those who came together to create this special project. I want to thank the editors of all the volumes; Peter Toohey and Mark Golden, Ruth Evans, Bette Talvacchia, Ivan Crozier and Chiara Beccalossi, and Gert Hekma for their sterling efforts in the face of my continual demands, and for helping to keep their contributors on track, especially when the occasional one dropped out with little warning. Huge thanks also go to all the contributors who freely committed their time and efforts. I also want to thank Tristan Palmer at Berg for all his support and Catherine Draycott from the Wellcome Trust Picture Library for making available the Wellcome images.

Julie Peakman, General Editor

ILLUSTRATIONS

CHAPTER 1

CHAPTER 3

CHAPTER 6

CHAPTER 7

CHAPTER 9

CHAPTER ONE

Introduction: What Was Sexuality in the Middle Ages?

RUTH EVANS

Sexual behavior and attitudes toward sex throughout the period 350–1450 were profoundly shaped by the beliefs of early Christians that sex was the source of original sin and that sexual continence was the road to salvation. St. Paul's letters to fledgling Christian communities around the Mediterranean in the first century C.E. did not directly condemn marriage (see 1 Cor. 7:27 and Eph. 5:22–33), but they counseled sexual purity: "It is good for a man not to touch a woman" (1 Cor. 7:1); "no fornicator … hath inheritance in the kingdom of Christ and of God" (Eph. 5:5).

The strong conviction that the Second Coming was imminent may in part explain why reproduction was not important for early Christians.[1] But this does not account for the disproportionate opprobrium directed toward women, and female sexuality in particular, that characterizes some of the early patristic writings. In *On the Appearance of Women*, the North African Christian convert Tertullian (ca. 160–ca. 225) urged recently converted women to don penitential garb in order to atone for Eve's first sin. Thundering, "You are the gateway of the devil," he advised these women that in order to achieve perfect chastity, they must "not only *not* seek to be the object of desire, but also despise the very idea of being one."[2] Tertullian's misogyny was extreme, but antifeminist attitudes ran deep, especially in clerical culture, and persisted throughout the period, though not without significant challenges.[3] But one risks endorsing the medieval stereotype by emphasizing clerical misogyny. The large number of medieval women who renounced sex in favor of lives of abstinence were not all repressing or sublimating their sexuality: they actively embraced the possibilities that virgin careers offered, including those that paradoxically may have included forms of erotic satisfaction not otherwise available to them.

Following the conversion of Constantine (313) and Emperor Theodosius's establishment of Christianity as the imperial religion (380), early Christian asceticism was somewhat tempered by the need for sexual reproduction to ensure the continuation of the state. St. Augustine of Hippo (354–430) argued in *City of God* that although celibacy was the route to spiritual perfection, marriage was a good in itself, and not just a means for preventing fornication.[4] Surprisingly, he even declared that Adam and Eve had sex in Paradise, but as a "calm act of will," not in "the turbulent heat of passion."[5] The problem for Augustine was not sex itself but lust, which arose because of sin, causing the sexual organs to defy the will.[6] In his influential account of the Fall, Adam and Eve do not immediately become aware of their nakedness, as in the biblical account in Genesis, but rather they feel "a novel disturbance in their disobedient flesh, as a punishment which answered to their own disobedience."[7] Involuntary sexual arousal thus becomes the primary distinguishing mark of humanity's sinful state.

Augustine's view that mind and body were separate entities, and that the mind or will must control the unruly body, informed medieval Christianity's view of sexual matters for most of the period. In the *Confessions* Augustine declared that "sins of self-indulgence are committed when the soul fails to govern the impulses from which it derives bodily pleasure."[8] That view is still broadly intelligible to us today. But whereas Freudian psychoanalysis sees sexuality as internal to the body and its drives, "a surging, hydraulic force that Western culture struggles to repress," Augustine saw sex as a divine punishment that needs to be mastered by the will.[9] And although Augustine regarded marriage as blessed by God and sanctioned it as a means for procreation, even sex between husband and wife was problematic. In his authoritative *Decretum* (ca. 1140) Gratian states that "coition is no sin, venial or mortal," if done for offspring or "to pay the debt," and a sin only for the man if done to guard against incontinence, "but when it is from lust or for the sake of pleasure, then the coition is a mortal sin and the man sins mortally."[10] But these orthodoxies did not go unopposed: Geoffrey Chaucer's Wife of Bath's "Prologue," with its frank refusal to see married sex as sinful, is an eloquent testimony to fourteenth-century lay protest against such strictures.[11]

Attitudes towards sexuality varied widely throughout the period. In opposition to the theologians' emphasis on chastity, some physicians believed that sex—even extramarital sex—was vital for a healthy regimen because it restored the body's humoral balance by purging accumulated "seed" (both male and female). Constantine the African, an eleventh-century medical writer and Benedictine monk, declared that "no-one who does not have intercourse will be healthy. Intercourse is truly useful and promotes health."[12] And whereas the thirteenth-century Statutes of Angers enjoined seven years' weekly self-flagellation for masturbation (an extreme punishment even within the penitential tradition), some physicians *prescribed* masturbation for men and women to prevent harmful seed retention.[13]

Medieval Christendom was not homogeneous or monolithic. The Orthodox Eastern Church (which split from the Western Church in 1054) not only preserved the institution of married clergy but also adopted a more moderate position on asceticism than the Western one: virginity was admirable, but marital sexuality was seen as tolerable and not as fraught with obsessive guilt.[14] Contact between Christian and Islamic cultures was strong: Arabic sources had a great impact on Western medical theory and practice, and on the tradition of courtly love; the French Dominican William of Adam, for example, writing circa 1318, was familiar with the phenomenon of the *mukhannath*, the effeminate cross-dresser recognized in Muslim societies.[15]

Today we think of sexuality as "an autonomous domain."[16] But in prebourgeois Western societies, "intercourse, kinship, and the family, and gender, did not form anything like a 'field' of sexuality" but rather they represented "institutions and thought patterns which we tend to view as political, economic, or social in nature, and the connections cut across our idea of sexuality as a thing, detachable from other things, and as a separate sphere of private existence."[17] As historians of sexuality have argued, our modern terms—"heterosexuality," "homosexuality," even "sexuality" itself—are late-nineteenth-century categories that cannot be blithely applied to earlier eras. They depend moreover on statistical "norms" that were unknown in premodern times.[18] The problem is not so much that the categories are unhelpful for understanding the Middle Ages, since we often need to impose modern categories in order "to achieve intelligibility,"[19] and because we need to approach the past, in James Schultz's words, "in terms that matter to us."[20] Rather, they present history as a continuum, when in reality it is full of gaps, hesitations, and discontinuities. Historians of sexuality have also tended to ignore or misrepresent the Middle Ages, either believing that medieval people were less interested in sex than we are (a view undergirded by the still-prevalent Victorian assumption that the people of the Middle Ages were "childish" or "innocent") or, conversely, caricaturing the era as one of unbridled sexual openness.

This periodization has been reinforced by Michel Foucault's influential but much-contested and misunderstood contention that in pre-nineteenth-century Western culture people performed sexual *acts* but did not believe themselves to have sexual *identities*.[21] But as more evidence emerges that sexual identity is not solely a modern phenomenon,[22] it is nevertheless important to be specific about the nature of medieval sexual identities. For example, it is doubtful that anyone in the Middle Ages would have considered his or her sexual behavior to be expressing the "truth of the self" or to be liberating him or her from repression. When Margery Kempe, a devout married woman of the merchant class living in early-fifteenth-century East Anglia, confessed that she had agreed before evensong to a sexual tryst with a man she was fond of,[23] her aim was not to liberate herself from the church's restrictions through intimate self-revelation. Rather, she saw her sexual desire as a sign of her "vnstabylnes" (unstableness): the man's offer (later retracted) was seen as a temptation to sin, and she acknowledged her temptation as a "creatur" (created being)[24] representing all sinful human creatures. Her guilt undoubtedly also derived from clerical misogyny: in portrayals of the sins, women are often represented as lustful seducers of men (fig. 1.1). But this episode, which preceded Kempe's "conversion," was nonetheless a self-defining moment.

The primary sources for the study of sexuality within this period are scarce. Much was not recorded and much evidence has undoubtedly been lost. The sources are overwhelmingly official: canon law, legal documents, and trial records. There are no medieval treatises called *On Sex*, no Kinsey Reports, no secret diaries, and very few first-person accounts that deal with sexual experiences. The penitentials catalog sexual practices in explicit anatomical detail, but we know nothing of the actual incidence of those behaviors or how the laity perceived them. The English theologian Thomas of Chobham (ca. 1160–1236) speaks of a husband pimping his wife,[25] and Bede's eighth-century *Penitential* requires seven years' penance for women who fornicate "per machina," that is, with a dildo,[26] but we do not know if these practices were common or if laypeople regarded them as serious offenses.

As Ruth Karras observes, medieval people were not incessantly bombarded with images of naked human bodies as we are today. Without mass media, sex could not be used to sell goods, pornography could not be distributed, and sexual subcultures could not flourish. There was no consumer capitalism to sexualize children in order to urge them to buy clothes or music, and no media representations of the sex lives of the rich and famous.[27] However, disabled or "eccentric" bodies were far more frequently on display than they are today and were eroticized (pace J. G. Ballard's *Crash*),[28] and even

FIGURE 1.1: Woman seduces a man at night in front of his house.
Personifications of the sins. German miscellany (ca. 1420–1430).
Wellcome Library, London.

hypersexualized, insofar as disability was linked with the sexual transgression of the parents.[29]

Despite the paucity of sources and the obscurity of the facts that we do possess, we can nevertheless reconstruct some of the cultural meanings that sexuality had in the Middle Ages. One is that the crucial distinction was not between heterosexuality and homosexuality but among forms of sexual activity: whether you were married, abstinent, or a virgin.[30]

CONIUGATI, CONTINENTES, VIRGINES: THE MARRIED, THE ABSTINENT, AND VIRGINS

As Karma Lochrie argues in chapter 2 of this volume, "the primary rubric under which sexuality in Nature is measured, at least in medieval theology, is not heterosexuality versus everything else, but abstinence versus sexual activity."[31] Chastity, not heterosexuality, was the medieval ideal, because all sexual activity carried the taint of original sin. The theologian Origen of

Alexandria (185–253) even went so far as to castrate himself; his action may have been an over-literal interpretation of Jesus's apparent approbation of those "who have made themselves eunuchs for the kingdom of heaven" (Matt. 19:12). But virginity was only counseled, not commanded. This made it more highly prized, in that it was freely chosen. In his treatise *Adversus Jovinianum* (ca. 393), written to refute the heresy of Jovinian (a monk living in Rome who declared that there was no difference between celibate and married clergy), St. Jerome declared: "Christ loves virgins more than others, because they willingly give what was not commanded them."[32] Virginity trumped even angelic chastity, according to Albert the Great (ca. 1206–1280), because of the constant battle required to overcome the corruptibility of the human flesh.[33]

Although there were some famous male virgins—Christ, St. John the Evangelist, St. Alexis—virginity and chastity were viewed as largely female concerns. In the traditional division of medieval women's "estates," virginity offers the greatest heavenly rewards. As the author of the thirteenth-century English treatise *Hali Meithhad* (*Holy Virginity*) puts it, "For wedlac haueth hire frut thrittifald in heouene; widewehad, sixtifald; meithhad with hundretfald ouergeath bathe." ("For marriage has its reward thirty-fold in heaven, widowhood sixty-fold; virginity, with a hundred-fold, surpasses both.")[34] To be a chaste wife is good, to be a chaste widow is better, but to be a virgin is best.

Men could transcend their gender identity in striving for the ideal of virginal wholeness and purity, but for a woman to achieve such an ideal she had to become, in effect, a man. According to St. Jerome, "As long as woman is for birth and children, she is different from man as body is from soul. But if she wishes to serve Christ more than the world, then she will cease to be a woman and will be called man."[35] Jerome was speaking metaphorically, yet some saints' legends tell of startling bodily transformations. When Uncumber of Wilgefortis wished to resist her impending marriage, she prayed to God and suddenly sprouted a moustache and beard. The intended groom refused to marry her, and her father had her crucified.[36] But by the late Middle Ages, virginity had come to be seen more as a mental state than as a physical one.[37]

Chastity was also important within the medieval Orthodox Eastern Church. The term for living in sexual abstinence in Church Slavonic was *celomudryj* ("full of wisdom"), which was applied not only to celibate monks and nuns, but also to married couples abstaining from sexual relations.[38] Orthodox parish priests and deacons were not required to be celibate, though marriage was not mandated.[39]

Next to the celibate or virginal elite was the married second tier. The three traditional justifications for marriage and married sex throughout the period were procreation, remedy against fornication, and payment of the so-called marriage debt. St. Paul's famous dictum, "it is better to marry than to be burnt [with desire]" (1 Cor. 7:9), assumed that sexual desire was an evil in itself, and that marriage represented the lesser of two evils. In his *Decretum* (ca. 1140), Gratian was less punitive, granting that although "it is clear that [the married] are not commanded to join together solely for the procreation of children ... marriage is not to be judged evil on that account, for what is done outside of the intention of generation is not an evil of marriage, but is forgiveable on account of the good of marriage which is threefold: Fidelity, Offspring, and Sacrament."[40] These last constituted the so-called *triplex bonum* (triple good) of marriage.

The church frowned on remarriage. Gratian grudgingly conceded that second marriages were to be allowed because they eliminated the danger of fornication,[41] but the Eastern theologian Gregory Nazianzen (329–390) declared: "The first [marriage] is law, the second is indulgence, the third is transgression, and anything beyond this is swinish."[42] But in post-Alfredian Anglo-Saxon England, at any rate, political expedience trumped the church's censure of multiple marriages: Edward the Elder married three times, Edmund twice, Edgar three times, and Æthelred twice, and Cnut abandoned Ælfgyfu, the mother of his oldest son, to marry Æthelred's widow, Emma of Normandy.[43]

Wives of the merchant class were expected to know their place, following the dominant Pauline model: "Let women be subject to their husbands, as to the Lord" (Eph. 5:22–25). This might mean providing sex on demand. The late-fourteenth-century *Mesnagier de Paris*, written by a forty-something Parisian *borgois* (burgher, townsman) to instruct his fifteen-year-old spouse in proper wifeliness, instructs her to always "have his shoes removed before a warm fire" when he returns home, and to comfort him "with other joys and pastimes, intimacies, loving caresses and secrets that I will not speak about."[44]

Marriage was often a social and economic arrangement rather than a matter of individual choice, especially among the middle classes and aristocracy. In 1478 the English gentlewoman Margaret Paston, in a letter to her eldest son, John, advised him that if he were to regain the land he sought to claim as a result of a proposed marriage, "out of respect for God do not abandon it, if you can find it in your heart to love her, and if she is such a one by whom you think you can have children. Otherwise, on my word of honour, I would rather you had never married in your life."[45] Land comes before love, and even before heirs.

But marriages were indeed also made for love. In 1469 Margaret Paston's daughter Margery Paston secretly married Richard Calle, the family's head bailiff (a servant, in other words), in defiance of both of her parents. Although Margaret tried to get the marriage annulled, the bishop of Norwich judged that the marriage vows were legally binding.[46] As Michael Sheehan argues, the consensual theory of marriage that was developed in canon law not only enabled clandestine marriage (a valid marriage being constituted by consent followed by consummation) but allowed individuals to escape the control of family.[47] But troth-plighting (engagement) could also be the grounds for acrimonious disputes. In 1418 Margaret Whitell of York enlisted her friends to compel her abusive partner, John Beaumunde, to honor the contract he had made with her. Armed with a knife and an ax, they persuaded John to make a contract *per verba de presenti* (by words of present consent), that is, an immediately binding contract, though made under duress. The marriage case that followed argued that John was bound to Margaret by virtue of a future contract followed by sexual intercourse.[48]

In Italy the age pattern of marriage was different from that in northwestern Europe. The Florentine *castato* (tax census) of 1427–1430 shows that the average age at the time of marriage was over thirty for men but below eighteen for women. One consequence of this was that before marriage men visited prostitutes and also had sex with other men.

One peculiarly medieval phenomenon is "spiritual marriage," defined as "chaste cohabitation within the context of licit marriage."[49] It was a predominantly female religious practice. St. Cecilia is the most famous legendary example; other historical examples include Mary of Oignies (ca. 1167–1213) and Bridget of Sweden (d. 1373). Christina of Markyate (ca. 1100–1155) desired chaste cohabitation but was forced to flee, like the fugitive St. Alexis.[50] Spiritual marriage represented a significant challenge to the marriage debt—as is demonstrated by the struggles of Margery Kempe with her husband, John, to achieve a chaste union[51]—but it was a variation of chastity, rather than of marriage itself. One chastely cohabiting couple, Mabel and Reynold Rich, the pious parents of St. Edmund of Abingdon (d. 1240), pursued extreme ascetic practices. Mabel, for example, wore two steel breastplates to make her hairshirt dig deeper into her flesh. But the details provided by Edmund's hagiographer are best understood as creating a context for Edmund's piety rather than revealing the reality of spiritual marriage.[52]

Even when sex within marriage was enjoyable, a lively sense of its sinfulness was often present. St. Jerome, for example, argued that loving one's wife too ardently was as bad as adultery.[53] When Margery Kempe had to care for her old and incontinent husband, John, she remembered "how sche in her yong age had ful many delectable thowtys, fleschly [carnal] lustys, & inordinate louys [desires]" toward her husband's body, but she considered her nursing of John a deserved retribution for her previous "inordinate" sexual pleasures.[54]

COURTLY LOVE

It has been argued that the European phenomenon of courtly love—emerging as if from out of nowhere in the poetry of the twelfth-century troubadours of southern France, and flowering in France and Germany (Gottfried von Straßburg's *Tristan and Isold* [ca. 1200] is a major landmark)—represents "an important milestone in the shift" from an ideology of sex for procreation to an ideology of sex for pleasure.[55] Courtly love significantly challenges Foucault's view that the medieval discourse of sex was "markedly unitary," organized solely around "the theme of the flesh and the practice of penance."[56] Drawing on classical conventions first established in Ovid's *Ars amatoria*, courtly love celebrated the cult of a passionate, idealized, and largely extra-institutional heterosexual love. *Fin'amor*, "refined love," involved no religious obligation to produce children, no economic ties, and no marital alliance.[57] Courtly love was an elite literary form enjoying immense cultural prestige, "firmly invested in the social and moral gulf dividing the refined (*courtois*) from their antithesis, the *vilain*."[58] It inaugurated new and enduring literary themes: individualism, pleasure in loving, and romantic love. It delighted in contradiction, weaving the sensual with the spiritual, the secret with the known, ecstasy with death. Gendered hierarchies were reversed: the lover became the humble servant of the lady (in troubador poetry she is *midons*, "my lord"), who was remote, haughty, and merciless. Love was suffering, with the man displaying absolute fidelity to the beloved, possibly throughout years of rejection. This marked him as *courtois*.

Courtly fictions did not directly represent sexuality, but they were nevertheless powerful sexual allegories. Male anxieties about female sexuality were often displaced from the category of sexual difference to that of class difference. In the thirteenth-century French *Roman de la rose*, the woman's Daunger (mercilessness) was represented as a club-wielding *vilain* (peasant). As Felicity Riddy argues, "The image of the woman as threatening peasant points … to a male sense that the ritualized reversals of courtly experience—which are engineered by him—are nevertheless at the same time humiliating and dangerous."[59] In a similar vein, René d'Anjou's sumptuously illustrated allegorical love-quest fantasy, *Livre du cuer d'amours espris* (1457–1477; *Book of the Love-Smitten Heart*),[60] which is in the tradition of the *Roman de la rose*, depicts the threatening figure of Jealousy as an unkempt female dwarf (fig. 1.2). Her appearance (bristling hair, hispid tunic, bare arms and legs) indicates not only dangerous sexual wantonness

FIGURE 1.2: Heart and Desire speak to the dwarf Jealousy. Barthélemy d'Eyck. In René d'Anjou, *Livre du cuer d'amours espris* (1457–1477). Cod. 2597, fol. 9v. Österreichische Nationalbibliothek, Vienna.

(signaled by the exposed breast) but also extreme uncourtliness—the very opposite of the demeanor of the elegantly costumed page Desire.

Compelling arguments have been made that courtly romances are not as heterosexual as they seem,[61] but same-sex desire was seen as uncourtly. In Marie de France's twelfth-century *Lanval*, Guenevere chides Lanval for preferring his male entourage to women: "People told me often enough that you don't go for women. You have well endowed young men/servants, and find your pleasure in them, base villain! Malformed freak!"[62] And with the idea of same-sex desire as improper and grotesque, we approach the tangled history of medieval sodomy.

THE "VICE AGAINST NATURE": SAME-SEX RELATIONS AFTER THE FACT

Because the "homosexual" is not a medieval identity for either men or women, we must retroactively reconstruct a history of homosexuality in the Middle

Ages, by analogy with Freud's concept of *Nachträglichkeit* (belatedness): the psychic process whereby an event that has taken place "is 'reactivated' at some later point, when new events and new knowledge endow it with a meaning it could not have had at the time."[63] Such a reconstruction means that our history will never be "on time," but it will be ethical, insofar as it refuses to equate modern and medieval identities and practices while also acknowledging that we bestow new meanings on the past in the light of present knowledge.

That past is often obscure. The seventh-century Irish *Penitential of Cummean* lists a number of sins that monks might commit, with a tariff of punishments: kissing ("simple," "licentious," and "with emission or embrace"); mutual masturbation (when committed by men over twenty, it warranted a penance lasting twenty or forty days, or a hundred days for a second offense); inter-femoral masturbation (a penance of two years, or a hundred days for a first offense and one year for a second); and fellatio and anal intercourse (seven years' penance).[64] The sliding scale for repeated offenses implies that the penance did not act as a deterrent, but that the monks committed them repeatedly or were believed to do so. But what we glimpse here of the medieval sodomite is elusive. We see him only as the target of prohibition. We do not know the actual incidence of the behaviors described or what they meant in terms of lived experience. Our reading of the sodomitical monk will thus never coincide with his time—but neither will it coincide with ours.

Ambrose (d. 397) was the first to give "the sodomitical vice" or "the vice against nature" the explicit meaning of same-sex copulation, but for Augustine it also meant simply disordered desire.[65] Mark Jordan argues that the noun "sodomy" (*sodomia*) was first invented in the eleventh century, in Peter Damian's rabidly denunciatory *Book of Gomorrah* (1049).[66] This text provides the most comprehensive medieval discussion of sodomy: "Four types of this form of criminal wickedness can be distinguished ... : some sin with themselves alone [masturbation]; some by the hands of others [mutual masturbation]; others between the thighs [thigh-fucking]; and finally, others commit the complete act against nature [anal intercourse]."[67] For Peter Damian, *sodomia* is "a cancer [or crab] of ... uncleanness[,] ... slithering through the clerical orders,"[68] a crime worse than bestiality because it drags others down with it to destruction.[69]

But by the reign of Henry I (1100–1135), "sodomy" had become a general term for a range of "non-natural" behaviors.[70] According to Thomas Aquinas (ca. 1225–1274), "sins against nature" were those forms of lust directed solely to the pursuit of pleasure and precluding procreation. These included, in ascending order of sinfulness, masturbation, deviation from the natural

manner of coitus (which was limited to face-to-face intercourse with the man on top), anal penetration, and bestiality.[71]

By contrast, medieval Slavic sources understood "sodomy" and "unnatural" sex differently from the Western Church: the passive sexual role for men, sex with animals, and incest were seen as "unnatural"; sex with the woman on top was sodomy.[72] But sodomy was also conflated with heresy in both the Western and Eastern churches. The English word "buggery" derives from "Bulgarian," after the heretical tenth-century Bogomils of Bulgaria, who attacked the institution of marriage.[73] The plagues of the later Middle Ages were blamed on sodomites and Jews.[74]

In Florence, sodomy became a matter of public morality: the Office of the Night (*Ufficiali di notte*) was established in 1432 so that Florentines could deposit accusations of male sodomy.[75] In Venice a *collegio de sodomiti* was established in 1418 to deal with offenders. John Boswell has argued that prior to the advent of the Inquisition, homosexuality, along with other behaviors ascribed to heretics, became utterly stigmatized, so that by 1300 "a single homosexual act was enough ... in many places to merit the death penalty."[76] Yet when we do find mention of various sins in earlier theological and penitential texts, they do not unambiguously refer to same-sex male copulation. Gratian's *Decretum* (ca. 1140) termed any sexual acts that were not related to procreation or in the missionary position as "sodomy." For unknown reasons, Dante put his former teacher, the Florentine magistrate and poet Brunetto Latini, among the sodomites in the seventh circle of hell in his *Divine Comedy* (1308–21), although there is no evidence to suggest that he was a sodomite in any of the medieval senses of the word.[77] "Sodomy" is thus a notoriously unstable and unspecific term that cannot be easily accommodated within a seamless history of homosexuality.[78]

Although it is vital to rehearse the meanings of sodomy, there is a very real danger that in universalizing sodomy as the defining feature of the medieval homosexual, we fail to trace the varieties of homoerotic desires and homoerotic subject positions. In medieval Islamic cultures there is also strong condemnation of male anal intercourse (*liwat*), but in the writings of the ninth-century Samarra and Baghdad court poet al-Jahiz we find evidence that male same-sex relations could be advocated as pleasurable and that adult males could have "clear, distinct sexual identities."[79] In an Arabic dialogue titled *Mufākharat al-jawāri wa'l-ghilmān* ("Boasting Match between Slave Girls and Page Boys"), the admirer of boys is known as a *luti* (from the name of Lot, the Old Testament figure involved in the destruction of Sodom and Gomorrah). In the dialogue, the opposing sides are spoken by an admirer/owner of slave girls and a *lūti*. The latter boasts: "I have no need for cunt/I think fucking is revolting/No one screws the cunt/Except those who are poor and needy./So if you screw, screw/A beardless youth, pale as a piece of ivory."[80] Even though the dialogue is ritualistic and deliberately outrageous (and misogynistic), as Hugh Kennedy argues, "the *lūti* of the Arabic dialogue is a recognizable type and it seems assumed that a man is either a *lūti* or not," in other words, that he has a sexual identity—and one, moreover, that he flaunts.[81]

WOMEN LOVING WOMEN?

"Sodomy" was also a term used in the Middle Ages to describe sex between women.[82] But unlike sexual relations between men, what women did together "often escaped categorization in the relevant sources."[83] But lesbian activity was not wholly invisible.[84] Tertullian (ca. 160–ca. 225) referred (disapprovingly) to the *frictrix* (female rubber), and the first known use of the term "lesbians" (*Lesbiai*) was in 914, by the Byzantine commentator Arethas.[85] In the seventh century, Donatus of Besan warned against what Jacqueline Murray calls "particular friendships" between enclosed women such as nuns, arguing that they "should not have the younger sisters with them in the bed but be joined by elders or groups."[86] The penitentials occasionally (but not always) singled out female homosexual practices,[87] but with penalties much less harsh than those assigned for male-male sexual activities.[88] In the Orthodox Church sexual intercourse between women was defined as a type of masturbation, incurring a penance of one year's exclusion from communion; this was more severe than the penance for male mutual masturbation.[89] Nevertheless, women's activities largely went unpunished and therefore undocumented. This makes it doubly difficult to construct a history of premodern lesbianism.

The earliest known medieval case of female same-sex genital contact concerns a woman known as Guercia, accused in Bologna in 1295 of sodomy with a widow and other women.[90] Legal records document only about twelve other women, all from the fifteenth century (the earliest is 1405). But only one— Katherina Hetzeldorfer in 1477—was executed for her activities.[91] In order to expand the social history of medieval lesbianisms, Judith Bennett has coined the term "lesbian-like" to describe women whose lives offered opportunities for loving or supporting other women, or who resisted marriage. According to Bennett, lesbian-like women might thus include an early-fifteenth-century cross-dressing Polish student from Krakow; Laurence and Jehanne, two wives from Bleury, near Chartres; prostitutes and ex-prostitutes in late-fourteenth-century Montpellier,[92] and (even) the several million adult women in Europe during the High Middle Ages who either never married[93] or lived abstinently within single-sex communities, such as the beguines of northern Europe and the *anacoreti* of Umbria and Tuscany in the thirteenth to fifteenth centuries.[94]

But evidence for lesbian genital contact or erotic desires is elusive. Agnes Grantham, a wealthy York widow staying in the house of William Pountfret, shared a bed with Dame Christiana, a relative of William's and a vowess (a woman, usually a widow, who had taken a vow of chastity). In a matrimonial cause paper of 1411 from the York church court, one of the deponents, a servant, Agnes Kyrkeby, stated that "frequently she [Agnes Grantham] went over to the bed with her [Christiana], often covering her naked in bed with sheets, as at times in like manner other women and servants of the same house often did in the sight and knowledge of the same witness."[95] But was this erotic for any of the parties? Did Agnes and Christiana do anything with each other in bed? And what else did Agnes Kyrkeby witness?

Thirteenth-century English anchoresses (women largely from the merchant class who voluntarily had themselves walled into anchorholds at the side of churches) may have used their private spaces to explore same-sex erotic desires, directing a lesbian gaze on their female servants, or participating in "worldly games" (forbidden by the thirteenth-century guide for anchoresses, *Ancrene Wisse*).[96] But it is not always clear that lesbianism is involved when we hear of female same-sex desires and sexual behaviors, or that medieval people would have described them as that or understood their erotic affect as lesbian.[97] Caroline Walker Bynum has argued that where we see the erotic or the lesbian in pictures of bared breasts or accounts of the medieval nuns Lukardis of Oberweimar and Margaret of Faenza "breathing deeply into their sisters' mouths," medieval people thought of the nuns' experiences as religious ecstasy, and of breasts as food. What mattered was not eroticism but whether such sensations and experiences were divinely inspired or came from the devil.[98]

Archival work on historical lesbians is importantly supplemented by queer readings of both male- and female-authored secular and devotional texts that imagine female homoerotic possibilities even if they do not openly endorse lesbian sex.[99] In Ovid's tale of Iphis and Ianthe, Iphis's mother brings her up as a boy to prevent her father from murdering her (he had vowed that if she were a girl he would do so). Iphis is married at the age of ten to a duke's daughter, Ianthe, and they become lovers. In Ovid's version of the story, Iphis laments that her desire for another woman is monstrous and unnatural, but this detail is importantly omitted in John Gower's late-fourteenth-century retelling of the story in his *Confessio Amantis*. Gower cannot quite envisage a woman loving another woman qua woman (he follows Ovid in having Cupid transform Iphis into a man), but neither does he condemn lesbianism.[100]

This is also the case in Etienne de Fougères' somewhat bizarre account of lesbian activity in his *Livre des manières* (ca. 1174; *Book of Conduct*). "These ladies," he says, "bang coffin against coffin,/without a poker to stir up their fire[,]/ ... join shield to shield without a lance./ ... They don't bother with a pestle in their mortar/nor a fulcrum in their see-saw."[101] Importantly, lesbian sex is not seen here as sinful or failing to provide satisfaction. Yet the coffin image suggests the traditional association of women's bodies with death (Peter Damian famously said that to embrace a female body is to embrace a corpse)[102] and the jousting involves the feared subversion of traditional hierarchical gender roles.[103] And Etienne cannot quite fathom what women actually do when they have sex: "They're not all from the same mold:/one lies still and the other makes busy,/one plays the cock and the other the hen."[104] In its veiled reference to dildos the poem may participate in the general male incredulity about lesbian sex, an incredulity that may have prompted one male witness in the 1295 Bolognese case to testify that Guercia used silk *virilia* (dildo-like objects) to have sex with women.[105]

"PERIPHERAL SEXUALITIES"

It is difficult to categorize medieval sexual practices as either "normal" or "perverse" when a great deal of what is nowadays in the West generally regarded as clinically or statistically normal (for example, oral sex or simply enjoying sex) was regarded as sinful by medieval Christian *pastoralia* and canon law. *All* masturbation was illicit in the Middle Ages, because it involved spilling one's seed outside the "proper" vessel. Within monastic culture there was a constant fear of autoeroticism, whether voluntary or involuntary.[106] Masturbation was associated with Jews, the devil, blasphemy, and apostasy. Guibert of Nogent's twelfth-century autobiography, *De vita sua*, relates how a monk seeking magic knowledge from a Jew asked him to mediate for him with the devil. The devil would only agree to share his knowledge if the monk made a sacrifice to him of a "libation" of his "seed," demanding "you shall taste it first as a celebrant ought to do." The "unhappy" monk agrees, thus renouncing his faith.[107] Playing with oneself is presented here not as a clinical perversion but as a horrifying sin that must be repressed. But this view is at odds with that of medieval physicians, who, as we have seen, *recommended* masturbation to restore the body's physical balance.

Different cultural formations affect our historical understanding of other "perversions."[108] Bestiality, for example, though clearly practiced, was strongly censured in canon law as an unnatural sin that tainted its practitioners with *infamia* (dishonor).[109] The fact that some canonists believed the animal should be killed[110] suggests ritual scapegoating: the removing of human responsibility in order to preserve the boundaries between the human and the animal and to expurgate the guilt of the community.

Conversely, medieval practices that now look perverse to us seem not have been considered so then. The explicit accounts by fourteenth-century witnesses in matrimonial litigation cases heard in York of overhearing rough sex between an older man and a twelve-year-old bride and of seeing couples naked in bed together have been described by the historian Jeremy Goldberg as containing "elements of paedophilia, of sadism, and of voyeurism."[111] But we do not know if the witnesses were aroused by what they saw, or the court by what it heard. And a category such as pedophilia is contingent upon the historical and legal definition of a child. From the eleventh century onward in Europe the canonical age of sexual consent for a woman was twelve (for a man it was fourteen). In Tuscany it was customary for child-brides to have sex at age twelve.[112]

The Bible prohibited cross-dressing (see Deut. 22:5). But the abomination has less to do with this being a sexual perversion than with the scandalous reversal of gender roles. Men cross-dressed for sexual reasons or to avoid violence.[113] Women (such as Christina of Markyate) cross-dressed to enter institutions from which women were excluded. It was acceptable for women to cross-dress in order to show their devoutness, for example, by becoming a monk, but intolerable when they entered the masculine sphere, since such competition, in Vern Bullough's words, "represented not a gain in the status of woman but a loss of status for men."[114] The medieval transvestite saints Marina and Thecla escaped impending marriages by dressing as men.[115]

A Latin document of 1394 offers the testimony of a London male prostitute known as John Rykener who occasionally passed as a woman under the name of Eleanor.[116] While wearing women's clothes s/he provided paid sexual services for three scholars, two Franciscans, a Carmelite friar, and six foreign men. S/he then had sex "as a man" with a certain Joan Matthew at Beaconsfield, and also with two foreign Franciscans "as a woman" ("ut cum muliere"), which may refer not to cross-dressing but rather to taking on the passive role in the sexual encounter.[117] S/he also claimed to have had sex with many nuns, and with married and unmarried women, as well as with many priests, "who had committed that vice with him as with a woman." But this evidence must be viewed with care, and the document is in any case unique. Rykener had a protean gender and sexual identity, and a sharp sense of a business opportunity, but any pleasure he took in these encounters is unrecorded.

Outside Europe, evidence from the Ummayad court in ninth-century Baghdad shows that slave girls were regularly dressed as boys and known as *ghulamiyat* (boy-like), and considered sexually attractive to men who liked boys.[118] In medieval Europe the almost universal practice of men playing women's parts on the stage also institutionalized cross-dressing, but there are few contemporary erotic reactions to the practice.

Conversely, some medieval behaviors that were regarded as relatively orthodox today look perverse: "Both male and female saints regularly engaged in what modern people call self-torture—jumping into ovens or icy ponds, driving knives, nails or nettles into their flesh, whipping or hanging themselves in elaborate pantomimes of Christ's Crucifixion."[119] Clare of Rimini (1282–1346) hired two men to tie her to a stone column in the church of St. Colomba, with her hands behind her, where she remained from Good Friday until the following Saturday afternoon. Afterwards, she visited local churches, scourging herself along the route with bundles of twigs.[120] Catherine of Siena (1347–1380) flagellated herself regularly with an iron chain. Peter Damian was a strong advocate of self-flagellation for monks ("the discipline").[121] Though apparently masochistic, these acts are located within a cultural formation that is radically different from today's. For Caroline Bynum these forms of self-harming were sometimes understood as the "chastening of sexual urges or as punishment for sin" but "were more frequently described as union with the body of Jesus."[122] They were empowering rather than pathologically destructive.[123]

It is important to remember, however, that the masochistic bond is "an essentially religious tie."[124] If we accept Georges Bataille's modern definition of masochism as "self-shattering,"[125] then there are similarities with medieval experiences. But for Peter Damian there is good self-shattering (penitential flagellation) and bad self-shattering (sexual excesses), and the road of sexual excess emphatically does *not* lead for Peter Damian to the ecstatic discarding of the self celebrated by Bataille.[126] Yet medieval accounts of the soul seeking annihilation in extreme acts do come close to modern experiences of masochism, in which the boundary between pain and pleasure is blurred: Catherine of Siena desires agony, because "in … knowing [Christ] the soul catches fire with an unspeakable love, which in turn brings continual pain."[127] And female abjection clearly did produce pleasurable effects for both its subjects and viewers. In Christ's words to Catherine of Siena, "this is not a pain that troubles or shrivels up the soul. On the contrary, it makes her [the soul] grow fat."[128]

Flogging was commonplace in the monastic education of boys. In his autobiography *De vita sua* (ca. 1114), Guibert of Nogent recalls one teacher who
repeatedly "showed excessive severity in his unjust floggings, and yet the great
care with which he guarded me was evident in his acts."[129] The perversity here
is equivocal; we simply do not know if the flogging was a source of erotic
satisfaction for Guibert's teacher. However, another twelfth-century pedagogi-
cal scenario explicitly sexualizes a master's beating of his pupil. This is Peter
Abelard's account of meeting Heloise: "All on fire with desire for this girl ...
I came to an agreement with her uncle [the Parisian canon Fulbert]. ... I was
amazed by his simplicity—if he had entrusted a tender lamb to a ravening wolf
it would not have surprised me more. In handing her over to me to punish as
well as to teach, what else was he doing but giving me complete freedom to
realize my desires, ... to bend her to my will by threats and blows if persuasion failed?"[130] There is no evidence, however, that Heloise did not consent to
Abelard's sexual coercion.

Another extraordinary case of what appears to be a perversion—fetishistic
serial killing—is that of Gilles de Rais (b. 1404), who held high office as a
marshal in France. Best known for his sexual abuse and murder of large numbers of children, mostly boys (it is not known how many, but it may have been
up to three hundred), in the Nantes area, he was tried and hanged in 1440.
His crimes included decapitation, disemboweling, and hanging the bodies on
beams and then strangling them. One witness, his servant and accomplice Henriet Griart, testified that Gilles kept the heart and hand of one young boy in
a jar and used them in diabolical invocations.[131] Sexual satisfaction was involved: in the case of one child, Griart claimed that, like all the others, it had
"served [Gilles'] libidinous purposes."[132]

But was Gilles perverse in the modern clinical sense? The new "world of
perversions" that arose in the nineteenth century was, Foucault argues, the
result of a shift in power mechanisms: from "law and penalty" to "medicine
and regimentation," the latter employing a very different set of tactics, not
to prohibit but to control, producing "an entire sub-race" of "scandalous,
dangerous victims, prey to a strange evil that also bore the name of vice and
sometimes of crime."[133] But Gilles is not a "victim": he is the subject solely
of tactics of prohibition, his actions viewed as both sinful and diabolical. Yet
there is some evidence that Gilles thought of himself as having a unique sexual
identity: Griart testified that "he had heard ... the accused say that he had been
born under a particular astrological configuration which meant, he said, that
no-one could know or understand the perversions or illicit acts that he could
be guilty of."[134] Although Gilles claims this identity as astrologically determined

and uses it not as the marker of his belonging to a biological "species" but as an excuse for his sin, his self-presentation is nevertheless analogous to Foucault's characterization of the late-nineteenth-century homosexual as a "perverse" type: "Nothing that went into his total composition was unaffected by his sexuality. … It was consubstantial with him, less as habitual sin than as a singular nature."[135] Gilles' case suggests, at the very least, some minor revisions of Foucault's claim that the perversions are a marker of the modern.

SEX, RELIGION, AND THE LAW

Perhaps the most significant piece of medieval legislation is the twenty-first canon of the Fourth Lateran Council (1215), which imposed the requirement of annual private confession of sins on every baptized Christian over the age of twelve. Confessional manuals before 1215, which had their roots in ancient monasticism, are customarily described as penitentials. After Lateran IV, which unleashed a flood of regulatory writings, there appeared two types of texts for priests: *summae confessorum* (summaries of sins for priests to consult) and manuals designed to aid priests in prompting penitents to speak the whole truth about their sins (where? when? with whom? how often?). Confessors were warned about questioning penitents too closely in case they learned new ways to sin. In one Russian Orthodox manuscript, by a question about sex after communion, a marginal note warns, "Don't ask virgins!"[136]

Pierre Payer, the leading authority on both the penitentials and the later confessional writings, demonstrates that in the latter there is an intensification of the trend that was already apparent in the former, namely, a disproportionate concern with sexual sins by comparison with other sins: in Alan of Lille's penitential (ca. 1191) about 36 percent are sins of lechery; in the statutes issued by the diocese of Angers, France (1217–1219), the figure is 50 percent.[137]

Throughout the early medieval period, public penance—for public sins—coexisted with private penance, for sins committed in private (although more so on the Continent than in England).[138] In the earliest Latin penitentials, from Ireland, the tariffs for nonreproductive forms of sex are severe (from two to seven years of fasting), but bestiality, fornication, and masturbation only receive a year's penance.[139] Critics disagree as to whether the lists of sins in these earliest penitentials were those that had actually been confessed.[140] In Cnut's reign (1017–1035) the penalty for adultery was severe for a woman: she had to give all that she owned to her husband, and her nose and ears were cut off.[141] Rhinectomy appears in Marie de France's twelfth-century *lai Bisclavret* as punishment for a disobedient wife.

The relative gravity of sexual offenses can be seen by comparing their tariffs with the nonsexual: in Theodore's penitential, revenge-murder for a brother's death incurs a penance of three to ten years, but sex with one's mother incurs fifteen years of penance or seven years with "perpetual pilgrimage."[142] In one tenth-century English vernacular penitential, priests and deacons are required to be defrocked for fornication, but not bishops (who had to submit to the king's judgment).[143] The pattern is one of gradual extension of penance from a practice once reserved exclusively to those in monastic orders to include the laity, and eventually (after 1215) all Christians. The focus on "unnatural" sex as sex that did not lead to procreation gave rise to some absurdities in Western canon law: for example, Aquinas deemed that because sex *a tergo* (doggy-style) and incest, even with a parent, could result in children, these practices were not "unnatural" and therefore incurred lesser penalties than masturbation.[144]

Raptus meant both rape and abduction throughout the Middle Ages. Rape was the violation of one man's property by another man, or the taking by violence of something that did not belong to the rapist. There is a complex continuum of behavior between abduction and rape, which makes it difficult for modern commentators to distinguish clearly between them. It was not uncommon, for example, for relatives to abduct young female relatives if they felt unhappy with a marriage arrangement—say, if the girl was only twelve. In England, in the late-twelfth and early-thirteenth centuries, rape cases focused on the physical violence the woman suffered. But from the late-thirteenth century onward, they focus on the issue of consent. However, the power that men had over women and servants meant, as Karras argues, that it is not possible "to draw a sharp line between consensual relations and rape."[145] There was no medieval law relating to marital rape. In the later Middle Ages "scandalous" crimes, especially rape, incest, and sodomy, were capital offenses. The punishments for rape varied, depending on the status of the person raped: rape of a child was punished quite severely, but rape of a marriageable woman relatively lightly. But very few cases were recorded.

Outside canon law, the crime of *raptus* might be dealt with very differently. In 1369 Michele Dolfin, a Venetian noble, was prosecuted for tying up Pietro Condulmer, also a noble, and violently beating him with a sword for breaking into his house and having sex with one of his slaves, Rubea. Sympathetic officials fined Dolfin only 100 lire, even though he had humiliated Condulmer, because the latter had violated Dolfin's property (both his house and slave). However, Condulmer's night of sex with Rubea was judged an infringement "of the honor of the government," and he was fined 200 lire.[146] What mattered was less the punishment of guilt than the re-establishment of public honor.

Divorce barely existed in the Middle Ages. Figures for the fourteenth and fifteenth centuries in York show that marriages rarely generated litigation.[147] A marriage might be annulled on the basis of a husband's impotence (fig. 1.3) or an impediment such as consanguinity (if this were discovered later), or, in England, if a previous marriage contract existed. Separations could be obtained, very rarely, on the grounds of the wife's adultery or the husband's cruelty, or if the husband wished to enter a monastery, but the separated partners could not then marry others.[148] Separations became more difficult to obtain after 1215, when the degree of consanguinity within which a relationship was viewed as incestuous was reduced from seven to four.

Sexual activity between married couples was strictly regulated, at least in theory. They were expected to abstain from sex at certain periods (Lent, Easter week, seven days before Pentecost, forty days after Pentecost, Advent), as well as on some days of the week (Wednesday, Friday, and Saturday) and at certain times of day (before communion on Sundays and feast days). Sex was prohibited during menstruation, three months before a woman gave birth, and

FIGURE 1.3: The dissolution of a marriage due to impotence. Gratian's *Decretum* (1310–1330). MS 262, fol. 86v. Fitzwilliam Museum, Cambridge. By permission of the Fitzwilliam Museum.

forty days after. In the words of the English abbot Ælfric (ca. 955–ca. 1010), "It is less harm for a Christian man to enjoy meat at Lent than to enjoy his wife sexually."[149] The diabolical consequences of infringement—and the magical powers of virginity—are well illustrated in a miracle attributed to the icon of the Virgin at Hilandar (a Serbian Orthodox monastery on Mount Athos in Greece). After a husband raped his wife on Holy Saturday, the wife vowed to dedicate the child she had conceived to the devil. But the boy was pious and beautiful and escaped the devil's claim on him by invoking the power of the Virgin.[150]

SEX, MEDICINE, AND DISEASE

Medieval medicine was influenced by several traditions from late antiquity and was not underpinned by a single, consistent biological theory.[151] Medical views about sex therefore varied widely. Religious and social values frequently intersected with "scientific" understandings because of the impact of the authoritative writings of natural philosophers and theologians on biological issues such as conception, infertility, and hysteria. But the need for practical solutions to sexual problems sometimes challenged biblical attitudes and scholastic theories. The value placed on virginity, for example, was somewhat undermined by certain late medieval physicians' views that coitus was part of nature and that sexual restraint might be harmful.[152] The Greek physician Galen (131–201), whose ideas were transmitted to the medieval West through Latin translations of the eleventh-century Arabic writer Avicenna, recommended masturbation as a cure for female hysteria.[153]

There were three important influences on medical understandings of sexuality. Aristotle (384–322 B.C.E.) held that in conception the male seed provided the active principle (form) and the woman was merely the inert vessel (matter). Hippocratic theory viewed human physiology as composed of four humors (yellow bile, black bile, phlegm, and blood) that were differently distributed in men and women (men were hot and dry, women cold and moist), and this, in turn, affected understandings of male and female libido.[154] Finally, Galen argued that the female anatomy was less perfect than the male, insofar as a woman's organs were inverted and inferior versions of men's: the vagina was an underdeveloped penis that had not been turned to the outside, making the male body paradigmatic (the so-called "one-sex" model).[155] A group of practice-oriented question-and-answer medical treatises known as the Salernitan questions, composed in northern France and England around 1200, were important for transmitting Galenic and Hippocratic ideas about sexuality and reproduction.[156]

Not all the experts were men: Hildegard of Bingen (1098–1179) composed theoretical medical works,[157] and there are many contemporary references to "the women of Salerno" and to one eleventh-century female healer known as Trotula (fig. 1.4).[158] But medieval medical textbooks rarely use images of women to illustrate diseases specific to parts of the body; figure 1.5 is relatively exceptional.[159] And there is a great deal of imprecision in descriptions of the female anatomy: the clitoris, described in some texts as the "nymph," or *tentigo*, was often confused with the labia and its sensitivity was poorly understood.[160]

One crucial but unresolved debate concerned the production of female seed. Aristotle believed that only men had the seed necessary for conception, whereas Hippocratic theories held that women produced seed as well.[161] Supporters of the one-seed theory saw menstruation as evidence that women's bodies lacked the vital heat that was needed to turn blood into semen.[162] These opposing views had enormous consequences for the understanding of female

FIGURE 1.4: A female healer, perhaps "Trotula," holding up a urine flask. Medical miscellany (early-fourteenth century). Wellcome Library, London.

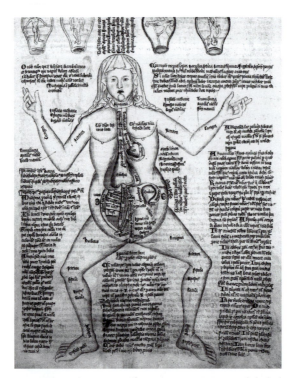

FIGURE 1.5: Anatomy of a pregnant woman, labeled with ailments ("Disease Woman"). On top are four fetal positions in uterus. German miscellany (ca. 1420–1430). Wellcome Library, London.

pleasure and its role in conception. Adherents of the Hippocratic two-seed theory believed that conception depended upon the woman emitting seed and having an orgasm (pleasure). Constantine the African even argued that women experience greater pleasure than men in intercourse because they not only expel their own sperm but receive male sperm "from the desire of their fervent *vulva*."[163] Prostitutes were believed to be largely infertile because they only had sex for money, not pleasure, and therefore would not produce the requisite seed or experience the pleasure necessary for conception.[164] This had an impact on rape cases: if a woman conceived as a result of rape, then it was deemed that she must have had an orgasm and therefore had not been raped.[165] An odd bit of folklore in King Alfred's Old English translation of Boethius—"A woman gives birth to children and suffers great pains according to the great physical pleasure which she has previously experienced"[166]—sounds like a combination of the orgasm/pleasure theory of conception and God's curse on Eve: "in sorrow shalt thou bring forth children" (Gen. 3:16).

Couples would go to great lengths to conceive. In 1393, after several years of infertility, Francesco Datini, age forty-one, and Margherita, whom he married when she was sixteen, had recourse to four different types of remedy but only one was medical: the others were a wise woman's poultice, a belt with special inscriptions to be placed on the belly accompanied by incantations, and pious acts of charity.[167]

Certain sexually transmitted diseases were unknown in the medieval period. Although gonorrhea is an ancient disease, syphilis did not arrive in Europe until 1493–1494 (the first outbreak was in Naples).[168] But leprosy, with its symptoms of "unclean" scaly flesh and bodily degeneration, was considered a retribution for sexual sins.[169] According to the widely disseminated twelfth-century *De secretis mulierum* (*On Women's Secrets*), men were believed to contract leprosy (and sometimes cancer) though intercourse with menstruating women.[170] The thousands of medieval European lepers were regarded as pariahs, subjected to strict segregation, and forced to sound their approach by ringing a bell. Cresseid, in Robert Henryson's *Testament of Cresseid* (ca. 1450–1500), is one such outcast, punished by God for her infidelity, her previously beautiful face "deformait" (deformed) by the ravages of the disease.[171] Mary Magdalene was the patron saint of both reformed prostitutes and lepers, reinforcing the link among women, sexuality, disease, and abjection. But it is vital to stress that the late medieval emphasis on the doctrine of the incarnation, with its focus on the sacrament of the Eucharist (bread transubstantiated into Christ's body) and on images of Jesus as mother, considerably modified pervasive views of the flesh itself as inferior and of the female body as polluting.[172]

SEX, POPULAR BELIEFS, AND CULTURE

Medical treatments for sex and old wives' tales coexisted with no apparent incompatibility, as we saw in the case of Margherita and Francesco Datini. Love-magic and sex-magic were rife across Europe at all levels of society and endorsed by medical textbooks. One tenth-century English aphrodisiac was semen mixed with food, reputed to make women more attractive to men. For increasing a woman's sexual responsiveness, the Anglo-Saxon *Medicina de Quadrupedibus* advises men: "mix the gall from a buck with frankincense and the seeds of a nettle," and "[g]rease the penis with this before intercourse."[173] The parts of virile animals were thought to confer virility.

Orthodox religion and popular superstition appear to be opposed in the sixth-century Irish penitential of Finnian, which prescribes six years of penance for anyone dealing in magic drafts "for the sake of wanton love." But a twelfth-century German source tells of a woman who held a consecrated host in her mouth while kissing her husband, to make him love her, and in 1376 a friar was tried for allegedly providing Alice Perrers with a potion to obtain the love of Edward III.[174] It would be wrong therefore to make an absolute distinction between Latin clerical culture and vernacular beliefs. Rather, their interactions were, in Valerie Edden's words, "a constant process of cross-fertilization."[175]

Collections of exempla (moralistic tales suitable for embellishing sermons) offered vernacular versions of the clerical tradition, albeit in more lurid form. But popular anecdotes often hold the clue to a culture's deep anxieties. In one exemplum from the early-fifteenth-century English *Alphabet of Tales*, "Chastity in a Wife Is Greatly to Be Praised," an old nobleman, Duellus, is told by his neighbor that his hand stinks and that this must displease his young wife, Yliana. Storming home, Duellus demands: "Why have you never told me ... that my hand stinks?' "Sir," Yliana replies, "I would have done so, but all other men's hands stink as yours does."[176] The fabliau-like punch line depends on the clerical commonplace that women will commit adultery at every opportunity. The wife is presented as both innocent and stupid, a woman who does not even realize that to have sex with other men is a sin, let alone that this should not be confessed to one's husband.

But even this apparently simple cautionary tale complicates orthodox religious teaching about the importance of wifely chastity. To what extent does the story condemn the husband for presuming to take a young wife when he is old and sexually incompetent? Should he have been more mindful of his personal hygiene and of his young wife's sensibilities? Has he been masturbating, a sin often described as "sullying oneself with one's hands"?[177] Or has he been "playing away," given that adultery is often referred to in the pastoral handbooks as a "stynkynge synne"?[178] Though ostensibly misogynist, the exemplum might have been interpreted by some women (and perhaps men) as being critical of old men taking young wives.

Popular beliefs also indicate that women feared the size of their husband's penis and the violence of sex. Though Innocent III permitted the dissolution of a marriage if there was a gross disparity between the size of genitals, William of Rennes argued that a woman ought to put up with a certain amount of violence in consummation. But John of Freiburg argued that "a wise woman" had told him that never, or very rarely, was a man's penis so large that his bride could not accommodate it.[179] In one interestingly pro-woman image in a miscellany of German provenance from 1420–1430 (fig. 1.6) a nude woman with a cut in her abdomen (perhaps a symbol of the result of violent penetration)

FIGURE 1.6: Genital disparity and violent sex. The text reads: "I have often been distressed, sister, by the size and length of the male member." German miscellany (ca. 1420–1430). Wellcome Library, London.

addresses another: the text reads: "I have often been distressed, sister, by the size and length of the male member."

Evidence that the church did not induce universal guilt about sex is found in the corpus of late medieval comic fabliaux from northern France (1150?–1340), which were notorious for their frank enjoyment of sexuality.[180] Their explicit naming of body parts and words for sex is an effect of their genre, not their addressees, since their intended audience appears to have been bourgeois, or even seigneurial—the same social groups that also enjoyed refined courtly romances.[181] Indeed, the fabliaux traded precisely on the knowing use of sexual double entendre. The coy virgin in "The Maiden Who Couldn't Hear *Fuck*" doesn't object to the act itself but only to the use of crude language with which to describe it, happily fucking a clever young man who guides her responses to him by using metaphorical language ("horsey" for penis, "fountain" for vagina).[182] In *Les quatre souhais Saint Martin* (The Four Wishes of St. Martin), St. Martin gives a peasant four wishes, but his wife wishes that her husband be endowed with pricks everywhere: "you'll then appear the prick you are!"[183] To her delight, pricks of every shape and size instantly sprout all over his body: "One prick alone's no good to me,/it's always soft as fur."' The peasant then wishes that his wife be covered with as many cunts as he has pricks—and so she is. Realizing their mistake, they wish them away, but finding themselves both cuntless and prickless, they must then use the final wish to restore their original organs.

While the joke here is at the expense of foolish peasants and self-willed wives, other fabliaux mock social climbing (revealing their audience bias) and celebrate female resourcefulness. In Guérin's early-thirteenth-century fabliau *Berangier au long cul* (*Berangier of the Long Asshole*), a lady who has been married off to the son of a social-climbing *vilain* (peasant) determines to teach her cowardly, boorish husband a lesson. Disguised as a knight, she discovers him defacing his shield to impress her with derring-do not done and forces him to kiss his/her ass.[184] When he/she bends over, he sees "the longest ass he'd ever seen." On returning home, he finds his wife in bed with her lover, but she threatens to call on "Sir Berangier of the Long Asshole," and the shamed husband must bear his cuckolding.

One of the most important literary miscellanies of the monastic Benedictine Reform, the Exeter Book (ca. 1000), contains about fifteen obscene riddles that depend on double entendre: a leather bottle being cleaned by a "lustful" slave woman is also used for masturbation ("she sticks me in her bosom" and "moves me about repeatedly, sweeps me through a dark place") (12); a "strange thing" that "hangs near a man's thigh" is a key/penis (44); a "marvellous creature" that brings pleasure to women and makes the "eye" wet is an onion/penis (25); a "boneless thing" that swells is dough/a penis (45).[185] The churn riddle plays with the analogy between making butter and making out (54); the keyhole riddle describes the manipulations of a key in a hole in sexually suggestive ways (91). Riddle 12's reference to a *wala* (Welshwoman/slave) crucially reminds us that in reading sexual otherness back into medieval texts, we must not ignore "other systems of (often violent) differentiation and opposition."[186] Like the Anglo-Saxon penitentials, the riddles furnish evidence of sexual practices at the beginning of the second millennium but say nothing about the incidence of these practices. However, given their appearance in a monastic miscellany, together with the fact that their idiom is found across a range of Anglo-Saxon texts, from penitentials to homilies and hagiographies, it makes little sense to see them as rebelling against the "officially repressive culture" of Anglo-Saxon England.[187] They are the very products of that culture.

A number of indecent poems survive from medieval Wales (fourteenth to seventeenth century). In the earliest, "Cywydd y Gal" (ca. 1330–1350; "The Penis"), the poet Dafydd ap Gwilym addresses his unruly member ("a bridle must be put on your snout") with a catalog of inventive soubriquets: "net quill of the cunt," "horn of the scrotum," "nut-pole of the lap's cavity."[188] The female poet Gwerful Mechain (active 1480) celebrates female (hetero)sexuality in "To Jealous Wives" when she claims that "every big-cocked lover is after me." Her poem "To the Female Genitals" matches Dafydd ap Gwilym's with its roll call of riddling synonyms: "tender frieze, fur of a fine pair of testicles,/a girl's thick grove, circle of precious greeting,/lovely bush, God save it."[189] Despite their openness about sex, these poems do not, however, seem to have been intended to be erotic.[190]

The popular equation of money and ejaculation that is found in the classical myth of Zeus and Danaë (the god appears to Danaë in a shower of gold) and in the numerous Renaissance puns on spending[191] is not found in the Middle Ages, although in Chaucer's "The Shipman's Tale" a French merchant, after substantially boosting his earnings abroad, celebrates his return home by having vigorous sex with his wife: "And up he gooth [gets it up/penetrates her] and maketh it ful tough [is very demanding]."[192] But just as today, one (misogynistic) term for an impotent man in the fifteenth century was "cuntebeten" (pussy whipped).[193]

One important popular superstition from the patristic period onward was the belief in *incubi* and *succubi*: demon lovers that invaded human bodies in their sleep (the names are not gender specific but refer to their position, on top or below). These fantasies represent an uncanny return of the repressed: their origins lie in clerical anxieties about nocturnal pollution, since the succubus can be blamed for inducing wet dreams.[194] The favored scholastic answer to the puzzle of demonic insemination was that a demon succubus obtained the seed from a man and then changed into an incubus in order to impregnate a woman.[195] Women were believed to be especially susceptible to incubi because of their greater libidinousness. This link between women and the diabolical provides, as Dyan Elliott puts it, "the gravitational pull toward the materialization of the witch" in the early modern era.[196]

At the end of the period we see the beginnings of a democratization of sexually explicit materials, especially in Italy. Antonio Beccadelli's collection of obscene and indecent epigrams, *Hermaphroditus* (ca. 1425), celebrates sodomitical practices.[197] The Florentine Poggio Bracciolini's *Facetiae* (1450), a collection of humorous and occasionally scabrous anecdotes (in one a prostitute claims damages against a barber who had cut her badly while shaving her pubic hair, thus causing her to lose clients; the court's verdict is not revealed),[198] was written in Latin to provide a veneer of propriety but was widely read in Italy, France, Spain, Germany, and England. The advent of print would of course enable this kind of material to circulate ever more widely but Poggio's jests are symptomatic of the permeable boundaries between high and low culture throughout the period. What is "popular" (of the people) is generically determined (just as fabliaux are rude because their genre demands it, not because their audience is uneducated), and what appears elite (by virtue of being written in Latin or circulating among a restricted group) may be "popular" in nature.

PROSTITUTION

The church condemned prostitution but tended to overlook it if it served to prevent worse sins.[199] Augustine held that "unnatural" acts between man and wife were worse than those between a man and a prostitute.[200] There is no censure of prostitution in the early Irish, Anglo-Saxon, and Frankish penitentials until the mid-ninth century, when a canon in the *St. Hubert Penitential* addresses the clients (including monks) of "women who have fornicated with others," but not the women themselves.[201] Even the infamous nineteenth book ("The Corrector") of Burchard's *Decretum* has one only canon dealing with prostitution. In fact, medieval canon law did not clearly define prostitution.[202] Neither are the demographics of prostitution clear, since the terms used for sex workers and (hetero)sexually active unmarried women are often the same: *meretrix*, for example, also meant a priest's concubine.[203] Although there is no case from the English courts, and apparently none anywhere else in Europe, of a man being accused or convicted of prostitution, not all prostitutes were female.[204]

We know very little about the lived lives of prostitutes or about secular attitudes toward them. Some held land: in 1002, King Æthelred confiscated land at Dumbleton, Gloucestershire, because its owner was a prostitute.[205] Prostitution appears not to have been the result of coercion, though popular stories recognized that women were driven to it by economic necessity.[206] But in his *Sermon to the English* (ca. 1014), Wulfstan, archbishop of York and bishop of Worcester, censures one especially nasty practice: a group of men buying a woman in common, gang-banging her, and then selling her out of the country to Vikings.[207] Official brothels existed in many later medieval towns in Continental Europe (less often in England), but prostitutes also worked out of rented rooms, taverns, the homes of their employers, and bathhouses.[208]

It is likely that prostitutes used contraception, though there are hardly any references to this.[209]

Prostitutes in many European towns had to wear distinctive clothing.[210] Defined as one community, they also served to define the boundaries of other communities. In Christian Spain, Christians could put to death a Jewish or Muslim man who had sex with a Christian prostitute, but there was little concern about Christian men having sex with prostitutes of other faiths.[211] Professional or semi-professional sex workers were employed as expert witnesses to determine a husband's alleged impotence in marriage annulment cases.[212] In 1432 Joan Semer, Margaret Bell and Joan Laurence—all known sex workers—were called in to the York court to expose their breasts and to fondle the "yard" (penis) and testicles of one John Skathelok to see if he could be aroused.[213] Prostitutes might also serve civic interests: in 1403 Florence's Office of Decency established a municipal brothel staffed by women from outside the city to provide an alternative to male sodomy and to deal with low population levels.[214]

The church made efforts to convert prostitutes. Gratian declared that "It is not a sin to take a prostitute as wife," because "an evil person becomes good if guided by a good person's example."[215] In 1198 Pope Innocent III praised men who gave prostitutes a second chance by marrying them, and in 1227 Pope Gregory IX approved the Order of St. Mary Magdalene for repentant prostitutes. Mary of Egypt was another legendary repentant prostitute. Margery Kempe of Norwich looked on both Mary Magdalene and Mary of Egypt as role models, because they demonstrated that women who had sinned might yet be sanctified.[216]

EROTICA

There is no recognized medieval category of "erotica"—erotic art or literature that is bought or sold by collectors and connoisseurs.[217] Neither is there pornography, which depends (like erotica) on technologies and systems of distribution that were unavailable in the Middle Ages. As Lynn Hunt persuasively argues, pornography emerged with the invention of printing.[218] Pornography, as Leah Price so deliciously puts it, is "one of the few genres to which readers' responses leave tangible traces,"[219] but semen stains on medieval manuscripts or artworks have yet to be discovered. In a vigorous penitential culture perhaps few medieval readers or viewers sought solitary sexual gratification through reading or looking at material intended to arouse. But this does not mean that medieval viewers were not aroused by what they read or saw.[220]

Some sexually explicit medieval imagery may have been intended to promote fertility or to be apotropaic, that is, designed to warn against illicit or
sinful behavior, especially if it appeared in an ecclesiastical context. But some
medieval viewers may have been titillated by even grotesque and un-erotic
art such as the stylized carvings of exhibitionist women with gaping vaginas
known as sheela-na-gigs, which are found only on British and Irish churches,
such as at Kilpeck on the Welsh border,[221] and the female and male exhibitionist figures (including acrobatic penis-swallowers, anus-showers, and ithyphallic men) found in western France and northern Spain.[222] Other medieval
monumental sculptures that occupy this ambiguous zone include phalloi as
corbels (France);[223] copulating couples; and one couple with haloes (unusually)
at Maillezais, France, the woman gently fondling the man's outsize penis.[224]
Another source of sexually explicit art is the wooden carvings under misericords ("mercy-seats": small shelves on the undersides of the wooden seats in
choir stalls that allowed clergy to lean against them for relief while remaining
upright) that are found in England, France, the Netherlands, Italy, Spain, Por-
tugal, and Germany from the thirteenth century onward. Examples include the
exhibitionist figures in the cathedral of Treguier (France) and a wooden sheela
at Strelley, in Nottinghamshire.

Also ambiguous, in terms of intent and reception, are the thousands of
curious fifteenth-century sexual badges that were first discovered in Paris in
the nineteenth century.[225] Mass produced from cheap lead and intended to be
worn, they depict sexual organs in various surreal postures, with human legs,
winged, ambulant, or riding: one depicts a vulva on pilgrimage (with pilgrim's
hat, rosary, phallus-shaped staff, and phallus epaulettes);[226] another shows
three phalluses on human legs carrying a vulva, crowned with three small
phalluses, on a litter;[227] another is in the shape of a phallus on legs, its glans
pecked by a bird (fig. 1.7). Their meaning is unclear. They may have been
apotropaic, but equally they may have been intended to bring good (sexual)
luck and fertility.[228] The winged phallus or phallus-bird was a popular three-
dimensional ancient Roman fertility talisman, which also appears carved on a
Roman stone from Wroxeter, Shropshire, as a winged or wheeled phallus with
the fica sign—a sexual hand gesture—and a bundle of phalloi.[229] The winged
phallus also appears in nineteenth-century eastern erotica (fig. 1.8). But while
the vulva motif is not found in Roman culture, the vesica/mandorla shape
of the vulva badges recalls medieval devotional imagery that represents the
wound in Christ's side as a vulva (punning on *vulnus*, "wound"), perhaps
suggesting (as with the badge sending up a Marian procession) a mocking
of medieval piety.[230] These highly visible, mass-produced, comic (rather than

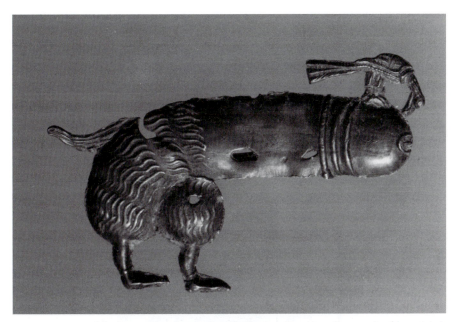

FIGURE 1.7: Lead badge in the shape of a phallus on legs, its glans pecked by a bird. Dutch (second half of fifteenth century). Rotterdam, Collection BOOR (Bureau Oud-heidkundig Onderzoek Rotterdam). In H.J.E. van Beuningen, A. M. Koldeweij and D. Kicken, *Heilig en Profaan 2: 1200 Laatmiddeleeuwse insignes uit openbare en particuliere collectives*, Rotterdam Papers 12 (Cothen: Stichting Middeleeuwse religieuze en profane insignes), fig. 1755.

erotic) badges perhaps represent the medieval commercialization of sex—the precursors of today's novelty underwear, T-shirts, and condoms.

Medieval iconography also included many cryptic sexual meanings. Rabbits, for example, signaled the female pudenda, through the pun on "con (coney/cunt)."[231] Another obscene pun is found in the *mise-en-page* of Glasgow MS Hunter 409, fol. 57v, the unique copy of Chaucer's translation of the *Roman de la rose* (fig. 1.9). The decorated border features the sexually explicit motif of the wild flower *Arum maculatum*, popularly known as cuckoopint from its characteristic erect spadix ("pint," meaning "penis," appears in English nicknames, such as Robert Pintel in 1177).[232] Although the *Roman de la rose* eschews direct sexual language, "it invites its readers to interpret it as a sexual allegory,"[233] an invitation that is extended by the illuminator of this beautiful presentation manuscript. The spotted brown leaf/spadix that pokes lasciviously through the hole in the roundel of the decorated initial capital *T* is simultaneously penis (albeit possibly diseased), tongue, and leaf and thus

FIGURE 1.8: A flying penis ejaculating into a
flying vagina. India (?) (nineteenth century).
Wellcome Library, London.

wittily conjoins page ("folio"/leaf) and language ("lingua"/tongue) under the
sign of phallic vulnerability. This reveling in sexual innuendo (here cued visually rather than verbally) is typical of courtly fictions, which substitute for
the act of copulation a pleasure in "obscene hermeneutics."[234] If we do not
find erotica in its modern sense in the medieval period, there was nevertheless
a taste for visual representations of the sexual that appealed to a group of
sophisticated cognoscenti.

CONCLUSION

Although medieval theologians weighed down human sexuality with a sense
of utter sinfulness and elevated sexual abstinence as the ideal, it is very far
from the case that sex was always and everywhere considered in relation to
"an absolute law of the permitted and the forbidden."[235] At the beginning of
the period, the prescriptions of Latin canonical law and the stern insistence

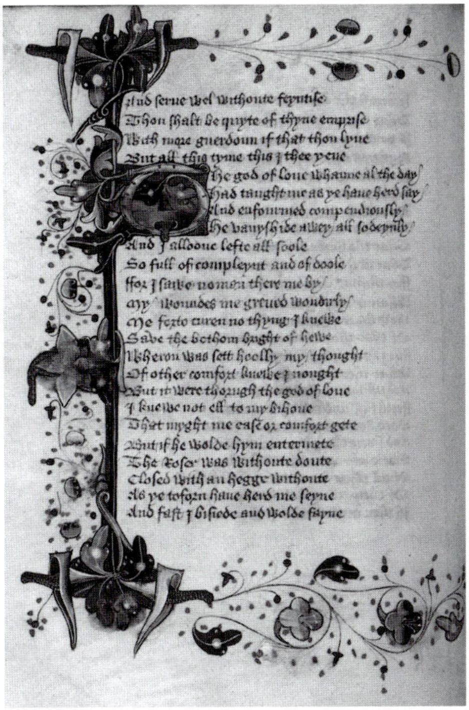

FIGURE 1.9: Cuckoopint (*Arum maculatum*) flowers and leaves border decoration. In Geoffrey Chaucer, *Romaunt of the Rose* (ca. 1440). MS Hunter 409, fol. 57v. Glasgow University Library Special Collections.

on sexual purity were largely aimed at monastic communities, though with an undoubted effect on the laity. It was only after the legislation that developed from the Fourth Lateran Council of 1215 that the church sought to govern the sexual activity of all Christians through a systematic program of pastoral instruction in the vernacular and the imposition of universal, annual confession. While these mechanisms of power focused disproportionately on sexual sins and especially on the relations between husband and wife, sex was far less regulated than it appears. The church was itself the sponsor of much that was smutty and erotic; medieval medicine contradicted church teaching; literary and visual texts played with the imaginative possibilities of bodies and desires, of cross-dressed women and improperly gendered men; anecdotes and fabliaux spoke of sexual pleasures as well as sexual anxieties.

But neither is it right to see this medieval sexual mosaic in terms of a dynamic of prohibition and resistance. Prohibition itself gave rise to new cultural formations of sexuality that were not expressions of resistance so much as creative resignifications. Medieval virginity, "one of the great inventions of medieval Christian culture," not only constituted a sexual category in its own right but opened up endless possibilities for self-definition, especially for women.[236] Courtly love was another great medieval sexual invention, endowing the West with an *ars erotica* (erotic art) and ushering in a new order of desire, one that shared with religious discourse an emphasis on the almost unbearable pleasure of suffering but in which pleasure itself became the only pursuit, without reference to any criterion of utility or transcendence.

Though surviving texts and artifacts bear only very limited and partial witness to the sexual lives of medieval people, we should not assume that the meanings of modern sexuality are any more coherent than those of the Middle Ages. As Karma Lochrie argues, "what we do not know about the past … can in turn help to reveal the incoherence of modern sexual categories, reminding us of what we do not know about the present either."[237] Medieval sexualities, precisely because they have to be retroactively constituted, thus provoke us to question the coherence of contemporary sexual categories and identities, and remind us of the difficulty of constructing any history of sexuality. The history of medieval lesbians and homosexuals, of sexual prohibitions and sexual possibilities, of erotic and scopophilic pleasures, is not delivered to us solely by "the physical traces of the past" but is "a construction of it under conditions and constraints determined by the present."[238] Our making of that history is driven by our desire.

CHAPTER TWO

Heterosexuality

KARMA LOCHRIE

Heterosexuality did not exist in the Middle Ages. It is true that acts of intercourse, reproduction, marriage, fornication, and prostitution were as common throughout medieval history as they are today, but the rubric under which these acts are classified—and the identities that they presume today—was not. In other words, the heterosexuality we know today as a category for understanding human sexual behavior and as a social and sometimes theological norm governing society—in short, heterosexuality as a given—was unknown to the Middle Ages. Since Michel Foucault's famous invocation of the difference between sodomy as a collection of acts and the sodomite as a species of individual in the first volume of *The History of Sexuality*,[1] historians of sexuality have debated the relative difference between sodomy and sodomites and modern homosexuality and homosexuals. The same historical and theoretical attention has not been devoted to heterosexuality as a category, despite Foucault's efforts in that same volume to elucidate the difference between medieval and premodern rules regarding the marriage relationship and the development of sexual norms that coincided with the emergence of heterosexuality as a concept in the eighteenth and nineteenth centuries.[2] Reading Foucault's first volume of *The History of Sexuality*, one learns that heterosexuality is as much about norms and processes of normalization as it is about particular kinds of sexual acts and desires. If Foucault is correct, then heterosexuality as a concept seriously skews—if it does not obscure—medieval, and indeed early modern, sexualities.

In order to understand fully why the Middle Ages was ignorant of heterosexuality as we know it, it is important to pursue Foucault's linking of the
emergence of modern heterosexuality with the evolution of norms and technologies of normalization. One of the more salient implications of Foucault's
remarks about the history of heterosexuality is that the category has less to do
with sexuality, ultimately, and more to do with the decidedly less sexy effects of
modern technologies of normalization. Because of the concomitant emergence
of heterosexuality and norms and the subsequent convergence of the concept
with its primary "operation," scholars use the term "heteronormativity" to
suggest the larger reach of heterosexuality into the "normative organization of
the world," by contrast with the category of homosexuality, which is marked,
in part, by the absence of the normative richness that heterosexuality enjoys.[3]
Heteronormativity includes more than the categories of sexual acts and identities: it is the "whole field of social relations [that] becomes intelligible as
heterosexuality" and as "that sense of rightness—embedded in things and not
just in sex."[4] No such sense of rightness or the intelligibility of social relations
in terms of heterosexuality was available to the Middle Ages as long as norms,
normalcy, and normalization had not yet been developed as technologies of
cultural regulation.

"Heterosexuality" as we understand the term came into being with the
advent of norms through which it became constituted. Not until the nineteenth century did norms evolve as both measurements and "means of producing a common standard" through the subjection of individual instances to
"an abstraction of commonality."[5] The entire process of normalization that
governs the production of heterosexuality as well as other areas of modern
life involves a complicated series of measurements, comparisons, and evalua-
tions that occur through the subjection of the individual to that abstraction of
commonality. Foucault provides one of the most extensive descriptions of this
process of normalization in the context of prison culture, but it applies equally
to modern sexuality:

> [The art of punishing] brings five quite distinct operations into play: it
> refers individual actions to a whole that is at once a field of comparison,
> a space of differentiation, and the principle of a rule to be followed.
> It differentiates individuals from one another, in terms of the following
> overall rule: that the rule be made to function as a minimal threshold, as
> an average to be respected or as an optimum towards which one must
> move. It measures in quantitative terms and hierarchizes in terms of value
> the abilities, the level, the 'nature' of individuals. It introduces, through

this 'value-giving' measure, the constraint of a conformity that must be achieved. Lastly, it traces the limit that will define difference in relation to all other differences, the external frontier of the abnormal. ... [To recapitulate, it] compares, differentiates, hierarchizes, homogenizes, excludes. In short, it *normalizes*. ... Like surveillance and with it, normalization becomes one of the great instruments of power at the end of the classical age. For the marks that once indicated status, privilege and affiliation were increasingly replaced—or at least supplemented—by a whole range of degrees of normality indicating membership of a homogeneous social body but also playing a part in classification, hierarchization and the distribution of rank. In a sense, the power of normalization imposes homogeneity; but it individualizes by making it possible to measure gaps, to determine levels, to fix specialties and to render the differences useful by fitting them one to another. It is easy to understand how the power of the norm functions within a system of formal equality, since within a homogeneity that is the rule, the norm introduces, as a useful imperative and as a result of measurement, all the shading of individual differences.[6]

There are at least three crucial pieces to Foucault's remarks that will help to differentiate modern *normalized* heterosexuality from the sexual organizations of the Middle Ages: first, it creates an abstract commonality, whether that abstraction is an average or an ideal. Second, the norm quantifies degrees of difference within that abstract commonality out of which the abnormal is created. Finally, the norm reinforces the homogeneity of the abstract commonality even as it measures, compares, and calibrates difference.

Heterosexuality as a norm (rather than just a collection of sexual desires, acts, and behaviors) thus emerges first as a calculated majority sexual practice of an abstract commonality, in this case, the "population," a concept introduced courtesy of the new science of statistics.[7] Second, heterosexuality represents both *the most common* and *the ideal*, constituting the ideal as majorative and the measure of all deviating degrees of sexual difference with respect to itself. At the same time that it results from an abstract homogeneous whole called the "population," heterosexuality as a norm also *confers* homogeneity, moral virtue, and reality on particular sex acts and the practitioners of those sex acts, as well as that "sense of rightness" that accrues to all normative organizations of the world. Heterosexuality has never existed apart from its normalization, and in fact, it is hard to imagine heterosexuality *strictly speaking*, since none of us has ever known it solely as a category of sexual orientation or identity.

The distinction that medievalist scholars sometimes make between modern heterosexuality and premodern heteronormativity is not a meaningful one. Heterosexuality is the effect of heteronormativity; neither exists without the other. Because it had no technology of norms or science of sexuality responsible for our modern notions of heterosexuality, medieval sexuality cannot be described in terms of heteronormativity. The stakes for preserving this terminology in the study of premodern sexualities are high: a world of sexualities before they became organized through norms around the binaries of heterosexuality and homosexuality will continue to elude scholars. An even more serious consequence is that the historical reach of heteronormativity threatens to become naturalized and universalized through continued deployment of the category for premodern sexualities. Only if we abandon heteronormativity as a category can alternative configurations of sexuality in the Middle Ages emerge and provide a corrective to the presumptive heterosexuality of the present.

Perhaps the closest that the Middle Ages came to the modern category of the norm was its category of the natural. It is often assumed, as one scholar writes, that "'natural' was being used as a stand-in for what a later age would call 'normal.'"[8] As the next section argues, medieval "Nature" and modern "norms" are not interchangeable terms, nor does heterosexuality necessarily find its medieval rationale in Nature, as we might suppose.

NATURAL AND UNNATURAL

Nature in the Middle Ages had none of the power, consistency, or technological force that modern norms have to rationalize and legitimize heterosexuality. First of all, as a moral authority, Nature was not as dependable in theological and philosophical discourses as one might think. Nature's lack of absolutism, its fragility, and its lapses often compromised the efforts of natural philosophy to develop a moral system for sexual acts and desires.[9] One reason for this instability in Nature's realm was that there were two natures in medieval theology: the more ideal prelapsarian nature and the more common and corrupt postlapsarian nature. The former represented all that is good and perfect—what Albert the Great calls Nature in its "maximally natural" state.[10] The Fall, however, introduced a corrupted Nature marked by the subversion of reason. It is this Nature that represents the human condition, what is "common" and universal to all, but in no sense is this Nature therefore regarded as a standard of human behavior the way a norm is. Medieval theologians appeal to a prelapsarian ideal in their discussions of natural and unnatural sexual acts, but this ideal is hardly "normative" in the sense that it predicates its desirability upon its sense of the average, common, and most widespread.[11]

The second problem with Nature's role in prescribing heterosexuality for the Middle Ages is that the taxonomies of sexual acts produced in medieval theological treatises were not organized according to a heterosexual norm or ideal. In Thomas Aquinas's discussion of sexual categories, for example, Reason and Nature are the two standards governing his hierarchy of species of lust. Together these standards do not so much guarantee a heterosexual norm as they limit legitimate sexual acts to marriage (according to Reason, since the desire for children is the main purpose of sex) and to procreation (according to Nature). Although this bar of legitimacy for sexual acts is narrowly heterosexual, it is important to recognize what it excludes: all "heterosexual" acts within marriage that do not lead to procreation, including oral sex, masturbation, sex with the wrong "vessels" or "instruments," or sex in gender-inappropriate positions. Furthermore, Aquinas's procreative ideal leads him to judge rape a less serious offense than masturbation or oral sex between husband and wife, because it can lead to conception, while the others cannot.[12] The procreative standard of Aquinas and others is focused more on reproductive intention, correct instruments (penises), and appropriate vessels (vaginas), than on the principle of male-female sexual relations.

Finally, the primary rubric under which sexuality in Nature is measured, at least in medieval theology, is not heterosexuality versus everything else, but abstinence versus sexual activity. The medieval ideal is thus chastity, or sexual abstinence, not heterosexuality, which falls into the category of "venereal acts," a category that is never completely exempt from sin. According to this rubric, "heterosexual acts" and "unnatural acts" are arranged along a continuum ranging from legitimate to increasingly illegitimate. The heterosexuality of the sexual desire or act does not determine its relative venality, as heterosexual and other kinds of acts are clustered together throughout the scale of species of lust.

The state of Nature, therefore, does not lend itself to any medieval heterosexual norm or ideal, since it is governed by principles other than the ones that determine modern heteronormativity. Moreover, Nature's prescriptive authority over sexuality is seriously compromised in some medieval accounts, such as Alan of Lille's *The Plaint of Nature* and Geoffrey Chaucer's *Parliament of Fowls*. Nature in Alan of Lille's work is beset by sexual anomalies, as Mark Jordan has shown, including "the drunkenness of desire, hermaphroditism, polygamy, and sexual self-mutilation."[13] Although Nature advocates orderly reproduction in Alan's work, her explanation of the various sexual disorders suggests otherwise. In a sequence describing the revolt of Venus from Nature's tutelage, Nature acknowledges a fundamental disordering of desire in her domain as a result of Venus's breakout from her control, causing mankind to "languish" from Venus's own "piercing fever" of lust.[14] Nature's fatal consignment of desire to Venus's purview explains the multiple and unsettling existence of unnatural sexual acts and desires within the realm of Nature.

Chaucer's Nature, too, is plagued by disorder, unreasonableness, and disruptive desire. The parliament of birds that Nature convenes in order to pair up members of each species with a mate ends in confusion and failure. Even though Nature suggests that Reason should reign over the female eagle's choice of a mate, she refuses to choose, postponing until the following year her choice of one of the male eagles as a mate. Nature's procreative agenda is humorously undermined in Chaucer's poem, attenuating the moral authority of Nature's realm in sexual matters.

DESIRE, SEX, AND LOVE WITHOUT HETEROSEXUALITY

How did the Middle Ages understand sexual desire? Specific sexual acts? Love? Insofar as heterosexual desire is understood narrowly in its modern sense of desire for someone of the opposite sex, it is safe to say that the Middle Ages did not entertain the default presumptions either that all desire is heterosexual or even that sexual desire is primarily a question of the gender of the object of desire. In fact, it is not even certain that sexual desire was itself a discrete category apart from other kinds of desire. It is true that medieval theology used the Latin term *luxuria* to designate a category of sexual sins; it is also true that *libido*, or "lust," is often the term used to describe that "integral part of the constitution of fallen human nature."[15] The difference between medieval sexual desire and modern sexual desire is that the former is not limited to sexual desire per se. According to Thomas Aquinas, lust is the opposite of temperance, and thus it includes *all* forms of excessive desire. In the *Summa theologica* he writes that "lust applies chiefly to venereal pleasures, which more than anything else work the greatest havoc in a man's mind, yet secondarily it applies to any other matters pertaining to excess."[16] Venereal pleasures, in turn, are viewed by Aquinas and other writers of the period as complicit in the larger arena of overweening desire, including ambition, greed, and luxuriousness (as in the inordinate craving for soft bedding and clothing). Sexual desire, therefore, is not configured around the sex of the subject or object of it, nor is it a separate species from other kinds of desire. One has only to observe Chaucer's representations of the Garden of Venus in "The Knight's Tale" and *The Parliament of Fowls* to glean the many affiliations of sexual desire—with prodigality, greed, courtesy, nobility, and pride in clothing.[17]

The medieval theology of desire, therefore, does not necessarily regard the various species of sexual sins as so many sexual preferences of particular sinners; rather, sexual sins are available to all humans, regardless of marital status, as part of the condition of fallen humanity. This is one reason that Chaucer's Parson and other authors of treatises on confession in which all of the seven mortal sins are extensively cataloged and defined were so careful not to name "thilke abhomynable synne, of which that no man unnethe oghte speke ne write" ("that abominable sin, of which no man ought hardly speak or write").[18] If sodomy is named, it might seduce unwitting humans to experiment in it. *All* humans were susceptible to *all* kinds of sexual sins because sexual desire was itself integral to the human condition and because it was complicit in the other kinds of excesses of desire—social, political, and selfish—to which humans were so susceptible. Sexual desire was not a discrete desire, but just one in a nexus of desires that are often inter-implicated with one another: ambition, greed, ungoverned speech, and lust, for example, would be seen as consistent symptoms of a Christian subject who has become enthralled by his or her own lusts.[19] The narrowing of the semantic field for "lust" from its medieval meaning of pleasure and desire generally to mean sexual desire in a pejorative sense exclusively did not occur until the sixteenth century.[20]

If medieval sexual desire was rather protean and portable, medieval sexual acts were narrowly prescribed, not according to modern identity categories of heterosexual or homosexual, but according to the principles of activity and passivity in conjunction with reproduction. The assignment of active sexual partner to the male and passive partner to the female might seem to resemble modern heteronormativity or gender ideology. In fact, however, the principles were more narrowly understood in medieval discourse than they are today, with activity signifying penetration, and passivity receptivity to penetration. Any sexual act that did not align with the strict rubric of the male-penetrator/female-penetrated sexual act was not "natural." What is perhaps more surprising is that this active-passive principle of "heterosexual" sex did not necessary correspond to the way in which men and women were regarded as sexual beings in the Middle Ages. The fact that women were assigned the role of the properly passive partner in sex did not mean that women's sexual appetites or courting behaviors were likewise expected to be passive. Women—not men—were generally regarded as the oversexed gender in medieval theology, literature, and medicine; that is, they were regarded as more sexual than men were thought to be. The image of the hypersexed woman is a common—but not a positive—one; it derived from the belief that women were less rational than men and therefore more susceptible to the polymorphous impulses of desire.[21]

One of the chief distinctions, therefore, between legitimate and non-legitimate sexual acts was the relative alignment or misalignment of gender roles with the active or passive principle. For example, the phenomenon of the woman on top in sexual intercourse between a man and a woman was regarded by William Peraldus, the Dominican author of the important treatise *Summa vitiorum* (1236; *Summa of the Vices and the Virtues*), as an unnatural sin precisely because it violated the active-passive manner or position associated with the active and passive principles.[22]

Likewise, men who engaged in sex with each other violated the same principle because one of the sexual partners would be seen as taking the passive (feminine) position. Alan of Lille provides the most famous and overwrought tropes for the violations against the masculine active principle in sex acts between men. The first trope is grammatical: the sex act between a man and a woman is like the grammatical relationship between subject and predicate, in which the subject is the actor and the predicate is the recipient of action. As in grammar, and so too in sex, meaning derives from the operations of activity and passivity (and masculinity and femininity). However, when man engages in sex with another man, he "becomes both subject and predicate: one and the same term is given a double application. Man here extends too far the laws of grammar. Becoming a barbarian in grammar, he disclaims the manhood given him by nature."[23] The activity of the subject is here equated with masculinity, and the implication for sexual acts is that only the receptive partner—the predicate, so to speak—is guilty of grammatical barbarism and sexual anomaly.

Immediately following this trope of sexual violations of the active-passive principle, Alan delivers his most notorious trope of the hammer and anvil. Alan's "sexual forge," in which the active hammer strikes the passive anvil to produce sparks, becomes disfigured in the male-male sexual act. Not only does the partner who occupies the anvil position assume a passive function, but the "striking" of hammer on anvil produces no sparks, or seeds, and the entire interaction is therefore "barren." The hammer, furthermore, "shudders in horror of its anvil" since it leaves no "stamp of the parent-stem."[24] What is remarkable about Alan's trope is that it does away entirely with the element of penetration in its image of hammer striking against anvil, construing the natural and procreative act to consist of a violent active principle that leads to reproduction on the strength of its activity alone. The trope omits penetration entirely in favor of a sexual activity rendered as a kind of cudgeling. The only difference, therefore, between male-male sexual activity and "heterosexual" sex lies in the gender of the anvil. Those men like Narcissus, who "converted Venus' hammers to the function of anvils,"[25] do not fundamentally change the nature of the sexual act, but they do change its meaning insofar as they adopt the passive/anvil position in sex.

Alan of Lille and medieval culture generally do not conceive of sexual acts, therefore, in terms of a heterosexual standard by which all others are judged. In fact, many sexual acts that are "heterosexual" fall into the category of unnatural acts. Furthermore, it is not so much the biological sex of the sexual partner that determines the licitness or illicitness of the act, but the active or passive position assumed by the sexual partner in sex. Women and men can easily commit unnatural acts with each other according to the same logic that designates same-sex sexual acts unnatural. The narrowly "natural" act of sex between men and women is hardly even recognizable as "heterosexual" in Alan's trope, where activity and passivity seem to override penetration as the reproductive ideal of sexual relations between men and women.

The medieval discourses of both sex acts and sexual desire were clearly gendered and gendering. The principle of activity and passivity, as I have shown, is crucial to the gendering of sexual activity in the Middle Ages, and in many respects it does not correspond to modern heteronormativity. Femininity was identified with passive receptivity of penetration, whether the person occupying that position was male or female. The masculine principle of activity, as Alan of Lille implies, trumps penetration as the natural rule of thumb. Sexual desire, too, was gendered in the Middle Ages: it was considered to be essentially feminine and feminizing. Insofar as inordinate sexual appetites were associated with women and femininity, sexual desire itself (even of the "heterosexual" variety) threatened to effeminize men. Whereas modern heteronormativity valorizes sexual promiscuity in men as an index of masculinity, medieval culture associated rampant sexual desires and practices with femininity, and therefore the same man who today might be regarded positively as a womanizer might have been viewed as effeminate in the Middle Ages. The entire cultural construction of cuckoldry in the medieval and early modern periods derives its humorous and murderous force from the degrading—because feminizing—effects of masculine "heterosexual" desire. Chaucer's "Miller's Tale" derives its humor, in part, not only from the effeminacy of John, the old and jealous husband, whose sexual possessiveness emasculates him, but by the end of the tale also from that of Absolon and Nicholas, the two competitors for Alison's attentions, both of whom are humiliated at the end of the story, and in the case of Nicholas, even symbolically castrated. Cuckoldry was not only the stuff of premodern comedy; it could also assume tragic dimensions in Shakespeare's *Othello*, in which the spectacle of a great man "loving not wisely but too well" provides a lesson in the unmanning effects of heterosexual love and their recuperation in tragedy.

There are two contexts in which the differing perspectives on male "heterosexual" desire are understood in premodernity and modernity. The first—the gendering of desire—has already been discussed. The second has to do with the differing roles that homosociality played in the two eras. Homosociality as an ideal governing masculine relations dates back to classical ideas of male friendship, and this idea is still fundamental to medieval ideas of friendship and love. This means that, unlike modern heterosexual desire, which exists within a "heterosexual imaginary," premodern sexual desire existed within a "homosocial imaginary," making it rank and "mean" differently from how it does today. In addition, homosociality and the patriarchal family (in the sense of a family organized according to the principles of guaranteeing and valorizing paternity) actually held a primacy in premodern culture that would have been threatened by the modern idea of heterosexual love.[26] Although a distinction would accrue in the sixteenth century between true love's companionate and sexual aspects and desire's "precipitate, inconsistent, turbulent, and dangerous" ones, no such clear difference between love and sexual desire can be mapped for the Middle Ages.[27]

The language of medieval Latin and vernaculars did not always make such a distinction, except, that is, in the language of courtly love. The phenomenon of courtly love in medieval culture seems to validate its predominantly heteronormative readings by scholars in the sense that it provided a space in that culture for the valorization of heterosexual desire, sentiment, and love. It is important, however, to contextualize this approbative discourse of heterosexual love alongside the "theology of aversion and instrumentalization"[28] that also characterizes medieval discourse on the subjects of love, desire, and marriage. This conjunction, at the very least, attenuates the "heteronormativity" of the period in that it produces the ideal of "heterosexual" love within a cultural context that neither recognizes nor supports it. Since the literature of courtly love is not, by any means, an insurgent or reformatory one, it is misleading to read it through modern heteronormative lenses. The phenomenon of courtly love is part of, rather than the exception to, a medieval culture that still did not understand sexual and romantic relations between men and women in terms of the category of heterosexuality.

One further observation to be made regarding medieval representations of "heterosexuality" has to do with the glaring absence of textual evidence for a shared medieval understanding of the pleasures and salutary effects of heterosexual love and sex. This is no small absence: apart from the rather legislative language of theological treatments of reproductive sex, there really is not much in the way of a sustained discourse about heterosexual pleasures. One of the only places in English literature of the Middle Ages in which the pleasures of heterosexual sex are extolled is so remarkable that it inspires comment for its anomalousness. This passage occurs in the Middle English poem *Cleanness*, in which God contrasts heterosexual pleasure to the sins of Sodom and Gomorrah:

> I compast hem a kynde crafte and kende hit hem derne,
> And amed hit in myn ordenaunce oddely dere,
> And dyght drwry þerinne, doole alther-swettest,
> And the play of paramorez I portrayed myseluen,
> And made therto a maner myriest of other:
> When two true togeder had tyghed hemseluen,
> Bytwene a male and his make such merthe schulde come,
> Welnyghe pure paradys moght preue no better.

> [I devised for them a natural craft, and taught it to them secretly,
> And regarded it in my ordinance uniquely precious,
> And set love therein, intercourse most sweet,
> And the play of lovers I myself portrayed
> And made for it a manner of behavior that is the most delightful of all;
> When two faithful ones have tied themselves together,
> Between a male and his mate such pleasure should come
> That well-nigh pure paradise might prove no better.][29]

The "natural craft" of heterosexual love is here the sweetest of sexual acts, and God claims to have endowed it with the most delightful of pleasures ("merthe"). Reproductive aims are noticeably missing from the scene of heterosexual love-play. Yet one should not forget that this encomium to heterosexual pleasure is situated within the story of Sodom and Gomorrah, and it betrays an anxiety about the failure of God's "natural craft" to dissuade some lovers from unnatural modes of sexual pleasure. The singularity of this kind of special praise for heterosexual love and sexual pleasure and its anxious concern for a courtly love-play that is not so admirable attenuates its apparent normative function.[30]

Contrary to our modern assumption, therefore, love between a man and a woman is not necessarily heterosexual.[31] Close readings of the mise-en-scène of courtly love and desire might arguably also reveal that courtly love is more about the "love of courtliness," or the qualities of nobility, than it is about sexual desire for the opposite sex, in which case James Schultz's term "aristophilia" might serve as a better description of the phenomenon of medieval romance that we call courtly love. The valorization of nobility and aristocracy in courtly love does not always resemble heterosexual romantic love, with its explicit eroticization of sexual difference.[32] It is important to attend to the ways in which love and desire are represented in courtly love without the presumption of heteronormative romance.

Another pervasive theme of some medieval romances that tends to be overwritten in some narratives of medieval courtly love is the failure of "heterosexual" love either as a prerequisite of chivalric masculinity or as a compensation for military prowess. Grail romances posit the masculine hero not after the pattern of Gawain, the successful and prolific courtly lover, but after the chaste heroism of Perceval, Galahad, and Bors. Although chastity is an ideal associated with Christian heroism, it is not so consistent with romance heroism in which courtly love/desire functions as an essential part of chivalric economies. The chaste masculine hero of the medieval Grail romances thus attests to at least one alternative to the conventional structure of medieval romance, one in which carnal desire is sacrificed to a spiritual desire.[33] It is also betrays its own anxious desire to realign masculine subjectivity with chastity, rather than courtly love for women, and to refocus the *telos* of "romance" on spiritual rather than earthly love.

Although it often involves romantic love between men and women, therefore, courtly love is not heterosexual in the modern sense because it is not supported by all the apparatus of modern heterosexuality, including the affective family, the domestication of desire and idealization of marital pleasure, and the widespread dispersal of the implications of romantic love for the nuclear family; the nation; concepts of human rights, intimacy, and happiness; freedom in a democratic society; and the social order itself. Although medieval courtly love served the ends of aristocratic self-definition and exclusion, it never assumed the literary, social, or political dimensions of modern romantic love, which are all effects of heteronormativity. As the next section of this chapter argues, heterosexual romantic love developed out of the institutionalization of desire within marriage and the concept of companionate marriage in the Renaissance. It is only after love and desire are fully domesticated by the eighteenth century that romantic love in its modern sense becomes an ideal. The dangerous nature of desire in the Middle Ages and through the Renaissance becomes transformed into modern heterosexual romance only after it is brought "in from the cold" by the "moraliz[ation] and domesticat[ion of] a destabilizing passion" that "confin[es] it within the safety of the affective family."[34] The ideology of heterosexual romantic love, in other words, cannot be separated from the relocation of idealized erotic desire into the domain of the family.[35] The romantic desire and love found in medieval courtly love then become transformed into a consummate social, political, and personal ideal that finds its most wistful expression in marriage.

MARRIAGE WITHOUT HETEROSEXUALITY

The extensive evidence for marriage as a desirable and widespread social arrangement during the Middle Ages does not mean that heterosexuality was equally pervasive. Like sexual desire, medieval marriage occupied a fraught cultural terrain generally marked by clerical condemnation, ambiguated status of sex within marriage, and inconsistency. Foucault has described the difference between premodern and modern marriages in terms of a shift from the "deployment of alliance" to the "deployment of sexuality."[36] Medieval marriage, according to Foucault, is organized around the "fixation and development of kinship ties" and the "transmission of names and possessions."[37] At the same time, marital relations were governed by a "system of rules defining the permitted and the forbidden, the licit and the illicit." This system of rules for marital sex, however, did more to catalog the illicit than it did to guarantee the licit nature of marital relations. If oral sex between consenting spouses was deemed unnatural as compared with incest because of the procreative possibility of the latter and the impossibility of the former, marital sex never enjoyed that categorical sanctity that modern marriage confers on it via heteronormativity. The "deployment of sexuality," which Foucault dates to the eighteenth century, configures sexuality around a strict definition of heterosexual monogamy at the same time that it proliferates and extends the regime of the perverse according to "the sensations of the body, the quality of pleasures, and the nature of impressions."[38] Foucault's distinction between the two deployments is not a successionist one; that is, he does not argue for the superimposition of the deployment of sexuality on the previous deployment of alliance. The modern family, according to Foucault, represents the convergence of these two deployments, one governing the rules of legitimate sex and one that has produced the "obligatory locus of affects, feelings, love."[39] If Foucault is right, the modern formation of marriage, family, and heteronormativity is not only a relatively recent phenomenon, but it differs fundamentally from the social and religious institution of marriage that obtained before the eighteenth century. More than anything else, marriage becomes the primary locus of the normalizing of a "heterosexual" sexuality, as well as the measure of the perverse in modern society.

One of the keys to the theological formation of sex in marriage in the Middle Ages was the concept of the marriage debt. An oft-cited passage in 1 Corinthians institutes the idea that would be quoted by Peter Lombard, St. Thomas Aquinas, and perhaps most famously Chaucer's Wife of Bath: "Let the husband render the debt [of his body] to his wife, and the wife also in like manner to the husband" (1 Cor. 7:3). Although this idea offered a "rhetoric of equality" regarding sexual obligations in marriage, it also advocated an instrumentalist construction of sexuality according to which the spousal subject was obligated to surrender her- or himself to the use of the other.[40] In addition, the increased interest in the marriage debt in theological writings from the twelfth century onward accompanied a focus on the woman's availability to her husband, rather than the reverse, inspiring protocols for women's adornment and her passive role in sexual intercourse.[41] At the same time, the exacting and rendering of the marriage debt was fraught with the danger and mortal sin for women. Once "every pretext for sexual refusal was inexorably removed from the woman," even the wife's exacting of the debt could be a source of sin.[42] In addition to the gender inequity that was built into the Pauline rule of the *debitum*, the language of economic transaction rendered the sexual act in marriage less of a "heterosexual" sex act in the modern sense and more of a business transaction—a rendering that the Wife of Bath would exploit to her own advantage in the prologue to her tale in Chaucer's *Canterbury Tales*. St. Paul's dictum for marital sexuality, with all its coercive and commercial language, could not be further from the exalted understanding of marital sex produced by modern heteronormativity.

In addition to its sanctification of sex and heterosexual monogamy, modern marriage (and heteronormativity) also differs from its pre-and early modern precursors in its fundamental social structure of intimacy. Many scholars have suggested that modern notions of heterosexual love and marriage are inseparable from the advent of intimacy, understood as that realm that unites the emotions and sexual desires to produce "a sexualized experience of others that stands apart from society and yet is recognized by it."[43] Far from representing a strictly sexual category of experience, intimacy comes to function as the salutary form of social interaction and self-cultivation that is born of the crisis of social hierarchies in the early modern period. In contemporary American culture, if not Western cultures generally, "a complex cluster of sexual practices gets confused, ... with the love plot of intimacy and familialism that signifies belonging to a society in a deep and normal way. Community is imagined through scenes of intimacy, coupling, and kinship. And a historical relation to futurity is restricted to generational narrative and reproduction."[44]

Before intimacy, sexuality did not quite function as a means of social interaction and self-cultivation. To be sure, sexuality is already a form of social interaction in the Middle Ages, but it is not a generalizable mechanism for imagining social interaction and sexual subjectivity. The sexual relations that are imagined in medieval texts, whether they are theological or romance texts, are hardly capable of sustaining this "love plot of intimacy," according to which not only are communities imagined but differences are bridged and a shared humanity (or citizenship) is implied. Although medieval marriage certainly provided a locus of intimacy for men and women, it never achieved the kind of cultural capital that it enjoys today as a chief guarantor and expression of this ideology of intimacy and as "the privileged institution of social reproduction, the accumulation and transfer of capital, and self-development."[45]

Intimacy is not the only factor that distinguishes modern from medieval marriage. Two others are equally important and arguably related: the shift to companionate marriage and the emergent distinction between lust and love. Companionate marriage emerged roughly in the sixteenth century, according to most historians, although medievalists have also argued for an emergent form of it in the late Middle Ages.[46] Unlike earlier dynastic or reproductive models of marriage, companionate marriage emphasized "the conjugal unit ... as a locus of domesticity, spiritual equality, and companionship."[47] In addition to promoting a new discourse of friendship, mutuality, and eroticism between spouses, companionate marriage also brought with it an array of social imperatives surrounding parenting and childhood education. Even more importantly, companionate marriage contributed to the development of the idea of the family as "private, autonomous, and affective, rather than public and permeable to kin and community."[48]

This idea of the companionate marriage was not a strictly Renaissance phenomenon, however; it developed out of the medieval church's insistence on consent between spouses as the foundation of medieval marriage in the twelfth century. The development of intimacy and its attendant notion of the "affective family," however, emerged in the late medieval and early modern periods. The association of heterosexuality with this emergent concept of the companionate marriage and affective family comes about, in part, through its eroticization of marriage. Medieval representations of the sexual relationship in marriage, as discussed previously, were highly fraught insofar as they were based on the economic trope of the marriage debt and the church's taxonomy of sexual sins, many of which included sexual acts within marriage. The eroticizing of the sexual relationship between husband and wife seems to accompany the emerging distinction between lust and love, and it resulted in the privileging of an idea of conjugal happiness born of equality, companionship, and erotic pleasure.

A shift occurred in the late medieval and early modern periods from an ideology of marriage that endeavored to accommodate the church's celebration of celibacy and minimalist approach to marital sex based on the Pauline admonition that it is "better to marry than to burn" to one that waxed rhapsodic over the "romantic and companionable happiness of married love and family life."[49] Thomas Hoccleve's *Regiment of Princes* (1411–1412), for example, argues for disciplining lust in marriage and choosing a wife based on her virtue rather than sexual attraction. Hoccleve engages in a discussion in which his own wistful contention that he married for love becomes exposed as lust. The marriage contracted through desire is doomed to become "an helle" once that desire has dissipated. The stark opposition between a chaste kind of love of virtue and lustful distraction leaves little room for an ideal of marital pleasure. Two centuries later Robert Crofts enthuses over "the multitude of felicities" in marriage, including the pleasure of "the sweet society of Lovers," the "sweet councell" spouses afford each other, and the incipient joy that pervades the rest of their actions.[50] The narrow interpretation of sex and desire in Lydgate seems to exclude the possibility of the kind of marital pleasure that Crofts idealizes.

This same contrast can be observed in late medieval texts, too. That famous cluster of tales in Geoffrey Chaucer's *Canterbury Tales* commonly referred to as "the marriage group" suggests that companionate marriage was already a matter of social debate. The Wife of Bath exploits the Pauline prescription of the "marriage debt" to wield power over her husbands. At the same time, she counters the theological endorsement of virginity over marriage, claiming the laudatory end of marriage to be sex. Despite all of the Wife's claims for the married estate and protestations that she "evere folwede myn appetit" ("always followed my sexual appetite"),[51] she is no advocate for companionate marriage. In fact, the Wife of Bath suggests that the fantasy of marrying for love and sexual attraction does not necessarily benefit the woman's position in marriage. The Wife's marriage to her fifth husband, Jankyn, "which that I took for love, and no richesse [wealth],"[52] turns out to be a huge mistake, as it causes her to surrender her sovereignty, and him to abuse her. Although the Wife's prologue and tale both end with a vision of companionate bliss, her own experience is an object lesson in the dangers of that ideal for women.

Other tales in the marriage group offer competing models of nuptial happiness. The "Clerk's Tale," for example, renders Hoccleve's preference for love of virtue over mutual attraction an ideal. Thus Walter chooses Griselda not on the basis of his attraction to her, but on the basis of her virginity, humility, steadfastness, obedience to her father, and allergy to idleness. The marriage agreement between Walter and Griselda is wholly devoted to Griselda's consenting to surrender her will to his. The problematic consequences of Griselda's consent—her agreement to Walter's "murder" of her children—suggests medieval awareness of the limitations of this model, even though the narrator translates his story into an allegory about the relationship of man and God.

It is in the "Franklin's Tale" that most Chaucer scholars have discerned a nascent medieval ideal of companionate marriage based on two aspects of the tale: it attempts to incorporate the courtly love of the main characters, Arveragus and Dorigen, into marriage, and it articulates an ideal of equal companionship between husband and wife. The Franklin who narrates the tale offers a kind of manifesto of companionate marriage in which he characterizes the spousal relationship as a friendship based on love and companionship. He argues that "mastery" and "sovereignty" are inimical to the freedom and equality that marital love demands for its sustenance and proposes patience as the supreme virtue in marriage. "Looke who that is moost pacient in love," states the Franklin,[53] and he goes on to suggest that mutual tolerance is the key to love and happy marriages. Of course, the tale ends up suggesting otherwise, insofar as Dorigen's freedom seems to get her into trouble, and Arveragus's vow never to exert authority over her nearly leads to disastrous consequences. Even more problematic is the Franklin's ultimate abandonment of the idea of companionate marriage in favor of a debate about the relative nobility of the men in his tale. Chaucer's implicit endorsement of companionate marriage in this tale, therefore, is arguable, to say the least, but the tale suggests that formative ideas of companionate marriage were circulating in late medieval England.

One last kind of marriage practiced in the Middle Ages and extolled in saints' lives in particular was the medieval phenomenon of "spiritual marriage." An idea that really finds no modern equivalent in modern heterosexual marriage, spiritual marriage was a "legally binding marriage in which sexual relations have been remitted by the consent of both parties for reasons of piety."[54] Because of the superiority of virginity over marriage, at least in the elite texts of theology and canon law, the incorporation of virginity into marriage became a method primarily for women to resist their society's reproductive expectations and overcome the institutional stumbling block to spiritual perfection that marriage was understood to pose. Spiritual marriage was emphatically not the consequence of diminished sexual relations between spouses, or age, but of a deliberate decision on the part of both spouses. Furthermore, unlike sexually active marriages, spiritual marriages were thought to offer "a profound intimacy and companionship between the sexes that is in no way contingent on sexual intercourse."[55] The tradition of spiritual marriage in the West stretches from the time of Christ until the end of the Middle Ages, around 1500. It can be found in the lives of St. Cecilia and Christina of Markyate and the fifteenth-century mystic Margery Kempe. Although it was controversial, as Kempe's experience demonstrates, it was also highly regarded as an alternative lay spiritual practice that emerged from the eventual democratization of sanctity. Far from representing a variation on a dominant medieval heterosexuality, spiritual marriage constitutes a variation on chastity that circumvents the parameters of the marriage debt and forges a pious companionship that was regarded as superior to ordinary marriage relationships. By most modern standards of heterosexual marriage, medieval spiritual marriages are off the grid insofar as they sacralize chastity over sexual union, resist the medieval church's understanding of marriage in terms of the marriage debt, and imagine a competing form of piety to ecclesiastical institutions.

HETEROSEXUALITY'S SINE QUA NON: HOMOSOCIALITY

Although modern heteronormativity is typically understood to mean male-female sexual relations and all the cultural capital associated with them, it also incorporates male homosociality in its very structure and meaning. Scholars have demonstrated the critical role that male homosocial bonding plays in the structures of heterosexual desire and narrative.[56] The section of this chapter devoted to the subjects of desire, sex, and love suggested that the premodern and modern periods are governed by two different cultural imaginaries, one homosocial and the other heterosexual, and that this difference structures the negative and positive associations with masculine desire in pre- and postmodernity. The difference between the homosocial and heterosocial imaginary is that in the former, male-male bonds are primary, while in the latter they are secondary (though no less crucial) to heterosexual bonds. The homosocial imaginary valued male-male friendship and spiritual ties over sexual relationships between men and women, in part, because sexual desire was associated with women, irrationality, and excess. The heterosexual imaginary, by contrast, configures masculinity in part through heterosexual relationships, while retaining the importance of male-bonding for the achievement of social, political, and economic power.

A structure similar to the homosocial triangle underlying heterosexual love plots can be found in medieval narratives of courtly love and fabliau cuckoldry. That is, many narratives of courtly love, like many fabliaux, construct erotic triangles between rival masculine lovers and the female object of desire, or husbands, cuckolders, and wives. Masculine rivalry is a common feature in medieval love plots, whether courtly or comic. Beyond the rivalry, however, some have argued that courtly love sometimes serves in medieval literature to compensate for and redirect the homosocial—and even sexual—ethos of chivalry and other masculine networks. Chaucer's "Knight's Tale," for example, places the heterosexual love interest on the periphery of a narrative about chivalric brotherhood and rivalry. In *Sir Gawain and the Green Knight*, Gawain's vows to the Lord of the Castle come into conflict with his obligations to the protocols of courtly love.

Another homosocial ethos governs medieval court culture, monasteries, cathedral communities, spiritual texts, and treatises on friendship. This form of homosociality has been called "ennobling love."[57] The extent and dominion of this sentiment extends beyond romantic love even for a culture known for its courtly love and the romance genre. This ennobling love found in courtly love represents a dominant and historically specific form of homosociality, and it is distinguishable from romantic love first in its publicity rather than its privacy. Second, it is a way of behaving primarily, and a mode of feeling only secondarily. Third, it is a social ideal for an aristocracy—lay, clerical, and monastic. Fourth, it is a social habitus that was available only to men from antiquity to the late eleventh century; from the twelfth century onward, it was available to women (as seen primarily in spiritual texts), but it continued to be primarily a male homosocial habitus. Finally, this ennobling love is a form of aristocratic self-representation in which the virtue and reputations of lovers are enhanced.[58] A "culture of love and friendship" can be seen in diverse texts as "letters of friendship from monasteries and cathedral communities, courtly romances, the biography of the English visionary recluse Christina of Markyate, love lyric in Latin and the vernacular, Ælred of Rievaulx's tract on friendship, and the treatises on love by Andreas Capellanus and Baldesar Castiglione in the fourth book of his *Book of the Courtier*."[59]

Whether such a rhetoric constituted a Platonic tradition of same-sex relations or a homoerotic one, or both, as scholars have argued, its importance for an understanding of medieval sexuality lies in the primacy of male homosocial bonds as guarantors of power and prestige, but also its idealized mode of affectivity, friendship, and passion.[60] An organization of the medieval world according to this dominant structure of public, affective male homosocial bonds modifies the meaning and prominence of the "heterosexuality" we might find in the same culture. Not only are heterosexual love and sex secondary to male homosociality in the cultural hierarchy of affect, but they are placed in tension with the ideals and virtues of that homosociality.[61] Even more importantly, homosocial love remains the primary "technology of the self," to borrow Foucault's language, by means of which one practiced self-mastery, self-cultivation, and virtue.[62] Romantic love and sex were derivative of the male homosocial ideal, and they never quite supplanted it until, perhaps, fairly recently.

CONCLUSION: HISTORY WITHOUT HETEROSEXUALITY

The power of heterosexuality to assume the status of normal, universal, and historical, and the essential organization of sexualities over time, is a tribute to the effects of normativity in the present, but it is not borne out by a study of past sexualities. While Foucault theorized the "perverse implantation" by which deviant sexualities came to signify a new category of individuals, he also implies in his *History of Sexuality* that a "normal implantation" was just as crucial to the modern regime of heterosexuality.[63] As I have shown, such a regime of the normal in and of itself did not exist in the Middle Ages—nor did anything like the modern expansion of heterosexuality as an ideal and a presumptive majorative sexual practice. The normal and perverse arose together in the history of Western culture. Perhaps one of the signal symptoms of the normativizing of heterosexuality in modern culture is the tendency of scholars of the past to presume its historical universality.

The Middle Ages and Renaissance offer modern scholars of sexuality the opportunity to investigate a world in which sexuality was not governed by a heterosexuality that also supported a normative organization of the world. Premodernity might not offer scholars a direct path to imagining a world after heteronormativity, but it does at least suggest the limitations of heteronormativity and, it is to be hoped, a vector into the conceivability of a modern heteronormativity with no future.

CHAPTER THREE

Homosexuality: Specters of Sodom

ROBERT MILLS

In many ways the topic of medieval homosexuality can only be approached through its ghosts. After all, the various activities, desires, and dispositions gathered together under the Christian theological heading of sodomy (and its non-Christian counterparts) can rarely be traced back to actual bodies and experiences with any clarity. This is not to say that women never had sex with other women in the Middle Ages, nor men with men, or that sodomy was principally a theory. Rather, the conceptual frameworks within which same-sex sexual practices were condemned in this period, which were often devised against the backdrop of religious and political hysteria, do not allow easy access to the "objective" truths of medieval sexuality. Accusations of sodomy cannot simply be treated as statements of fact, and "sodomite" itself is hardly a neutral label, one that leads historians logically to homosexuality. Sodomy's rhetorical coloring defies attempts to construct an orderly archive of sexual experience, let alone to gain direct access to the "real" voices of medieval sodomites. What remains, for the most part, is a mishmash of scapegoating recriminations, unreliable recollections, and half-spoken fantasies, one that haunts more recent conceptions of homosexuality but is in no way identical to it.[1]

This is not to say that medieval sodomy and modern homosexuality are totally distinct: the metaphor of haunting gets at the ways in which the roles assigned to medieval sodomites continue to exert a spectral presence in the present. This occurs most explicitly in the context of recurring religious debates about the "sinfulness" of same-sex sexuality; but secular jurisdictions that have, until very recently, continued to prohibit "sodomy" or crimes "against nature" (notably certain North American states) also betray the persistent influence of medieval theological principles on modern attitudes.[2]

Identify medieval sodomy and modern homosexuality too closely with one another, however, and we are confronted with major interpretive difficulties. Some contemporary understandings of sexuality—which assume, for instance, that individuals who love one another passionately and those who have sexual relations can both be described by the single term "homosexual"—meet a challenge in situations where expressions of homoerotic affect and acts of same-sex copulation are viewed as distinct phenomena, the former publicly validated and the latter vigorously condemned. "Homosexuality," like "heterosexuality," potentially produces more confusion than clarity when projected onto such situations. How does one square the anxieties of the early church father Augustine (d. 430) that "immodest women" were shaming themselves in jesting and playing, "even with other females," with poetry, sometimes written by women themselves, testifying to passionate same-sex feelings within medieval convents? Why was an influential churchman such as Anselm (d. 1109), who regularly wrote ardent love letters to his male friends, the motivating force behind a piece of church legislation designed to root out those who "commit the shameful sin of sodomy" from the English clergy? How could medieval intellectuals in the Arab-Islamic world who did not mince words in denouncing the crime of *liwat*—a category derived from the Koran that generally denoted male anal intercourse—simultaneously condone, or even compose, poems encouraging the appreciation of beautiful beardless boys? Applying the category of homosexuality to these examples may produce visions of a religious culture simultaneously "tolerant" and "intolerant" of homoeroticism, or of individuals suffering from "internal" homophobia, when in fact very different modes of understanding were playing out.

Imagining a Middle Ages "before homosexuality" offers one way around this problem: instead of pushing medieval sexualities into heterosexual or homosexual boxes, we can set about documenting taxonomies of identity and desire that resist this particular organizing binary. Focusing on the ways in which distinctions of age, gender, role, religion, and social status structure same-sex relations can point to aspects of medieval sexuality that override or significantly inflect considerations of same-sex object choice, showing up, in the process, a much more diverse field of sexual possibility than the modern hetero-homo division arguably allows.[3] However, the risk is that articulations of a time "before" leave in place notions of modernity as a conceptual unity fully at ease with its homogenized conceptions of gay and straight identity.[4] This binds researchers into false narratives of temporal progression and cultural uniformity, when the modern world itself has no commonly agreed-upon criteria for designating who or what is homosexual in a given context: for all the cultural dominance of the hetero-homo binary, we have learned to accommodate a fair amount of imprecision in the term's application, both globally and locally. Labeling some contemporary individuals who have same-sex contact "homosexual" produces its own categorical confusions. Those who engage in occasional sex with same-sex partners without compromising their "normal" status (say, married men who enjoy sexual relations with other men as well as with their wives) do not always assume the mantle of gay identity willingly or comfortably; we may be doing violence to the complexities of their daily lives if we assume that we can simply resolve these questions of sexual identity by transforming them into questions about "homosexual" acts.[5]

In order to address these complications of evidence and interpretation, this chapter is organized around three principal sites of haunting and confusion. The first section, "Punishment," considers religious attitudes to same-sex sexuality in the Middle Ages and the uneven influence of these viewpoints on secular law. The second, "Publicity," asks what happens when same-sex acts deemed illicit by religious or secular authorities meet discourses of same-sex love and friendship, and whether there are circumstances when the two become confused. The last, "Possibility," foregrounds the particular role gender plays in medieval sodomy polemic, as in the trope of "lesbian" impossibility (which emerges toward the end of the Middle Ages) and tales of gender trouble or transformation (which were popular throughout the period); it also considers the effect that attitudes in medical writings and natural philosophy had on these other perspectives. Sodom's specters, these examples demonstrate, often repeat themselves in the present, but they do not necessarily recur in ways that allow them to be identified as precise precursors.

PUNISHMENT

The Latin word *sodomia*, "sodomy," was first coined by the Italian monk Peter Damian in the eleventh century. In 1049 Damian wrote a polemical treatise called the *Book of Gomorrah*, which was designed to persuade the pope at the time to stop the spread of a vice variously identified with masturbation, mutual rubbing of "manly parts," fornication "between the thighs," and penetration "in the rear."[6] Damian's use of the term *sodomia* is ultimately derived from the Old Testament story of the punishment of Sodom. The account of the city's destruction in Genesis 19 narrates a cruel breach of the obligation to provide hospitality to strangers. Two angels come to Sodom one evening to investigate vice in the city. Lot, seeing the angels at the city gates, offers them lodging in his quarters. Before the household goes to bed, Sodom's inhabitants besiege the residence and order Lot to deliver his guests "that we may know them." Lot offers his two daughters instead but, threatened with a violent rebuff, is eventually escorted out of the city with his family by the angels. Subsequently, the Genesis narrator recounts, the Lord "rained upon Sodom and Gomorrah brimstone and fire" and destroyed the cities and their inhabitants. Although Sodom was taken up in other Old Testament books as an image of sudden divine retribution, it was not generally understood as a story about male-male copulation in Jewish theology.[7] Only in the fifth century, with Augustine, do we find explicit references to the crimes of Sodom's inhabitants as a variety of same-sex passion, and even then Augustine condemns not male-male relations per se but the general eruption of "debaucheries in men."[8] It was not until the seventh or eighth century that Sodom began to be used as a means of identifying particular kinds of sexual practice in the handbooks on penance compiled for the use of confessors in Irish and Anglo-Saxon monasteries: these penitentials refer to "Sodomites" or copulation "in the Sodomitic manner."[9] Only with Damian's coinage of "sodomy," influential even into modern times, did Christianity possess a word capable of reducing the practitioners of these vices to a single essence: sodomites, who perform acts of sodomy, and who will trigger divine anger as a consequence.

The censure of *liwat* in Islam, like Christian denunciations of sodomy, has its roots in the story of Lot and his guests. *Liwat* literally refers to "the doings of Lot's people," as discussed in the Koran, which relates how God sends messengers to the prophet Lot (*Lut*) but the inhabitants of the town "hurry" to the host to rape his guests; as in the biblical account, Lot puts his daughters forward as an alternative but is refused. God subsequently destroys Lot's people (*luti*) by raining down stones and by "making high parts low parts." Several of the statements or hadith attributed to Muhammad condemn *liwat* severely. Like sodomy, though, a number of different activities seem to be included: one of these refers under this heading to men who "adopt the antics of women" and vice versa, males who commit bestiality, and males who penetrate males. Nonetheless, the schools of law based on Muhammad's customary practice, or sunna, narrow *liwat* down considerably, referring specifically to male anal penetration as the activity deserving of punishment.[10]

At first sight women do not appear to have been included in these religious rulings, but a closer look reveals a different picture. One of the hadith already mentioned makes reference to "women who adopt the antics of men" (though as a mode of gender transgression rather than same-sex desire), and some Arabic moralists treated women who indulge in nonpenetrative rubbing (*sahq*) with one another as a distinct variety of sexual irregularity.[11] Likewise Christian penitentials sometimes assign penance for women who fornicate with other women, and moralists from Ambrose of Milan (d. 397) to Thomas Aquinas (d. 1274) include women in their definitions of sodomitical or unnatural desire.[12] In 423 Augustine addressed a letter to consecrated virgins: his epistle, which subsequently became the basis for regulating several women's monastic communities, warns that the love a sister bears for her companions "ought not to be earthly but spiritual," for the things that "shameless women do even to other women" in jesting and playing are to be avoided.[13] It is not clear what these things are, and Augustine does not explicitly refer to the story of Sodom in this context; his reference to outbreaks of carnal love among women is typically allusive. Centuries later, however, the French theologian Peter Cantor (d. 1197) explicitly includes women in his treatise "On Sodomitic Vice." Referring to Genesis, Cantor contends that God's creation of male and female should be taken to mean "There will not be intercourse of men with men or women with women, but only of men with women and vice versa," and he goes on to cite Romans 1:26–27, which refers to women who have "changed the natural use into that use which is against nature" as well as men who have "burned in their lusts towards one another."[14] Hincmar, archbishop of Reims (d. 882), objects to women who "do not put flesh to flesh as in the fleshly genital member of one into the body of the other" but instead use "instruments of diabolical operations" (presumably dildo-like objects) to excite desire. Moreover, there is a sense in which Christian theological traditions of sodomy implicated women from the very beginning, based as they were upon the misogynist desire to banish outbreaks of "feminine" perversity—a horror about women provoked, ultimately, by Eve's temptation prior to the Fall. Damian refers in his *Book of Gomorrah* to the "utterly diseased Queen of Sodom," who defiles her male victims and takes them captive "under her domineering yoke," pointing to a very real sense in which sodomy came to be identified conceptually with women.[15]

Occasionally, visual images themselves testify to the role played by women as well as men in conceptions of same-sex desire. In the first half of the thirteenth century two large manuscripts containing numerous scenes illustrating and passing comment on the Bible were produced in Paris for the royal circle. These *Bibles moralisées*, or "moralized bibles," each include a scene commenting on the Fall of Adam and Eve in Genesis, which represents, as the accompanying texts make clear, those who "through the desires of their bodies" transgress God's commandments. The accompanying miniatures depict two couples, one male, one female, kissing and embracing. In figure 3.1, the participants also lift or remove clothing in a seductive manner.

By the time these unique images had been incorporated into the iconographic schemes of the *Bibles moralisées*, a more coordinated response to sodomy had been formulated by churchmen. In the eleventh century the Roman Church underwent a program of moral and religious revitalization, during which the papacy strengthened its authority. During this period of so-called Gregorian Reform, attitudes to sodomy were codified in the form of canon law, which included decrees clearly condemning same-sex acts.[16] Burchard, bishop of Worms (d. 1025), includes in his influential collection of canons a book of "corrections for bodies and medicines for souls," in which a male

FIGURE 3.1: Transgressive bodily desires. Moralization of Genesis 3:1–6 in *Bible moralisée* manuscript (1220s). Cod. 1179, fol. 4r (detail), Österreichische Nationalbibliothek, Vienna.

sinner is asked whether he has inserted his rod ("virga") into the backside of a male ("in masculi terga et in posteriora") in the Sodomitic manner ("more sodomitico"); the book also contains canons prescribing penalties for women, including three years' penance for those who use artificial phalluses.[17] Other bishops likewise sometimes took it upon themselves to legislate against sodomy as part of a general effort to enforce clerical celibacy: the Council of London, instigated by Anselm in 1102 when he was archbishop of Canterbury, passed a statute condemning those who indulge in unnatural sex acts, especially those "who of their own free will take pleasure in doing so"; clerics found guilty of the vice are to be deposed, lay folk deprived of legal status.[18] In 1179 the Third Lateran Council, an ecumenical meeting of Christian bishops, imposed sanctions against clerics and laypeople who have been found "to have committed incontinence which is against nature, on account of which the wrath of God came upon the sons of perdition and consumed five cities with fire."[19]

While sodomy began to be policed more stridently by the church in earthly settings, churchmen also sometimes dreamed up fantastical punishments for sodomites in the afterlife. Visual images of these punishments, while rare, afford a unique glimpse into the mind-set of Christian moralists in the later Middle Ages. A fresco depicting hell on the south wall of the Camposanto (fig 3.2), Pisa, painted in the second quarter of the fourteenth century, incorporates a special zone entirely devoted to the chastisement of the lustful. Included within that category is a pair of sinners, one of whom is penetrated

FIGURE 3.2: Punishments for lust. Detail of engraving in Giovanni Paolo Lasinio, *Pitture a fresco del Camposanto di Pisa* (Florence, 1832) depicting Buonamico Buffalmacco's *Last Judgment* (ca. 1332–1342) at Camposanto, Pisa.

from his anus to his mouth by a spit, in an allusion to anal intercourse; the spit, twisted by a devil to the left, enters the mouth of the penetrated victim's accomplice to the right, in an allusion to oral sex. Both sinners wear paper miters (just like punished criminals in Italian temporal justice of the period), which may originally have had labels identifying the sins in question. Although the Pisa fresco is heavily damaged as a result of a Second World War bomb and exposure to the elements, engravings made in the early-nineteenth century help with the comprehension of this particular allusion. The scene's significance also becomes apparent when viewed alongside another fresco painted several decades later: a late-fourteenth- or early-fifteenth-century fresco by Taddeo di Bartolo in the Collegiata, San Gimignano, where the spit-roasted figure is clearly labeled "sotomitto."[20]

The take-up of these religious viewpoints in civil law was inconsistent. Indeed, the earliest known execution for "sodomitical vice" in western Europe is recorded in a chronicle from Basel in 1277, which may come as a surprise to those who have inherited an image of the Middle Ages as an era of unremitting bloody punishments.[21] In regions such as England, there are no records of executions taking place for sodomitic activities throughout the period. All the same, in the Byzantine Empire centered on Constantinople (modern-day Istanbul), a different picture emerges: the reign of Emperor Justinian (d. 565) was marked by a comprehensive rewriting of Roman law, the legal system inherited from ancient Rome, which included rulings making sex between men a capital offense. This harsh treatment was justified, according to Justinian's logic, by the fact that "because of such crimes, there are famines, earthquakes and pestilences," thus harking back to the biblical destruction of Sodom.[22]

Echoes of such fears can be heard in subsequent jurisprudence cast in the Roman tradition. A collection of capitularies fabricated in the mid-ninth century by a monk calling himself Benedict the Levite falsely ascribes to the Frankish king Charlemagne (d. 814) a series of laws that were not his, including a spurious decree stipulating the burning of sodomites on the basis that they provoke divine wrath.[23] Notably, though, Benedict has in mind here all sexual acts "against nature" (i.e., not related to procreation), and his reasons for inventing the fake capitulary may have been to justify the dominance of ecclesiastical authorities over worldly institutions. There is no evidence that the penalty of burning was applied during Charlemagne's reign itself, and it was not until the thirteenth century that legal authorities began pursuing sodomy with any regularity, partly because of a conflation of sodomites with heretics. Inquisitions, which were originally designed to eliminate unorthodox behavior in communities such as monasteries, were later extended to include investigations of heretical activity in the lay population; crucially they involved secular authorities in their operations. From the thirteenth century, inquisitors undertook a sustained investigation of religious sects in Languedoc, a region in southwestern France, condemning the so-called Cathars or Albigensians for a whole host of transgressions, including sexual deviance.[24] Occasionally heretics were questioned about sodomy, and while no one was ever put on trial for sexual misdemeanors alone, in 1323 a lowly subdeacon called Arnaud de Verniolle confessed to having sex with a number of males in the town of Pamiers, as well as posing falsely as a parish priest who could hear confession. Arnaud's fate was to be deprived of his ecclesiastical office and, for the "horrible and damnable crime of sodomy," to be "placed in iron chains in the strictest prison, [and] to be fed a diet of bread and water for life."[25]

From the fourteenth century, certain European jurisdictions systematically persecuted sodomites, though again same-sex contact tended to be tainted with the brush of heresy. City governments north of the Alps (in what is now south Germany and German-speaking Switzerland) began enforcing severe penalties against males who indulged in *ketzerie* or "heresy," an expression that generally denotes same-sex behavior in the documents. This was stepped up in the fifteenth century, when a number of men were sentenced to death for the "heresy" they had committed with each other, though it is worth remembering that death sentences for sodomy were still extremely rare compared with other offenses such as theft or murder.[26] In certain cities in Flanders, sodomy, or *bouguerie* (a term derived from the name for another heretical sect called the Bulgars, who supposedly originated in Bulgaria), was punished by death during the fifteenth century, though the greatest period of repression occurs at the end of the Middle Ages: most of the ninety executions for sodomy in Bruges between 1385 and 1515 took place after 1450.[27]

The level of legal activity in Italian city-states such as Florence and Venice dwarfs that north of the Alps by comparison. Because the Italian proceedings often ended in fines rather than executions, conviction rates were dramatically higher.[28] The legal records that these proceedings left behind have generated some rich insights into the structures of male-male contact in this region of Europe. Statistical analysis of prosecution records in fifteenth-century Florence, where a new judicial commission called the Office of the Night was set up specifically to root out and punish sodomites, has shown that Florentine same-sex encounters assumed a hierarchical rather than reciprocal or egalitarian form: they took place between adult and adolescent males. Moreover, the men who assumed the dominant roles in these liaisons with younger sexually receptive partners were often also sexually active with women.[29] We should not project the Florentine situation onto the rest of Europe, of course: because of different marriage patterns in Italy, where women married in their teens and men in their late twenties or thirties, men in this region may have found different outlets for same-sex encounters than they did in other parts of Europe.[30] Nonetheless, the records uniquely provide insights into the ways in which, in one region in the late Middle Ages, same-sex sexual activity was integral to mainstream masculinity. In this location, at least, a polar opposition between "homosexuality" and "heterosexuality" simply did not hold.

In Florence itself sexual relations between women failed to attract the attention of authorities, and prosecutions for sodomy between males and females were also rare before the 1480s and 1490s: the Office of the Night viewed sodomy as a vice mainly pertaining to sexual contact between males.[31] In northern Europe, by contrast, women offenders were pursued with greater vigor, though actual convictions were still infrequent.[32] A transcript of a letter recording how, in 1444, two women pursued the "vice against nature which is called sodomy," survives from Rottweil in southwest Germany, and three women were found guilty of the crime in fifteenth-century Ghent.[33] Nonetheless, it was not until 1477 that a woman was actually executed for same-sex sexual contact. Trial records from Speyer on the Rhine describe how Katherina Hetzeldorfer successfully passed as a male and sought out two other women as sexual partners; she was drowned for her transgression.[34]

Since Islamic law placed a great deal of emphasis on the need for eyewitnesses to an offense—in practice, it was the public transgression of sexual morality that was uppermost in legislator's minds—convictions for the crime of *liwat* may have been quite rare in premodern contexts.[35] Although one of the hadith ascribed to Muhammad prescribes stoning (so long as four upright Muslim men can attest to the fact that they have seen the "key entering the key hole"), there is little indication that Lot's people were systematically persecuted in Muslim states in the Middle Ages.[36] It was only in the late-twentieth century that explicit laws criminalizing same-sex practices began to be included in the penal codes of certain Muslim countries, probably influenced by more recent Western models of homosexual "deviance."[37] While in theory medieval Islamic moralists were quick to condemn sexual offenses, in practice punishments for illicit same-sex contact were probably reasonably uncommon.

The considerable increase in records of penalties for sodomy in Europe at the end of the Middle Ages, and in subsequent centuries, does not necessarily mean that before this time religious or secular authorities were more "tolerant" of same-sex sexual activity. Tolerance may not be the most useful framework for understanding attitudes to same-sex sexuality in medieval cultures.

After all, there is plenty of evidence to suggest that throughout the period sodomy and its cousins were viewed as morally troubling, even if the activities in question could sometimes be ill defined. It is probably closer to the truth to imagine a world in which same-sex behaviors *that had no social implications* were entertained habitually and without consequence; only those that threatened prevailing distinctions of gender, religion, or social status were legislated against with any force, and it was only in the later Middle Ages that certain civic authorities became interested in policing these distinctions systematically. Indeed, it is arguably the very publicness of certain modes of same-sex contact that put them at risk of sodomitical readings.

PUBLICITY

Although attitudes vary considerably according to generational and other cultural factors, in modern Europe public displays of affection tend to be socially acceptable as long as they conform to certain rules. Acts such as kissing, embracing, or holding hands, if they occur between individuals roughly similar in age, status, and ethnicity—and especially if the two participants are gendered male and female—are more likely than not to escape notice. Conversely, pairings that transgress these codes may elicit comment, derision, or even legal censure. For instance, into the 1990s same-sex couples were periodically arrested in Britain for showing affection in public, under laws that were only reformed in 2000. The reverse appears to hold in some other locations (parts of the Middle East, for example): male-female couples may be harassed, while males who express affection toward each other in public do so without fear of reproach. This is because the gestures in question resonate very differently according to their cultural settings; although acts such as kissing potentially signify erotically in many different societies, gender especially inflects the ways in which those acts are read in a given situation. It is important to bear this in mind when confronting medieval attitudes to same-sex affection. Whereas today we would probably be surprised and shocked if two politicians of the same sex went as far as sharing a bed with one another and notifying the press of their desire to do so, or if male religious leaders published poems or letters expressing ardent love for other males, medieval societies generally took a different attitude. The language used by medieval writers to express love for same-sex companions contains elements that seem, by modern standards, startlingly erotic. The lines dividing eroticism from affect seem to have been drawn differently in the Middle Ages, and "friendship," in the modern sense, may be too mild a term to capture this depth of feeling.

A handful of examples will suffice to outline the particular qualities that set this pattern apart from some more recent understandings. Condemnations of "particular friendships" were common from the earliest days of medieval monasticism, embodied in conduct books such as the *Rule of St. Benedict*.[38] Yet Anselm, the same archbishop who oversaw the passing of the London ruling condemning sodomy, took the view that the invocation of passionate feelings for his friends, both male and female, was entirely appropriate for someone in public office. Indeed, following in the footsteps of classical philosophers such as Cicero and early church fathers such as Augustine, who treated friendship between men as a relationship potentially superior even to the relationship between a husband and wife,[39] Anselm used surprisingly passionate language to talk about his bonds with fellow male religious; these outpourings of emotion are recorded in his letters. Grieving his separation from Gilbert Crispin, abbot of Westminster, Anselm prays that "when we see each other again we should once more revive, face to face, lip to lip, embrace to embrace, our unforgotten love," and writing to his "beloved" Gundulf, a monk in the priory of Bec, where Anselm was abbot until 1093, he says, "Everything I feel about you is sweet and joyful to my heart. ... Wherever you go my love follows you; and wherever I may be, my longing for you embraces you."[40] Some historians have asked whether these epistolary outpourings provide evidence of Anselm's homosexuality: John Boswell presents him as one of the forerunners of a movement "to formulate a theology which could incorporate expressions of gay feelings."[41] But we need to recognize the communal function of this correspondence. Letters were not simply expressions of personal affection but also gifts and tools designed to foster benefits such as mutual prayer or the sharing of advice. Thus Anselm also adopts comparable language in his missives to nuns and kinsmen.[42] Moreover, his declarations of love derive their ethical value principally from their interaction with philosophical and spiritual traditions of idealized public friendship.[43] Recent constructions of homosexuality arguably fail to capture this reliance on stylized convention.

In monastic settings some writers also had the opportunity to compose poems expressing erotic affection for members of the same sex. There are quite a number of verses in which male authors dwell on the sexual desirability of other males, especially youths; occasionally we also find lyrics or epistolary poems apparently exchanged between nuns. The poet Marbod (d. 1123), who became bishop of Rennes in France, wrote several poems meditating on the attractions of beautiful young males, including a lyric reflecting on the ephemeral nature of youth and human desire:

The little flower of youth is fleeting and too brief;
It soon withers, falls, and knows not how to revive.
This flesh is now so smooth, so milky, so unblemished,
So good, so handsome, so slippery, so tender.
Yet the time will come when it will become ugly and rough,
When this flesh, dear boyish flesh, will become worthless.[44]

A twelfth-century manuscript from the Bavarian community of Tegernsee contains a poem apparently placed in the mouth of a woman, A., who laments her separation from G., "her unique rose":

When I remember the kisses you gave me,
The way you refreshed my little breasts with sweet words,
I would like to die
Since I cannot see you.[45]

These texts elaborate certain classical, biblical, and courtly topoi—motifs of worldly transience or longing for an absent beloved. As such they remain embedded in literary traditions and it is impossible to ascertain whether the passions behind the words are "real." Then again, the same can be said for almost all the love poems of the Middle Ages, and indeed for the lyrics of modern pop songs. Although the attitudes they convey can be instructive, once again we shall have to make do with ghosts.

In the Muslim world expressions of male-male passion were as intense as their Christian counterparts, if not more so, a situation that has led some commentators to romanticize the culture as an erotic paradise "tolerant" of homosexuality. The poet nicknamed Abu Nuwas ("the kiss-curled one," d. 810), one of the most renowned Arabic lyricists of the Middle Ages, wrote numerous poems of boy love that became points of departure for much subsequent Abbasid poetry. (His legacy continues to be celebrated into the twenty-first century in Baghdad, where a street and a park are named after him.) Nuwas, and poets like him, wrote verses that today would be characterized as "pederastic": the genre demands that attention be lavished on features characteristic of youth, such as beardless chins or downy cheeks.[46] As in certain Christian debate poems of the twelfth-century, which compared the relative merits of boys and girls, some Arabic poets also devoted verses debating their preference for male or female lovers.[47] The Iberian Peninsula, dominated for half a millennium by Muslim rulers, developed its own tradition of poetry celebrating the sensuality of male adolescent beauty, so much so

that the German playwright Hrotsvit of Gandersheim (d. after 973) wrote a
saint's life satirizing the Cordoban ruler Abd al-Rahman III (d. 961) as a man
"corrupted by sodomitic vices," desperate to "steal kisses" from a Christian
youth called Pelagius, whom he subsequently martyrs.[48] Jewish poets in Spain
also got in on the act, writing comparable verses addressed to young male
beloveds.[49]

Intent on fostering new national identities, commentators in the nineteenth and twentieth centuries began disowning these medieval poetic legacies,
influenced in part by modern European notions of normativity and sexual
identity. Arabic scholars characterized the desires expressed by Abu Nuwas
as "deviant" or "debauched,"[50] and in 2001 selected volumes of his poetry were
reportedly withheld from publication or burned by the Egyptian Ministry
of Culture in Cairo; in the same year, fifty-two men were arrested on the
Queen Boat, a disco on the Nile, and alleged to be members of a cult devoted to the poet's memory.[51] Yet intolerant as such contemporary attitudes
appear, medieval poets were not working with the concepts of homosexuality
(and pedophilia) that have arguably contributed to these purges: the aesthetic appreciation of boyish beauty was viewed as morally distinct from
sexual inclinations that result in *liwat*. Some Islamic traditions, such as Sufi
mysticism, even viewed aesthetic appreciation of boys as a "witness" to divine
beauty itself.[52] We should also remember that within a culture valuing a strong
polarity between male and female, age-structured desire itself was strongly
gendered and potentially available to *all* adult males: the beardless boy was
not necessarily perceived as being of the same sex as the poetic narrator, but
rather celebrated for the facial features that set him apart from adult men; the
desires at stake were not perceived as being confined to a small minority of
"perverts."[53] Christian poets likewise wrote within such frameworks. Many
of the twelfth-century Latin lyricists who composed poems celebrating youth-
ful beauty—often in terms that fail to distinguish sharply between masculine
and feminine perfection—also devised verses condemning all expressions of
amor lascivus, or sexual love. Marbod of Rennes argues in one of his lyrics
that "copulation performed by members of a single sex, a crime less serious
than none, is punished more severely than any other" and in another poem
spurns the kisses of a "shameless woman":

When I reject her kisses, even as I spurn them I feel other kisses,
And as for her words, so sweet with their sound,
ready to move even a eunuch's spirit,
Although I hear them, I cannot help but reject them.[54]

On the surface this literature seems to convey contradictory impulses, switching between tolerance and intolerance, heterosexuality and homosexuality; but such a view fails to appreciate the delicate balance between sexuality and spirituality, lust and aestheticism, that these writers endeavor to strike in their compositions. In the same way, it would probably not make sense to see medieval Christianity as a culture that "tolerated heterosexuals," despite the apparent contrast between stark condemnations of fornication and adultery in religious writings and celebrations of adulterous relations in the literature of courtly love. These concepts are simply not fine grained enough to work as universal descriptions.[55]

One image that potentially bears witness to the condemnation of sexual love between men and boys in monastic settings is a sculpted capital in the nave of the abbey church of Vézelay (fig. 3.3). The capital represents a boy being violently abducted by a large eagle-like bird as two adults look on and protest (to the left) and a devil grimaces (to the right). The abducted boy, suspended upside down, does not appear to be deriving any pleasure from his ordeal.

FIGURE 3.3: The rape of Ganymede. Nave capital in church of La Madeleine, Vézelay (first half of twelfth century). Photo © Robert Mills.

The scene has often been interpreted as a Christian spin on the legend of the rape of Ganymede, an attractive young prince who, according to classical myth, was carried off by the king of the gods, Zeus—disguised as an eagle—to serve as cupbearer to the gods. Representing the seduction of a young male by a powerful predator (figured as a bird of prey), the capital appears to paint a thoroughly negative picture of such a relationship: it is figured as the devil's work. In twelfth-century Vézelay, this message would have been understood not only by the community of monks who used the nave every day, but also by the pilgrims who visited to glimpse the relics of Mary Magdalene rumored to be buried within the church. The capital sends a message that lascivious behavior of any kind will receive its just deserts; only love that is not physically consummated is acceptable in the sphere of monastic asceticism.[56]

Of course this is not to say that the line separating sex from love was never crossed in practice, or that the distinctions did not occasionally become blurred in representation. The category of sodomy became important in the later Middle Ages precisely to the extent that it was politically useful, as a slur that could be employed against enemies. Sodomites were essentially bogey-men, like the communists of the 1950s or the terrorists of the early-twenty-first century—the basis for a powerful scapegoating rhetoric. Used to disparage po-litical opponents, hazily conceived social, religious, or military threats, words, and phrases that alluded to sodomy were deployed to undermine precisely the kinds of socially sanctioned same-sex relationships that some authors were so quick to venerate.[57] Whereas a twelfth-century chronicler could describe the relationship between the future king of England Richard Lionheart and King Philip Augustus of France as "vehement love"—a love so strong that "they ate every day at the same table and from the same dish, and at night their beds did not separate them"—historians casting their eye retrospectively over the reign of one of Richard's successors, Edward II, sometimes expressed the suspicion that the monarch's bonds with his male favorites were simply a cover for sod-omy. One chronicle goes so far as to claim that Edward indulged in sodomitic vice "excessively," despite the fact that during the reign itself chroniclers ini-tially described the king's relationship with Piers Gaveston—later murdered by Edward's enemies—as an "unbreakable bond of love," ritually sealed with a covenant of brotherhood.[58] Rituals celebrating male-male love as a mode of voluntary kinship were not uncommon in medieval Europe: distinct from marriage but nonetheless borrowing some of its language, "wed" or "sworn" brotherhood was an ideal immortalized in secular romances (including certain works by the fourteenth-century English poet Geoffrey Chaucer).[59] When aspersions of sodomy were cast over such bonds, the point was to undermine their capacity to be socially and politically meaningful. Sodom's phantomlike attributes had the power to transform a public relationship connoting order, spirituality, and equality into something secretive and suspicious, an alliance characterized by disorder, carnality, and inversion.

Although medieval women tended to be classified by their sexual or marital status (i.e., as virgins, wives, or widows) rather than by their mutual interactions, looking beyond those rigid classification schemes, it is clear that writers were capable of imagining women sharing physical intimacy with one another.[60] One glimpse is contained, perhaps surprisingly, in a popular satire attacking sexual relations between males: Alan of Lille's *Plaint of Nature* (ca. 1160–1165), which spares no effort in condemning men who turn from female to male sexual objects. Referring to the classical Greek hero Paris, he laments: "No longer does the Phrygian adulterer chase the daughter of Tyndareus [Helen of Troy] but Paris with Paris performs unmentionable and monstrous deeds."[61] Yet in the same text the satirist idealizes exchanges of affection between female allegorical figures that would, in many modern European settings, probably be deemed overblown: Nature, personified as a beautiful maiden and queen, uses passionate bodily gestures to receive a series of female virtues. Upon the arrival of Humility, the narrator tells us, "Nature went to meet her with strenuous haste and sweetening the feast of her greeting with the sauce of kisses, showed a countenance betokening a love in the very marrow of her bones." Generosity announces to Nature that "a golden chain of love links me with you," and even Chastity is welcomed by Nature with a "prefatory kiss" and a "marital-like embrace."[62]

The apparent contradiction between Alan of Lille's allegorical celebration of intense female fellowship and his condemnation of male-male relations in his allegory may be symptomatic of the difference gender makes to the interpretation of same-sex bonds. In a culture where men tended to hold more power, women may have possessed less public significance than their male counterparts; medieval writers may therefore have had less reason, or found it less useful, to police the borders separating affect from eroticism when they tackled the issue of female fellowship.[63] Yet an ethical uncertainty could still be imparted to women's relations with one another when they mattered spiritually or socially. One example can be found in guidance literature designed to regulate the lives of female recluses, or anchorites, women who dedicated themselves to a life of chastity by shutting themselves off permanently from the world in a cell. In a thirteenth-century English rule book called *Ancrene Wisse*, the anchorite is warned not to indulge in a certain unmentionable activity "with or without a partner," for fear of feeding the "unnatural young" of her lustfulness.[64] The next section will show how transgressions of gender ideals occasionally offered another opportunity to bring female interactions into contact with sodomitical frameworks. But misogynistic ascriptions of inordinate desire to women also created a climate in which women were viewed as always already sexually perverse, and capable of unnatural relations on this basis.[65]

POSSIBILITY

Gender deviance was crucial to medieval efforts to render sodomitical relations intelligible, as some of the examples already cited make very clear. The handful of women put to death in northern Europe at the end of the Middle Ages for sodomy suffered this fate not simply because they had slept with other women but also because they had appropriated masculine identity. The judges who put Katherina Hetzeldorfer on trial obsessed about how she forced her sexual partners to submit to her "manly will," how she described herself as her lover's "husband," and how she fashioned a dildo-like device from stuffed leather and a stick. In such cases—rare as they are—the gender-conforming parties do not seem to have been punished as severely as their gender-bending associates.[66] Switching from male to female also provided a lens through which male-male relations could be conceptualized, both by legal authorities and by the participants themselves. Arnaud de Verniolle, condemned for sodomy with "heresy" by the papal inquisitor in southern France, testified to practices that amounted to moving his penis between his partner's legs and ejaculating "as with a woman," even when—as he himself admits—he was often perfectly happy to switch roles. While statements from some of his sexual partners suggest that Arnaud was the dominant actor in these deeds of thigh-fucking (even sometimes forcing himself violently on his younger male companions), in his own deposition the cleric himself is at pains to present the desires as reciprocal and mutually fulfilling. Thus his trial records betray a curious ambivalence regarding the degree to which the sexual relations he enjoyed had de-virilizing consequences for himself and his partners.[67]

Other judicial records likewise suggest that gender inversion was conceptually significant but that its consequences for sexual identity were relatively transitory: an entry in the Plea and Memoranda Rolls for London in 1394 records the case of one John Rykener, "calling him/herself Eleanor," who, "having been detected in women's clothing," was discovered by city officials "committing that detestable, unmentionable, and ignominious vice" with a man called John Britby. Britby, we are told, thought John/Eleanor was a woman all along and asked if he might "as he would a woman" commit a "libidinous act with her." In return the streetwalker wanted money for his/her "labor." Other men also had sex with him/her "as with a woman" ("ut cum muliere") for money, but strikingly John/Eleanor also bedded numerous nuns and both married and unmarried women, "how many s/he did not know," and had sex with them "in a manly way" ("modo virili") with no expectation of a fee in return.[68] John/Eleanor's case in fourteenth-century London bears comparison with the prosecution of Rolandino Ronchaia in fourteenth-century Venice. Ronchaia was a biological male or intersex person who developed female physical attributes such as breasts and, living as a female prostitute called Rolandina, had sex with an "infinite number of men." We do not know if or how John/Eleanor was punished, but Rolandino/a was eventually burned for his/her sins.[69]

In contrast to these legal cases, polemicists such as Alan of Lille were in no doubt about the dire and enduring consequences of same-sex relations for gender binaries: hammers are turned into anvils, he splutters, and defy Nature's rules: "thus man, his sex changed by a ruleless Venus [the Goddess of Love], in defiance of due order, by his arrangement ... falls into the defect of inverted order."[70] Such notions of prolonged or even permanent inversion affect numerous accounts of same-sex contact in the Middle Ages, so much so that at times it seems as if gender deviance trumps aberrant same-sex behavior as the phenomenon at sodomy's definitional center. Hugh of Flavigny, a French abbot who records in his chronicle some of the "marvels" that preceded the death of the Anglo-Norman king William Rufus in 1100, mentions the case of one Peter, a royal chaplain who confesses to being impregnated by another man ("masculum a masculis impregnatum"), after which he subsequently conceives a monstrous child. This story encodes the belief that a receptive male acts so like a woman that he becomes pregnant, but it also renders the idea of male femininity impossible: dying of the abominable growth, the chaplain is refused Christian burial and laid to rest beyond the cemetery walls "like an ass."[71]

Just as for many centuries sodomy had been characterized as an "unspeakable" or "unmentionable" vice—a rhetoric of inscrutability that endowed it with a peculiar ability to fulfill any number of political, moral, and social requirements—writers toward the end of the Middle Ages exploited motifs of "lesbian" impossibility as a means of making female same-sex relations visible.[72] This is a ploy that emerges especially forcefully in late-fifteenth-century texts. *The Revelation of the Monk of Eynsham*, a translation of a late-twelfth-century Latin afterlife vision first published in London around 1483, contains an extended sequence recounting the unspeakable torments doled out to "sodomites" in purgatory, in which the narrator also reflects briefly on female practitioners of the vice. As he puts it, "I never heard before neither had any suspicion hitherto that the kind [race] of women had been depraved and defouled by such a foul sin."[73] The narrator's incredulity here performs a rhetorical function. Expanding the original monastic vision, which makes only passing reference to female sodomy, the English translator makes a concession to the mixed audience of the printed text, which would have included laypeople, by supplementing the text with another statement that imagines women corrupted by the vice.

A moralized version of a tale by Ovid, translated by William Caxton in 1480, contains an even stronger statement of denial about the possibility of female sexual couplings. The story of Iphis and Ianthe, from book 9 of the *Metamorphoses*, tells how Iphis's mother saves her daughter from death at the hands of her father—who has issued an decree stating that any girl child born to his wife will be slain—by raising her from infancy as a male. During her adolescence, however, the girl's father (who still thinks she is a boy) betrothes Iphis to the maiden Ianthe, the two girls fall passionately in love, and finally, after Iphis has been magically granted a sex change by the gods, the pair marry and live happily ever after. In keeping with the sex-change device's ultimate erasure of the same-sex component of the coupling, Caxton's narrator refuses to contemplate the episode's homoerotic potential. Placing the trope of impossibility in the mouth of Iphis herself, we are informed: "There is no female that desireth to a-couple her to another female." Nevertheless, in the moralizing passage that concludes the narrative, female same-sex relations *are* rendered intelligible, albeit through a prism that makes them completely anachronistic. The moralist imagines a woman dressing as a man "in ancient time," whom a fair maiden desires to marry but who, deprived of the "instruments of nature," achieves her "foul desire" by the art and craft of an evil old bawd who fashions for her a "member apostate," that is to say, a substitute penis. Just as certain penitentials and legal documents refer to women making use of makeshift dildos, Caxton's moralist raises the specter of the lesbian phallus as a tantalizing but repulsive possibility, only to reject it as impossible in the present: "Now there be none that have to do with such work," he announces, "for it is overmuch villainous and dommageable [harmful]."[74]

Medieval Islam presents a contrast to the Christian outlook. Although one of the sayings attributed to Muhammad does imply that men and women who switch gender roles will face the anger of God, men who penetrate other men sexually are treated as a separate category.[75] The eleventh-century scholar al-Raghib al-Isfahani (d. 1060) refers to dildos but only mentions them in the context of women who penetrate men; when he does discuss women who initiate sexual contact with other women, he stresses that they have an intrinsic dislike for phallic penetration. This suggests that Arab thinkers were perfectly capable of imagining mutual, non-hierarchical sexual relations. The eleventh-century medical writer al-Jurjani (d. ca. 1078) likewise imagines women who engage in sexual activity with one another without resorting to phallic substitutes: he describes them as fighting a "war" without "spear-thrusting," the parry of a "shield with a shield."[76] Nor were the boys with whom poets were infatuated characterized as transgressing their designated gender roles. Although, as we have seen, they were sometimes compared with female be-loveds, they were not necessarily "feminized" (a term that implies some kind of switch), since their youth already made them differently gendered. Age-structured or "pederastic" relations were gender inflected rather than gender transgressive: once the youths grew beards, they became less attractive, and notions of "same-sex" sexual orientation may well distort the place assigned to role differentiation in these literary encounters. What oriented the poets' desires was precisely the difference of the boyish love objects from their own adult masculinity.[77]

For adult men to adopt the penetrated position, it was necessary to endow them with an aberrant pathology. In societies that forge a link between active penetration and domination, men who seek out subordinate positions tend to be viewed with suspicion; their desire to be sodomized is usually explained by one of two means—as a sign of gender deformity or as a mark of bodily de-ficiency. In the Middle Ages, the Arab-Islamic world generally viewed adult males who were sexually passive as being afflicted by a medical condition rather than being marked out as effeminate. Al-Jurjani writes about the phenomenon of *ubna*, a kind of physical ailment that makes men want to be fucked, but this does not assimilate them, as such, with women. (Nonetheless, some writers did refer to a separate category of *mukhannathun*, or "effeminates," who from the ninth century were often assumed to adopt the passive role with men.)[78]

Some of these ideas were taken up critically by Christian natural philoso-phers, who absorbed Arabic medical learning through the Latinized teachings of Avicenna, or Ibn Sina (d. 1037). Avicenna devotes a whole chapter of his *Canon of Medicine* to *ubna*, which becomes corrupted in Latin translation to *aluminati*. This disease, we are told, occurs "in him who is accustomed to have men lie on top of him. And he has much desire, and there is in him much unmoved sperm, and his heart is weak. And his erection is weak in the root, or it has become weak now that he is habituated to copulation." The passage seems to treat the condition as involuntary: "men who wish to cure them are stupid," Avicenna announces, since the cause of *aluminati* is a malformed penis; the author draws here on another text, formerly attributed to Aristotle, that puts the desire for sexual passivity down to a buildup of semen around the anus caused by irregular spermatic ducts. At the same time, the Latin translation of the Arabic includes interpolated sentences alleging that the physiological arguments are products of "wicked science," "empty," and unreliable.[79] This was the viewpoint inherited by Christian theologians who took an interest in medicine. The Dominican scholar Albert the Great (d. 1280) engages with medical analyses when he treats other sexual topics, but not when he turns to male-male copulation, which he condemns purely on moral grounds. Sodomy is unnatural, against reason, and against God, he argues, "a contagious disease" that jumps from one person to another.[80]

Although theologians treating medical topics generally characterized male sodomy as a "wicked act," some Christian writers did adopt naturalistic explanations for males who indulged in "womanly" sexual behavior. The Italian physician Peter of Abano (d. ca. 1316), commenting on Avicenna, seems to have considered the condition innate and thinks that effeminates have blocked or malformed passages in their penises. At the same time, he does append a second category to his discussion: "sodomites" who, he says, are not born with such desires but come to them "on account of depraved and filthy habit."[81] This dual attitude of naturalistic understanding and moralistic censure does not simply surface in theoretical discussions. The trial records of Arnaud de Verniolle also demonstrate the social impact of ideas from natural philosophy. Arnaud's deposition records a statement he made to one of his sexual partners that "in some men nature demands that they perform that act [i.e., sodomy] or know women carnally" and that "he very much felt himself that his body would suffer if he should abstain for more than eight or fifteen days if he did not have sex with a woman or did not commit that crime with a man."[82] Arnaud's views were probably influenced by medical and philosophical arguments counseling against sexual abstinence, which was assumed by some authors to be detrimental to the balance of humors in the body.[83] While he admits that he sometimes occupies the penetrated position himself, he is not suggesting that nature produces gendered passivity. Instead he makes an argument for the "naturalness" of male sexual activity, a penetrative ethos in which the gender of the sex object is neither here nor there.

On one level there was less need to pathologize female same-sex relations as sick.[84] According to medieval Christianity, women were already dangerously perverted or, as the anchoritic guidance text *Ancrene Wisse* puts it, nurturers of an "unnatural" lust. Transgender narratives offered one way for authors to conjure up homoeroticism as a spectral presence. But so long as either the gender performances were stabilized through sex-change miracles or the cross-identifying protagonists refused to engage in sexual activity (as was the case in stories of chaste transvestite saints), the homoerotic potential was kept at bay.[85] Yet confused ideas about female genitalia did surface in anatomical writings available to medieval authors, some of which associated an enlarged clitoris—or some organ like it—with masculine impersonation and women-desiring women. Some surgical manuals even likened the hypertrophied clitoris to a penis or implied that the deformation made the owner susceptible to homoerotic cravings.[86] William of Saliceto, a thirteenth-century surgeon based in Bologna, describes how sometimes a "thing" appears on a woman that is "just like a penis" (*sicut virga*), and "sometimes it occurs to her to do what men do with women, that is, have coitus with women."[87]

Although some Christian moralists do appear to have been working with ideas of sinful, sodomitical essence, natural philosophers only intermittently endowed their subjects with identities. Avicenna divides the men suffering from *aluminati* into identifiable groups or *secta* who enjoy being sexually passive in different ways, whereas William of Saliceto implies that women afflicted with fissures and growths in the womb (which may include a "great clitoris or protuberance") are victims of circumstance—say, a tricky childbirth or a ruptured abscess—and therefore not subject to any effort to classify them as a separate category. It is hard to get from here to Michel Foucault's "hermaphrodism of the soul," the psychiatric model of homosexuality that arose, according to him, in the nineteenth century.[88] Indeed throughout this chapter we have confronted medieval same-sex contact through its ghosts: slippery sodomy, with its elusive rhetoric; penal institutions, with their inconsistent paradigms; friendship discourse and lyric poetry, with their delicately drawn aesthetic codes; transgender narratives, which introduce the possibility of homoeroticism precisely at the moment when it slips away. We cannot say that we have found "our" homosexuality in these spectral encounters—or at least, not a homosexuality that elicits total recognition. But the enigmas and confusions that linger in the archive remind us not to view our own sexual categories as universally applicable or fully formed.

CHAPTER FOUR

Sexual Variations

CORY JAMES RUSHTON

Sexual "variations" or perversions (to use the language of nineteenth-century sexology) depend on the prior constitution of sexual norms that both create and regulate them. Yet, as Karma Lochrie argues in this volume, the Middle Ages may not have had an idea of a norm from which one could deviate. Nevertheless, medieval texts describe a very narrow range of licit sexual activity. They also identify as variant a number of sexual phenomena that are markedly different from the ones we recognize today, such as being too attracted to one's spouse. It is important to be clear from the outset that no one in the Middle Ages would have described him- or herself as a pervert, fetishist, or necrophiliac. Not only did the terms not exist, but medieval people for the most part did not think of themselves as having a sexual *identity*—rather, they engaged in a range of sexual *behaviors*.

Sodomy—in its modern definition, the act of anal penetration—represents one preeminent medieval sexual variation. The word was coterminous with anything beyond the licit, particularly any sexual activity that was not intended for the purpose of procreation.[1] When the French king Philip the Fair (r. 1285–1314) wished to ensure that the Templars would not escape his kangaroo court with their lives, he augmented the heresy charges with one that was ubiquitous in ecclesiastical courts: sodomy. The very ubiquity of this term is both instructive and problematic. As John Boswell noted in his landmark study of homosexuality in the late antique and medieval eras, the word "sodomy" "has connoted in various times and places everything from ordinary heterosexual intercourse in an atypical position to oral sexual contact with animals," while at other times it exclusively referred to male homosexuality. For those reasons, Boswell avoided the term altogether.[2] Therefore, while Philip's charge of sodomy primarily refers to same-sex sexual behavior at this period, it can also refer to any form of illicit sexual behavior.

An additional problem is that our modern understanding of medieval secular love as divided into good and bad—exemplified by the division of the classical figure of Venus into twin and opposed representatives of spiritual and physical love—has been useful as an organizational principle but still obscures a wide range of sexual possibilities in the Middle Ages in favor of a binary we still share: good and bad sex, good and bad love, the heterosexual norm and its "perversions," with homosexuality only recently and imperfectly moving from the latter category into the former.[3] This division has medieval origins: Bernard Silvestris's twelfth-century commentary on the *Aeneid* distinguishes between the lawful Venus, who stands for harmony and natural justice, and the wanton Venus, who is "the mother of all fornication."[4] The ninth-century Benedictine monk and grammarian Remigius of Auxerre puts it even more starkly: there is a love "good and chaste, by whom virtues and wisdom are loved; the other unchaste and evil, whom we call 'loves,' in the plural, for the sake of distinguishing the good love."[5]

Just as "sodomy" could act as a catchall word for any sexual misconduct, so too could "lechery," or *luxuria*, which was divided into several categories in the penitentials: simple fornication, adultery, incest, violation or *stuprum*, abduction/rape (*raptus*), and "vice against nature." This last category comprises many of the behaviors that are still today considered "perverse," including fetishism and bestiality.[6] But the first category reminds us that several sexual modes that appear perfectly normal today were considered sinful in the Middle Ages: sexual positions beyond the missionary, for example. For many medieval people there is a sexual norm defined, largely, by the vast penitential literature, and this is opposed to a variety of other activities that either do not fit our current classifications of sexual variations or are categorized in significantly different ways from those current today.

At the same time, medieval culture accepted some behaviors that look "perverse" to us: an intense and possibly conflicted interest in the sexualized torture of female saints, or the eroticization of the relic, to take two examples. The present chapter will therefore deploy the clinical term "paraphilia" (sexual diversity, in other words), rather than the modern notion of perversion, and its search will be for evidence of what Remigius might have included under the category of "plural loves." The search for medieval sexual variation will bring us uncomfortably close to the human capacity for the extreme, and perhaps even more uncomfortably (even perversely) near an admission that our modern idea of sexual heteronormativity is descended from a medieval struggle to define what sex was, and what gendered individuals were meant to *do* with sex. To some modern eyes, this struggle will look more than metaphorical; medieval texts seem to acknowledge that sexual attraction carries within itself elements of power and control that seem potentially dark and troubling.

To some degree, it is possible to see medieval confession as the origin for modern sexual classifications, as legions of priests attempted to discover evidence for behaviors that did not yet have names, let alone a fully articulated definition. In the first volume of his *History of Sexuality*, Michel Foucault argues that the medieval confessional created a discourse concerning sex in which it was necessary to speak the most intimate truths about one's sexual practices, and thus to reveal the "truth" of the self: to define oneself as a (sexual) subject. A direct line, argues Foucault, runs from the medieval confessional to late-nineteenth-century psychoanalysis, which invented the "talking cure," and which deployed the categories for describing sexual identities that are so familiar to us today.[7] Medieval writers were aware of the potential dangers of confession; the thirteenth-century Dominican writer William Peraldus was one of many medieval theologians to urge vigilance in extracting sexual confessions: "There is to be great caution in speaking and preaching about this vice [lechery] and in asking questions about it in confession so that nothing is revealed to me that might provide them an occasion for sinning."[8] In other words, the confessor should not put ideas into his subject's head. Any attempt to read medieval sexuality must bear in mind that Foucault did not aim to develop, and was perhaps even opposed to, a fully articulated theory of sexuality; rather, the *History of Sexuality* in particular is best seen as a "critical antitheory" that was intended to act as a resistance to "the circuitry that connects sexuality, truth, and power," an attempt "to make sexuality available to us as a possible source for a series of scholarly and political counterpractices,"[9] to bear witness to the diverse.

This chapter will focus on four types of paraphilia: fetishism; transvestism/cross-dressing; algolagnia, which encompasses both sadism (active algolagnia) and masochism (passive algolagnia);[10] and pedophilia.[11] I will make considerable, although by no means exclusive, use of literary texts, alongside medieval canon law, romances, and court trials, as a way of getting at the *mentalité* at work in medieval culture. As scholars have argued, any literary text composed within a historical society is itself a historical document; in Jacques Le Goff's words, "to study the imagination of a society is to go to the heart of its consciousness and historical evolution."[12] At times it will be difficult to determine unambiguously whether something we find sexually suggestive today would have been understood the same way centuries ago, and, if it was so understood, whether it was suggestive for the same reasons.

THINGS OF THE BODY: LOOKING
FOR THE MEDIEVAL FETISH

Chrétien de Troyes' *Lancelot, or the Knight of the Cart* (1170s) contains the first-known version of the story of Lancelot's adulterous love for King Arthur's queen, Guenevere. Throughout the poem Lancelot displays skilful martial ability in the unquestioning service of a beloved woman. When they first have sex, in the stronghold of an enemy knight who is keeping the queen captive, Lancelot approaches Guenevere, bowing to her "in adoration, for no holy relic inspires him with such faith."[13] This erotics of idolatry depends on the overturning of the proper function of both the saint and the traditionally dominant medieval man. Lancelot's absolute submission to the queen has previously resulted in his willing self-humiliation, as he rides in a cart to rescue her after his horse has been killed; to do so is to appear to be a condemned criminal, and Lancelot hesitates only briefly before climbing in.[14] That hesitation is enough to anger Guenevere, who somehow hears of it and initially refuses to see her rescuer.[15] Part of his path to redemption in the queen's eyes is her insistence that Lancelot fight his worst in a tournament, introducing a very real element of physical pain to their relationship, with the queen entirely in control of Lancelot's physical well-being. The trajectory of humiliation and pain has led at least one commentator to declare Lancelot a kind of masochist,[16] and it is apparent from even a cursory reading of the text that Lancelot's actions when in Guenevere's presence are always dictated by her.

An even more suggestive example of Lancelot's worship of the queen comes when he finds a comb of gilded ivory with some hairs in it. Lancelot faints when he learns that they were once on the head of the queen and carefully removes each hair from the comb so as not to break them, behaviors that look very much like a hair fetish, or trichophilia, to a modern reader:

> Never will the eye of man see anything receive such reverence; for he begins to adore them, putting them full a hundred thousand times to his eyes and mouth, to his brow and face, with every show of joy. They are his great treasure and his delight. He places them against his breast,

between his shirt and flesh, next to his heart. He would not exchange them for a cartload of emeralds or carbuncles. Now he is confident that he will never suffer from boils or any other illness.[17]

The symmetry between the way a medieval Christian should treat the relic of a saint and the way in which Lancelot treats Guenevere's hair forces the reader to pronounce the action either sublime or parodic. The narrator himself states that the hairs would compare favorably to "gold refined a hundred thousand times and melted down again as often,"[18] hinting that he shares Lancelot's devotion to Guenevere, however blasphemous it seems. Jeffrey Cohen notes that Lancelot and text alike "make a fetish of these locks"; Guenevere's hairs "are simultaneously saint's relic, metonymy for Guenevere, and substitute trigger for the mystical feelings of completeness that overwhelm Lancelot in the queen's presence."[19] But does this suggest that Lancelot suffers from trichophilia in the modern clinical sense of the word? In the medieval cult of saints, which Lancelot's worship of the hair alludes to, body parts were invested with enormous healing power. The fifteenth-century Augustine friar Osbern Bokenham claims to have been protected from physical harm by a ring that had touched St. Margaret's foot, kept at a Dominican priory near his birthplace (albeit without the heel and great toe).[20] But we cannot be sure that this religious talisman did not also have an erotic dimension.

Freud's definition of the fetish was that it was "a substitute for the woman's (the mother's) penis that the little boy once believed in and ... does not want to give up," and this disavowal on the subject's part manifests itself in a fetish based on the last thing seen or experienced before the moment of trauma when the mother's "castration" is first experienced: the shoes or feet, because the boy sat there to stare up at the genitals, "pieces of clothing" that "crystallize the moment of undressing."[21] We now know that the phenomenon has more diverse and complex origins. Modern definitions of the fetish complicate the search for past evidences of fetishistic behavior, largely because the specifics and results of an encounter with a fetish object were often not recorded. As L. F. Lowenstein argues:

There are a number of definitions of fetishes. One of the psychological definitions is that a fetish is an "object" providing sexual gratification. It is also often defined as a "form" of perversion in which sexual gratification is obtained from other than the genital parts of the body. A more detailed and expanded definition is that fetishism is a condition wherein non living objects are used as the exclusive or consistently preferred

method of stimulating sexual arousal. There are many different kinds of fetishes and many are socially acceptable. Among fetishisms that are acceptable is the use of perfumes, seductive clothes and mementos. Usually the fetishist obtains sexual excitation by kissing, tasting, fondling, or smelling the object. It appears that most fetishists are males and most use such objects while masturbating alone or with another. It is often used as a form of foreplay which progresses towards coitus. In fetishism purely, however, the fetishist's action or behaviour takes primary attention.[22]

Lowenstein also notes recent studies in which pets and even shopping can be fetishes, evidence perhaps—contra Freud—of female fetishism.[23] Most readers, however, would think immediately of the more common fetishes: feet and shoes (podophilia), underwear or stockings, hair (trichophilia). The fetish object, read here as a thing of the body, begins as a synecdoche for the whole but comes to take on the force of that whole: not merely a symbol, but the object of desire itself, only tangentially related to the body to which the foot or the hair properly belong. Evidence for this phenomenon in the Middle Ages will be difficult to find, but romance—with its legion of knights engaged in ostensible worship of women—is a good place to start.

The word "fetish," from the fifteenth-century Portuguese word used to describe the magical objects found among the newly discovered peoples of West Africa (fetiço "charm, sorcery"), is conceptually closely related to "relic" (although sixteenth-century Europeans would be unlikely to apply the term directly to their own collections of spiritualized body parts). However, the medieval idea of the relic is in all major respects identifiable with that of the fetish: objects associated with the bodies of the saints were reputed to have spiritual power that looks very much like magic today, and the Host (the consecrated wafer in the communion ceremony) was supremely a cult object. Hundreds of stories detailing how Jews attempted to destroy the Host, as well as similar stories in which Muslims attack depictions of the Cross, read like rehearsals for later Western accounts of fetish objects outside Europe (and for anti-Catholic stories within Europe).[24] This is fetish in its religious, and far more ancient, sense, even though the cult of the saints could itself be eroticized at times. Just as an ancient pilgrim conflates the saint's forearm with the spiritual entity residing in heaven,[25] so the modern fetishist mistakes the foot or an object of clothing for the sexual whole, especially in the absence of that whole—the fetish is an attachment to the material object without there necessarily being any understanding of the real relationship between that object and the thing represented. For the fetishist, a shoe or a lock of hair carries with it a promise (a substitute for the woman's missing or invisible penis), in Freud's words becoming "a kind of token of triumph over the threat of castration and a protection against it."[26] Yet if this phenomenon exists in the Western Middle Ages, the originary relationship between the fetish object and the threat might very well be different.

The enormously popular thirteenth-century French courtly poem *Le roman de la rose* includes numerous references to feet, which appear to be among the first of their kind; the lyrics of the troubadours also contain what has been called the first "aesthetically idealized woman's foot," seen as narrow, high arched, and long toed.[27] For some researchers, there is a high coincidence of references to foot fetishes at moments in which sexually transmitted diseases are on the increase, the first being a remarkable outbreak of venereal disease in thirteenth-century Europe, when numerous contemporaries record a "burning" disease that appears to be gonorrhea.[28] Presumably, men find substitute behaviors when sex itself becomes dangerous. However, it must also be acknowledged that the periods in which venereal disease was on the rise were also moments of relative or apparent emancipation for women: the submission of the male lover in the courtly code, however seriously we take that submission, would be likely to manifest itself partially through the ancient pre-medieval symbolism of kissing the feet. The root cause of this sudden historical interest in the foot is not the young boy's fear of castration, his own or his mother's, although it is still a substitute of the foot for the penis. There may, of course, be multiple origins for behaviors that look similar on the surface, and this would imply that fetishes arise at particular moments in time in culturally specific ways.

The rules of "courtly love," as set out in Andreas Capellanus's twelfth-century *Art of Courtly Loving* and the poetry of the troubadours, demand that the lover worship from afar and be content with little signs of grace (a glance, a smile, a physical favor such as a piece of cloth). This suggests that fetishistic behavior may be a substitute for actual contact—and indeed, this is implied in Chrétien's *Lancelot*, where the queen's hair does seem to bear (in Freud's phrase) "an assignable relation to the person whom it replaces and preferably to that person's sexuality."[29] For Freud, that person would be the mother or primary female caregiver for the child, but while Guenevere may qualify as a mother figure by virtue of her office as queen, Lancelot is not a child, even if his unmarried and possibly landless state is one of relative dependence. The scene of courtly love typically occurs between a married lady and an unmarried man of lower rank; it is not difficult to extrapolate a family drama operating within the feudal system.

To whatever extent we believe that courtly love existed in reality, the ideology operates as a site for exactly these kinds of behaviors (worship of woman, a cult of erotic relics): in Slavoj Žižek's words, "The knight's relationship to the Lady is thus the relationship of the subject-bondsman, vassal, to his feudal Master-Sovereign who subjects him to senseless, outrageous, impossible, arbitrary, capricious ordeals."[30] Žižek exaggerates, but there are many examples of heroines imposing mysterious rules on their lovers, as with the infamous Felice ordering Guy of Warwick on "increasingly dangerous and time-consuming journeys to win her love, journeys which eventually take him to Constantinople."[31] In the courtly code, the beloved woman is analogous to both the political tyrant (before whom the subject might prostrate himself) and the saint (who deserved a similar level of diffidence).

Lancelot's discovery of the queen's hairs is accidental, and female hair per se is not a fetish for him. Only when he knows these are Guenevere's hairs does Lancelot indulge in some fetishistic behaviors: kissing the hairs in a clearly erotic fashion, and keeping them close to his heart. But despite Lancelot's deep reverie and strong emotional reaction to the hair, his eroticization of the hairs ends not with erotic reverie—of the kind Chrétien's Perceval experiences when he sees blood in the snow that reminds him of his mistress's cheeks—but with a reference to their magic properties: the hairs will protect him, he believes, from illness. Although Freud pointed to the talismanic function of the sexual object, its protection against castration or sexual impotence, this does not seem to be what Lancelot intends in his worship. He is passive in the face of the queen's desires, obeying her in all things; perhaps that does imply that her hair is both trophy and relic, sexual prompt and protection against danger. If members of the culture could act in a proprietary or even aggressive way toward the actual saint in his or her shrine while still speaking the language of devotion, then so can the ostensibly submissive lover. This would reinforce the idea that, for Lancelot, Guenevere's hair is more relic than fetish, a metonymy for the queen but not a substitute for her absent penis; more importantly for a popular understanding of the fetish, no other woman's hair would have a similar effect.

If Lancelot has any fetish, it is specifically for Guenevere. As someone in love with another man's wife, Lancelot cannot hope to achieve a socially appropriate relationship with Guenevere. In an oedipal reading of this story, Lancelot would figure as the child, with Arthur as symbolic father and Guenevere as mother. Threatened by the father, Lancelot falls into fetishistic reverie over the queen that is prompted by her hair, here not the last physical object seen by the child as his gaze moves up, but the individuating characteristic of a sovereign figure (that which crowns her)—and one that is gender specific only in its style and length from that of the husband from whom she gains that power. In essence, it would be a fetish located in the homosocial—the realm of male bonding—and not in traditional Freudian absence. When the queen invites him into her bed, "pure sexuality" briefly takes the place of the pseudo-religion in which the hair stood in for Guenevere; Lancelot is described as eminently happy at this turn of events, and in some sense Chrétien's poem appears to testify to a sexual maturation—touching Guenevere's hair is a stage on a path to something else, where the hair will cease to matter in the presence of the queen's living, desiring body. Once Lancelot enters the queen's bed, there is no further mention of hair or combs.

A superlative male figure often the object of sexual attention, Lancelot can be seen as a location for medieval speculation about sexual extremes—just as his overpowering love for the queen may result in fetishistic behavior, so Lancelot's body is the focus of sexual obsession in others. In Thomas Malory's *Morte Darthur* (ca. 1470), the young Sir Lancelot encounters a woman named Hellawes, who desires a kiss from him. When Lancelot refuses, she explains her motivations in true self-revealing super-villain style:

> "Well, sir," seyde she, "and [if] thou haddyst kissed me thy lyff dayes had be done [your life would be over]. ... I have loved the [thee] this seven yere, [but] there may not woman have thy love but quene Gwenyver; and sytthen [since] I myght nat rejoyse the nother thy body on lyve [I am not able to enjoy your body while you are alive], I had kepte no more joy in this worlde but to have thy body dede. Than wolde I have bawmed hit [embalmed it] and sered [preserved] hit, so to have kepte hit my lyve dayes; and dayly I sholde have clypped [embraced] the and kissed the, dispyte of quene Gwenyvere."[32]

Lancelot laconically, and somewhat oddly, responds by telling her she speaks well and asks Jesus to preserve him from her "subtyle crauftys [cunning arts]."[33] Hellawes is not the only medieval literary character to contemplate necrophilia (a nineteenth-century term, but it is difficult to imagine a better one in this case). In the fifteenth-century *Alphabet of Tales*, a collection of popular exempla, we are told of a monk who became obsessed with a woman he had seen.[34] When she dies, he digs up her grave and, admiring her fine burial clothes, takes her body back to his cell. Predictably, the body begins to stink as it decomposes. The monk himself pronounces the moral: the rotting corpse is a reminder to him that desire goes the way of all flesh, and he gradually weans himself from the temptation he had felt earlier.

These stories contain a number of details that appear deviant in both modern and medieval terms: Hellawes wishes to embalm Lancelot's body so that she can hug and kiss it (euphemistically, have sex with it); she also wishes to do the same thing to Gawain, which would create a bizarre necrophiliac ménage à trois. The monk initially seems to feel that the woman's body is at least as attractive in death as it was in life. He merely lacks Hellawes's ability to embalm the object of his desire. Hellawes creates a sacred space (a chapel) intended for deviant erotic play that invokes the spiritual, Lancelot's body taking the place of a saint's in a profane parody of the medieval relics system. Hellawes will engage in something that looks like worship but has clear connections with sexuality: her fondling and kissing of Lancelot's corpse will be against the wishes of the woman who has access to his living body and thus could be understood as something erotic (even if many readers and listeners might feel horror rather than titillation). The monk does not create a sacred space in which to house the object of his desire, but the urge to collect and to keep seems much the same. This seems to be fetishistic in its desire to collect the object, but that object is not a substitute for the whole, unless we view Lancelot as the knight who stands in for all chivalry. That still does not seem to qualify as a fetish in the modern sense—can an embalmed body be a substitute for a body animated by a soul? Hellawes is both a character who is willing to go to illicit extremes to win power and a literary figure who testifies to male fears that women will go to perverse extremes. Leo Bersani has argued for the inherent sociality of sex, that the individual's struggle is not with a castrating loss (as implied in Freud's view of the fetish) but with a desire for "nothingness," the state of being before the individual falls into the social world that defines him or her.[35] Hellawes offers a vision of Lancelot as desired without himself desiring, a vision of his negation for her pleasure, which she intends to take in solitude. Lancelot and Gawain's bodies will become symbols of their former selves; more than mere trophies, they will be toys, their chivalric selves reduced to a kind of pure masculinity that utterly lacks agency. To the medieval mind, to desire was to court trouble, even when—especially when—that desire is achieved. For Hellawes, to achieve her desire outside the social world, the objects of her desire will have to suffer.

TRANSVESTISM

The impossibility of knowing the mental state of historical individuals is particularly acute when it comes to male and female transvestism. There are many possible motivations for cross dressing, not all of them sexual or erotic. In most of the well-known medieval examples, a woman cross-dresses either to avoid marriage (as in many saints' lives) or, as in the popular but apocryphal legend of Pope Joan, to stay close to a man who is entering religious life.[36] Pope Joan's story is instructive: falling in love with a monk named Ulfilias, Joan enters his monastery in male disguise in order to be with him and later travels with him to Athens. Upon his death, Joan travels home via Rome, where she is urged to lecture and has great success within the church, rising to the rank of pope under the name John VII Anglicus (because she is said to be English). Her female nature betrays her, however, when she meets another monk who closely resembles Ulfilias. She becomes pregnant, giving birth while in procession and dying soon after. There is no evidence that the male disguise is to be seen as sexual in nature rather than gendered. Clearly, Joan speaks to a medieval anxiety about women's ability to act as men do: to lecture or preach, to enter sacred spaces reserved for men, to have names that can slip across gender easily (Joan/John). Jacopo de Voragine added woman's failure to hold to a wise course as another moral of this story.[37] There is no reason to believe that Ulfilias, Joan, or the second monk are sexually excited by Joan's male guise—her clothing is simply a means to an end (a career in the church) within the narrative, and outside the narrative they serve various ideological ends, few primarily having to do with sexuality (although they have a great deal to do with gender).

There seem to have been strict if unspoken guidelines governing the ways in which each sex could impersonate the other. For women (particularly in hagiographies), dressing as men could indicate virtue or an attempt to achieve some worthy end. When the heroine of the *Roman de Silence*, a thirteenth-century French romance, is not permitted to inherit her father's property, she impersonates a knight in order to pursue her inheritance. When her sex is revealed, she marries the king, and the female right to inherit is eventually restored—although her voice is lost when the narrative no longer requires it, as Silence never speaks again within the text.[38]

In a society where men were considered physically and spiritually superior to women, for a woman to wear men's clothes was often seen as a signal that an individual woman aspired to a masculine type of sanctity, however impossible that would be in practice (as the story of Pope Joan implies). For men, the possibilities for cross-dressing were narrower. Men were permitted to dress as women on the medieval stage, or in the context of festivals or carnivals. Men who dressed as women, when not looking for covert heterosexual opportunity, did so for comedic value or to gain glory, often on a stage of some kind. The thirteenth-century knight-errant Ulrich von Lichtenstein dressed as the goddess

Venus for a number of jousts, ostensibly to bring glory to women.[39] His disguise also brought glory to him as the man who could defeat his foes even after lowering his gendered status. In both cases, the status of the male remained unaffected by the clearly theatrical nature of the cross-dressing. What is at stake in cross-dressing in the Middle Ages is status rather than sexuality.

One prominent exception is Joan of Arc, burned when she broke a promise not to resume wearing men's clothing as part of her recantation. Joan was tricked by her English captors into wearing men's clothing, a tactic that Vern Bullough rightly pronounces "a fascinating comment upon the attitudes of the time that they used the resumption of male dress, something which they undoubtedly engineered," as their basis for her subsequent execution.[40] Here, at least in this one moment, history and literature radically differ: what is possible for the heroine of the *Roman de Silence* is not possible for Joan of Arc. In neither case is there evidence that for these women cross-dressing is an erotic, rather than a pragmatic or political, mode of behavior.

There also seems to be little evidence of either men or women living as the opposite sex in order to engage in sexual behavior associated with the other, apart from one Spanish woman in the sixteenth century, Eleno/Elena de Desopedes, who apparently posed as a man and married a woman (and twice passed physical examinations designed to reveal her "true" sex).[41] An unusual case from late-fourteenth-century London provides a glimpse of a cross-dressing man motivated by something like the idea of modern sexual identity. In December 1394 a certain John Rykener was arrested in women's clothing while having sex with a man named John Britby, who claimed not to realize Rykener's biological sex.[42] Rykener called himself Eleanor and is said to have been taught to dress as a woman by Elizabeth Brouderer and taught to practice sodomy by a woman named Anna, "the whore of a former servant of Sir Thomas Blount"; he admitted to having sex with men for money, sometimes with priests. He also "often has sex as a man with many nuns and also had sex as a man with many women both married and otherwise." He also confessed to what appear to be several attempts at blackmail when Elizabeth prostituted her daughter to men in darkened rooms; in the morning, she would claim that it was Eleanor who slept with them. It seems that no further legal action was taken in relation to Rykener.

Our interest lies in the evidence of the scribe's attempt to deal with Rykener's fluid gender: Rykener was alternately demarcated as male or female depending on what he/she was doing at the time. Still, even here, we must admit partial defeat in our search for medieval paraphilia: Rykener had sex with both men and women, hinting that he may be what we now call bisexual, but he only slept with men for money, implying that "his motivation ... was more financial than libidinal." Furthermore, he is first encouraged to cross-dress by a woman who seemed to have sensed an "earning opportunity."[43]

Even if there were unambiguous evidence that Rykener's cross-dressing brought him sexual gratification, it is doubtful whether medieval culture would have the means of describing it. Even Chaucer's Pardoner, whose elusive sexual identity is the subject of many modern inquiries, is presented with an ambivalence that allowed scribes to rewrite him as heterosexual with little complication: Chaucer's narrator tells the reader that the Pardoner seemed to be "a geldyng or a mare,"[44] that is, either a eunuch (castrated like a gelding) or the passive partner (a female horse) in same-sex affairs. Even if we agree that the Pardoner does have a sex life or could be a sexual object, he potentially acts sexually as a eunuch. Are the physical manifestations of his difference themselves an indication that someone found them attractive (some critics argue that the Summoner did)? If so, does that reinforce the possibility that Rykener would have found other individuals eager to have sex with him, not as a substitute for woman, but specifically as a man dressed as a woman? Again, the evidence is equivocal, but we cannot rule out this possibility.

THE SEX LIVES OF SAINTS

We have become accustomed to the idea that sexuality and spirituality have fluid borders in the Middle Ages, particularly in mystical experience. Union with the divine takes the form of sex with the divine, partially under the influence of Bernard of Clairvaux's influential metaphorical reading of the unabashedly erotic Song of Songs, a reading partly designed to defuse its powerful eroticism. Nuns were *sponsae dei*, brides of God, which implied an intersection of sexuality and the divine (as it did for Julian of Norwich, the late-fourteenth-/ early-fifteenth-century English recluse and mystic). Unlike male saints, virgins in hagiography were often threatened with marriage, rape, or both. Saints of both sexes were tortured, the women in ways that often stressed their gender attributes, their sanctity rooted in their corporeal selves and not primarily in their spiritual virtues.[45] One telling example is the virgin-martyr St. Barbara, as depicted in a painting by Master Francke composed of eight panels, now held at the National Museum of Finland in Helsinki. Robert Mills has noted how the images of Barbara bound, her torturers slicing and burning her breast, look superficially like extreme pornographic scenes.[46] In the story of St. Agnes, the saint's tormenters persistently attempt to display her body, even to the point of throwing her into a brothel, where that body would become common property (a not-unfamiliar motif in hagiographic texts about female saints). God consistently and miraculously covers the body of Agnes, allowing her hair to grow with unnatural speed or throwing a divine mantle over her.[47] St. Margaret is suspended by her feet and whipped; St. Barbara's most common iconographic depiction is with a bared breast, always about to be cut or otherwise mutilated. In a sense, the conflict is over who has access to the body of the female saint: her tormenters or her God. The audiences, however, occupy a third voyeuristic space. The viewer's eye lingers at the edge of the threat, encouraged to look, implying that medieval audiences may have thrilled to the imagined scenes of torture (whether in horror or titillation, or both).

Criticism has recently moved beyond the assumption that medieval people voyeuristically enjoyed the depictions of suffering saints, particularly female saints. Hagiography seems to call for the reader's identification with the tortured saint, the masochist in the service of the divine, but it may also allow (in Mills's words) "the viewer a licence to take pleasure *in* violence ... [and] may on a different level have fuelled sadistic inclinations in the minds of the audiences, modes of aggression that contradict martyrdom's dogmatic premise." The masochist-saints are themselves in the process of transforming their experience into heavenly reward and social efficacy (they will be permitted to help others after death), but it is possible that the torture of saints allows "medieval Christians ... to enact fantasies of aggression against God himself"—after all, between the promise of reward and the emphasis hagiography puts on the saints' resulting delight in the torture, the saints do not actually suffer.[48] A saint is the perfect outlet for sexual sadism: a victim who desires pain and who thus "gives the viewer a licence to take pleasure *in* violence, as well as identifying, imaginatively, with the position of the violated saint."[49] To feel sexual desire for a virgin-martyr is already to defy God; indeed, her resistance to male lust brings about the performance of her martyrdom and guarantees the achievement of her sanctity. For the man who feels lust for the future saint, his desire looks normative but is always already deviant. The *South English Legendary* version of the St. Anastasia story makes this clear when a prefect attempts to rape three Christian virgins. He is miraculously made to think that a set of dirty pots and pans are the virgins and sets about sexually assaulting the inanimate objects. The narrator remarks that the prefect "had his lover according to his desire, but he went a little wrong."[50] The humor appears to acknowledge that men can be expected to lust after virgins, in just the same way that the fabliau and its modern descendent, the dirty joke, often link sex and humor of a dark kind. The prefect's misguided vision, what he thinks he sees and feels, is a fantasy that is simultaneously invoked and mocked.

In the story of the virgin-martyr St. Juliana, as Gayle Margherita notes, "The romance hero is metamorphosed into mere sadist, the would-be courtly heroine becomes the victim of this unbridled passion: lust passes easily into torture, romance into violence."[51] But the "mere" is too dismissive. These metamorphoses are not due to the genre of hagiography but reveal a medieval attitude toward the dangers of desire itself. While courtly love ostensibly shows the woman controlling the man, in reality it is more about controlling the woman. Indeed, seen from a modern algolagnic viewpoint, the saint is a perfect submissive partner, capable of an almost infinite absorption of pain and infinite resistance to the sadist's desires.

SEXUAL VIOLENCE AND CONTROL

If we now see a strict division, in most cases, between heteronormative behavior and the language of power and control associated with sadism, masochism, and bondage, the Middle Ages saw it quite otherwise. Medieval heterosexual relationships can themselves seem deviant to modern eyes, and literature across the period consistently deploys the language of "power negotiation" (to borrow a phrase from modern BDSM communities). The Wife of Bath and her five husbands engage in sometimes violent negotiations: older wealthy men controlling a young bride in the case of the first three, and a wealthy older woman dominating young husbands in the case of the last two. Her fifth husband, Jankyn, constantly reads from a book of wicked wives, a book she eventually destroys; in revenge, he hits her, causing permanent deafness in one ear. She pretends to be dead, and he is so frightened by the possibility that he has murdered her that she is able to gain complete control of their marriage: "He yaf [gave] me al the bridel [bridle] in myn hond,/To han [have] the governance of hous and lond,/And [Both] of his tonge, and of his hond also."[52] Her tale includes a similar, if more fantastical, negotiation between an old hag capable of magical transformation and a rapist-knight who needs an answer to the question of what women want in order to be spared his life. The hag trades that answer for his hand in marriage and then negotiates with him: in return, does he want her ugly and old (and faithful) or young and beautiful (and desired by many)? Meekly, he allows her to make the choice, and his reward for granting her sovereignty is that she will be both beautiful and faithful.

Critics have been troubled by the tale's contradictory female and male wish fulfillments: the woman gains the upper hand but the rapist-knight obtains a perfect trophy wife. The sexual violence we see as deviant (rape) has led directly

to a version of medieval society's ideal marriage, with the man in control of
the very appearance of his spouse. But if we see this as an example of Bersani's "inevitable play of thrusts and relinquishment,"[53] a constant struggle
between lovers for supremacy in any relationship, then the old hag, at least, is
playing by the rules of the exchange of power, an essential element in partner
play within modern sadomasochistic relationships. The Wife of Bath and her
literary avatar are not alone in playing this game. Kristina Hildebrand argues
that even some of the historical Pastons, in their letters between husbands and
wives, write to each other within a playful system that borrows heavily from
the language of "eroticised power difference."[54] Chaucer provides a perfect
example of the couple that negotiates its power exchange, this time in the
"Franklin's Tale." Dorigen, taking pity on Aurelius as a courtly lady should,
promises to "take hym for hir housbonde and hir lord" while he swears never
to "take no maistrie [dominion]" and to "obeye and folwe hir wyl in al [her
will in everything],/As any lovere to his lady shal," reserving only the respect
his rank should accord him.[55] Chaucer's Franklin explains that there is good
emotional reason for this:

> Love wol nat been constreyned by maistrye [dominion].
> Whan maistrie comth [comes], the God of Love anon
> Beteth [beats] his wynges and farewel, he is gon![56]

Neither sex likes to be "constreyned as a thral [servant],"[57] although in
Chaucer's romantic tragedy *Troilus and Criseyde*, a story of lovers who come
together only to be driven apart by war and infidelity, love is only consummated when the language of conquest is present.

When Troilus and Criseyde make love for the first time, their foreplay
is both sweet and a little embarrassing: Troilus faints with emotion and
must be hauled "aswowne" (fainting) into his beloved's bed; when her
kisses wake him up, his first words indicate that he doesn't know where
he is or what Criseyde is doing.[58] She wonders, and many readers wonder
with her, "Is this a mannes game?"[59] Nevertheless, it is Criseyde who soon
seems dominated by her fears: "Right as an aspes lef [aspen's leaf] she gan
to quake" when Troilus at last embraces her,[60] a mood that the narrator
heralds by drawing a parallel between sexual activity and the hunt: "What
might or may the sely larke [innocent lark] seye/Whan that the sperhauk
[sparrowhawk] hath it in his fot [has it in its talon]?"[61] Troilus's timidity
is ironically highlighted by the narrator's insistence on the predator-prey
metaphor; when Troilus himself turns to this language subsequently, it sits

uncomfortably on his shoulders. Either finding his confidence or trying to act as he thinks is expected, Troilus now tells Criseyde that she is caught and has no choice but to give him what he wants (what Criseyde has struggled to give him, in fact):

> This Troylus yn armes gan hire streyne [pressed her in his arms],
> And seyde, "O swete, as evere mot I gon [as long as I live],
> Now be ye kaught, now is ther but we tweyne [there is only us two].
> Now yeldeth yow [submit], for other bote is non [there is no other remedy]."[62]

But that is not necessarily what Criseyde wants—a more active lover is not the same thing as a ruthless hunter—and she tells him that if she had not already agreed to yield, she "were now not here."[63] Although they took a rocky path, the negotiations between Troilus and Criseyde eventually arrive at their destination, an apparently uncomplicated heterosexual union, but that should not obscure the fact that one of the great medieval heterosexual romances utilizes the language of conquest and violence. To some extent Troilus succeeds or fails as a lover inasmuch as he can accommodate himself to this violent trope.

This use of imagery associated with hunting and capture for the purpose of sexual seduction is not unique to *Troilus and Criseyde*. In *Sir Gawain and the Green Knight* (ca. 1360–1380), the wife of Gawain's host attempts to seduce a naked Gawain by trapping him in his bed. Calling him an unwary sleeper, she claims he is "tan astyt [quickly caught]," and that she intends to bind him in his bed.[64] She is flirting and playful, but she is simultaneously speaking the language of erotic bondage. For Gawain to be "taken" and bound has sometimes been read as mild threat to Gawain's masculinity. At the beginning of Jerome's *Life of Paul* (repeated in the *Alphabet of Tales*, no. 138), the threat is stated more strongly. Jerome tells two stories, one of a Christian bound and covered in honey by the devil (no fate is given), and the second the story of a young man tied up with "caressing garlands" and laid on a bed of feathers in an idyllic garden. The youth is discovered by a prostitute who happens to be wandering by and who, impressed by his beauty, proceeds to fondle him to arousal. Just as she straddles him with a view to taking his virtue, the youth finds the ideal solution: he bites off his own tongue and spits it into the prostitute's face.[65] Jerome paints the scene with a hardly disguised and barely sublimated eroticism: the garden and the binding garlands do not only explain the youth's helplessness; they allow, albeit temporarily, a surrender in the reader, who watches the tableau until the victim rescues himself. The gaze lingers not on the biting of the tongue, but on the bondage that required it. The lady may have reason to believe that the claim to have captured and thus controlled Gawain is not just a threat but part of the foreplay that her words imply he would avoid if he could. Gawain is not the youth in Jerome's second story, and he needs his tongue to talk his way out of trouble (even though the tongue's flirtation is a less thorough solution). If medieval desire is linked to the language of the hunt and of force in a way that seems less problematic than it would today, it is nevertheless to be expected that desire would occasionally run to the extreme.

SADISM WITHOUT CONSTRAINT

If it is difficult, and even impossible, to determine when a certain historical or literary behavior is a sexual one, there is one medieval case that is assuredly sexual. The trial of the fifteenth-century nobleman Gilles de Rais, the companion of Joan of Arc and perpetrator of the ritual and sexual murder of dozens of children, is often taken to be the "first recorded case of a sadistic sexual offender" in history, not just by medieval historians but by experts in the psychology of today's sexual predators.[66] Gilles de Rais is a prototype of the figure of Bluebeard, who murders his wives and keeps their bodies as trophies in a locked room, and for the child-murdering aristocrats in films such as *The Hour of the Pig* (1994, called *The Advocate* in North America) and *The Reckoning* (2003, based on Barry Unsworth's novel *Morality Play*). To a lesser extent his figure lies behind the cinematic allusions to the droit du seigneur (or *droit de cuissage*), a modern myth that states that a lord has "first night" sexual rights to any new bride from his lands (used in *Braveheart* [1994] with no historical basis in its fifteenth-century source, and in *The Warlord* [1965]).[67] The specter of Gilles de Rais has a double power to terrify, as the first known sexual serial killer, but one with both the aristocratic power and the resources to commit his crimes on a huge scale, and to hide those crimes for some time.

Gilles's case is a rarity in that both the medieval and modern interpretations of his crimes are relatively close: although the ubiquitous charge of sodomy is applied to his crimes (the warrant was issued on the authority of Jean V, duke of Brittany), a more accurate modern diagnosis would be biastophiliac pedophilia (paraphilia that depends on the rape of children to achieve arousal). Although he was charged with heresy through a related series of alchemy charges, Gilles raped and murdered somewhere between sixty and three hundred children, and while medieval and modern commentators often disagree about what constitutes a sexual crime, de Rais seems terrifyingly familiar to modern eyes. One accomplice, Henriet Griart, testified that Gilles took more pleasure in the murders than in the pedophilia and often played with the severed heads and limbs of his victims:

> When the said children were dead he kissed them and those who had the most handsome limbs and heads he held up to admire them, and had their bodies cruelly cut open and took delight at the sight of their inner organs; and very often when the said children were dying he sat on their stomachs and took pleasure in seeing them die.[68]

While this is a record of a trial—and thus subject to the mediation of court authorities—the behavior seems familiar from modern examples of similar sexual killings, most notoriously the case of John Wayne Gacy (executed in 1994 for killing thirty-three young men and boys). Even when Gilles assaulted girls rather than boys, he is said to have avoided their genitals altogether, preferring to stroke himself to erection before "rubbing his member on the bellies of the said boys and girls with great delight, vigor and libidinous pleasure until the sperm ejaculated on their bellies."[69] The graphic nature of the trial records, almost unprecedented in their wealth of detail, is largely responsible for Gilles' place as Western history's first known serial killer.

Gilles was assisted in his crimes by a number of courtiers and servants, including a woman named Perrine Martin, who became known as Le Meffraye: the Terror. Among his close servants was Etienne Corillaut, called Poitou in the trial documents. J. Benedetti thought Poitou's story "perhaps the most tragic; corrupted and perverted as a child, he was drawn willy-nilly into a situation from which ... there was no escape."[70] The trials record two contradictory moments at which the young Poitou discovers his master's crime, the first occurring just after he goes into service with Gilles, when Gilles molests him in the manner already described (the testimony quoted in the previous paragraph Poitou's). On both occasions, Poitou is saved from murder by the actions of other servants. It seems clear from the records that if Gilles is one of the earliest recorded sexual serial killers, Poitou is the first recorded example of a person so badly abused that he become his abuser's accomplice. Poitou was executed in 1440, on the same day as Gilles (who asked to be executed first, so that he could set a good example to those he had previously led astray).

Bersani has often repeated the claim that sexuality, for our culture, as for others, is wrapped in comfortable lies, "the redemptive reinvention of sex" being understood as one of mutual tenderness and emotional depth rather than penetration and power.[71] Although Bersani may overstate his case, it remains true that the Middle Ages largely imagined sex without any comfortable lies concerning tenderness and affection. While these existed as an ideal, sex was intimately related to power and control.[72] If there is a depiction of mutual and emotionally resonant sexual activity, it usually comes as a result of negotiation like the ones explored in this chapter. In fact, even Chaucer seems to view sex as something inherently violent and competitive. Even "the English canon's favorite 'wayside drama' [the *Canterbury Tales*] has this specific, jaundiced bodily economy of the erotic: males pierce; women bleed."[73] This is undoubtedly a dark view of medieval sexuality that is not universally accepted. Yet the language of power and hierarchy is so omnipresent in the literature that it is perhaps possible to claim that the category of deviant sexuality in the Middle Ages is much wider than has been previously thought.

CONCLUSION

Medieval classifications of the diverse and the deviant have porous boundaries and are ambiguous. Easy categorization both within a period and between periods is ultimately difficult to achieve. Medieval society, like our own, reveals diverse sexual behaviors, but medieval sexuality has many violent elements that reinforce gender and social hierarchies.

CHAPTER FIVE

Sex, Religion, and the Law

IRINA METZLER

The foundations of medieval attitudes to sexuality, and the condemnation of what were deemed to be sexual transgressions, lie in late antiquity. In 309 C.E., a number of bishops and presbyters met at the synod of Elvira (modern-day Granada) and imposed legislation on their congregations. A number of their eighty-one canons directly condemned certain forms of sexual behavior. For example, canon 13 related to virgins who had dedicated their lives to God but then turned to "lust" instead; canon 18 related to clerics who were placed in the ministry and then committed a sexual offense. The canons minutely distinguished between adultery committed once (canon 69), twice (7), frequently (47), with Jews or pagans (78), by bishops, presbyters or deacons (8), by a cleric's wife (65), or a layman's wife (70); divorce was addressed (8, a woman leaving her husband); fornication (*fornicatio*) (7 and 30, seen as something that young people are particularly prone to); prostitution (12, women engaged in pandering others or selling their own bodies); men abusing boys (*De stupratoribus puerorum*) (71); and abortion (63, seen as something a woman does to disguise the consequence of an adulterous affair).[1] In all, 45 percent of the total of eighty-one canons dealt with matters of sexual conduct. All the major themes that were to reappear later in medieval texts, over and over again, can be found here already.

Later medieval legal views of sexuality derive from rulings made at such synods and from early Christian moral theology. These notions were crystallized in late antiquity by two patristic authorities in particular: St. Jerome and St. Augustine.[2] Broadly, their main arguments are that sexuality per se is denounced as evil; virginity is the state one should aspire to; and if one must have a sexual life, then only within legitimate marriage. Sex within marriage was a licensed but fundamentally sinful act, only permissible with the express aim of begetting children. The sex of one's partner (though same-sex activity was illicit) was less important than the concept that *all* sexual activity had to be potentially reproductive. A fourteenth-century preacher's manual by an anonymous English Franciscan friar reiterated these patristic views, stating that adultery could even be committed by a lawfully wedded couple: "namely when husbands become adulterers with their own wives, using sex not for procreation but for their lustful pleasure alone,"[3] although this was not as bad as adultery between a married and an unmarried person, or between two people married but not to each other.

Sex in what has come to be called the "missionary position" was deemed to be the only natural, and therefore the only permitted, position, so that all other heterosexual variations were often classed as sodomy. The regulations governed not only physical position but also temporal correctness. There were numerous restrictions placed on permissible times for sexual intercourse, and if a married couple strictly adhered to them, then that left about half of the year out of bounds. Sex was taboo on Sundays (sometimes extended to Fridays and even Wednesdays), the feast days of saints, periods of fasting such as Lent or Advent, and during a woman's life when her body manifested physiological processes which were held to render her "impure" (menstruation, pregnancy, the first forty days after parturition, and lactation).[4]

Sexual activity by clerics was of far greater concern to the church. Throughout the early Christian centuries there were various drives to enforce clerical celibacy, but it was the eleventh-century Gregorian Reform that concentrated on attempting to eliminate clerical marriage (Nicolaitism). Degradation, removal of clerical rank and "house arrest" in a monastery were possible consequences for sexually active clerics who had been convicted of misdemeanors. In practice, clerical celibacy was never truly implemented, since in the High and later Middle Ages priests and even higher-ranking clerics still kept concubines.[5] Following greater emphasis on "standards" within the church and enforcement of celibacy for priests from the eleventh century onward, the church tried to remove priests' concubines. For example, one of the reform popes, Pope Urban II (1088–1099), placed particular emphasis on enforcing legislation against simony, clerical marriage and sexual misconduct.[6] The First and Second Lateran Councils (1123 and 1139 respectively) established canons that invalidated clerical marriage and lowered the status of any family members (wives or children) that might have arisen from a clerical marriage. Many former wives therefore were legally degraded to "concubines" and, in theory at least, were to be expelled from clerical homes. Canon law, unlike secular law in England, ruled that children born illegitimately because their parents were unmarried subsequently became legitimate if their parents married at a later stage.[7] Church reformers of the eleventh century, however, keen to impose higher moral standards on both clergy and laity, tried to get canons enacted that reduced the likelihood of illegitimate children gaining an inheritance through their deceased parents.[8]

Since so many kinds of sexual activities were now prohibited, or regarded as permissible only at certain times, the potential for sexual misconduct (and thereby committing a sin) was therefore increasingly likely. Penance and confession were offered as two means of expiating such sins. Penance, the earlier form, usually took place in public, but was gradually supplanted by private confession. Hence we have two types of sources for the church's attitude toward illegal sexual activity: penitentials and confessors' manuals. Over the course of the earlier Middle Ages up to about 1200, the church came to distinguish between sins and religious crimes, which the early church had treated as one and the same. By the High Middle Ages, although sins could be confessed in private, religious crimes continued to be dealt with in public in a canonical court, just like the earlier penances. Church courts policed behavior deemed immoral, including sexual misconduct of both clerics and the laity: "The issues that brought the largest numbers of people into personal contact with canonical courts at the local level had to do with marriage, family, and sexual behavior."[9] A religious crime constituted a sin that had become publicly known; for example, if, as the result of adultery, a man abandoned his wife and moved in with another woman, this would be a publicly visible crime and would be handled in an ecclesiastical court, while the protagonists might still privately confess their sins as a separate atonement.[10]

The earliest penitential from the first half of the sixth century is attributed to the Irish cleric Finnian of Clonard. As in later penitentials, sexual offenses form the greatest number of items, more than any other category.[11] In Finnian's text, sexual offenses make up almost two-fifths of the total.[12] For example:

> If anyone has defiled a vowed virgin and lost his honor and begotten a child by her, let such an one, being a layman, do penance for three years; but in the first year he shall go on an allowance of bread and water and unarmed and shall not have intercourse with his own wife, and for two years more he shall abstain from wine and meats and shall not have intercourse with his wife.[13]

The innocent wife is punished just as much, in our understanding at any rate, as the offending husband, by being denied intercourse with her husband through his penance.[14]

The refinement of categories of sexual behavior culminated in the *Decretum* of Burchard of Worms (bishop 1000–1025). Although this dealt with *all* types of sin the nineteenth book dealt specifically with a catalogue of sexual offenses.[15] Penitentials dating from the earlier Middle Ages remained in use for centuries, but by the High and later Middle Ages began to be supplanted by confessors' and preachers' manuals, model sermon books, exempla, and saints' lives. An intellectual break with the penitential tradition of categorizing and listing types of sin purely by the act itself comes with Peter Abelard's work on ethics in the twelfth century. For Abelard, a subjective intention matters more than an action. On their own, actions, including sexual actions, are neither good nor bad: it is the agent's purposeful intent (or lack of it) that makes it sinful or not.[16] Henceforth it was not simply a matter of whether someone had committed adultery but also question of whether they had deliberately and purposefully done so—a "premeditated" sin, to use a term from modern criminal law. The confessors' manuals provide sample questions with which the confessor could draw out from the penitent the intent behind the sin. A wonderfully detailed fictitious dialogue between a confessor and his penitent, "which summarizes the sexual sins prohibited in church law" is given in the *Summa confessorum* (1208–1215) of Robert of Flamborough:

PRIEST: There remains coitus which is lechery in the strict sense of the word. Have you ever been polluted with lechery?

PENITENT: Lots of times.

PRIEST: Ever against nature?

PENITENT: Lots of times.

PRIEST: Ever with a man?

PENITENT: Lots of times.

PRIEST: With clerics or with laymen?

PENITENT: With both.

PRIEST: Married laymen or single?

PENITENT: Both.

PRIEST: With how many married people?

PENITENT: I don't know.

PRIEST: So you don't know how many times?

PENITENT: That's right.

PR: Let us find out what we can. How long were you with them?

PENITENT: 7 years.

PRIEST: In what Order?

PENITENT: (I have been) 2 years in the priesthood, 2 in the diaconate, 2 in the sub-diaconate, a year as an acolyte. I sinned with unattached people, but I don't know the number of people or times.

PRIEST: Did you sin with clerics?

PENITENT: I sinned both with seculars and with religious.

PRIEST: Tell me how many seculars and how many religious, and what Order you and they were in when you sinned together, and whether they possessed the dignity of archdeacon, dean, abbot or bishop? Did you ever introduce any innocent person to that sin? Say how many and what Order you were then in?[17]

By the High Middle Ages, there were well-established sliding scales of penalties that could be handed out to sexual offenders. In addition to penances and monetary fines, in church courts the accused sometimes had to produce oath-helpers, known as compurgators. In the late-thirteenth-century court of the archdeaconry of Sudbury (Suffolk), five compurgators were required in cases of adultery, rising to either five or seven in cases of incest; and in mid-fourteenth-century England archbishop Stratford specified a maximum number of six compurgators for a crime like fornication, and a maximum of twelve in cases of adultery and other more serious crimes;[18] hence adultery was regarded as graver than simple fornication. Certain types of people were deemed to be more prone to sexual misconduct than others: among them, prostitutes, but also sailors. The idea of a sailor "having a wife in every port"—that is, of having adulterous liaisons—already features in one mid-fourteenth-century English confessors' manual, the *Memoriale Presbiterorum*.[19]

To understand the "formal enforcement mechanisms that medieval ecclesiastical courts employed to implement the Church's sexual norms,"[20] it is necessary to give an outline development of canon law. In the very strict procedural rulings of canon law, the onus of proof was on the accuser who had to find two impeccable witnesses who would swear they had in fact seen the accused act in the way complained about. Since that was very unlikely, in reality much sexual misbehavior, especially by clerics, was probably unreported. Sexual misconduct more often than not was a hidden crime. Understandably, the church found this situation untenable. Thus a decision in canon law was handed down by Pope Innocent III (1198–1216) which effectively removed the need for witnesses should the misdemeanor be so "public that it can properly be called notorious."[21] Further developments within canon law, also instigated by Pope Innocent III, led to the inquisitorial procedure.[22] Under this procedure, it was no longer necessary for an accuser to bring a case. Instead the judge could launch an investigation on the basis of any information that was presented to him, including hearsay and rumor: he effectively became the prosecutor. The inquisitorial system is of course most widely associated in the modern mind with heresy trials and the post-medieval witch hunts, but this procedure could be used for any prosecution under canon law. By the early-thirteenth century the onus of proof was loosened yet further. The notion was introduced that several partial proofs could add up to a full proof (which the two-witness requirement had been). A partial proof could be a sworn statement by someone who only believed that a crime had been committed but who had no actual eyewitness knowledge of the fact, and their testimony was allowed to have some judicial weight as evidence. According to James Brundage, "These developments in the law of evidence, combined with the introduction of *per notorium* [Pope Innocent III's notoriety clause] and inquisitory procedure, made it much easier by the end of the thirteenth century to prosecute and convict offenders against the Church's rules about sexual behavior than it had been in 1200."[23]

The Fourth Lateran Council of 1215 instigated two further demands; that everyone must make confession at least once a year (which meant the local priest knew more about his parishioners' sexual behavior than previously when confession had been a more random affair); and that preaching was to be specifically addressed to the laity (most surviving sermons prior to 1215 were composed in Latin, and therefore intended only for educated clergy).[24]

With greater legislation, came more cases of sexual misconduct to the extent that the overwhelmed bishops began to delegate routine offenses to their archdeacons. Unsurprisingly, archdeacons were not the most popular clerics, and were frequently the object of satire and ridicule.[25] By the end of the thirteenth century, canon law and its enforcement had developed to such an extent that supervision and control of sexual activity constituted the main offenses dealt with by church courts. Fines imposed on people convicted of sexual misconduct provided the economic basis for their perpetuation since the money was ploughed back into the system, keeping all the archdeacons, judges, and court recorders in business.

Some people came before the courts requesting a judicial decree of separation or annulment (divorce in modern parlance) for reasons of sexual incompatibility. This could imply anything from frigidity to impotence to infertility. An allegedly impotent husband was examined by "experienced women" to see if he reacted sexually at all. These women "were not always respectable matrons but in fact prostitutes, who were in a sense acting as expert witnesses."[26] In the fifteenth-century case of John Scathelok in York, he was examined by women, one of whom "exposed her naked breasts, and with her hands warmed at the ... fire, she held and rubbed the penis and testicles of the said John. And she embraced and frequently kissed the same John ... the whole time aforesaid the said penis was scarcely three inches long, ... remaining without any increase or decrease."[27] Witnesses might also be asked to testify that in bed the couple were trying hard enough. Women too, not just men, could be examined by other, matronly, women to establish if they were physically capable of intercourse.[28]

The guilty parties might be publicly humiliated (even using physical punishment) if they had committed a sexual crime, a practice known as the charivari, or "rough music." Adulterous women might have their heads shaved and be paraded through the streets of a town, while men might be publicly whipped. In some towns in southern France, if an adulterous couple had been caught in flagrante delicto (the man with his trousers down, or both found undressed behind closed doors), then they were made to run naked through the streets from one town gate to another.[29] By the fourteenth and fifteenth centuries, however, the guilty party could be punished with a fine instead of physically, as stipulated in the French royal ordinances.[30] Confessors might also impose penalties, such as fasting on bread and water for a given period commensurate with the sin being atoned for, or could order the repentant sinner to go on a pilgrimage.

In secular law, early medieval regulations on sexual activity can be found in the Germanic law codes, which covered most of northern and western Europe, including Visigothic Spain as well as Burgundian France and Anglo-Saxon England, as well as Germany.[31] Various hierarchies of compensation for physical injuries of all kinds are listed in these texts, including for injuries that may have had more social impact ("losing face") than actual bodily harm. Such a scheme of sliding penalties was applied in eighth-century Frankish Salic Law to the deliberate touching of women's bodies by unauthorized males; for example, touching a woman's finger or her head was fined fifteen shillings (half the fine for attempted abduction) and touching a woman's breast (the same as for illegal sexual intercourse with a married woman) was fined forty-five shillings.[32]

English common law and manorial records show fines for extramarital sexual activity in the form of *leyrwite* to be paid to the lord of a female serf.[33]

There was a common law belief that husbands had the right to kill unfaithful wives and their lovers (in effect, this was private individuals taking the law into their own hands: "vendetta justice"), but if they went too far, or if the punishment was too brutal even by the standards of the time, then there might be royal intervention. Matthew Paris in the thirteenth century related one dreadful episode, where the lynch mob who had castrated an adulterer were themselves tried and convicted. Subsequently, the king proclaimed as law that "no one dare to mutilate the genitals of adulterers."[34] In a later case from 1476 in Normandy, the husband killed not just his wife's lover but his wife, too, resulting in the conviction of the vengeful husband, although he simply had to pay an enormous fine.[35] By the late-fifteenth century, private revenge was seen as contravening royal justice. Authorities in the later Middle Ages used capital punishment for "scandalous" crimes, especially rape, incest or sodomy (crimes that were held to undermine sexual morals); in Ferrara during the 1490s, "a peasant burned to death for impregnating his sister and for bestiality with asses, a 17-year-old youth from the suburbs burned for sodomy, another peasant hanged for theft and incest with his sisters, ... [and] an 80-year-old draper convicted of sodomy and sentenced to death by burning was spared his life,"[36] showing that old age did not necessarily curb sexual desires or sexual activity.

Neither secular nor canon law was very effective at implementing its regulations. Offenders were difficult to pin down in confession, since for someone to make confession, they had first to acknowledge that they had committed a sin. In cases of "simple fornication" (sexual relations between unmarried men and women) the confessing couple often refused to believe they had sinned, pointing out that many ordinary people behaved in this way.[37] One fourteenth-century preacher's manual went to great lengths to counter the claim "that simple fornication is not a mortal sin because it is a natural act,"[38] using copious arguments from the Bible and classical texts. Although fornication meant any forbidden sexual intercourse, for the author of this manual it particularly referred to intercourse with widows, prostitutes or concubines.[39] Various other religious tracts claim that most people considered fornication to be no sin.[40] The medieval theologian Thomas Aquinas observed: "although some believe adultery is a sin, nonetheless they do not believe that simple fornication is a sin."[41] Some theological writers cautioned against a lenient view of fornication, believing that to treat it as a venial sin would undermine the institution of marriage; if people believed that fornication would not lead to damnation, they would see no reason to bind themselves to each other in marriage.[42] One might also argue that the "constant thundering from the pulpit against sexual temptation and extramarital sexual behavior"[43] reflected the reality that people from all levels of society did not in fact pay very much attention to exhortations to repress their sexual desires.

Pre-Christian marriage rules allowed various methods of marriage,[44] but from the later seventh century onward, changes in marriage regulation were introduced. There was a shift from an earlier notion of marriage primarily as a political-economic, contractual arrangement between families (a model that allows for divorce at will) toward the clerical notion of marriage between consenting individuals—in its widest sense, the birth of the romantic notion of marriage. Some historians have seen a conflict between clerical and secular notions of marriage based on tensions between the church's view of marriage as an indissoluble, permanent union, and secular views where marriages were made (mainly amongst powerful families) as a convenient political and economic tool "to optimize the interests and fortune of the family as a whole."[45]

Rules governing incest or consanguinity were often used to gain divorces that would be otherwise impossible in the church's eyes, as was the canonical notion of free and voluntary consent, without which a marriage could also be declared invalid. Such compromises could allow a continuation of ecclesiastical notions of marital permanence while allowing secular society a form of "get-out clause" from inconvenient marriages. Adultery could also be used as means of escape from an unwanted marriage. A double standard applied whereby rules against adulterous women were much more strictly enforced than those for men; Mary, Duchess of Brabant and wife of Duke Louis II of Bavaria, was beheaded in 1256 after she had been mistakenly convicted of adultery.[46] The accusation was never proven because the adulterer was never identified. Mary's husband went on to found a Cistercian abbey, in pious expiation of his doubts, and married twice more.

Sex before marriage, although condemned as fornication, was deemed acceptable as long as the couple intended to marry in the future. In the practice known as *abjuratio sub pena nubendi* (forswearing on pain of marriage), the fornicating couple repeated marriage vows in the future tense.[47] Even if such vows had been taken without witnesses, they were still valid as a marriage agreement according to canon law; the couple were deemed married in the eyes of God. This legal provision seems to be another expression of the theological view that taking the path leading to a lesser evil is preferable to trying to enforce absolute moral standards that few can actually uphold—better to marry even in a clandestine marriage, than have sex and not be married at all.

Incest was another sexual danger. The medieval definition of incest was much stricter than in modern Western society; some sexual relations with non-blood relatives were also labeled incestuous. A fourteenth-century preacher's manual defines incest as sexual intercourse with a person related by blood or "spiritual kinship."[48] Earlier authorities, such as the so-called *Roman Penitential of Halitgar* (ca. 830), included a man's stepmother, or the widow of a man's uncle, or his wife's sister in a list of close relatives. A man thus committing incest "shall be canonically condemned."[49] The Fourth Lateran Council in 1215 defined incest as any sexual activity with persons related to within the fourth degree, where each degree meant one generation from a common ancestor. One of the reasons often given by moralists as to why prostitutes should be avoided was the danger of incest: a man had no way of knowing whether a prostitute had previously had sex with his brother, father or other relative, and according to ecclesiastical definition she might therefore be related to him and he would then unwittingly be committing incest.

Christian moral theology also condemned the excessive consumption of alcohol because it led to illicit sex. The biblical precedents were Noah, the first vintner, whose sons saw him shamefully naked when he was drunk (Gen. 8:20–23) and the daughters of Lot, who deliberately made their father drunk so that they could commit incest without him noticing (Gen. 19:31–36). The first-century Pope Clement I cautioned young men and women against drinking wine because alcohol aroused the passions.[50] The Augustinian canonist Peter the Chanter (d. 1197) cited the biblical story of Lot's drunkenness, as well as the classical author Terence's observations on the connection between Ceres (goddess of corn and therefore of alcohol) and Venus (goddess of love and therefore sex), to conclude that there were strong links between gluttony, of which drunkenness was a prime example, and sexual sins.[51] The Fourth Lateran Council in 1215 specifically mentioned that clerics ought to drink only moderately to avoid sins of the flesh.[52] Due to the link between alcohol and sexual sins, taverns and other drinking places were also regarded as places of dubious sexual morals: prostitutes frequented taverns, and women working in taverns were morally suspect. Bernard of Pavia (d. 1213), a canon lawyer, went so far as to argue "that a man who permitted his wife to work at a tavern could not charge her with adultery if the sin was associated with her work."[53] But canon lawyers also argued that alcohol was a mitigating factor in sins of the flesh. In the eleventh century Burchard of Worms in his *Decretum* reduced the penalty for married couples having sexual intercourse on holy days (normally forty days) to half if the man was drunk.[54] In canon law, if men or women committed adultery while drunk, they received milder penances than those who had committed the same sin sober. Marriages that were consummated while under the influence of alcohol might not be regarded as legally binding; in one case from York in 1418, a couple agreed to marry, then broke off the engagement, but then had sex (that is, consummated their promise of marriage) while one of them was drunk. The question arose whether the couple were legally married or not: "According to a fourteenth-century treatise on ecclesiastical discipline the answer was no, because the drunkenness did not indicate consent."[55] Medieval men appear to have used drunkenness as an excuse for sexual misconduct. As the thirteenth-century text *La clef d'amour* puts it: "When man behaves like arrant sot,/The drink is blamed, the drinker, not."[56]

Earlier medieval law did not have a concept of rape as a separate offense. The Germanic law codes of the early Middle Ages treated rape and abduction together; women were defined by their status (free/slave, married/virgin) and punishment was meted out according to whether a man raped a slave girl or a free woman. Furthermore, most passages on rape in these laws mentioned marriage (or lack of it) in the same section, or the payment of a bride-price as compensation, or the punishment of the man for refusing to marry the raped woman rather than for the forced sex.[57] Rape was seen primarily as abduction and as violation of women within the context of women as members of a certain *familia*. The main purpose of the codes was to protect property and the correct channels of inheritance, not to protect women from non-consensual sex.

In canon law, extramarital sex was an offense, and in secular law violence was an offense, but no law of the earlier period combined the two offenses. Rape in the modern sense did not exist as a legal category. *Raptus* in earlier medieval texts tended to mean the abduction of someone's daughter with a view to marrying her without the permission of her father or guardian—her own consent was deemed irrelevant.[58] Sexual intercourse was not necessarily included in the offense of *raptus*, since the crime lay in the abduction, the stealing of the woman from the person (generally male) who held legal power over her.[59] In England it was only in 1275, enshrined in the Statute of Westminster I, that rape became a crime that could be prosecuted by royal justices:

> And the king forbids anyone to rape, or take by force a damsel under age, either with her consent or without it, or a married woman or a damsel of age or any other woman against her will; and if anyone does so the king will, at the suit of him who will sue within forty days, do common justice therein; and if no one begins his suit within forty days the king will sue in the matter; and those whom he finds guilty shall have two

years' imprisonment and then shall make fine at the will of the king, and
if they have not the means from which to be fined at the king's pleasure,
they are to be punished by longer imprisonment, according to what the
offence demands.[60]

Even here rape (sexual violence) and abduction (taking by force) are still
linked, and the assumption persists that a male relative, husband or guardian
will make legal representation and accusation on behalf of the female victim.
Theoretically, the king, that is, the king's judge, might initiate proceedings if
no one else did within the forty-day period. But in practice most accusations
had to be made privately by women, and it seems that in many cases legal
actions initiated by women were simply dropped at an early stage in the proceedings.[61] One reason given by historians as to why so few rape cases resulted
in the conviction of the rapist is the severe punishment in earlier secular law.
While the punishment for rape was mutilation or even the death penalty, male
jurors were likely to weigh up the punishment against the perceived suffering
of the victim, and in many cases the actual rape, and more specifically the loss
of virginity, were deemed not to warrant as harsh a penalty as sentencing to
death. However, there is no indication that the conviction rate for rape trials
improved even when later statutes commuted capital punishment to imprisonment or monetary fines. What status a woman had also defined her success or
not in cases of rape accusations, since, for example, the rape of a prostitute
was often not considered a crime, but rape of a child (a girl under the age
of twelve) was punished more severely than rape of a widow. Since rape was
regarded primarily as a violation of a woman's marriageability, those women
who would have had more success in the marriage market were also more
likely to have success in a court of law.

Further statutes in 1382 and 1487 pushed English law on rape in a direction
that removed injury to the woman even more and placed greater importance on
injury to her family (by way of ruined reputation and damaged marriageability).[62]
Rape and abduction became again entangled in legal thinking. In other European regions, too, these features of the evolution of rape laws can be found.
One historiographic interpretation is that while there was a tension between
canon law (which did not require parental consent to a couple's marriage) and
secular law (which did require parental consent), secular rape laws existed primarily to uphold property values: what the law wanted to avoid was young
women eloping with the man of their (but not their parents') choice and jeop-
ardizing planned family unions; rape legislation therefore increasingly became
concerned with abduction legislation.[63]

An important absence in medieval law was any consideration given to the concept of rape within marriage. Canon law had by the thirteenth century defined a valid marriage as a union that initially required consent but was also ratified by sexual intercourse:

> The canonistic texts thus show that ... when a couple married and consummated their union physically through an act of sexual congress, consent to that first act of marital intercourse implicitly carried with it unconditional consent to future intercourse at the will of either party through the remainder of their natural lives.[64]

The niceties of canon law deemed a wife guilt free and sinless if she submitted to sexual intercourse that her husband demanded of her, for example, during Lent, but that was a far as it went—the fact that the wife may not have wanted intercourse herself is of no consequence; instead the importance of "rendering the conjugal debt" is paramount. How strongly this view was held is demonstrated in theological and canonist texts by William of Rennes and Bonaventure. Both discuss a fictional case where a newly married woman wishes to become a member of a religious community. Under ecclesiastical law, both parties to the marriage had a period of two months from the initial giving of consent to decide whether either wished to enter a religious life (the highest aspiration in ecclesiastical thinking) and so to refuse sex to the other. William and Bonaventure both argue that in this case of forced sex, priority was taken by "the rights and obligations attached to the marital debt over the right to enter religion."[65] So even in cases of contradictory legal stances a woman's wishes and rights were subsumed under those of a man.

Unlike rape, prostitution was a sin (in canon law), but not a crime (in secular law). Activities associated with prostitution, however, such as procuring (sometimes by raping a girl which subsequently might make her unmarriageable) and pimping, were considered crimes. Many late medieval towns in Germany, England, Italy, and France legalized and regulated prostitution in municipal brothels. The reasoning behind the legality was that by providing a regulated outlet for sexuality, greater sin (through indiscriminate fornication) would be prevented; better to have a few sinful women than potentially many women sinning. Secular legislation concerning prostitution went through phases; firstly, a restriction of prostitution (or expulsion of the prostitutes themselves from certain towns) in the thirteenth century, followed by a phase of toleration in the fourteenth century, and finally a phase of acceptance with regulation in the fifteenth century (even going so far as the establishment of municipally run brothels in some towns).[66] However, according to church law of the twelfth and thirteenth centuries, toleration for prostitution as a "necessary evil" was already present in theological thinking. It was in fact the secular authorities who were most eager to restrict or regulate prostitution: "Any clerical ideas of the protective value of prostitution in greater battles against sin seem not to have been transmitted to the lay population."[67]

Because prostitutes often had to be readily identifiable, the law required that they wear distinctive garments (a yellow scarf in Vienna, a red cap in Berne and Zurich, a striped hood in Bristol).[68] Places where they lived and worked might also be regulated. A proclamation on August 4, 1416, ordered all prostitutes in Milan to wear a cloak, and a further proclamation on May 18, 1417, ordered them to return to the brothel[69]—visibility and spatial control were important regulating factors. In medieval London, the punishment for prostitutes who failed to keep to their designated areas (Cokkeslane and Southwark) was the relatively lenient one of a humiliating public parade at first offense, and only at the third offense the shearing of the woman's hair in public.[70] In many English towns, as was also common in other European cities, prostitutes were forbidden from plying their trade in the center of towns and were banished to special, generally outlying areas—or so the texts relating to municipal laws tell us. But the onomastic and archaeological evidence provided by street names (the evocative Gropecunt Lane/Street found in many larger English towns) and those streets' location in, or near, the center of these towns indicates that far from being at the margins, prostitutes worked or resided, or both, in the central urban areas.[71]

A singular case of a male prostitute has been discovered in the legal records of medieval England. In December 1394 one John Rykener, "calling himself Eleanor," was found dressed in women's clothes "having sex with another man in a London street one night."[72] This discovery poses problems, both for the medieval legal recorder, as for the modern historian trying to interpret the acts, since John Rykener could not be ascribed a sexual category: "He was not a prostitute as medieval people understood that concept, and it was unclear whether he was a sodomite."[73] Rykener was not in fact prosecuted, not through lack of evidence, but because the authorities did not know precisely what to prosecute him for.

The most troubling type of sexual behavior for both ecclesiastical and secular authorities was what was termed "sodomy," a term that covered many more practices than buggery. One medical writer commented on some women of Florence delighting in a most shocking practice; when these women were widowed, or their merchant husbands were away on lengthy business, and

sexual desires overcame them, they satisfied themselves by the use of elaborately crafted dildos, of which the writer had seen "a small stuffed bag in the
shape of a man's penis." For the writer, these women were not just passively
partaking in a morally reprehensible action, but actively sodomizing themselves, and therefore committing the worst of sexual sins. Far better for them
to "have sexual intercourse with men, and so commit a lesser sin."[74] The sin of
fornication (or adultery, if the woman was married) was preferred as the lesser
evil. Sodomy in medieval thinking therefore did not mean only homosexual
activity.

The problem with homosexual acts was not so much that non-legitimate
sexual intercourse may have taken place, but that it involved an inversion of
established gender roles. Men were always deemed the active sexual person,
women the passive.[75] In same-sex relations between men, one had to take the
passive role even though men were meant to be active; in relations between
women, one of them had to be active. It is this gender role "inversion" that
upset medieval moral sensibilities more than the actual physical activity. The
author of the fourteenth-century preacher's manual that discusses fornication,
adultery, and incest at length refuses to countenance any discussion of sodomy,
which he calls "the diabolical sin against nature," adding: "I pass over it in
horror and leave others to describe it."[76] Sodomy is therefore a sin against the
perceived natural order of things. An early medieval text, the Irish *Penitential
of Cummean* (ca. 650), simply states: "So shall those who commit sodomy
do penance for seven years. For femoral masturbation [the precise meaning is
not defined], two years."[77] Whether either of these behaviors was a one-time
offense or became habitual was also distinguished in the same penitential,
so that men guilty of sodomy first-time round had to do penance for a year,
but for two years if they repeated the offense.[78] Female same-sex relations
hardly mattered in the earlier penitentials only in the late-seventh century were
women specifically mentioned, and then with less severe penalties imposed on
them.[79]

Some distinction needs to be made between legal texts originating from
religious sources and those originating from secular ones. In the earlier Middle Ages, although there were plenty of religious texts legislating against
"sodomy" in the widest sense, there were few secular law codes that took
any interest in the matter: "Although sexuality occupies a considerable
portion of such legislation [that is, local secular law codes] and Christian
teachings regarding rape, adultery, incest, illegitimacy, marriage, fornication,
etc., receive the sanctions of the civil authorities which promulgated the
codes, homosexual relations are not proscribed in any of them."[80]

Like the development of legislation on prostitution, legislation on sodomy went through different phases. During the eleventh and twelfth centuries theologians had worked out the definitions of "sodomy" and it became one of many sins to be confessed, as part of a program of enforcing Catholic morality on a not exactly enthusiastic populace. The eleventh-century Gregorian Reform led to a systematization of the material that was sometimes quite random and contradictory in the earlier penitential literature: "The penitential came into its own by the end of the twelfth century, as the various vices were systematically organized and the suitable penance clarified in accordance with universally accepted canons."[81] In the thirteenth century secular law began to formulate legislation against sodomy (for example, at Siena in 1262 and Bologna in 1265),[82] and by the fourteenth century it was often punishable with the death penalty, although there were great regional variations in how far legislation was taken and in how far the letter of the law was applied.[83] One of the severest punishments was advocated in the mid-thirteenth-century laws of Alfonso X of Castile:

> Although we are reluctant to speak of something which is reckless to consider and reckless to perform, terrible sins are nevertheless sometimes committed, and it happens that one man desires to sin against nature with another. We therefore command that if any commit this sin, once it is proven, both be castrated before the whole populace and on the third day after be hung by the legs until dead, and that their bodies never be taken down.[84]

The development of theological definitions and scholastic condemnations of homosexuality was achieved by the thirteenth century, and secular law caught up with canon law developments; nevertheless, "persecution was still episodic and a willingness to prosecute homosexuals by burning as prescribed by law did not become evident until the fourteenth century."[85]

The fifteenth century saw the greatest fear of sodomy throughout western Christian Europe and the most stringent application of capital punishment. One notorious sexual criminal of that century, Gilles de Rais, has come down to us as the Bluebeard of modern fiction. The real Gilles de Rais was a French nobleman who was hanged in 1440 for the sexual abuse and murder of apparently hundreds of children, most of whom were boys. Additionally, during the fifteenth century, "public enthusiasm for such punishments produced what may be the first 'news report' of contemporary homosexuals."[86] An illustrated chronicle (Diebold Schilling's *Die große Burgunder-Chronik*) depicts two men being burned at the stake for sodomy at Zurich in 1482. Coincidentally, it was at Zurich in a legal accusation of 1422 that the term *florenzen* was coined, "meaning to commit the 'vice of Florence,'"[87] that is, sodomy. Florence, like Venice, saw a rise in legal accusations of sodomy during the fifteenth century. In Florence in particular, the "problem" was highlighted by St. Bernardino of Siena in a concerted campaign of preaching against sodomites during 1424–1427.[88] Bernardino's preaching was so successful that one can directly link the legislation passed in the Italian cities of Perugia, Siena, Todi, and Massa Marittima to his activities.[89] A case of a woman being put to death apparently for her transgressive sexual behavior comes from Speyer (Germany), in 1477, where Katharina Hetzeldorfer was accused by other women of wanting to "have her manly will" with them, and of behaving "exactly like a man with women" with them, by using a "piece of wood that she held between her legs," and making "an instrument with a red piece of leather, at the front filled with cotton, and a wooden stick stuck into it."[90]

From the later Middle Ages onward, sexual activity between members of different ethnic as well as religious groups was legally regulated and curtailed. This mainly affected Jews. Sexual relations between Jews and Christians were forbidden and sometimes punishable by death, as in the laws of King Juan I of Aragon (1387–1395). The thirteenth-century English law collection known as *Fleta* bundled together sexual offenses such as bestiality, sodomy, and cohabitation "with Jews and Jewesses." Those who were convicted of such crimes were to be burned alive.[91] In many places throughout western Europe, Jewish men were forbidden from visiting Christian prostitutes. Inter-ethnic and inter-religious sex was therefore sometimes regarded as among the most serious forms of sexual misconduct. However, legislation was never consistent or very clear cut, varying across time and place, and according to the sex of the offenders. Padua in 1420 had a range of punishments, from the death penalty for a Jewish man if he had sexual intercourse with a married Christian woman to a lesser punishment if a Jewish man had sex with a Christian prostitute; a Christian man who had intercourse with a Jewish woman got away with "flogging and prison or a fine."[92] Different gender, ethnicity, and social statuses dictated the severity of the offense and the degree of corresponding penalties. The aim of such legislation was to ensure exclusive access to one's "own" women, and women of one's own group were to be protected against predatory males of the "other" group. Hence sex between Christian women and Jewish or Muslim men was punished more severely than sex between Christian men and Jewish or Muslim women.

Accusations of sexual impropriety could also be used to tarnish the reputations of and label as deviant groups of people that the clerical and secular establishments wanted to prosecute for other reasons. A link was made "between sexual nonconformity and theological heterodoxy in the eyes of the Church,"[93] so that people accused of being heretics were often also accused of sexual crimes: in the fourteenth-century heresy inquisitions centered on Montaillou in the Pyrenees, many of the apparent heretics were also accused of adultery, incest, and other sexual misdemeanors. The case of Arnaud of Verniolle, who was investigated in the series of trials in 1323 that stemmed from the inquisitorial procedures instigated by Jacques Fournier, bishop of Pamiers, has been cited in modern histories of homosexuality as a prime example of the medieval repression of sexual deviancy in general and homosexuality in particular. But in context, Arnaud's case is more about heresy and his posing as a priest than about his sexual behavior.[94] Precisely because of the church's long-established and minutely detailed involvement in legislating and regulating what we would now call the private sex lives of consenting adults, it is extremely difficult to draw distinctions between prosecutions for sexual matters and prosecutions for wider religious irregularities, and we must resist imposing such ahistoric distinctions on the Middle Ages.

CONCLUSION

Legislation on sexual conduct was a way of strengthening social cohesion, of establishing a sense of identity for a group,[95] and of ultimately creating a mentality that set apart Christians and heretics (or Jews or sodomites), leading to a legitimated "us" and a marginalized "them." This is not a novel development of the Middle Ages, since ancient Mediterranean and Near Eastern societies had similar concepts of cultural exclusivity through marriage laws, or of religious purity and the prevention of pollution through sexual renunciation.[96] What was new about the legal developments of the Middle Ages, in both canon and secular law, was that regulation of what we call private life became regarded as something the authorities of church and state had a right to do. But this also requires a revision of the stereotype of the rulers of the Middle Ages as interfering in the lives of its people more than occurs in the modern period. As Karras argues, "placing the government in the bedroom is a medieval development," but "it was the modern period that brought it to a fine art."[97]

CHAPTER SIX

Sex, Medicine, and Disease

JACQUELINE A. TASIOULAS

Medieval medical texts only occasionally deal with sexuality directly, and any such attempts are accompanied by self-justification on the part of the author, solemnly insisting upon the legitimacy of the subject as it is presented to a world ready to censor and condemn. Far more common is the material on sexuality that emerges within the framework of other concerns, such as gynecology, anatomy, even astronomy and physiognomy. Any study of medicine and sexuality in the later Middle Ages must therefore draw upon a wide range of texts, from the learned tomes of the accepted scientific authorities to scattered chapters in encyclopedic works to references in herbariums. But even beyond this is another layer of texts: penitentials, saints' lives, medieval romances, all of which are a rich source of medical material, for the authors of these works are themselves drawing upon both popular and learned medical theories about sex, sexuality, and sexual disease. It is a vast, unregulated, and contested body of material, and while there is frequently a strong desire in evidence in these medieval texts to establish "norms," there is frequent admission too of the difficulties involved in establishing scientific models that can synthesize popularly held beliefs, concur with practical observation, and fit teleologically with a view of the universe that requires everything to exist for a purpose. "To what conclusion," asks Chaucer's Wife of Bath,

Were membres maad of generacion …?
Trusteth right wel, they were nat maad for noght.
Glose whoso wole, and seye bothe up and doun

That they were maked for purgacioun
Of urine, and oure bothe thynges smale
Were eek to knowe a femele from a male, ...
So that the clerkes be nat with me wrothe,
I sey this: that they maked ben for bothe;
That is to seye, for office and for ese
Of engendrure, ther we nat God displese.[1]

[To what ends were our reproductive organs made? Believe me, they
weren't made for nothing. People might try to gloss over the matter,
saying that they were created in order to pass urine, or that our little bits
were made so that we can differentiate female from male, ... Well, so that
the scholars aren't angry with me, I'll argue this: that they were made for
both purposes; by which I mean useful function but also the pleasure of
reproduction, and in that we don't cause God any displeasure at all.]

Chaucer's imaginative encounter between the sexually voracious Wife and St.
Jerome is a miniature scientific treatise on sex: the church patriarch's argument
that purging the body of impurities is the primary end of sexual organs together
with an acknowledgement of procreative purposes and the Wife's own insistence
upon pleasure are the three key elements in any scientific discussion of sexuality
in the Middle Ages. And "differentiating a female from a male" is, much as the
Wife disparages it, the starting point of many scientific texts of the period.

That the reproductive organs constitute the essential difference between men
and women was not a matter of anatomical debate, but there were various
ways in which that difference might be interpreted. Since the time of Aristotle
(384–322 B.C.E.) there had been a tendency to define male bodies as "external,"
possessing genitals on the outside, while the female was thought to possess
"internal" genitalia, which remained inside on account of the female's perceived
lack of heat.[2] The significantly warmer male body, Aristotle argued, enabled
the sexual organs to develop until they showed themselves externally, while
the colder female body retained them (it was even a commonly held belief that
if a woman were to spread her legs very wide apart, the latent testicles would
descend and reveal themselves, and the woman would become a man).[3] This obvious difference of location aside, the male and female sexual organs themselves
were frequently viewed as similar. For some writers, they were essentially equivalent, merely arranged differently; others, including such influential figures as
Albertus Magnus and Thomas Aquinas, took the protruding male genitalia
as the standard, the female sexual organs being viewed as an imperfect and
under-developed version of those of the male. The Greek physician Galen, one

of the most influential anatomists of the early Christian period and highly es-
teemed by the medieval West, was among those who believed that a female was
an incomplete male, her sexual organs being unable to develop fully through
lack of heat. Famously, his treatise equates the female genitalia with the eyes of
a mole and describes the female body as an "advantageous mutilation":

> Just as the mole has imperfect eyes, though certainly not so imperfect as
> they are in those animals that do not have any trace of them at all, so
> too the woman is less perfect than the man in respect to the generative
> parts. For the parts were formed within her when she was still a foetus,
> but could not because of the defect in the heat emerge and project on
> the outside, and this, though making the animal itself which was being
> formed less perfect than one that is complete in all respects, provided no
> small advantage for the race; for there needs must be a female. Indeed,
> you ought not to think that our Creator would purposely make half the
> whole race imperfect, and, as it were, mutilated, unless there was to be
> some great advantage in such a mutilation.[4]

The benchmark here is the male, and the female body is deficient, and indeed
this is the predominant view throughout the Middle Ages: the male body is the
physical norm and the female by her very nature deviates from that norm. Nevertheless, the perceived similarity in design between the sexes remains striking.
Medieval drawings of the uterus frequently emphasize this similarity, the same
diagram being easily adapted for both the female reproductive tract and the
penis. The idea of a bicornuate uterus made the equation with the male testes
a natural one, and it can be difficult to distinguish between the two in the
illustrations that accompany the anatomical texts. Similarities were emphasized further by the insistence of many medical writers on the Hippocratic idea
that the female, just like the male, produced "seed." Galen, once again, was
a chief exponent of this view, which was transmitted to the medieval West by
Avicenna, among others, and eventually made its way to the Middle English
encyclopedias. John Trevisa's translation of Bartholomaeus Anglicus's *De proprietatibus rerum*, for example, insists on the existence of a female sperm and
a functional equivalence between the sexes:

> The mater of the childe is mater seminalis, that is ischad by worching of
> generacioun, and cometh of alle the parties of the fadir and the modir.[5]

> [The child's body is formed from seminal fluid, which is produced during
> sex and is contributed by both the father and the mother.]

The form and nature of this female seed were, however, much debated. Aristotle had denied the existence of any kind of seminal fluid in women, arguing that the female contribution to the fetus was menstrual fluid. The menses provided the formless matter that the male seed then worked upon in order to create the fetus. Various analogies were used: menstrual fluid was the wood to the seminal carpenter, a mere ball of wax to the male shaping principle.[6] Indeed, the notion of waxlike matter being provided by the woman becomes one of the most popular ways of explaining the Incarnation. Christ's human body, derived from the Virgin Mary, is frequently described as a candle, occasionally even as a candle for which Mary herself becomes the candlestick.[7] The same Aristotelian idea lies behind Isidore of Seville's etymology of "mother" in his highly influential encyclopedic discussion of the derivation of words, the *Etymologiae*. Isidore claims the derivation of *mater* (mother) from *materia* on the principle that it is the mother's sole function to provide the base matter of the embryo:

> A mother is thus called because from her something is made. For "mother" [*mater*] is, as it were, "matter" [*materia*]; while the father is the cause.[8]

Medical diagrams also make manifest another widely held belief about the female body: its status as "vessel" in reproduction. Illustrations of the uterus often have a marked similarity to some kind of vase, and indeed the woman is occasionally referred to as *vas* in medical texts. The result is a suggestion that the woman is merely a passive receptacle for the male seed, and yet the equation of uterus with penis in illustrations such as figure 6.1, as in many other medical texts, results in the womb itself being viewed as the primary female sexual organ: the female equivalent of the penis. Such equivalency, however, leads to a fundamental question regarding the production of female "seed," and consequently to a consideration of female pleasure. Writing in the twelfth century, Hildegard of Bingen, one of those who employs the term *vas* as a synonym for "woman," argues that the woman produces some kind of emission during intercourse, but that what she produces is merely a "small foam" (*parvam spumam*), a mere crumb to the male loaf.[9] Hildegard, like Aristotle, is not a believer in female semen. For her, the seed either is, or is contained in, the male semen alone. She does, however, believe that the female *spuma* is essential to conception, and that it is an emission that corresponds to male ejaculation. While it is the result of less violent agitation of the blood on the part of the woman, pleasure is nevertheless a prerequisite for its production.

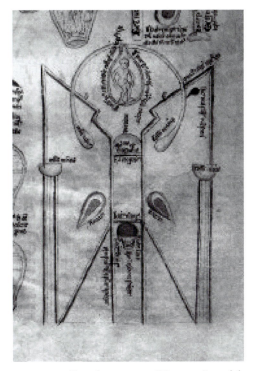

FIGURE 6.1: Female anatomy: "One-sex" model.
German miscellany (ca. 1420–1430). Wellcome
Library, London.

Constantine the African, writing a century earlier than Hildegard, and one
of the most influential medical theorists of the earlier Middle Ages, had also
taken up the question of male and, to a lesser extent, female pleasure. In the
Pantegni (late-eleventh century) he insists that the female too produces seed,
and that both male and female sperm are required in order for conception to
occur. The emission of such seed in the male is the source of pleasure, and a
necessary act in order to avoid a harmful accumulation of sperm. Women similarly derive pleasure from the voiding of superfluities, and in fact their pleasure
is considered by Constantine to be the greater, a view that helped substantiate
and explain the prevalent clerical belief in women's voracious sexual appetite:

> Women derive greater pleasure from intercourse than men, since male
> pleasure comes only from the expulsion of superfluities. Female pleasure
> is twofold, in that they both expel sperm and also receive the male's
> sperm into their fervently desirous *vulva*.[10]

Slightly later, the prostitute, that favorite exemplum of medieval writers on sexuality, would be invoked to substantiate the claim that a pleasurable emission of male and female seed must accompany conception. A long Salernitan sequence of medical and scientific questions and answers that originated in the twelfth century demands to know why prostitutes, who engaged so frequently in sexual acts, rarely become pregnant. The answer given is that, as in the case of the man, female emissions are the result of pleasure, and that the woman engaged professionally in sexual activity for money simply does not feel such pleasure and consequently does not produce the necessary sperm for conception.[11] The same text then goes on to consider the case of the victim of rape, who in spite of clearly suffering both violence and trauma, nevertheless conceives. In such instances the woman surely could not have produced "seed" as a result of pleasure, and the problem is therefore that either female semen is not necessary for conception or the substance does not require pleasurable stimulus for its production. The answer offered to this conundrum attempts to preserve the need for both pleasure and the production of female seed but does so in a way that divides the woman into rational agent and uncontrollable pleasure-seeking carnality. It argues that women who are raped might initially resist but that the weakness of the flesh means that they will also experience pleasure. The will is therefore divided into "rational" and "natural," and while the raped woman does not rationally desire the act, the author argues, there is nevertheless a possibility of carnal pleasure, which will lead to orgasm and the emission of the woman's "seed."[12]

The exact nature of the female "seed" is contested throughout the early Middle Ages, but that it did exist and that it was induced by sexual pleasure were the foundations of most theories until the middle of the thirteenth century. The challenge would come with the reappearance of the works of Aristotle, systematically translated into Latin in the second half of the thirteenth century, and with them a return to the idea of passive female matter and active male form.

The medieval followers of Aristotle had their own favorite exempla, notably the almost ubiquitous late medieval account of the woman who became pregnant after bathing in water into which a man had ejaculated.[13] There is no question here of female pleasure being a necessary part of conception. The woman is, once again, merely a fertile vessel, open and ready to receive the male seed. Such female "seed" as was thought to exist merely acted in conjunction with the menstrual fluid to provide the material substance of the child, at most serving to dilute the hot, thick fluid of the male. Galen, writing in the second century, and with knowledge of the existence of the ovaries, was not content to ascribe to women the role of provider of formless matter that had satisfied Aristotle. Like Hippocrates before him, he argued strongly for the necessity of active female seed in reproduction. The medical and philosophical writers of the Middle Ages had, therefore, a range of options on the subject, and their writings tend to reflect this, various opinions emerging in the course of a single work, or the exact definition of "seed" never becoming clear. Albertus Magnus (d. 1280), for example, wavers in his view but ultimately decides against active female sperm in his *De animalibus*, refuting the widely held notion that as women experience more pleasure in intercourse than men do, they not only must produce semen but must do so in greater quantities:

> Some have erred ... because they thought that the woman herself has a sperm because she sometimes emits a white fluid during intercourse. In reality, she has no sperm save that which would take the name of sperm equivocally.[14]

Whatever the woman produces merely contributes to the matter of the child and does not have the active properties of the male seed. But the great medieval encyclopedia *De proprietatibus rerum* is ultimately a lot less clear in its explanation of conception; John Trevisa's Middle English translation emphasizes a shared contribution to the formation of the fetus, but the actual contribution is less specific beyond the idea that the woman's "blood" serves in some way as a dilutant to the hot, thick substance of the male:

> The mater of the childe ... is sched in the place of conceyvynge abrood, that is by the drawinge of vertue of kyne igadred togedres in celles of the modir, and is medled togedre by worchinge of kinde hete. For but digest blood of the fadir and the modir were imedled togedre there mygte be no creacioun nothir schapinge of childe, for the mater of blood that cometh of the male is hote and thicke, and therfore for the grete thickness it may nougt sprede itself abrood. And also for passinge hete the mater of the childe schulde be destroyed and wasted but it fongith temperament of womannes blood, that hath contrarie qualitees.[15]

> [The matter from which the child is formed is deposited in the place of conception and by its own innate power is drawn into the chambers of the womb, where the two are mingled together by the natural force of heat. For without the refined blood of both the father and the mother being mixed together there could be no creation, no formation of the

child, because the kind of blood that comes from the male is hot and thick, and this very thickness means that it has limited mobility. And also [the semen's] intense heat would mean the death and destruction of the child if the semen were not tempered by the woman's blood, which has the opposite properties.]

That the female body was colder than that of the male was accepted by medieval authorities almost without exception, and many basic assumptions about sex followed from it. These ranged from the widespread belief that women experienced stronger sexual desire than men because their cold bodies were constantly craving the superior heat of the male to the idea that the female body was in itself deficient in its formation because of its essential coldness.

According to Aristotle, male semen had sufficient inherent heat to produce a child in the likeness of itself in terms of both sex and physical resemblance. If, however, the natural cold of the womb managed somehow to overpower this natural male heat, then nature would deviate from the norm, and the first stage in this deviation would be the formation of a female fetus instead of a male:

> Anyone who does not take after his parents is really in a way a monstrosity, since in these cases Nature has in a way strayed from the generic type. The first beginning of this deviation is when a female is formed instead of a male.[16]

A female child is thus merely an incomplete version of the superior sex, "as it were a deformed male."[17]

The explanation for the initial "failure" of heat is often linked to the placement of the seed within the uterus. For Bartholomaeus Anglicus, male children simply developed on the right side of the womb, while females grew on the left.[18] The right side was held to be hotter and thus superior to the left, possibly for the reason outlined by William of Conches in the twelfth century: the womb did not generate its own heat but was instead warmed by its proximity to the liver, the right side of the womb being closer to this organ and thus hotter than the left.[19] Both views are linked to the popular notion of the seven-celled uterus, which originated in Byzantium but was wholeheartedly embraced in the West by the thirteenth century. According to this theory, the womb had seven compartments: three of these were situated on the warmer right-hand side and engendered male infants; the three chambers on the left were cooler and produced female children. The final compartment was situated in the middle, and the sex of any embryo formed within this area was a matter for debate. *The Knowing of Woman's Kind in Childing*, a Middle English translation of the very popular *Cum auctor*, provides a lengthy and detailed account of the seven-celled uterus and its effects in determining the sex of the child:

> The matrice ... ys partyde into seven vessellys, of the wyche thre lyth in the party touarde the ryght side, and thre in the party touarde the lyfte syde, and the seventh evyn in the myddys betuene the navyll and the wykket. ... And yf hit so be that the sede fall into eny of the chambyrs of the ryght syde, hit shall be a man chylde yf hit therin abyde and be con-ceyvydde; and yf hit fall into eny of the vesels of the lyfte side, hit schall be a maydyn child. And yf hit fall into the vesyll that ys in the myddes, hit fallyth owt and perysch fro the place of creacyon ... and yf it so befall that hit be conceyvyde ther, hit schall have the tokyn bothe of man and of woman, that ys, bothe yerde and wikket.[20]

> [The womb is divided into seven cells, three of which are positioned on the right side, three on the left side, and the seventh in the middle between the navel and the vagina. ... And if it happens that the seed falls into any of the chambers on the right, if conception occurs then the child will be male, and if it falls into any of the compartments on the left, the child will be a girl. And if it falls into the middle chamber, it is likely that it will not become embedded and will be lost from the place of conception ... but if conception does occur there, the child will have the organs of both man and woman, that is to say, both penis and vagina.]

By no means did all authors agree with the notion of the seven-celled uterus, but the theory was a popular one, providing a simple and systematic way of answering questions on sex differentiation and multiple births.

The same material appears in another late-thirteenth- or early-fourteenth-century treatise that derived much of its authority by claiming to be the work of Albertus Magnus. The Pseudo-Albertine *De secretis mulierum* offers the advice that any woman wishing to conceive a male child should therefore lie on her right side after intercourse, or the left side if a daughter is desired.[21] As a text it is much concerned with the reception of seed into the womb and its positioning once there, recommending that after ejaculation the man should lie on top of the woman "for about an hour, so that the seminal matter does not scatter and form a monster."[22] Similarly, the potentially harmful results of "unnatural" coitus are spelled out:

> Some monstrosity is caused by an irregular form of coitus. For if a man lies in an unusual manner when he is having sex with a woman, he creates a monster in nature. I have heard tell that a man who was lying sideways on top of the woman during sexual intercourse caused the woman to produce a child with a curved spine and a lame foot. ... Irregular and extremely violent coitus is to be avoided in order for the fetus to be produced in the proper manner, and to avoid having the seed received in the wrong way in the womb. Coitus that is performed standing up is irregular in nature ... because the seed cannot be received as it ought to be.[23]

The text's main objective in discussing these matters is successful reproduction, and to this end it is even willing to sanction a discussion of female sexual arousal, a necessary part of the process because the colder female body is slower to produce its "seed." Nevertheless, so this author asserts, conception requires both male and female seed to be present together in the womb. While none of this material is directly attributable to Albertus Magnus, his genuine works do indeed contain passages on arousal and sexual position. The emphasis, however, is entirely on aiding conception:

> [The woman] will be naturally positioned if she is on her back with her legs spread well apart and quite elevated so that the opening of the vulva is raised toward the thighs. For this is where the hollow of the womb is and the sperm is then projected directly into the womb. ... When the woman mounts the man, the womb is twisted around and that which is in it is therefore poured forth. ... A woman that has relations from the rear only takes in the semen between the lips of her vulva because the thickness of her buttocks hinders the penis from reaching to the mouth of the womb.[24]

Passages on female arousal are, therefore, to be found in a large number of later medical works, even, for example, in those of authors such as Bernard of Gordon, a favorite of Chaucer's Physician, who were not always happy to translate everything they encountered in their source texts. The majority of authors, however, are keen to stress that their discussion is intended to aid the emission of female seed and consequently to promote successful conception. To this end a smaller number of texts discuss male arousal and techniques that might be employed by a woman should difficulties arise.

In spite of tacit references to erogenous zones and the necessity of arousal, nearly all scientific texts are conservative in the matter of sexual positions, and any deviation from the accepted horizontal mode was regarded as both morally and medically problematic. The *De secretis mulierum* even goes so far as to state that not only should the man always lie on top of the woman, but he should ensure that he does not raise himself too high, his chest always being in contact with that of his partner.[25] Avicenna, who provides a surprisingly explicit and forward-thinking description of ways in which to arouse women, nevertheless declares that the man's position is naturally on top, and that reversing this is potentially very harmful, the sheer effort of ejaculation being likely to cause lesions on the penis.[26] Together with the warnings, there were also amusing tales that suggested that medieval life did not always conform to medical and theological sanctions, as in the case of the inexperienced monk who breaks his vow of chastity and urgently questions his servant:

> "I have often heard that when a man and a woman have been together, children are born. But tell me, by your faith, which of the two bears the child?"—"I will tell you everything," replied the servant. "It's the one underneath."—"Woe is me," thought the monk, who was starting to realise the extent of his misfortune. "Alas," he said to himself, "whatever can I do? What a disaster! I was the one underneath. I'm going to have a baby!"[27]

No doubt there is also the fear of the dominant, insatiable woman lurking behind this tale, and indeed the very science that was employed to explain the formation of the female fetus was frequently used to present women as sexually voracious and insatiable creatures. The innate coldness of the female body that was accepted almost ubiquitously in the medical texts was also invoked in passages relating to sexual appetite, where the woman's lack of heat and craving to rectify this deficiency was given as an explanation for her "burning desire." To turn to the *Etymologiae* of Isidore once again:

> Some say that the name "female" derives from the Greek for "burning force," because of the intensity of her desire. For the female is more lustful than the male, among women as much as among animals.[28]

Indeed, a number of authors were keen to point out that a woman, alone of all female animals, continues to desire intercourse even when already pregnant and thus can be considered to be the most sexually voracious creature in existence.[29] Like damp wood that burns all the more fiercely once ignited, the cold female body was thought to rage with desire—a desire that went beyond psychological need in many texts and became biological necessity. The woman's body was thought to be in danger of possible suffocation if the womb was not satisfied; although nearly all the medical texts are in agreement about the dangers that the womb might pose, they are not agreed about the precise nature of the threat. According to one school of thought, the woman's heart and lungs were forced together by an accumulation of superfluous female "sperm" that leads to uterine migration. Another popular theory was that the humors being emitted by the retained substance became poisonous when the retention of seed or blood became too much for the womb to bear and spread through the woman's body to the brain. The symptoms of the disease included anything from a need to pull the knees up to the chest to convulsions and derangement, and the death of the patient in such circumstances was considered likely.[30]

While symptoms could vary, the cause was clearly the female body's need to purge itself of reproductive fluids in the same way as the male body. As one early-fifteenth-century gynecological treatise puts it:

> And this syknesse comyth of diuerse enchesons as of withholding of þe blode that they shuld ben purged of; other of sume corupt humours & venomous that ben in þe moder as men ben deliuered of sede that they shuld ben purged of; other of sume corrupt humours & venomous that ben in þe moder as men ben deliuered of sede that passith from her stones that ben by her yerde.[31]

> [And this sickness has various causes, such as retention of blood or else corrupt and poisonous uterine humors, all of which should have been purged, just as men are able to be purged by the expulsion of semen from the testicles via the penis.]

The idea of a migratory uterus is only one instance of the emphasis that many medical texts put on the importance of sex to the human body, and particularly on the benefits of ejaculation in maintaining good health for both sexes. The expulsion of excess fluid from the body was thought to be both physically and psychologically beneficial, and the majority of scientific treatises maintained that moderate sexual activity was preferable to abstinence. The emphasis is certainly on moderation, and indeed the whole basis of the argument depends on the idea that the body is a delicate balance of humors. While the essential warmth of the male body was generally regarded as positive, it was nevertheless argued that retention of semen over too long a period would lead to an intolerable buildup of heat that would lead to illness. The colder female body was obviously less prone to such risks and had the added benefit of menstruation to void superfluities, but a woman could, nevertheless, succumb to ill health if her own physical balance became disturbed through sexual abstinence. In a society that valued chastity so highly, it is not surprising that the first recourse of medical practitioners faced with such cases should be medical prescriptions, or a change of diet. But there are others who recommend simply that the seed must be emitted, including Albertus Magnus:

> Thus, when bodies cannot be purged because of the amassed sperm, too many infirmities and even sometimes death occur from sperm that is held in immeasurably long. Thus some are made healthy by intercourse.[32]

And in the case of those who had no immediate access to a legitimate partner, medical intervention could be sought. Both Galen and Avicenna, for example, recommend manipulation of the genitals by a midwife for virgins and widows who are affected by the retention of excess "seed"; and in the case of celibate men they simply recommend masturbation.[33] However, the majority of medical texts are not so explicit. The prohibition against the "sin of Onan" was so strong that while such a remedy is often implied, the first recourse is always a "cooling" diet, or the application of cooling poultices. This is the advice of Arnald of Villanova, though he too suggests "massage" for women in cases where the medication fails to relieve the symptoms.[34]

But the secret to sexual health in all cases is moderation. While the medieval *medici* advocate the expulsion of some seed as healthy, the nature of sperm was thought to be such that excessive sexual indulgence was considered to be harmful, or even fatal. There were various ancient theories about the semen's point of origin in the body: for some it was a substance that was drawn from all parts of the body; for others it originated in the brain; and for others it was a residue produced by the heat of the heart transforming waste into blood, and thence into a further refined and whitened sanguineous substance.[35] Medieval texts often attempted to reconcile these theories.[36] The notion of semen as "dealbated" blood—blood that has been heated and therefore whitened—allowed for a temptingly neat parallel with the menstrual contribution of the female in conception, while the idea that the white seminal humor arose in the brain was also visually apt. Indeed, it lent itself to a number of memorable warnings about sexual excess, notably the case cited by Albertus Magnus of a young monk who, having had intercourse with a woman seventy times in the course of one morning, died. The autopsy performed on him subsequently discovered that his brain had shrunk to the size of a pomegranate, and that his eyes had completely dried up, leading to the conclusion that coitus drains the body, and especially the brain, of its vital fluids.[37]

While Galen's acceptance of the Aristotelian theory of blood as the origin of semen was influential, some belief in a connection between semen and the brain still lingered, partly, no doubt, because many medical practitioners believed that sex was not merely a physical matter, but that the mind played a crucial part in many aspects of human sexuality.[38] In relation to the much-discussed case of pregnant women who nevertheless desired intercourse, the medical writers could only conclude that as the need was not physical, the womb already having achieved its reproductive goal, the source of the desire must be mental. The woman was responding not to a biological impulse, but to the promptings of her memory and the imaginative capacity of her brain, which recalled the pleasure of intercourse and desired the sensation again.[39] Texts that concerned themselves with male sexuality also often emphasized the importance of the brain as the point of origin for the whole sexual process. Gilbertus Anglicus, for example, puts forward the argument that it is the idea or memory of pleasure that leads to arousal, and that it is this mental stimulus that affects the body's vital spirits and leads to male erection. Indeed, many texts dealing with sexual problems advised the physician to enquire first about the mental state of the patient. As for Avicenna's *Canon* (early-eleventh century), it authoritatively put forward the idea that the emission of seed not only purged the body but also purged the mind of worries, obsessive thoughts, and the vapors that accumulated in the brain and could lead to melancholy.[40]

Melancholy was, of course, the lover's disease: a retentive illness that mirrored psychologically the retention of sperm that was often, at least imaginatively, the corollary of unrequited love. A surprisingly technical description of the extreme form of the disease is to be found in Chaucer's "Knight's Tale," where one of the young knights is said to be suffering from an advanced form of lovesickness. The disease is known as *amor hereos* and was, in its final stages, regarded as a fatal mania:

> Nat oonly lik the loveris maladye
> Of Hereos, but rather lyk manye,
> Engendred of humour malencolik
> Biforen, in his celle fantastik.[41]

[Not just like the lovesickness known as "Hereos," but rather an
advanced mania brought about by a melancholic humor dominating
the "fantasy," the anterior cell of the brain.]

Amor hereos was not a mere literary phenomenon; it was considered to be a
serious psychological illness worthy of study in the medieval universities.[42] The
key text was the *Viaticum* of Constantine the African, but there were numerous
medieval commentaries, including a thirteenth-century one by Peter of Spain,
the future Pope John XXI, who does not shrink from discussing the sexuality of
men and even defends the idea that women have passions strong enough for diseases such as *amor hereos* to develop.[43] Wild mood swings, deathly pallor, and
continual swooning were all considered symptoms of a disease that was widely
considered to originate in the brain and not, as some argued, in either the testicles or the heart. While both the heart and the sexual organs could be affected
by strong passions, the true locus of sexual mania was the estimative faculty of
the brain: the cell that allowed rational thought and judgment to take place. It
was bluntly stated in some texts that the application of "women or plasters to
the testicles" would cure most cases of "lovesickness." For those patients who
proved less easily treated, there was also Arnald of Villanova's (ca. 1240–1311)
prescription of "aversion therapy" in the form of aged women, or such objects
as menstrual rags, intended to appall the male victim and return him to a state
of right judgment. The beautifully named but otherwise enigmatic Bona For-
tuna, practicing medicine in France at approximately the same time, went one
step further and allegedly cured one young man of his lovesickness by having
him accused of homicide, thus occasioning a change of scene, separation from
the beloved, and a redirection of the patient's thoughts, all at the same time.[44]
But none of this would be at all beneficial to the true sufferer of morbid love.
Such people are so psychologically impaired by their obsession that they become incapable of making judgments about their situation and can focus only
on the object of his desire. In those affected by love sickness, the body's vital
spirits, the same that produce seminal fluid, are retained, returning to the brain
and further fueling the mania of obsessive love. The excess heat dries out the
anterior cell that houses the imagination (Chaucer's "celle fantastik"), and the
image of the beloved is retained even more adhesively, leading to yet further
rushes of the vital spirit. It is a circular process that cannot be stopped by any
external impetus except coitus with the object of desire. If the mania is allowed
to continue unchecked, the eventual outcome is death.

If *amor hereos* represents the extreme example of a body being overcome
by its own vital sexual heat, then the other end of the spectrum was occupied

in the Middle Ages by leprosy. Leprosy was a relatively common disease in Britain until around the fourteenth century, many towns having designated leper hospitals, some of them complete with their own gallows, a deterrent to those who wished to stray from their own contained communities.[45] The disease was greatly feared and, to a certain extent, misunderstood, as various forms of it were classed together as leprosy, together with certain skin conditions that manifested some similar symptoms but were not in fact leprous.[46] In spite of the difficulties in diagnosis, medieval physicians did go to great lengths to establish whether or not a patient had leprosy, for their verdict affected not just treatment but the way in which the patient would be received by society; even to the extent of whether they were regarded as living or dead, for the fate of a leper, at some points in place and time, was to be declared officially dead, the mass for the dead being said over him or her, and his or her goods being distributed.[47] Attitudes were extreme, partly because of the imagined danger of contamination, and partly because the origins of the disease were thought to be sexual. While some texts, such as the *De proprietatibus rerum* of Bartholomaeus Anglicus, were willing to consider that excessive consumption of garlic or else overexposure to the wind and cold might generate the disease spontaneously, the vast majority believed leprosy to be simply a venereal disease contracted through coitus with a leprous partner. The womb was once again an object of fear, as it was viewed as an ideal environment for leprous semen, incubating the disease so that its poisonous vapors would then infect the next man to come along, his warm genitalia porous and ready to absorb the fumes. The woman, it was believed, had the opportunity to purge herself of the disease during menstruation, but this was not a possibility for the man, and medical texts describe the leprous ulcers that would tellingly first appear on the penis.[48] The menses were not, however, always regarded as purgative and there are many medieval texts that regard menstrual fluid itself as the cause of leprosy. The commentators on the *De secretis mulierum* deliver a standard explanation for the origins of the condition:

> It is harmful for men to have sexual intercourse with menstruating women because should conception take place the fetus would be leprous.[49]

One commentary adds the observation that the man too will contract leprosy through intercourse with a menstruating woman.[50] The physiological principle behind this was once again a belief in the innate coldness of women: contact with the menses would deprive a man of his essential health-giving heat, and a child formed from such matter would, in the same way, be devoid of natural warmth. Similarly, any woman having contact with a leprous man could become a carrier of the disease, while being protected from exhibiting any symptoms by the coldness of her own body. As the twelfth-century philosopher William of Conches explains it,

> Even the hottest woman is colder than the coldest man: her complexion is unyielding and extremely resistant to any corruption from the male; even so, the putrid contagion that results from coitus with lepers, remains in the woman's womb. Then, when a man has intercourse with her, his sinewy penis penetrates her vagina and, on account of its force of attraction, draws this contagious matter to itself and to the surrounding organs, and transmits the disease to them.[51]

It is likely, as Danielle Jacquart and Claude Thomasset argue, that the folds and interiority of the female sexual anatomy mean that symptoms of many venereal diseases were simply not so apparent in women as in men, but the explanations show a fear of the female body as contagious and poisonous, and many a text offers advice to men similar to that given by John Gaddesden in the *Rosa Anglica* (ca. 1314):

> If you wish to preserve your organ from all harm, should you suspect your partner of being corrupted, purify yourself, as soon as you have withdrawn, with cold water in which you have mixed vinegar, or with urine.[52]

It was thought that in order for a woman to manifest the symptoms of leprosy herself, she must have had intercourse with not just one but many leprous men, a belief that made the female leper a particularly reviled creature.[53] It is not surprising, therefore, to find Criseyde, guilty of one of the most infamous acts of sexual betrayal in medieval literature, suffering from leprosy in a text from late medieval Scotland. While Chaucer's *Troilus and Criseyde* is silent on the subject of his heroine's eventual fate, Robert Henryson's *Testament of Cresseid* (ca. 1500) describes her rejection by a lover who had "fulfilled all his appetite, and more," her subsequent life as a prostitute in the Greek camp, and her contraction of leprosy and eventual death. Whether or not she is redeemed in the process, Henryson clearly regarded her leprosy as befitting her sexual crimes.[54]

Of course, while leprosy was the extreme case, the Middle Ages was aware of a range of venereal diseases. William Dunbar, another late medieval author,

gives a particularly evocative description of the young man who, having led a lecherous life, has succumbed to disease and impotence:

> His lume is waxit larbar and lyis in to swonne.
> Wes never sugeorne wer set na one that snail tyrit,
> For eftir sevin oulkis rest it will nought rap anys. ...
> He dois as dotit dog that damys one all bussis,
> And liftis his leg apone loft thought he nought list pische. ...
> He is for ladyis in luf a right lusty schadow,
> Bot in to derne, at the deid, he salbe drup fundin.[55]

> [His tool is now impotent and lies in a swoon. That weary slug is a
> complete waste of time, for even after seven weeks' rest it won't stay
> hard even once. ... He's like a stupid dog that pees on all the bushes,
> cocking his leg even though he can't piss. ... For ladies looking for love
> he's the very image of lustiness, but when it comes to the private act
> they'll find him droopy.]

Actual syphilis may not have swept Europe until the sixteenth century, but the medical texts contain descriptions of numerous infections relating to the sexual organs that can be identified as herpes, for example, or gonorrhea. And indeed, any abscesses or growths in the genital area were readily diagnosed as the result of sexual sin or excess. The *Life of St. Hugh of Lincoln* gives an account of a young man whose thigh bones gangrened and two holes, or rather caverns of terrible size and depth, appeared and yet he felt no pain at all from these immense wounds. The proximity of the affliction to his penis arouses suspicion, and he admits to the saint that he has "sinned, led astray by the persuasion of another person," and is cured when warm candle wax is applied to the wounds.[56]

While there is naturally not a great deal of sympathy for the victims of sexual disease, many of the medical texts do contain recipes to cure impotence of the kind suffered by the young man in Dunbar's poem, or even by his elderly counterpart whose aged member is dismissed as "soft and soupill as the silk" by his more nubile wife.[57] Certainly, Hildegard of Bingen believed that men and women were capable of sexual pleasure into old age.[58] Her compassionate approach to medicine, however, is not matched in all texts, and while physicians generally seem to have assumed that men of all ages might have wanted recipes to stimulate sexual desire, and to prolong their capacity for intercourse, the aged female body was widely thought to be a foul and even poisonous thing. In the fifteenth century, for example, John Lydgate's

"Dietary and Doctrine for Pestilence" advises that to maintain good health, men should "with women aged flesshly have na a do."[59] Women have their own specific medical needs catered to in, for example, the treatises attributed to Trotula of Salerno, one of which notably contains a recipe to restore the appearance of virginity; but aphrodisiacs as such generally belong to the male domain, and there existed a considerable number.[60] The longest section of Constantine's late-eleventh-century *De coitu* is given over to a discussion of aphrodisiacs (and, admittedly, anaphrodisiacs), some considered so powerful that merely their touch is enough to stimulate desire. A diet that induces heat was generally believed to be beneficial in aiding male sexual performance, and conversely, food that was traditionally viewed as "cooling" was believed to inhibit desire. Potions and ointments were also prescribed:

> An electuary concocted by Isaac to prolong intercourse: 10 drams Artemisia; 20 drams cleansed pine-nuts; 10 drams colewort, ragwort; 15 drams ginger; 7 drams anise; grind and rub for a very long time with butter and temper with honey, Give 5 drams to the patient on going to bed, then let him drink syrup or broth of parsnips; also, let his stomach and testicles be rubbed with oil of elder in which camomile is steeped.[61]

Constantine, of course, is the "cursed monk" of Chaucer's "Merchant's Tale" precisely because of such material as this. But Peter of Spain, no less a religious figure than future pope, is also interested in aphrodisiacs. In his earlier incarnation as a teacher of medicine in thirteenth-century Siena, his works included the *Thesaurus pauperum*, a medical compendium that contains thirty-four recipes to enhance sexual desire and performance. It also contains twenty-six contraceptive recipes, including, for example, the suggestion that a plaster of hemlock on the testicles might prove effective, together with a number of recipes that would have been likely to induce an abortion.[62] Some texts that supply information about contraceptives do so with the explicit aim of ensuring that no one should happen upon these ingredients by accident and thus inadvertently prevent conception. Certainly, this is what the manuscripts of the *Thesaurus pauperum* assert, although the text itself is most instructive.[63] Others, such as Hildegard of Bingen, omit the disclaimer, and simply give information about menstrual stimulants that would clearly have been potential abortifacients. She also gives direct information about such drugs in order to help women whose pregnancies have become life threatening. For example, a recipe for a plant she calls "oleaster" is accompanied by the explanation: "It induces an abortion in any woman in mortal danger."[64] However, much of the material was copied without any such justification for saving the life of the pregnant woman, and indeed the later Middle Ages had access to a considerable amount of information about contraceptives and abortifacients, some of it in texts such as Avicenna's *Canon,* which formed part of the syllabus in the universities. Recipes for contraceptives included highly effective ingredients, such as juniper berries, but they also made use of ingredients that simply looked the part, such as the voluptuously shaped pear. It is no accident, for instance, that Chaucer's May chooses a pear tree in which to have sex with her lover, though drinking the powdered root with water would have generally been thought a more effective contraceptive.

The Wife of Bath's question, "To what conclusion were membres maad of generacion?" finds an answer, therefore, in the medical texts, and it is an answer in keeping with her own explanation of "office" and "ese of engendrure." While the scientific authors firmly acknowledge that reproduction is the proper outcome of coitus, the question of pleasure is an essential part of this. For some authors, the pleasure of sex was nature's way of ensuring the continuation of the species through an act that would otherwise be regarded as repugnant by all. But for others, pleasure comes to dominate the narrative, and texts supply information designed to enhance the sex lives of both men and women. While most stress that the material they convey is intended to facilitate reproduction, there is a great deal in many of them that is designed to enhance performance, increase desire, and even terminate the pregnancy that they claim is their raison d'être. And while there are boundaries imposed as to with whom and in what way one should have sexual relations, it is nevertheless the verdict of almost all the scientific treatises that a moderate sex life was best for maintaining the health of the body. For those unable to adhere to such moderation, there were ointments and therapies, together with dire medical warnings, but the texts also provide assistance for those whose health is threatened by inability, on moral, psychological, or physiological grounds, to have sex. The male body and male sexuality are the norm, but a significant proportion of texts consider women too, in a way that goes beyond their role as receptacles for male seed.

CHAPTER SEVEN

Sex, Popular Beliefs, and Culture

MALCOLM JONES

LATE MEDIEVAL PHALLIC CULTS?

The Norman Welsh cleric Gerald of Wales (Giraldus Cambrensis), writing circa 1188, chronicles an apparently bizarre equine sexual rite that purportedly took place in Ireland:

> There is in the northern and farther part of Ulster, namely in Kenelcunill, a certain people who are accustomed to appoint their king with a rite altogether outlandish and abominable. When the whole people of that land have been gathered together in one place, a white mare is brought forward into the middle of the assembly. He who is to be inaugurated, not as a chief, but as a beast, not as a king, but as an outlaw, has bestial intercourse with her in front of everybody, professing himself to be a beast also. The mare is then killed immediately, cut up in pieces, and boiled in water. A bath is prepared afterwards for the man in the same water. He sits in the bath surrounded by all his people, and everyone, he and they, eat of the mare's meat which is brought to them. He quaffs and drinks of the broth in which he is bathed, not in any cup, or using his hand, but just dipping his mouth into it round about him. When this unrighteous rite has been carried out, his kingship and dominion have been conferred.[1]

Although many scholars have dismissed this account as fantasy, twentieth-century comparativists have shown its close relationship to the ancient Vedic rite of the *aśvamedha*, seeing it as the Celtic reflex of a widely attested Indo-European rite. Gerald's account would seem to imply that such a rite was still being observed in the north of Christian Ireland as late as the twelfth century.[5]

Over a century earlier on a remote promontory in the still-pagan north of Norway, the missionary king St. Olaf encountered another equine sexual rite. The sole witness to the episode is the fourteenth-century *Flateyjarbók*,[2] but the account of the incident—known as the *Volsaþáttr*—can be precisely dated to 1029. It relates how the penis of a horse that had just died and was being butchered in preparation to be eaten was rescued by the son of a woman who wrapped it in a linen cloth, together with leeks and other herbs to preserve it, and laid it in a chest. Every evening she prayed to it as if it were a god and persuaded the rest of the household to follow her lead, and then "by the power of the Devil, the thing grew and became so strong that it could stand upright beside the old woman when she wanted it to."[3] King Olaf and his companions arrive at the house in disguise and witness the ritual passing round of the pizzle and the verses recited over it by each recipient. Eventually the king reveals himself and converts them all to Christianity—even the old woman, who is markedly reluctant.

The *Volsaþáttr* is perhaps best understood as a somewhat garbled account of a ritual attached to the worship of the god Freyr, with whom both horses and phallicism were associated in Scandinavian paganism. In his Latin *History of the Archbishops of Hamburg-Bremen* (early 1070s), one of the most important sources of early Northern German and Scandinavian history, Adam of Bremen states that the Swedes have a well-known temple at Uppsala that houses the statues of three gods: Thor, Wotan (Odin), and Freyr. Freyr governs peace and pleasure, and to his statue, fashioned with an immense phallus, the priests offer sacrifices for happiness in marriage.[4]

A late-thirteenth-century English chronicle compiled by a Franciscan monk at Lanercost in Cumbria, and contemporaneous with the events it describes, records two further phallic rituals. Under the year 1268 it notes an outbreak of cattle plague in Lothian, Scotland, and the extraordinary steps taken by certain Cistercian monks to contain it. They "taught the country people to extract fire from wood by friction, and set up an effigy of Priapus" ("docebant idiotas patriae ignem confrictione de lignis educere et simulacrum Priapi statuere").[5] It is unlikely that an actual image of the Roman god Priapus was erected; rather, the words strongly imply the fashioning of a statue—presumably of wood—of prominently phallic appearance. In addition, one of the laybrothers "sprinkled the animals with the testicles of a dog that had been dipped in consecrated water" ("intinctis testiculis canis in aquam benedictam super animalia sparsisset").[6] This is also, incidentally, the earliest recorded instance of the kindling of a "needfire" in Britain, a practice that long retained a pagan feel to it, as well as being an extraordinarily late manifestation of phallic ritual.[7]

The same chronicle records how one day during Easter week 1282, John, the parish priest of Inverkeithing in Scotland, recruited a group of young girls and made them follow him as he held aloft before them images of the human sex organs.[8] It seems that it was principally the phallus that was involved, for the anonymous chronicler refers both to the profane rites of the blatantly phallic Priapus and to round dances performed in honor of "Father Liber," the old rustic Italian god of procreation and fertility. Singing and capering extravagantly like a mime actor, John encouraged the dancers, inciting them to lust with filthy language. The girls' mothers were scandalized, but attempts to remonstrate with him only caused him to attack his objectors.

We are not told of any official action taken by his bishop as a result of this remarkable episode. John does not seem to have been defrocked, for the chronicler goes on to report with evident satisfaction that during Penance week later that same year, he died of a mysterious stab wound. It is, of course, difficult to interpret John's behavior historically. Despite its blatantly sexualized nature, categories such as "pervert" and "pedophile" are uncomfortably anachronistic, and in any case John's actions were very public. While he certainly seems to have taken advantage of his respected position in the community, it also appears that he may have been a relic believer in an ancient, pre-Christian fertility or phallic cult of the type noted here. Both the priest's actions and the villagers' reactions are important here. The latter's evident outrage (and the mysterious stabbing) shows this cannot have been traditional, customary practice—as, indeed, does the very fact of its reporting, which reinforces its singularity.

RECONSTRUCTING MEDIEVAL FOLKLIFE

Phallic cults of course existed, especially in the pre-Christian era, but this apparently unique report from the British late Middle Ages does not allow us to generalize about phallic religious practice. But it should, nevertheless, give us pause. What do we know of such sexual folklife and lore in the late Middle Ages? How *can* we know anything about beliefs and practices that by their very nature—largely existing within oral culture, not sanctioned by the medieval church—are unlikely to have been recorded? In short, what sources do we have?

Paradoxically, one of the most valuable was produced by the very authorities who, so curiously, seem to have taken no action in the case of the Inverkeithing priest: the church. Many early manuals for priests taking confession survive, often prescribing the exact form of words to be used when interrogating parishioners, and detailing the appropriate penances, for which reason they are known as penitentials. One of the most famous is by Burchard of Worms, the nineteenth book of which is nicknamed "The Corrector" and offers 195 extremely detailed questions for priests to put to penitents about their sexual lives.[9]

One underexploited resource is the treasury of medieval nicknames, which shed a fascinating sidelight on sexual folklore—not just personal names but place-names too. And last but not least, there is the artistic and artifactual record. The presence of male and female sexual organs (often disembodied) carved on the stonework of medieval churches was by and large ignored until the late-twentieth century. While some recent scholars have seen them as "images of lust," that is, depictions of the vice of *luxuria*, visual displays of behavior to be abhorred, others regard them as *apotropaia*, protective devices, put in place to repulse the powers of Evil. Typical of these are the grotesque British female exhibitionist figures known as sheela-na-gigs.

Sexual exhibitionist carvings are sometimes found set into city walls or over important gateways, where such placing again argues for their apotropaic function, that is, as averting bad luck in general. In 1569, in his book on the history of Antwerp (Belgium), Johannes Goropius Becanus notes that Ters (English, Tarse) was the tutelary deity of the city, the local Priapus,[10] and a phallic stone sculpture now known as Semini set into the Burchtpoort gateway to the city survives. Formerly set above the Porta Tosa in Milan is the twelfth-century image of a woman lifting up her skirt to expose her nakedness, and who is furthermore trimming her pubic hair with a rather alarming pair of shears. A similar though much more crudely carved figure (now known only from a photograph) was found at Egremont in Cumbria, and it has been plausibly suggested that she too is "removing her pubic hair, so exposing her pudenda more completely, in order to ward off bad luck the more effectively."[11]

The question of whether or not such images can be regarded as pornographic is an extremely fraught one. Female pubic hair shaving later became a recognized pornographic subgenre, the earliest example being Peter Flötner's 1520s woodcut image showing a woman, wearing only an extravagantly feathered hat of the sort conventionally characterizing the typical mercenary's whore (*Landsknechthure*), trimming her pubic hair with a pair of shears, attended by a standing maidservant bearing a basin, the operation illuminated by a candle held in front of her crotch by a kneeling fool.[12] Both the mode of illustration and the medium—a woodcut—suggest private, voyeuristic consumption and thus argue for its being pornographic. But the medieval monumental pubic hair trimmers seem rather to have had a predominantly protective function.

Graphic pornography in its modern sense begins in the final decades of the fifteenth century, in Italy. In the decades immediately before and after 1500, scenes of female same-sex sexual activity were engraved on copperplates by Zoan Andrea (Giovanni Antonio da Brescia, 1464–1526) and Giovanni Battista Palumba (Master IB with the Bird, active circa 1500–1516 in Bologna).[13] To Marcantonio Raimondi—notorious as the engraver of *I modi*, illustrating Aretino's sonnets (ca. 1525)—is also attributed a unique engraving of a standing woman employing a dildo, preserved uniquely in Stockholm.[14]

SEXUAL BADGES

Though what remains today of medieval stone sculpture of a sexually exhibitionist nature (where it has escaped the attentions of the prudes and iconoclasts of later centuries), whether ecclesiastical or civic, is often obscurely placed, it is undeniably in the public domain. It is on a literally monumental scale, and yet similar motifs may be found on an important class of late medieval artifact that has only come to light in modern times: the lead badge. First described in Arthur Forgeais' 1858 book about the Parisian material dredged from the Seine,[15] the extraordinary and frequently bizarre corpus of late medieval lead badges recovered by archaeology (and as casual metal-detector finds) has only in the last few decades become more widely known. It is precisely because these tiny, seemingly inconsequential badges were mass produced in the cheapest of materials that they have such a disproportionate significance and why—despite the problems of interpretation—they are absolutely fundamental to our understanding of late medieval art and "popular" culture.

One cannot but be powerfully impressed by the surreal nature of the iconography of the sexual badges. We are ushered into a bizarre world populated only by male and female sex organs going—as it were—about their everyday business. Phalluses crew ships and are planted like bulbs; vulvas walk on stilts, hunt on horseback, and spin wool; the organs of both sexes climb ladders, go on pilgrimage (fig. 7.1), and are basted on spits. This motif of dismembered members, presented in a comic manner that is the very opposite of uncanny, is also found in literary sources, notably the thirteenth-century medieval French fabliaux. But the badges embody just that combination of bizarrerie and visceral shock that, from Roman times, was considered the perfect antidote against the Evil Eye.[16] Such indecent or ridiculous images were thought to draw the eyes of evil-disposed persons and spirits to themselves, thus averting the malignant gaze from the wearer.

FIGURE 7.1: Lead badge in the shape of a vulva as pil-
grim. Dutch (late-fourteenth/early-fifteenth century).
Inv. 3301. Collection Van Beuningen, Cothen. In H.J.E.
Van Beuningen, A. M. Koldeweij, and D. Kicken, eds.,
*Heilig en Profaan 2: 1200 Laatmiddeleeuwse insignes
uit openbare en particuliere collectives*, Rotterdam
Papers 12 (Cothen: Stichting Middeleeuwse religieuze
en profane insignes, 2001), fig. 1774.

Whether any of these individual sexual motifs in badge form are meaningful iconographically—in a narrow, rather than a generic apotropaic, sense—is
uncertain. On the one hand, the Evil Eye is repulsed by the exposure of the
genital icon, or amused and thus distracted—"diverted" in both senses—from
its malign intentions; on the other hand (by analogy with those lead badges
in the form of coin-filled purses), on the principle that like attracts like, such
badges may have been worn by persons of either sex attempting magically to
attract good luck in sexual matters. The repulsion of bad luck may also be considered a negative way of promoting good luck, as seems to be the implication
of an important Dutch badge in the form of a walking phallus, on the shaft of
which a now-headless figure holds out a banderole bearing the Middle Dutch
inscription *de selde*, "the good luck."

Ancient Rome, and those parts of the world it conquered, was a particularly "phallic culture"—and here I invoke not the evidence for ancient
ritual defloration associated by early Roman historians with the name of
Mutinus Tutinus, or later priapic rites and the poetic corpus of *Priapaea*,
for instance, but the ordinary, everyday *domestic* presence of the phallus.
Images of the phallus protected doorways and other vulnerable entrances to
the household, with perhaps little more real belief in its efficacy than is held
by those who similarly nail up horseshoes today. Phalliform *tintinnabula*
(bronze creatures cast in the round and hung about with bells for suspension
in domestic interiors as amulets to protect the house from evil) of the sort
recovered from Pompeii and Herculaneum protected particular rooms, and
innumerable phallic *fascina*, or bronze amulets incorporating the phallus,
often augmented with what we have come to term "phallic symbols," such
as the horn, were worn on the person.

There is certainly ample evidence for amuletic phallic ornaments throughout the countries that were conquered by Rome. The winged phallus or
phallus-bird is an iconographic motif already present in the classical world
that enjoyed another spell of popularity in the late medieval lead badge corpus, possibly via the accidental discovery of caches of late Roman small
bronzes. Some of the badge phallus-birds are shown perched on top of vulvas, perhaps indicating that we might read them as predatory—as raptors.
A unique late-fifteenth-century Ferrarese copperplate for producing prints
(from which only modern impressions survive) is engraved with the image of
an outsize phallus-bird apparently watching a human couple copulating; the
telltale detail of a bell around the "neck" of the phallus-bird harks back to
the ancient Roman *tintinnabula* (fig. 9.11). The frequent placing of bells in
similar position around the necks of the Dutch lead badge phalluses seems to
be a conscious echoing of this ancient Roman practice and even suggests an
"archaeological" origin for these objects, which suddenly appear in the late
Middle Ages. On the other side of the same copperplate three peasants are
depicted: a woman spinning, a man carving spoons, and a bagpiper sitting on
a closestool (a commode, in use from the sixteenth century). From the drone
of his instrument hangs a small model phallus—important evidence for the
late medieval currency of the phallus as *apotropaion*. Very similar-looking
phalluses cast in wax were still being offered for sale, though here as votives,
in a church near Naples dedicated to saints Cosmas and Damian, as late as
the end of the eighteenth century.[17] But an unnoticed passage in Sir Thomas
More's *Dialogue Concerning Heresies* (1529) attests to this votive practice
in sixteenth-century Picardy. It relates how a newly married English couple

visited the church of St. Valéry, where they found to their astonishment that the preventative of choice against "the stone" (gallstones and bladder stones) involved the measurement of the sexual organ of the pilgrim in question, for the manufacture of a votive model of it:

> For lyke as in other pylgrymages ye se hanged vp legges of waxe or armes or suche other partes so was in that chapell all theyr offrynges yt honge aboute the walles none other thynge but mennes gere [sexual organs] & womens gere made in waxe.[18]

In the Italian context of the Ferrarese engraving, however, there is a most suggestive letter written by the poet Pietro Aretino in 1537, ten years after the scandal caused by the publication of his pornographic *I modi*:

> A me parebbe che il cotale datoci da la natura per conservation di se stessa, si dovesse portare al collo, come pendente, e nella beretta per medaglia.

> [It would seem to me that the thing which is given to us by nature to preserve the race, should be worn around the neck as a pendant, or pinned onto the cap like a badge.][19]

We must note, however, that Aretino specifically says that such is *not*, in fact, the fashion, but it seems not unreasonable to suspect that this was indeed the practice in some quarters of contemporary Italian society, at least, in the light of the Dutch badges, the Ferrarese bagpiper, and ancient, as well as surviving, amuletic practice.

In recent years, the number of "small finds" of medieval metalwork has increased exponentially with the popularity of metal detecting. Three such finds relevant to this chapter are a circular badge/button found near Worksop in Derbyshire in 2008, the matrix of a personal seal found at Wicklewood in Norfolk in 2001, and a bronze pendant excavated from a Thames-side site. The Worksop badge (fig. 7.2) is particularly important in that it includes a legend. Although (as so often) the reading of the lettering is not certain, the imagery is, at least, unequivocal: engraved on the roundel are a main central phallus depicted in profile entering a vulva depicted frontally and two smaller phalluses below the main one. The first line of the inscription clearly reads "have," the second line is less clear, but one plausible reading is *þ:isheo* (the first letter, "thorn," represents *th*), that is, "th[ou] issue," the whole representing a prayer/invocation of fertility: "May you have issue!" If this reading

FIGURE 7.2: Bronze badge with traces of red enamel, incised with phalluses and the legend *have þ:isheo* ("May you have issue!"). English (?fifteenth century). Private collection.

is correct, then we have here a clear function for at least some of this sexual imagery (and one that might have been assumed on commonsense grounds): the promotion of human fertility.

The English bronze piece (fig. 7.3)—seemingly a pendant, as it has a cast suspension loop—recently came to light in an unstratified context from a rescue dig in London. Perhaps fourteenth-century in date, it takes the form of a stylized open vulva with—for once—a clearly legible inscription in Anglo-Norman, the variety of French employed in England at this period for inscriptions. To the right of the opening is the word "AMOVRS," and to the left, but retrograde, the words "CON POR," giving unmistakably—in modern spelling—"con pour amour" ("cunt for love"). It was cast as one piece, so the taboo word must have been deliberately—rather than mistakenly—written backwards, not necessarily out of coyness, but perhaps as a magical reinforcement of the impact of the icon.

At least two of the contemporary Dutch sex organ lead badges also unequivocally spell out the names of the organs. In Figure 7.4, a belled phallus walks toward a standing vulva, both mounted on legs, which stand on the label,

FIGURE 7.3: Bronze pendant in the shape of a stylized vulva inscribed "CON POR AMOVRS" (first two
words retrograde). English (?fourteenth century).
Excavated from a site beside the Thames. Museum
of London. Photo © Malcolm Jones.

"PINTELIN." I take this to be an injunction, or optative formation, composed of
the cognate Dutch noun *pintel*, "pintle"[20] plus the adverb *in*, "in" (i.e., "May
the cock go in!" or "Cock, go in!"). "CONTEN" ["cunts"] is the caption of a
sadly fragmentary fifteenth-century badge from Nieuwlande[21]—of which all
that remains otherwise, puzzlingly, is a somewhat limp phallus above the label.
Is this a deliberately mischievous mislabeling, or is it perhaps also an optative
formation ("Let's have cunts!")?

If we accept the "optative" interpretation of the badge legend, then it suggests the possibility that at least some of the sex organ badges—the functions
of which I have formerly tended to see as broadly apotropaic—might perhaps
be better interpreted as *bringing* good luck in the particular sphere of sexual
opportunity. Since there are English examples of nonsexual purse badges that
include (separate) miniature coins entrapped within the openwork casting and
that were surely intended to bring good monetary luck, we may reasonably

FIGURE 7.4: Lead badge in the shape of a phallus on legs approaching a vulva on legs, inscribed "PINTELIN." Dutch (mid-fourteenth century). Inv. 3161. Collection Van Beuningen, Cothen. In A. M. Koldeweij, *Foi et bonne fortune: Parure et dévotion en Flandre médiévale* (Arnhem: Terra Lannoo, 2006), cat. 7.27.

suggest that at least some of the sex organ badges were worn in the hope of attracting good sexual fortune.

The lead badges that have surfaced in recent years—in particular, those from the drowned villages of the Scheldt estuary in the Netherlands—have enormously increased the available corpus of late medieval sexual iconography but, frustratingly, no contemporary written documentation offers a hermeneutic key, and so interpretation has to be speculative. Their technical production details are identical to those of the so-called pilgrim badges. The Dutch catalogs reproduce 111 sexual badges (though many more have surfaced in the past decade) but classify them under the unsatisfactory heading *erotisch*.[22] Within this corpus alone, we can identify a number of motifs (for most of which there are several examples).

The first major taxonomic division is between those badges representing real men and women, and those that feature disembodied sex organs. In the former category are couples engaged in intercourse, male and female sexual exhibitionists, men and women brandishing phalluses, and male same-sex pairs. The rather more numerous second group may be divided into badges depicting the organs of both sexes, those featuring just phalluses, and those featuring just vulvas.

Beginning with the sex organ badges, in the first two-sex category are arboreal scenes with phalluses and vulvas shown as the fruits or leaves of trees, a striking instance of a crowned vulva being carried on a litter by three phalluses (fig 7.5: perhaps an outrageous parody of processions in honor of the Virgin), and images of both organs climbing up a ladder, or pierced on a spit, with the vulva acting as drip tray. The phallus badges may be divided into two thematic groups: those in which the phallus is depicted engaged in some sort of (human) activity, such as riding a horse, crewing a ship, or—the most

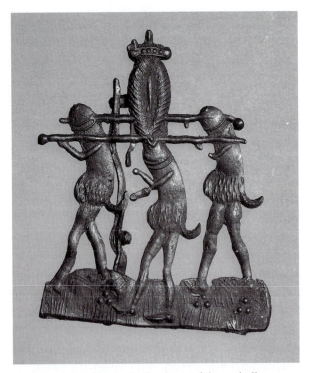

FIGURE 7.5: Lead badge in the shape of three phalluses carrying a crowned vulva on a litter. Dutch (late-fourteenth/early-fifteenth century). Inv. 0967. In A. M. Koldeweij, *Foi et bonne fortune: Parure et dévotion en Flandre médiévale* (Arnhem: Terra Lannoo, 2006), cat. 7.29.

numerous—just walking (though sometimes surmounted by a small human, for example, barrowing phalluses). In the other group the phallus is depicted passively, being planted like a bulb or roasted on a spit or projecting from a hood or back basket, lying in a purse or frying pan, caught in the jaws of a cat, or being brandished by a man or woman. The vulva badges may be similarly divided thematically: again there are vulvas riding or walking (some of which are clearly identified as on pilgrimage)—even walking on stilts—or spinning. One amulet—if that is what it is—takes the form of the two valves of a mussel shell that contains an engraved or separately cast vulva.

Some of these configurations appear to realize traditional erotic metaphors; others exhibit varying degrees of surreal fantasy. The 3-D badges in the form of couples having sex in a winnowing-fan are clearly punning on the fact that one meaning of Middle Dutch *wannen* ("winnow"), attested in contemporary Dutch *Boerden* [jests], is "copulate," presumably from the repeated action, and the fiddler who bestrides one walking phallus recalls the Middle Dutch *vedeln* ("fiddle") of similar import, but what are we to make of the couple having sex on the knife-edge, the rake, or the handbarrow? The man and woman copulating on the frame of the hair-comb miniature occupy the space that, on sumptuous full-size contemporary ivory combs, is often decorated with one or more courtly couples, perhaps from a romance. Are the lead lovers parodic? Is their designer mocking the aristocratic taste for *amour courtois* by cynically revealing what all that conventional dalliance is really about? Another badge (fig. 7.6) depicts the popular late medieval legend of the courtesan Phyllis, riding the philosopher Aristotle, another staple of the iconography of courtly love—though no other such representation reveals such a prominently phallic philosopher—are we again to suspect parody?

Probably the best-known medieval symbol of the female sex was the rose, as alluded to in the thirteenth-century French courtly love classic, *Le roman de la rose*, and possibly understood metaphorically in such medieval nicknames as the late-thirteenth-century Pluckrose. Descriptions of the extraordinary Brussels snow sculptures of 1511, recorded in some detail by Jan Smeken, include one female nude that must have been based fairly closely on a genre of late-fifteenth-century print in which the rose is strategically placed:

In the Rosendal a wonder was to be seen: a huge plump woman, completely naked, her buttocks were like a barrel, her breasts were finely formed, a dog was ensconced between her legs; her pudendum was covered by a rose; the "coffer" beneath the rose, once you taste it, causes many a man to lose his silver-plate.[23]

FIGURE 7.6: Lead badge in the shape of Phyllis riding an ithyphallic Aristotle. Dutch (first half of the fifteenth century). Inv. 1917. In A. M. Koldeweij, *Foi et bonne fortune: Parure et dévotion en Flandre médiévale* (Arnhem: Terra Lannoo, 2006), cat. 0.4.

In his late-fifteenth-century poem *Nouveau calendrier,* Jean Molinet pairs the female sexual *saincte Rose* with the burlesque phallic *sainct Vital* (punning on the Middle French *vit*, "penis").[24] The inevitability of the French pun on *vit* ("penis") and *vie* ("life"), besides appearing circa 1500 in riddles[25] and visually in *rébus de Picardie,*[26] was even the subject of an early-sixteenth-century satirical procession: a daring political charivari entitled *Le vit de François Premier,* in which a gigantic phallus in a pageant car was pulled through the streets of Paris and onlookers were invited to flagellate the royal member.[27]

One of the less common symbols of the female sex was the mussel shell, represented in the small lead mussel shell amulets that open to reveal a stylized vulva, either separately cast or inscribed on the inside of one of the valves. Clearly, the secret, hidden nature of the symbol is significant here. For centuries in Europe, certain shells, the exotic cowrie, for example, have been regarded as visual equivalents of the vulva and traditionally served as amulets, but native bivalves such as the scallop and the cockle have also played this role, leading the folklorist W. L. Hildburgh, incidentally, to suggest that the original intention of the Compostella pilgrim's cockleshell badge—and the millions of lead badge souvenirs that derive from it—may have been apotropaic. The tradition is ancient; apart from the evidence for such shell or shell-shaped amulets from burials, the Roman writer Pliny recorded the talismanic use of the shell named, significantly, *veneria* (suggesting a link with Venus, the goddess of sexual love), and J. N. Adams has shown how the Romance shell name represented by French *porcelaine*, Italian *porcellana*—literally, "piglet"—derives from Roman nursery usage, as noted by Varro, in which the vulva was referred to as *porcus*. Undoubtedly, the best visual parallel in late medieval art, however, is a detail from Bosch's *Garden of Earthly Delights* triptych (ca. 1510); in the central foreground of the middle panel is a naked couple copulating inside a huge mussel shell, open sufficiently to allow a voyeur's-eye view of the man's bare buttocks, scrotum, and legs, and his partner's bare feet, a motif later copied by Bruegel in his 1557 drawing of the vice *luxuria*.

The badge of a cat with a dismembered member in its mouth may be compared with a marginal drollery in a late-thirteenth-century Flemish illuminated manuscript of Vincent of Beauvais' *Speculum doctrinale*, in which a cat with a purloined penis is hotly pursued across the top of the page by a woman brandishing a distaff. Both may be allusions to the episode in the beast epic *Le roman de Renart*, where the cat Tibert, cornered in the priest's house, manages to escape after biting off one of the priest's testicles.[28]

THE BATTLE OF THE SEXES

Depictions of sexual activity in medieval manuscripts are relatively rare but have undoubtedly been made rarer by the tendency to destroy such material in post-medieval times on the grounds of obscenity. Quite exceptional is the series of six Flemish drawings of sexual metaphors executed circa 1470, in one of which a soldier brandishing a spear in obviously symbolic proximity to an aperture in the castle wall tells the chatelaine that he will enter her castle by *la basse court* (the Lower Court).[29] Like all thrusting weapons, of course, the spear is an ancient metaphor for the penis and, like the staff, an unequivocal phallic symbol; for example, in Lydgate's mid-fifteenth-century *Pain and Sorrow of Evil Marriage* (a free translation of a popular late medieval misogynist classic, the *De Coniuge non Ducenda*),[30] it is said that the husband will be cuckolded if "he be no spere-man good."[31] In similar vein, John Skelton's early-sixteenth-century Malkyn is said by her lover to be "trussed for to break a launce,"[32] further hinting that at least some Middle English surnames of the *Brekelaunce* type are not nicknames of the battlefield or tiltyard but commemorate more amorous jousts.

The vagina is correspondingly described as a "pavys or a target [both meaning "shield"] for a sperys heed" in the poem "Whan She Hath on Hire Hood of Grene," formerly attributed to Lydgate,[33] but another of the Flemish drawings perfectly illustrates such a metaphoric encounter. The Knight of the Drooping Lance (as I dub him) approaches on horseback a lady who holds a large shield out in front of her at waist height. His quatrain reads:

> How come, no matter what I do,
> That my thrusts don't strike
> Your shield as they should do?
> They're always too high or too low!

To which the lady responds:

> The fault is not mine, love,
> It's because your lance is bending;
> You can't strike it right
> If your shaft isn't stiffer![34]

An especially interesting instance of this phallic symbolism appears in the form of a haft borne by a particular type of late medieval dagger, referred to in England, at least, as a *ballok-knyf*, or a *ballok-hefted* knife.[35] Attempting to gloss Langland's use of the former in *Piers Plowman* (1377–1379) where worldly priests are satirized for wearing "A baselard or a ballok-knyf with botons overgilte,"[36] but unfamiliar with the *realium*, the *OED* unarchaeologically explains this sort of knife as "?one worn at the girdle."[37] In the London Museum's 1940 *Medieval Catalogue* they were still euphemistically styled "kidney daggers,"[38] but by 1978 A.V.C. Schmidt, in his edition of *Piers Plowman*, provides the right gloss: "A fashionable ornamental dagger or a knife with a knobbed (= testicle-shaped) haft, covered with gilt-studs."[39] Worn at the girdle, the handles of these daggers present an obviously phallic appearance, as sported, for example, by the young noblemen who surround the duc de Berry's table in his celebrated *Très riches heures* (1412–1416), or by the jaunty gallant in the foreground of Bruegel's *Netherlandish Proverbs* (1559).

Scenes of intercourse of any kind are comparatively rare in medieval manuscripts, but an illustration of a stall selling knives and sheaths in a fourteenth-century English manuscript includes an unusual scene of rape in the foreground.[40] The symbolic sexual counterpart of the sword or knife is the scabbard or sheath (*vagina*, "sheath"), and the relationship of the two is occasionally explicit in late medieval literature, as in *Der kurz Hannentanz*, a fifteenth-century German *Fastnachtspiel* (carnival play) in which the maiden says to the young man, "Ich pin di schaid, ir seit das schwert" ("I am the sheath, you are the sword").[41] The dream of a husband who feared he was being cuckolded, related in the Middle English version of *Partonope of Blois*, is as transparent to us post-Freudians as it must have been to its original late-fifteenth-century audience:

> He thogte he sawe hys neygbore drawe owte hys swerde,
> And fulle hys scawbarte he thogte that he pyssed.

> [He thought he saw his neighbour draw out his sword,
> and he thought that he pissed his scabbard full.][42]

In another late Middle English poem, *The Epistle of Othea to Hector* (ca. 1450), the danger to the male of "vncouth straung love" is encapsulated in the maxim "Owte of a cankred sweerd is hard to rubbe the rust,"[43] and the "rusty blade" that Chaucer's Reeve is said to bear by his side is perhaps similarly symbolic of his self-confessed lechery and indeed his comparison of himself to a rotten fruit.[44]

SEX IN VISUAL CULTURE

Before the time when single-sheet prints first become available (after 1500), only a very few Italian prints feature overtly sexual scenes. Wall paintings where they have survived—especially those not in the public domain—are another perhaps surprising genre in which to portray sexual scenes. One thirteenth-century fresco, discovered ten years ago in the Tuscan village of Massa Marittima on the wall of the building that houses the public fountain, features a bizarre but widespread medieval European motif: the phallus-tree. The motif also appears in late medieval wall painting (Schloss Lichtenberg in the Tirol), in the margins of a *Roman de la rose* manuscript, carved on a wooden German *Minnekästchen* or trinket box, in a late-fifteenth-century German drawing preserved in Istanbul, and as a fourteenth-century Dutch lead badge, on which, beneath the tree (bearing the legend "AMOVRS"), a couple copulate. The phallus-tree was also a feature of carnival time: civic records inform us that at Nördlingen in Germany in 1510 a branch bearing phallus-fruits was borne about the town. It is probable that the motif was intended to encourage fertility.

Recently a number of extraordinary late medieval pictorial graffiti have been published from the underground Caestertgroeve chalk mines at Sint-Pietersberg, near Maastricht on the Dutch/Belgian border. They date from the very end of our period, the late-fifteenth century. The subject matter is diverse; there is a fine jester's head, another jester talking to his bauble, two wildmen (one apparently a king, as he wears a crown), many religious scenes such as a man receiving the host from a priest with St. Veronica showing the *sudarium* in the background, a crucifixion and other images of Christ as *Salvator Mundi*, the Mount of Olives, the tree of the knowledge of good and evil, a skeletal death aiming his dart at a fleeing huntsman on horseback, the Virgin and Child, St. Francis, a reliquary bust of St. Servatius and—of particular interest here—a man buggering a dog (fig. 7.7).[45] Such scenes are understandably rare

FIGURE 7.7: Charcoal graffito depicting man buggering dog. Caestertgroeve chalk-mines at Sint-Pietersberg near Maastricht (late-fifteenth century). Photo © Jean-Jacques Spuissers.

in medieval art, but then, as now, the imputation of bestiality was commonly hurled about as an insult, and perhaps that is the case here, and perhaps the miner would have been instantly identifiable to his fellow workmen.

The bronze matrix of a personal seal (ca. 1300) recently discovered at Wicklewood, Derbyshire, shows a phallus penetrating a vulva, but on this piece the legend is not a caption, but the personal name of the seal's owner, one James Tibblecock. The perimeter inscription reads "IAS: TIDBAULCOCK"; the surname is etymologically a compound of one of the numerous Middle English forms of *Theobald* and the element *cock*, which often functions as a diminutive in the surnames of this period (see *Simcock* = Little Simon; *Wilcocks* = Little William, etc.). It is clear, however, that the seal-designer was punning on the sense of "penis," and probably on *ball* = "testicle" too. What we do not know is the reaction of those who came across James's seal attached to letters and other documents, but it is unlikely that they were offended or scandalized.

WHAT'S IN A NAME?

Medieval nicknames cast a fascinating sidelight on medieval sexuality. But uncontextualized onomastic evidence is fraught with difficulties of interpretation. The moniker of Geoffrey *Boresballok*, recorded at King's Lynn, Norfolk, in 1318, most probably invokes the virility and potency of the boar (meaning "prince" in the Viking era, and borne as a helmet crest by Germanic warriors). The late medieval Dutch lead badges in the form of ithyphallic bagpiping boars may also be in this tradition, as is the following recommendation offered in a mid-fifteenth-century English medical manuscript to a woman who is having trouble getting pregnant: "Let hyr ete the balockis of boris and sche schall conceyue." A text known as *The Diseases of Women*, popularly ascribed to Trotula of Salerno (eleventh to thirteenth century?), recommends for help with conception that the woman "take the stones [testicles] of a bore & drye hem in a potte," as well as eating fresh meat and—specifically—"the stones of bestes, as of bores, of boles, of wolues," all animals regarded as virile.[46] Other English thirteenth- and fourteenth-century nicknames include *Buckeballoc*, *Assbollok* and *Tupballok*, invoking another trio of animals traditionally seen as sexually potent: goat, ass, and ram. Ralph *Whiteballoc* (1197) and Robert *Blakeballoc* (1243) are somewhat put into the shade by Roger *Gildynballokes* (1316), a nickname found as early as the Domesday Book (1086) in Latinized guise as *aurei testiculi* and in Anglo-French guise as *Coyldeor* (1297). The Parisian tax roll of 1292 further includes a Eude *Coille-Noire* ("Blackballs") and Geffroi *Coulle-Mole* ("Softballs"). Exceptionally, we also know the name of a London prostitute (almost certainly her professional name): Clarice la *Claterballock* (1340).[47] Because the language of sexuality and the names of sex organs are often euphemistic or metaphoric, it is not always easy to be categorical in interpreting nicknames—"stone" can mean "testicle" in many vernaculars (see the two instances quoted previously from *The Diseases of Women*) and is a frequent literary pun, but in some names it will have had its more usual literal meaning. We cannot therefore be certain if the early-thirteenth-century Leicester man nicknamed *Smalstones* had a tiny scrotum or collected or dealt in pebbles or cobblestones.

A late-fourteenth-century anatomical work preserved in the Wellcome Library in London offers fascinating sociolinguistic data. Its author refers to the penis as the "yard," the polite term for that organ "whiche men callen a ters but for curtesie wymmen callen it a yerde" ("which men call a 'tarse' but out of politeness women call it a 'yard'"), suggesting that women habitually use the polite term, but that men use the less polite term "tarse." Similarly, in describing the scrotum, he lists a number of vernacular terms, "the cheste or the purs or the cod of [the] ballokis," but again notes that "of wommen it is y-callid a purs for curtesie" ("by women it is called a 'purse' out of politeness"), implying that "purse" was then the most polite term for the scrotum.[48]

A sense of the register of cod may be gleaned from the advice given in John Russell's mid-fifteenth-century courtesy manual, *The Book of Carving and Nurture:* "Put not youre handes in youre hosen, youre codware for to clawe."[49] Perhaps Robert *Scrattayl* (1327) was infamous for ignoring this advice, scratching his "tail" in public rather too often, and Roger *Holdballych* too perhaps—or was he a flasher? And what of John *Shakebollok* (1381)? Though not mentioned by the Wellcome MS author, *Pintle* was evidently the most common Middle English term for penis; simplex and compound nicknames featuring the word are surprisingly common and include *Pyntylwagge* (1379), *Wytepintell* (1313), *Silvirpintil* and *Scharpyntil* (both 1296),[50] *Swetpintel* (1275), and two animal-themed names, *Coltepyntel* (1276) and *Doggepintel* (1361). The first element in Hugo *Humpintel* (1187) is mysterious, though may be for *Huni-* (see in 1268, Thomas *Hunicod* [= Honey Scrotum] and, semantically, *Swetpintel* and Peter *Huniteil* [= Honey "Tail"]). Names employing the element "tarse" are not common, but concern with penis length is implied in the nickname of one Langgeters,[51] bizarrely interpreted as "Long Gaiters" by one authority, even though gaiters did not appear until the late-eighteenth century. The correct interpretation—Long Tarse—is confirmed by the cognate names of two contemporary medieval Germans, Urbanus and Zacher *Langzers*.[52] The writer of one of the Paston Letters of 1470 gleefully records of one man that "It is reportyd that hys pyntell is asse longe as hys legge," and in the extraordinary contemporary "Talk of Ten Wives on Their Husbands' Ware" (1453–1500), in which ten gossips sit drinking and comparing their husbands' penile inadequacies, one complains that her man's "pentyll pepythe owte beforn/Lyke a warbrede" ("peeps out like a maggot").[53]

The English medieval name corpus also provides our earliest evidence for words for the female sex organs. Godwin, a late-eleventh-century Winchester man, was given what David Postles has characterized as the "spectacularly salacious" nickname Clawcunte.[54] At this early date, bynames seem not to have been inherited as surnames, so we can probably assume the name was indeed originally conferred on Godwin, but the range of meanings of the verb "claw" in Middle English ranges from "clutch, grasp," via "scrape or claw at," to "scratch gently" (e.g. at an itch). A century later (1167) we find the extraordinary phrasal nickname given to Simon *Sitbithecunte*, suggesting that he waits like a cat to pounce on his prey. Records refer to Gunoka *Cunteles* (1219) ("cunt-less") and Bele *Wydecunthe* (1328). All the other such names I am aware of are attached to men: the apparently synonymous Richard *Luffecunt* (1276) and Robert *Quinteluue* (1222), Robert *Clevecunt* (1302), a man named *Cruskunt* (1338), Richard *Twychecunt* (1319; Middle English *twicchen*, "pull, tear, pinch"), John *Fillecunt* (1246), and another man nicknamed *Pinnecunte* (1272), this last perhaps referring to a husband who sought to control his wife's sexuality. Comparable names are found in other medieval European vernaculars: the Parisian Jehan *Condore* ("Golden Cunt," 1292) either inherited the name from a female ancestor or was perhaps willingly pimping out his wife.

The plant name "orchid" derives from the Greek word for "testicle," "so called from the shape of the tubers in most species" (*OED*). In his *Herbal* of 1562 Turner rightly notes that "There are diuers kindes of orchis, ye other kindes ar in other countrees called fox stones or hear [i.e., hare] stones, and they may after ye Greke be called dog-stones" (ii. 152), perhaps forgetting that he had earlier referred to "Whyt satyrion, or in other more vnmanerly speche, hares ballockes" (ii. 128 b). *Satyrion* itself—from the Greek word for "satyr," "in allusion to the reputed aphrodisiac properties of the plant so named" (*OED*)—was similarly a name given to various kinds of orchid, so that *ballokwort* means *Saturia* in one late-fourteenth-century glossary, while another contemporary list describes the plant as having "knobbis in the rotis lyke ballok stonys." It is difficult to be sure that *dog-stones* was a real vernacular name for various orchids rather than just Turner's translation of the medieval Latin botanists' name, *Testiculus canis*, though, curiously, *dog-ballokes* is recorded as a fifteenth-century name for the notoriously phallic plant now known as cuck-oopint.[55] *Wolvys-ballock* is recorded as a fifteenth-century name for the soldier or military orchid (*orchis militaris*).[56]

These orchid names provide a context for the four Dutch badges in the form of a gardener who appears to be stroking or planting a phallus that has been placed in the ground; in one, a person leads on a spade while another bends down to stroke the phallus, the shaft and glans of which have emerged from the soil, while its bulblike testicles are still rooted below, invoking the popular metaphor, via Latin *semen* ("seed"), of the man's "seed" being planted in the "fertile soil" of the woman's womb. Catherine Johns has drawn attention to a detail of the decoration on a red-figure vase by the Hasselmann Painter (ca. 430–420 B.C.E) that depicts a woman sprinkling phalluses set in the ground with water as a probable fertility ritual to encourage seed to grow.[57] This may also be the function for some, at least, of these badges.

The first element in Adam *Prickproud* (1466) may refer to *prick* ("penis");[58] *pride* in the sense of "erection" is attested in the poem "A Talk of Ten Wives on Their Husbands' Ware,"[59] so "proud" might mean "erect," but we should expect the adjective to precede, not follow, the noun it qualifies. The Paris tax roll of 1292 records a Guillaume *Fout-Vielle* ("fucks the old woman"), a Jehan *Fout-en-Paille* ("fucks in the straw"), a Maci *qui ne fout* ("who doesn't fuck"), and a Renodet *Fout-Oe* (1292) ("fuck the goose"), while Villon's *Testament* (1461) mentions one Michault "qui fut nommé le Bon Fouterre" ("who was called the good fucker"). From an English document comes the byname *Futladame* ("fucks the lady"),[60] but the corresponding English verb is noticeably absent from the onomastic record, although it has recently been plausibly explained as present in what sounds like a late medieval Lovers' Lane, *Fokkynggroue* ("Fucking Grove"), near Bristol (see the rather more euphemistic *Louyndgreues* (ca. 1301; "Loving Groves," in Cheshire).[61] The second edition of the *OED* is properly cautious, suggesting that in the surname Fuckebegger (1287), the first verbal element may merely be used in the sense "to strike," comparing "the Anglo-Norman surname *Butevilein* (literally 'strike the churl or wretch'), found in the 12th and 13th centuries."[62] However, a remarkable but unnoticed bronze personal seal matrix of circa 1300 in the British Museum (fig. 7.8) may have light to shed on this problem; in contradistinction to Maci *qui ne fout*, the Jean Grunard[i] who commissioned the present seal "FOCATOVT" ("fucks everyone")![63] The museum Web site blazons the facetious coat of arms within the perimeter legend as "cusped panel with saltire between three erect phalli and quatrefoil in chief."

FIGURE 7.8: Wax impression from the personal seal of Jean Grunard engraved with his name and nickname, Focatovt, as well as a facetious coat of arms featuring three phalluses. French (fourteenth century). British Museum. Photo © John Cherry.

It is an interesting sidelight on changing sensibilities that all the numerous Gropecunt Lanes of English medieval towns and cities have now disappeared, though the offending element occasionally survives in other place-names. The place still called Cunliffe, near Blackburn, Lancashire, is recorded as Kuntecliue in 1246 (Cunteclyue in 1276, etc.), and the authoritative English Place-Name Society considers it to be a compound of the two elements *cunt* and *cliff*.[64] In Anglo-Saxon times, *cunte* is found as a topographical element elsewhere in England—in Hampshire, for instance, where it occurs in two late Anglo-Saxon charters, combined with the element *halh*, which has the general meaning "nook or corner of land," but also "secluded hollow in a hillside." A lost Cuntelowe is attested, probably the name of a tumulus (Old English, *hlaw*), in the parish of Parwich, Derbyshire, in a thirteenth-century document. From documents of circa 1400 we learn of the now-lost name of a watercourse in the Macclesfield area recorded as Swylecuntdyche, that is, "Swill-cunt-ditch" (see the similarly lost stream or spring [Old English, *wella*] named Shauecuntewelle in Kent, i.e., "Shave-cunt Well").

THE CHURCH AND POPULAR BELIEFS

The penitentials attest to, or at least imply, a range of sexual practices. Bishop Burchard of Worms, compiling his Latin penitential around the year 1000 in Germany, expected his confessors to inquire of the female penitent whether she had ever ingested her husband's semen or mixed her menstrual blood in food or drink that he then unknowingly consumed in order to increase her husband's love for her. Or had she ever placed a live fish in her vagina and kept it there until it was dead and then cooked it and given it to her husband to eat, or kneaded dough with her naked buttocks and then baked it and given her husband the bread to eat, with the same end in mind?

All these appear to be genuine practices of popular sexual magic—menstrual blood used in this manner is attested in early-fourteenth-century Montaillou, for instance, while the specially prepared dough—remarkably—bears a distinct resemblance to the "Cockle-bread" mentioned by the antiquary John Aubrey in 1697.[65] Some penitentials envisage the use of aids to masturbation in both male and female contexts: Burchard describes the use of a dildo ("molimen aut machinamentum") or a piece of wood with a hole in it ("lignum perforatum"). In one of the branches of the literary French beast epic, the *Roman de Renart*, Reynard the fox constructs an artificial vagina out of rabbit fur ("parfist le con"), punning on *con* ("rabbit/cunt").

In a late-fifteenth-century edition (ca. 1475) of the *Somnia Danielis*, one of the acknowledged authorities for the interpretation of dreams in the late Middle Ages, occurs the following dream interpretation: "Perdere virgam virilem significat perdere connationem" ("To dream that you have lost your virile rod signifies the failure of an undertaking").[66] In the late Middle Ages, the discourse of witchcraft speaks of male castration anxiety.[67] In the influential *Malleus Maleficarum*, first published in Strasbourg in 1487, we read of

> those witches who … sometimes collect male organs in great numbers, as many as 20 or 30 members together and put them in a bird's nest, or shut them up in a box, where they move themselves like living members, and eat oats and corn. … A certain man tells that, when he had lost his member, he approached a known witch to ask her to restore it to him. She told the afflicted man to climb a certain tree, and that he might take

whichever he liked out of a nest in which there were several members. And when he tried to take a big one, the witch said: "You must not take that one because it belongs to our parish priest."[68]

Notwithstanding the fabliau-like gibe at the parish clergy, the disembodied yet evidently still mobile penis seems to have enjoyed a surprisingly eventful independent life. One almost tasteful Dutch badge depicts what is perhaps just such a nest of magically removed phallus-birds.[69] Hans Vintler's *Blumen der Tugend* (1486) refers to various superstitions current at that date in his native Tyrol. Referring to the deeds of the *Zaubrerin* (sorceress), he writes, "[sie] etleich stelen aus der pruech dem man sein geschirre gar" ("they will even steal a man's tackle from out of his breeches"); the accompanying woodcut shows the witch adding another purloined penis to her collection.[70]

If this suggests male fear of female sexuality, what then of the powers of the female sex organs? In mid-sixteenth-century Dubrovnik, Fiorio Petrovich lodged a complaint with the authorities that a woman named Mara had come to his house and called him a "sodomite" and a "horned goat," accompanying the insult with "appropriate" gestures, and then "to spite me, she lifted her clothes, showing her private parts."[71] Though evidently here used insultingly, the simple exposure of the vulva by the raising of the skirts is a well-established apotropaic gesture, technically known by the Greek term *anasyrma*. The episode is depicted in a mid-thirteenth-century French manuscript in which a group of mounted knights are confronted by three women who have raised their skirts, thus exposing their pudenda.[72] It is also the subject of a late-sixteenth-century Dutch painting in the Kunsthistorisches Museum in Vienna.[73] The same gesture is made by the Old Woman of Papefiguière in chapter 47 of Rabelais' *Quart livre* (1551), where, however, it has the traditional apotropaic effect of frightening away the devil, who is under the naive impression—traditional for ogres[74]—that the old woman's exposed pudendum is a "wound" that her husband, the farmer with whom he has come to fight, inflicted upon her with his "little finger."

Modern German *Scham* still means "genitals," as *shame* did in Middle English (surviving in the usage of the King James or the Authorized Version of the Bible), and that is also the literal meaning of the common Latin euphemism for the sex organs, *pudenda* ("of which one ought to be ashamed"): "also for schame these partyes hatte [are called] *pudenda*, the schamelich parties," as John Trevisa rendered Bartholomaeus Anglicus's Latin in the late-fourteenth century,[75] a sense vividly attested in the following passage in the medieval Welsh laws, concerning the bride who falsely claims to be a virgin:

> Neither is there any redress to her for the thrust he [the bridegroom] made into her with his penis; however, let her shift be cut as high as the top of her buttocks, and in front as high as the top of her cunt, and she is released with that thrust in her without compensating her for it. And that is the law of the bride who falsely claims to be a virgin.[76]

CONCLUSION

In this chapter I have only been able to sketch out some of the terrain relating to popular sexual beliefs and practices in medieval Europe, but I hope I have at least been able to indicate the kinds of sources to which readers might turn to discover more evidence.

CHAPTER EIGHT

Prostitution: The Moral Economy of Medieval Prostitution

KEVIN MUMMEY

Medieval prostitution can be understood as a daily, and nightly, ritual control of the body and as part of a larger project of moral hygiene. Attempts to identify, regulate, and segregate the prostitute, and the resistance to and compliance with that control, formed a complex network of institutions and quotidian interactions through which society struggled to find an equilibrium between what was and what ought to have been. E. P. Thompson used the phrase "moral economy" to analyze peasant discontent by linking social norms and obligations to a sense of appropriate economic behavior.[1] David Nirenberg employed the metaphor to describe royal stewardship of the social body, itself understood through metaphors of disease and corruption.[2] Others subsequently expanded the concept in a variety of ways. Here I apply it to the economic and social implications of illicit sex, which ramified across the entire social spectrum.

Like its commercial counterpart, the moral economy is a product of countless choices and circumstances. Civic leaders, ecclesiastical authorities, and canon lawyers recoiled at the specter of uncontrolled female sexuality. Yet a toleration of prostitution was often justified as the cost of placating the natural desires of unmarried males. Even those devoted to reforming prostitutes—among them the relentlessly crusading Louis IX—had to come to grips with the daily reality of illicit sex in streets, alleys, church graveyards, and crusaders' tents.[3] The prostitute was formally accepted as the receptacle of a society's filth, a necessary, if odious, evil. She also served as a societal release valve, a source of profit, and a sacrificial lamb for female honor.[4] Each day medieval societies made choices that put prostitutes in an intriguing gray area where they were both marginal and central, persecuted and accepted. Prostitution was an omnipresent municipal institution and a part of the history of women's devalued work, but it also degraded and damned its practitioners.

Medieval people—theoreticians as well as members of the communities in which prostitutes lived—were as aware of the moral price as they were of the economic costs and benefits. In theory, the presence of some sexually available women protected the honor of the rest of the female population. In practice, the supply and demand for illicit sex was complex and pervasive, making the identification and containment of women of ill repute a never-ending problem for civic authorities. Consumers of licensed and clandestine prostitution included clergy and married men as well as bachelors, notably students and traveling merchants.[5] Prostitution was available to every man who could afford to pay. The prostitute's acceptance of payment, however, was not the key to medieval societies' need to control her. More important was that she was promiscuous and willing to engage in sex with more than one partner. Prostitution was driven by the demand of a male clientele whose activities, while not necessarily condoned, were less closely surveilled and less frequently punished than those of the women who constituted the supply.

Countless informal arrangements and sexual circumstances existed alongside commercial sex. Women negotiated sex for protection and shelter as well as cash. Some engaged in sex for pay briefly or sporadically, as economic, political, or domestic circumstances dictated. No doubt some women chose this path because they found it lucrative; others were coerced and manipulated either by individuals or by circumstances. The actual practice of prostitution and related systems of sexual barter in medieval society far exceeded the boundaries of the system in which certain promiscuous women were supposed to be available to a population of bachelors with sexual license.

The moral economy of prostitution displays both elements of long-term continuity (the persistence of religious norms regarding sexuality in general and prostitution in particular; venerable assumptions about the nature of women) and change over time (the growth of urban centers and the effects of war, disease, and economic cycles on opportunities for women), and new understandings of penance. Different regions developed different negotiations and strategies within this moral economy. The circumstances of Muslim slave prostitutes in thirteenth-century Mallorca, for example, were different from those of adolescent Flemish prostitutes in late medieval England, yet their respective societies shared similar assumptions about the role of prostitution in the moral order of their polities, and they also shared a basic currency: the female body and access to that body.[6] The control of that currency involved the investment of elites: brothels, penitential (Magdalene) houses, enforcement mechanisms, ideological buttresses, and moral compromises. It also encompassed a vast array of daily choices and necessities: the commercial negotiations of prostitutes, procurers, and customers, and the informal decisions of men and women engaging in clandestine sexual arrangements. At the edges of the picture were the prying eyes and perked-up ears of the neighborhood, village, and parish—and the ever-present threat of ill *fama*, the loss of honor and rank through one's public reputation.[7]

The Christian Roman emperors and church authorities of late antiquity inherited the legal practice of prostitution in the Empire. Early legislation attempted not to abolish prostitution but rather to prevent women from being prostituted in certain circumstances. In 343 Constantius II prohibited the resale of Christian women as prostitutes, though he permitted them to be prostituted by their current owners. In the next century (428) the emperor Theodosius condemned the prostitution of daughters by their fathers and slave girls by their masters, though the need of successive emperors over the next century to repeat this legislation speaks to the persistence of the practice. Among these was Justinian, who in the 530s attempted to clear Constantinople of brothels and pimps. He also established the Convent of Repentance for former prostitutes, though Procopius reports that some of the women chose suicide over confinement.[8]

Though the record of prostitution in the early Middle Ages is undersourced, recent scholarship arguing for greater persistence of economic activity and urban life in this era than has been previously assumed suggests that the sex trade may have been active as well.[9] Whatever the volume of their activity, early medieval prostitutes attracted the attention of legislators and clerics. In the early-seventh century, St. Columban accused Theuderic II of fathering children with prostitutes, though it is difficult to disentangle the saint's moral outrage from his feud with Theuderic's grandmother, Brunhild.[10] Two hundred years later Louis the Pious attempted to regulate prostitution, making prostitutes and their clients liable to public whipping.[11] The Visigothic kingdoms of Spain threatened their own judges with punishment for failing to prosecute prostitutes, though these measures met with little success, as did a series of draconian whipping penalties aimed at women convicted of prostitution.[12]

With the growth of towns, and the increasing enforcement of clerical celibacy from the eleventh century on, sources more and more reveal the presence of commercial and other forms of illicit sex. The presence of prostitutes and "wandering women" especially concerned the organizers of the First Crusade, but prostitution in the towns too was a concern for canon lawyers and theologians. The twelfth-century jurist Gratian focused on the promiscuity of prostitutes rather than commercial motives, arguing that what marked a prostitute was that she took many lovers. Other jurists stipulated the number of lovers it would take for a woman to be promiscuous, and the benchmarks ranged from two to several hundred thousand. Medieval intellectual elites never reached a consensus on the motives for women to engage in prostitution, which ranged from poverty to greed (Aquinas) to lust (Hostiensis).[13]

As legal and theological attitudes changed over time, so did the way that church and municipal authorities treated prostitution in the central and late Middle Ages, a process that can be divided into three general periods. The first period, which lasted roughly through the thirteenth century, was marked by limited toleration, on the one hand, and a zeal for reforming prostitutes on the other. Repentant houses flourished particularly during the twelfth and thirteenth centuries, though they enjoyed a resurgence in the late-fifteenth century, especially in Germany.[14] During the fourteenth century a second phase of prostitution developed. Despite, or because of, the natural and anthropogenic disasters that threatened Europe, city governments grew increasingly sophisticated and active in establishing institutions for the maintenance of civic order, among them the civic brothel. Though prostitutes had in many places been relegated to an extramural existence, through the course of the century they were typically moved within the city walls, first to red-light districts and then to municipally run brothels. The city could provide security and maintenance while leaving day-to-day operations to a middling-status operator, who acted as a tax farmer. The fifteenth century has been characterized as the "century of the brothel,"[15] though civic brothels were opening in the early-fourteenth century and a few cities did not open their brothels until the mid-sixteenth century. Though outside the scope of this chapter, the closing of civic brothels in northern Europe and southern France marks a third phase, but it should be noted that civic prostitution in Spain lasted until the seventeenth century, and some Italian cities retained their public brothels until the twentieth century.

There are important exceptions to the civic brothel periodization. Paris did not open an official public brothel, instead tolerating prostitution in various red-light districts. The City of London never formally opened a brothel, and the only legally tolerated stews, those of Southwark across the Thames, belonged to the bishop of Winchester.[16] Bruges neither institutionalized prostitution in the fourteenth and fifteenth centuries nor enacted sumptuary legislation.[17] But the existence of public brothels in many towns in Germany, and some in England and northern France, means that civic brothels, although characteristic of the Mediterranean region, were by no means exclusive to it.

From a modern vantage point it has been tempting for some scholars to look back at the late medieval period as a relatively benign era for prostitutes, one in which they enjoyed the protection of the brothel in a society that lacked the sexually repressive atmosphere of the Victorian era. Others, notably Judith Bennett, have stressed the continuity in the plight of low-status women across eras, characterized by low pay and low skills.[18] Generally, the record tends to support her assertions. While there were exceptions, public brothels did not necessarily make life easier for their inmates. The moral-economic tradeoff that held that prostitution was a necessary evil—what was going on was allegedly better than sodomy, adultery, or adolescent violence—led not to protection of the prostitutes themselves, but to their close policing. Civic authorities tended to focus on who the prostitutes were and especially where they were, or should have been, practicing their trade.[19]

The placement of prostitution in a city was an important structural component of the moral economy; it involved a balance of moral oversight and financial interest that bound ecclesiasts, elites, workers, and marginals in the business of commercial sex. The attempt to define a restricted space for prostitution, whether a single civic-run bordello or a red-light district, was central to the moral topography of a city. The allocation of civic property and resources to prostitution and the decisions made about the behavior of those involved in the sex trade occurred in response to immediate local concerns and were affected by long-term economic, political, and demographic forces. Those cities that established civic brothels did not do so all at once, and the houses and red-light districts were organized with differing combinations of public and private financing and authority.

The first stage, of limited toleration and emphasis on repentance, was also often characterized by efforts to expel prostitutes from the city, a heavy-handed solution that was as impractical as it was short lived. Presumably to win God's favor as he left for the Crusades, in 1254 Louis IX of France ordered the expulsion of all public prostitutes (*publice meretrices*) from villages and towns, and the confiscation of all their property, even their clothing.[20] But only two years later, though this prohibition was repeated, a clause was added that they be kept out of the middle of town, respectable streets, churches, monasteries, and cemeteries and, if possible, driven out of the city walls. This grand, and failed, gesture of moral hygiene left historians with an inventory of where prostitutes were, or at least where the authorities were afraid they might be.[21]

Bologna also attempted to eliminate prostitution in the thirteenth century, in 1259 ordering prostitutes to leave, with little effect.[22] A 1276 Augsburg civic ordinance ordered "wandering women" (*femmes errantes*) to be chased outside the walls, but the same law called for public women to pay a tax.[23] By the 1330s, Bologna had replaced intermittent expulsion with the establishment of a public brothel. Venice also attempted expulsion in 1266 and 1314 before turning to less drastic zoning efforts in the mid-fourteenth century. Florence attempted a series of regulations in 1287 aimed at expelling prostitutes, but the persistence of clandestine prostitution led, beginning in 1325, to ordinances calling for identification and segregation.[24] In York, which shared with most of England the absence of institutionalized brothels, civic authorities created ordinances aimed at keeping prostitutes out of the city in 1301 and, despite decades of commercial and illicit sex, again in 1482.[25]

By the fourteenth century, prostitution had proved impossible to expel—too many men demanded it, and the lack of economic opportunities for women ensured its supply. Civic ordinances moved from a desire for expulsion to the second stage, an often-grudging admittance of prostitution within, or at least near, the city walls, and cities began to grapple with where to sanction and control illicit sexual activity. As with other complex historical processes, there is no single identifiable cause for the development of municipal brothels. That institutionalization accelerated after the Black Death has led some to connect the involvement of civic authorities in prostitution to concerns about sodomy, masturbation, and male homosexuality and their effects on the birthrate.[26] Peter Schuster has suggested that the profound psychological impact of the plague may have provided impetus for institutionalization.[27] This is not, however, a sufficient explanation. Prague, for example, established civic brothels long before it was assaulted by the plague in 1380. The best, albeit less dramatic, explanation for the rise in civic brothels is that they parallel the increasing complexity in urban institutions in general.[28] Cities, despite the demographic pummeling they took in the fourteenth century, were becoming wealthier and more administratively complex, and were attracting more immigrants from a rural population increasingly less tied to the land.[29]

The reasons behind municipalities' segregating and regulating prostitutes often centered on order, honor, and security, though different cultures tended to have different emphases. Elisabeth Pavan suggests that Venice's decision to establish a public brothel (1360) was part of an attempt to clean up the Rialto, in keeping with its role as the center of Venetian commerce.[30] The Lübeck authorities dryly asserted that they had opened their brothel (1442) "for the advantage of the community and the benefit of the state."[31] In 1445 in southwest France, the civic fathers of Castelnaudary were concerned with the large number of young men and unmarried servants and lack of public women and girls. Their solution to the problem of public disturbances arising from this state of affairs was to confine public women to a brothel on the outside of town, thus separating them from "honest folk" and providing a sexual outlet for their burgeoning bachelor population.[32] The honor of "decent" women was typically given as a reason for building a brothel. As late as the first decade of the sixteenth century, Bilbao's Juan de Arbolancha offered that the building of public houses outside the town would spare the citizens, especially honest women, daily contact with prostitutes. City fathers did not take his suggestion—apparently the risk of female honor was not worth the cost of a municipal brothel, or perhaps several centuries of contact between prostitutes and "decent" women in this busy mercantile center had proved not to be so great a danger.[33] Regardless of emphasis, late medieval ordinances regarding the establishment of brothels typically describe a crisis in morals and the necessity of segregating public women as a way to solve it, even though illicit sex had been practiced, tolerated, and taxed for decades or even centuries.

The municipal brothel, whether controlled directly, tenant farmed, or privately held, was not the only means by which cities attempted to segregate prostitutes.[34] Many cities were content, or at least resigned, to assign red-light districts and bathhouses as areas of officially sanctioned prostitution. By the fourteenth century, prostitution had become such a part of Parisian life that authorities there limited themselves to listing the streets where prostitution should take place, the times it should be practiced, and some behavioral rules, including sumptuary laws.[35] In Avignon, prostitutes were officially confined to two official red-light districts, the Bourg Gigonghan and the Bourg-Neuf, but they enjoyed, with few restrictions, the run of the city, and commercial sex was openly practiced in taverns, inns, and bathhouses. Institutionalization only came to Avignon with the departure of the curia in the mid-fifteenth century.[36]

Regulating and isolating prostitution was never a simple task, as civic authorities wished both to make prostitution available and to keep it out of sight. Many cities relegated their red-light districts, and even the civic brothels, to areas outside or just inside the city walls. Relatively cheaper real estate outside the walls was a natural gathering place for prostitutes, who had been banned from living in the town center. But as Leah Otis has pointed out in her study of prostitution in the Languedoc, whether a brothel was placed within or without the walls was not as important as finding a place for it where nobody would be offended. The visibility and accessibility of public brothels was often the product of negotiations between city elites, as well as the daily practices of prostitutes and their customers. In Montpellier, a special council drawn from all four quarters of the town had to be summoned to choose a site.[37] The placement of the brothel was a gauge of power relationships within the town—distance from the brothel and status were often one and the same. From the 1330s until the middle of the sixteenth century, Valladolid's brothel, while on the margins of the city, was situated uncomfortably close to the Puerta del Campo, at the end of one of the most important roads, the Calle de Santiago. Access to the brothel was in plain sight of the Puerta and the town fountain, causing city fathers great concern that *buenas mujeres* (prostitutes) might mix with honorable women who went to the water. It was not until 1500, however, that civic authorities ordered the religious confraternity who ran the brothel to close the main door and open another adjoining an alley. The confraternity did not comply. Several ordinances and forty years later the brothel was finally moved to another site.[38]

Schuster has argued that the most important characteristic of the placement of brothels in the cities of the empire, including Vienna, Leipzig, and Hamburg, was their proximity to the city wall, whether inside or outside. Natural as well as constructed boundaries were also used to keep brothels out of the public eye. In Lindau the civic brothel was banished to an island, while Constance placed its facility near the Rhine, and Frankfurt located its *Frauenhaus* on the Main River.[39] The placement of brothels near rivers and other bodies of water was hardly a coincidence, inasmuch as city waste was pushed out of the cities into the water, and the banks were often malodorous places where elites would not be likely to gather, and prostitutes were not likely to be seen. The three legally distinct districts of medieval Prague that contained prostitutes employed three common strategies of marginalization: the infamous Hampays brothel of the Old Town district lay between the Jewish neighborhood and the river, the prostitutes of the Obora area lived outside the town walls under the protection of the city magistrate, and the clandestine prostitutes of Krakow Street lived on the extreme edge of the city.[40] Bruges was an exception, in that many brothels there were located in the wealthiest parts of town, where they served the needs of merchants, foreigners, and important citizens.[41]

While a concern for civic decency kept the brothels on the physical margins, demand for prostitution required that customers still have easy access. Some city ordinances negotiated this contradiction by allowing prostitutes access to the center of town, while marking their perpetual state of dishonor. Augsburg's brothel, though placed by a minor gate near the city wall, was conveniently close to the city center, yet a statute of 1276 put its inhabitants under the control of the hangman, himself the most notorious outcast of the town.[42] The presence of prostitutes in Venice's center reveals particularly clearly the fluctuations of a volatile moral economy. As noted previously, a by-product of the city government's increasing power and confidence was the establishment of a civic brothel, the Castelleto, in San Matteo di Rialto parish.[43] The confidence of the mid-fourteenth century was followed by the demographic trough of the fifteenth, and a growing concern for the debilitating effect of sodomy. In connection with a rise in sodomy cases before the Committee against Sodomy, in 1444 prostitutes in the Rialto were allowed to work longer hours and were officially permitted to eat and drink in taverns. Fourteen years later city fathers had enough of this cure and, citing the threat to the moral traditions of the city, once again banned prostitutes from San Marco.[44]

Many brothels took the form of bathhouses (stews). Bathhouses in medieval cities were essential for public hygiene and also useful sites for social bonding. Not infrequently these bathhouses unofficially doubled as brothels, part of the "gray market" of the moral economy, on the margin between the ideal of civic order and the reality of the sex trade. Lyons boasted seven bathhouses, the most famous being the Etuves Tresmonnoye, near the seat of royal justice. Bathhouses and prostitution were so closely linked in that city that the expression *aller s'estuver* had a meaning that everyone understood.[45] Ordinances from German-speaking lands reflect the ambiguous status of bathhouse workers. Most German cities tried to prevent prostitutes from operating in bathhouses, though the commonly used expression "bath whore" points to the extent of their success. While Bruges had a number of legitimate bathhouses, many were notorious bordellos, judging by the yearly fines for prostitution levied against them. The famous bathhouse-bordello Weiter Balx was fined almost every year between and 1305 and 1355.[46] The presence of bathhouses as well as countless other venues of clandestine prostitution outlines the difficulty that municipal authorities had in confining prostitution to the civic brothel, and the many sectors of the population with financial interests in prostitution highlight that the municipality was one player among many in the sex trade.

The players who profited from the trade included prominent churchmen. The closest things to official civic brothels in London were the stews of Southwark, across the Thames, controlled by the bishop of Winchester (though it is not clear how many of them were actually bathhouses).[47] While by the fifteenth century the bishop directly owned only two of the "stewhouses" (brothels), he maintained jurisdiction over all of them and hence profited from the fines levied against those who violated the local ordinances.[48] The bishop of Albi in the south of France claimed jurisdiction over the prostitutes there and in 1366 moved them from the customary red-light district to a rather poorly chosen site opposite the abbey church of St. Anthony.[49] Churchmen not only occasionally governed the supply of prostitutes; they sometimes had an effect on the demand for their services. Avignon's thriving sex industry can be attributed in large part to the presence of the papacy (1309–1378).[50] Organizers of the Council of Constance (1414–1418) estimated that seven hundred prostitutes had descended on the proceedings, where they were reported to have charged exorbitant fees for their services.[51] In Dijon, clergy made up 20 percent of the clientele of the bathhouses and brothels and represented the entire spectrum of the church hierarchy, from mendicant friars and priests to high officials.[52]

Notable families also profited from brothel activities. The Este family of Ferrara seems to have owned the brothel on the Via del Gambaro, intermittently renting it out to overseers in exchange for rent and taxes.[53] The Venerio and Maureceno families, among others, enjoyed rents from Venice's Castelleto.[54] The Fajardo family monopolized the brothels of Granada, and the municipalities in the region did not benefit from regulating the trade there.[55] In Palencia, Fernando Gutierrez de Villoldo, a local noble and vassal of the king, controlled the town brothel and willed it to his heirs.[56]

Though prostitution could be lucrative, in many towns it provided a modest living for middling level proprietors. Juan Guzman de Molina, the proprietor of the brothel in Albacete, collected rents between 4,000 and 4,500 *maravedis* per year, a sum small enough that the city fathers could not justify the expense of building a new civic brothel away from the center of town.[57] In some cities the tenant farmers were of modest means and reaped equally modest incomes. Brothel renters in the town of Millau included a locksmith and a saddler, and until 1473, a number of relatively poor women. The brothel was apparently not a hot property—between 1418 and 1492 there were twelve years when the brothel was not rented at all.[58] Inhabitants of small villages, deprived of the relative anonymity of the big city and its brothel, probably sought outlets for illicit sexuality that tend to escape the record. The moral economy there may have been governed as much by prying neighbors as by local officials, the ordinance and the tax roll replaced by the knowing glance and the accusatory whisper.

Where prostitutes were supposed to be in a medieval city was contingent on a number of factors—the moral and physical topography of the town, real estate struggles among elites, and the response of cities to demographic and epidemiological crises, to name a few. But prostitutes were not always where, or who, they were supposed to be, and the persistence of clandestine prostitution and the flouting of regulations by sanctioned prostitutes illustrates another aspect of the moral economy—that the ordinances in a given locale were not only designed to regulate the behavior of those involved in the sex trade but were themselves shaped by the behavior of those they wished to control.

Less is known about the women who engaged in commercial and illicit sex than about the churchmen who wrote about them, the city fathers who regulated their behavior, and the buildings in which they worked. Their families, places of origin, ages, personal relationships, living arrangements, and survival strategies remain largely unknown. Despite these difficulties, the growing number of regional and city studies has made it possible to paint a general portrait of the medieval prostitute. While time, place, and culture account for significant differences in the lives of prostitutes, women involved in illicit and commercial sex throughout medieval Europe—often, though not always, single, young, alone and away from home—were expected to make themselves available to (almost) all men. Prostitutes filled larger European cities in significant numbers and were concurrently a fiscal asset associated with civic hygiene and a moral deficit associated with crime and disorder. It is as solution and problem that these low-status women occasionally peer through records commonly concerned with the interactions of male elites.

No matter where they were working, medieval prostitutes were often from somewhere else, though it seems that women in many places did not move very far.[59] Jacques Rossiaud found that two-thirds of Dijon's prostitutes were from the city or its surrounding region.[60] Most women who practiced prostitution either professionally or occasionally in the town of Manosque (Basses Alpes) in the fourteenth century came from within fifty kilometers of there, most of the rest coming from within one hundred kilometers.[61] Larger cities, while still drawing regionally, also housed prostitutes from farther away. The Florentine Office of Decency recorded the presence of prostitutes from Dalmatia, the Low Countries, Spain, France, Germany, and Poland.[62] Flemish prostitutes were a focus of Londoners' anger during the Peasants' Revolt.[63] Seville's prostitute population was marked by a predominance of Castilian and foreign-born women.[64] Though family and local pressure often kept women from practicing their trade locally, some towns made this explicit, as in the Andalusian town of Ronda, where married women who had parents in the city were prohibited from making a living as prostitutes.[65] Despite evidence from smaller towns, like Exeter, where only 20 percent of prostitutes had no family there, the mass of evidence suggests that for a variety of reasons—the lack of opportunity in the countryside, the ravishments of pestilence and war—many women were driven into cities where they were the prey of the prostitution industry.[66] The moral economy of a town required that some women be available sexually to protect the honor of others. Yet at the same time it preferred, and sometimes insisted, that they come from somewhere else. An outsider would not shame a local family and would not have a local kin network to protect her.

Prostitutes—for example, in Valladolid, Marina de Sicilia, Elionor de Pamplona, and Catalina de Burgos—were far from the only people whose names indicate their place of origin. But prostitutes also used names that point to their need for anonymity and perhaps in some cases highlight their marketing strategies. The potential customers of Clarice la Clatterballock or Guillemette la Chatte must certainly have known what was being offered.[67] Other names require more careful decoding, as Kathryn Reyerson has done with the fourteenth-century Montpellier prostitute Bonela Bonafossia. *Bonafo* is a troubadour word that may mean "grants her favors," while *fos* is a subjunctive tense of a verb that would make her name something like "she'd be good." *Fossa*, a ditch or marker, has an equally earthy anatomical connotation, while the name Bonela might be a reference to *bonila* (i.e., good quality).[68] Bonela's choice of name indicates an ability to play with the language to promote her business and while at the same time protecting her anonymity. While a pseudonym can be treated as evidence of subaltern agency, it also indicates the marginal status of these women. A family name connected women to the rest of society—both morally, in terms of reputation, and financially, in terms of inheritance, dowry, property, and so forth. When they used a pseudonym, women traded an essential currency of the moral economy, a family name, for one that spoke directly to her lack of honor.

Some prostitutes had more choices than others, and though the record is mute about many prostitutes' lives, different levels of circumstance can be discerned from the available evidence. Slaves constituted an often-overlooked segment of medieval prostitution, especially in the Crown of Aragon. Muslim women who were arrested for practicing prostitution without a royal license were sold into slavery. Their masters, despite regulations to the contrary, often forced them back into prostitution and kept the profits.[69] King Pere III of Aragon issued an ordinance in 1374 forbidding the prostituting of slaves in the Ciutat de Mallorca (modern Palma).[70] Slave prostitutes suffered from a uniquely oppressive double bind—they were legally owned by one, yet morally available to all.

At the other end of the spectrum were prostitutes like some in Paris who were able to buy or rent property and more or less openly conduct business in a tavern or under the thinly disguised cover of a shop.[71] Some of Montpellier's prostitutes were active in buying and renting houses in the red-light district and can also be seen purchasing wardrobe chests.[72] The shadowy world of clandestine prostitution—illicit and commercial sex practiced outside official brothels and bathhouses—presents the possibility that some women were able to choose from a select clientele or even a single customer, from whom they would receive decent wages and treatment. Evidence of a few relatively well-off prostitutes should be read carefully. Images of comfortable Parisian prostitutes, lust-happy Florentine prostitutes appearing in fifteenth-century tour guides, and high-placed Venetian courtesans served to reinforce long-held notions of the greedy prostitute who combined lust with avarice.[73] Creating an image of the prosperous whore was a way of segregating her—if she alone was responsible for, and wallowing in, the wages of her sin, respectable society was distanced from her dishonor—and a way of ignoring the effect of the moral economy on the poorest women.

In between these two extremes of prosperity and abject poverty were the majority of medieval prostitutes—women, typically young and single, who were either tricked into prostitution or chose it as full- or part-time work because they had no other choice. There were many reasons for entering the sex trade, chief among them the absence of economic opportunity, loss of virginity (either voluntarily or through rape), and the disruption of family ties (orphanhood or widowhood). Some women were forced into prostitution, often at very young ages, by employers or family members. In fifteenth-century London, thirteen-year-old Joan Hammond was "let to hire to divers persons for divers sums of money" by her employer Alison Boston, and Isabella Lane was sent by two women to the "houses of divers Lombards," where she was raped.[74] In late-fourteenth-century Mislata (near Valencia), Joana was accused of prostituting her daughter Maria. The poorest of families may often have resorted to sending daughters to brothels or bawds as a means of confronting the dilemma of too many children and too few economic opportunities.[75]

Most medieval prostitutes did not practice their trade independently but were in some way connected to someone else who was policing their behavior and profiting from their labor. Beneficiaries of illicit sex ranged from family members and employers to a collection of hustlers, bawds, and pimps to the civic authorities, church officials, and elite families, who benefited from the rents of brothels and red-light districts. A few semi-legendary procurer figures arose in the thirteenth and fourteenth centuries, such as the *rei d'arlots* of the Crown of Aragon—but the reality was far more mundane.[76] Many municipal brothels were in the charge of an "abbot" or "abbess" who maintained the facilities and oversaw the well-being of the prostitutes. In Toulouse, the oldest prostitute in the brothel was assigned the role of abbess and was charged with justifying expenses to the town council as well as keeping *ruffiens* (pimps) away from her flock. The better brothel keepers took care of their prostitutes when epidemics curtailed their work. Jeanne Robelot, Dijon's long-time proprietress, paid her workers living expenses during one such outbreak and was forced to petition the town for reimbursement.[77] The stews in the bishop of Winchester's manor in Southwark were subject to regulations designed to govern the behavior of stew holders and prostitutes, but they appear to have been regularly flouted.[78] Despite civic ordinances charging "padres" and "madres" in Cordoba and Málaga with protecting, housing, and feeding brothel prostitutes, in practice they frequently abused their power, requiring women to eat meals and have their clothes washed only at the brothel, at prices as exorbitant as those charged for their rooms. They routinely advanced money to prostitutes against their future wages, thus entrapping them in a form of debt servitude.[79] In 1415 and again in 1442, Perpignan issued brothel regulations citing complaints about widespread extortion of money from prostitutes.[80] Without family or honor in the city, the only protection prostitutes had were ordinances that were intermittently enforced and that often reflected the situation as it ought to have been, not as it was.

Besides the "abbots" and "abbesses," "padres" and "madres" and "stew holders" who operated public brothels under the gaze of the authorities, a variety of characters were associated with the clandestine sex trade, either as an occupation or to supplement their income. While procurers (who might be called "bawd" in English, "maquerelle" in French, and "lena" in Latin, and who included what we might today call pimps as well as go-betweens) faced greater punishment under canon and civil law than prostitutes, they were integral to the moral economy. They were cast in the role of lead villain, as the evil manipulators of innocent girls, for whom society claimed an interest in repentance.

The world of clandestine procuring covers countless illicit arrangements that took place in an equally countless number of places. Those who attempted to profit from the labor of prostitutes could be family members, lovers, spouses, employers, members of the clergy, and even other prostitutes. In late-fourteenth-century Valencia, witnesses at the robbery trial of Francisco de Varea declared that his only sources of income were from games with loaded dice that he ran and his wife's prostitution.[81] Katherine the Dutchwoman in London was accused of acting as a bawd for her daughter, and for beating her when she refused to sleep "with a certain Lombard."[82] Some women engaged in prostitution were accompanied by companions, who were sometimes their partners or husbands, sometimes just their pimps. Marion de la Court, a linen weaver and prostitute in Paris, confessed to a string of thefts undertaken to placate her "boyfriend," who would beat her if she did not bring him money. The companion of Marion la Liourde passed himself off as her husband and worked as a pastry chef, while also engaging in theft and living off the income she earned as a prostitute.[83]

Women as well as men were actively engaged in procuring. In Dijon, the majority of procurers in the record were wives of middling sorts, including artisans, carters, and innkeepers, and engaged in procuring (*maquerellage*) to supplement the family income. These women often recruited rape victims, women in bad marriages, and poor girls who been abandoned in the local hospitals for their private bordellos.[84] Perhaps the largest category of procurers consisted of those who employed women in low-status service occupations—servants, tapsters, laundresses, and the like—and also profited from their labor as prostitutes. In London, Robert Cliff and his wife were charged with selling their servant Agnes Smith to Lombards for forty pounds.[85] Tavern owners and hotel proprietors were often associated with prostitution, supplementing their incomes by having their employees provide sexual services to their clientele. Although the procuress (more than her male counterpart) became a vilified figure in literature, throughout late medieval Europe every stratum of society can be found involved in the trade, from the highest royal and civic officials to the lowest street corner hustler.

By the sixteenth century, the rules of the game would change, and cities would begin to close their civic brothels, choosing instead to criminalize prostitution. As with the opening of the municipal brothels, there is no easily identifiable cause for their closing. The Reformation has been put forth as a reason for brothel closings in Germany, but not all German cities followed this pattern. Cologne, Freiburg, and Soest opened houses in the 1520s, shortly before other cities began closing their houses.[86] The pressure of the Protestant Reformation and its critique of moral laxity, and the Catholic Reformation response, have been connected to the closing of brothels in Catholic cities, but many cities, especially in Spain and Italy, did not close their brothels and red-light districts until well after the sixteenth century. Syphilis has been cited as a reason for brothel closings, but the Nuremberg city council complained that it would be necessary to build three syphilis clinics instead of one if their house were closed, because they were concerned with the rise of illicit sex in other cities that had already closed their brothels.[87] Syphilis could also be a reason for expanding rather than contracting municipal brothels, as in Seville, where in 1570 city fathers felt that civic prostitutes could be kept under tighter medical and moral surveillance.[88]

Brothel closings may have been the product of changes in the view of male sexuality in popular culture and in Protestant and Catholic Reformation teaching. The encouragement of marriage, and a sterner view of male fornication in the sixteenth century, created an atmosphere where men were not always able to act with the sexual license of earlier eras. In many places, the well-ordered household became the engine of the moral economy. Prostitution remained a survival strategy for low-status women, but the conditions under which they operated had clearly changed. Throughout much of Europe, clandestine prostitution became the norm, and the surveillance of the policeman began to replace that of the civic father and the brothel padre.

Much of the scholarship on medieval prostitution has attempted to peer through the smokescreen of subalternity to determine where prostitutes fit on particular continua—continuity/change, agency/victimhood, worker/deviant, insider/marginal, and so forth. These conceptualizations, however useful they may be, do not take fully into account the network of social forces that were involved in prostitution. Women could be found selling or bartering sex in the richest palace and the foulest stew, on the Rialto and in the loneliest country inn. They could be relatively well off financially or, more likely, desperately in debt. Some prostitutes worked in well-managed brothels, others in those less scrupulously managed. Even more worked independently of brothels, and they ranged from the well-kept concubine to women chasing farthings in churchyards and under bridges. The compromise of seeing prostitution as a necessary evil, the attempt to exile prostitutes and then placing them within town walls, struggles over moral topography, and the various segregation strategies—sumptuary laws, red-light districts, brothels, and Magdalene houses—were reflective of cities' acceptance of the reality of the sex trade and their desire to organize, contain, and control its perceived corrosive effects. But the moral economy was not a one-way street. The controlling efforts of elites affected and were affected by the decisions of elite as well as middle- and low-status individuals engaged in the day-to-day business of the sex trade. Prostitution in cities could be influenced by something as small as the accusations of a neighbor or as large as a war or plague. While general traits of prostitution—loss of honor, poverty, assumptions about men's and women's sexual nature—were universal across medieval Europe, the values placed on them were determined in a negotiation that combined economy and morality. Illicit sex was traded everywhere, but its worth—in terms of its role in the health of the society and its street value—was not everywhere the same.

CHAPTER NINE

Erotica

SARAH SALIH

The exhibition *Seduced: Art and Sex from Antiquity to Now* opened at London's Barbican Centre in October 2007, announcing that "*Seduced* explores the representation of sex in art through the ages. Featuring over 300 works spanning 2000 years, it brings together Roman sculptures, Indian manuscripts, Japanese prints, Chinese watercolours, Renaissance and Baroque paintings and 19th century photography with modern and contemporary art."[1] That 2,000-year span, however, conceals an empty millennium, for the exhibition included not a single object or image from the medieval West. The erotic arts of Europe, to judge from this selection, originated in antiquity, revived in the Renaissance, achieved full fruition in the present day, but simply did not happen in the Middle Ages. This omission reproduces a consensus that medieval erotic imagery was significant only by its absence. General histories of eroticism in Western art regularly pass over everything between Pompeii and Aretino with a generalization such as "Eroticism is rare in the art of the Early Christian period and the Middle Ages. ... Christian art shunned the world of physical love and concentrated instead on spiritual upliftment."[2] Such a summary depends upon a narrow definition of erotic art and a long-standing denigration of the medieval. Yet again, "the Middle Ages are debunked as static, hieratic and unchanging"—characteristics that comfortably accommodate "sexless"—by narratives that require the period to represent all that is not modern.[3]

However, and inconveniently, initial consideration suggests that there may be some truth to the claim that medieval culture was not conducive to art that we can recognize as erotic. Visual stimulation was considered to be necessary to Eros. Love at first sight is the rule in medieval romances, for, as Andreas Capellanus wrote, "Love is an inborn suffering which results from the sight of, and uncontrolled thinking about, the beauty of the other sex."[4] Optical theory understood amorous looking as "an extension of the flesh," and so a bodily, sexual act.[5] But it was the objects of desire themselves, not representations of them, that provoked such looks. Medieval lovers, when separated, were more likely to treasure a beloved's jewelry, letters, or hair than to sigh over each other's portraits. Penitential discourse exhaustively catalogs every variant of sexual sin to which the human mind and body are subject, for confession must be precise, but is silent about the use of erotic art. In a substantial anthology of extracts from penitentials from all over Europe, from the seventh to the sixteenth centuries, the topic is not mentioned once.[6] A fourteenth-century English penitential, *The Book of Vices and Virtues*, misses every possible opportunity to condemn erotic response to the visual arts. It encompasses sexual fantasy, explaining that the "spirit of fornicacioun … maketh thoghtes [makes thoughts] come on the figures and liknesses of that synne in a mannes or a womannes herte, and maketh hem thenke ther-on [makes them think of it]"; visual temptation "to bihelde thes ladies and thes maidenes and damselles araied and apparailed [dressed and decked out]"; the sensual stimuli of "outrageous etynges and drynkynges and esy beddynges and delicious and softe schertes and smokkes and swote [sweet] robes of scarlet."[7] Amid this wealth of para-erotic pleasures, it is never envisaged that an individual might need to confess having been enticed to sin by looking at sexy pictures. Even Master Gregorius, an English visitor to Rome who was so taken by a nude statue—possibly the Capitoline Venus—that he felt drawn as if by magic to view it repeatedly, did not articulate his response to it as erotic and perhaps did not feel it to be so.[8] Given his enthusiasm for classical artifacts, admiration of the antique aesthetic was probably as important a component as admiration for a female form. His encounter with the statue is far more decorous, and his appreciation of it more diffuse, than the classical man-meets-statue narrative that leaves semen stains on the Venus of Cnidos.[9]

Two further tales of desire for statues offer only very qualified testimony to the erotic affect of images. The classical story of Pygmalion, who fell in love with his own handiwork, a statue of a beautiful woman, was included in the *Roman de la rose* and appealed to many of its illustrators.[10] Another story, equally popular, reversed the genders. In the Alexander romance, Queen

Candace, having failed to persuade Alexander to visit her, settled for a statue of him, made to his exact likeness by a skilled craftsman:

> He cast a fourme the kyng liche
> Jn face, in eighe, in nose, in mouth,
> Jn lengthe, in membres—that is selcouth! [marvelous]
> The quene it sette in her boure [bower]
> And keped it in grete honoure.[11]

Illustrators of this narrative, however, often substituted a two-dimensional painted portrait head for the three-dimensional whole-body statue specified in the text, thus drawing attention away from the hint that the queen gained some satisfaction from its life-size "membres."[12] They do not depict Candace alone with the artifact: both text and illustrative cycles are more interested in the subsequent meeting of Alexander with the artifact than in any erotic function it may have had in his absence. It is a story about the uncanny power of verisimilitude, not sex. Both these narratives imagine the person-statue relationship as primarily social: Candace shows "honoure" to her statue, and, according to the *Roman de la rose*, Pygmalion obsessively clothed and reclothed his statue, more interested in giving it a social identity than exploring its bare ivory/flesh.[13] The tales imagine an affective relationship with a particular image as a preliminary to more satisfying—because sexual—relations with the living referent of the image. The use of the image is more like erotic magic than like erotic art.[14]

Significantly, the Pygmalion and Alexander narratives occur in exotic pagan settings. The Middle Ages persistently associated erotic art with paganism and idolatry. Indeed, sexual subjects had been widespread in classical art. As they very often had religious functions, they were readily perceived as not only indecent but impious. Early Christians such as St. John Chrysostom decried theatrical and pictorial depictions of sexual behavior as dangerous to Christians' spiritual health.[15] The identification of obscenity as a defining feature of paganism is evident in the convention of depicting pagan idols with prominent phalluses, and in Master Gregorius's misrecognition of the classical statue of a thorn puller, or *spinario*, as a Priapus.[16] Christian rhetoric delegitimized pagan religious art and practices by reading them through an insistently sexualized hermeneutic. Ancient Roman celebrations of the phallus were not only about sex: though the form was not chosen by accident, it had a wide range of symbolic meanings and a long history of veneration.[17] But to St. Augustine, who saw the involuntary character of erection as evidence of humanity's fallen state, such activity must have seemed to be a demonically inspired surrender to the sign of original sin.[18] Acknowledging the apotropaic and fertility-enhancing intentions of phallic worship, he nevertheless denounced it as an affront to sexual modesty:

> It was obligatory for the most respected mother of a family to place a crown on this disreputable organ in full view of the public. This was how Liber had to be placated to ensure successful germination of seeds; this was how evil spells had to be averted from the fields. A matron had to be compelled to perform an act in public which even a harlot ought not to have been allowed to perform in the theatre if there were matrons in the audience.[19]

Augustine's objection is as much to the publicity and the inclusive character of the ritual as to its indecency, for its inclusivity obscures the crucial difference between matron and harlot. Refusing to accept it as a sacred act for a whole community, he rhetorically relegates it to the theater, the most profane of spaces.

Though Christianity succeeded in eliminating phallic worship, at least one fifteenth-century observer thought that sexual imagery remained as severe a threat to public morals as it had been in pagan times. In 1402 Jean Gerson, chancellor of the University of Paris, declared that one might see daily

> the most filthy corruption of boys and youths by shameful nude images [*imaginibus*], which are offered for sale in the very temples and on holy days, like idols of Belphegor, to which Christian children—o horrible shame—are introduced by impious mothers or sluttish maidservants, and the senseless laughter of damnable fathers, even to the most obscene songs, gestures and behaviours and to many other abominations, even in the churches, in holy places and on holy days.[20]

It is difficult to know which objects Gerson had in mind, though it has been suggested that he might have been referring to sexual badges.[21] Nevertheless, his polemic against the sexualization of public space is continuous with Augustine's, a millennium earlier. Obscenity is linked to idolatry, reawakening a latent anxiety that visual representation is inherently unchristian. Belphegor, or Baal-Peor, was indeed a fertility god whose worship is equated in the Old Testament with the impurity of sexual relations with foreign women.[22] Depictions of his worship in the picture cycles of the *Bibles moralisées*, shown here from the Rohan Hours (fig. 9.1), imagine looking at nude images—in this instance an elegantly elongated golden-haired male—to be idolatry, which results in sexual transgression. The nudity of the image is a medieval addition to the biblical source: while for the Old Testament writer, idolatry simply was sexual transgression, the postclassical Christian interpreter understands the sexual stimulus to be mediated through art. Gerson, like this illustrator, imagines a seamless unity of the form, the content, and the affect of the images; obscene pictures of obscene things have obscene results. The indiscriminate availability of such images to the vulnerable and hermeneutically naive general public makes them especially dangerous. These assumptions are shared with later anti-pornographic campaigners.[23] However, the social profile of these objects differs from that of much later pornography. They were on display in public spaces—indeed, in churches, much to Gerson's horror—and were surveyed collectively by family groups, whose response was dominated by amusement rather than arousal.

FIGURE 9.1: Worship of Baal-Peor. Rohan Book of Hours (1419–1427). MS lat 9471, fol. 235r. Bibliothèque nationale de France, Paris. By permission of the Bibliothèque nationale de France.

Gerson's polemic enables us to look more closely at the terms of the statement that the medieval lacked erotic art. Medieval sexual representations did not necessarily constitute a discrete category. If "pornography" is, according to the *OED*, "the explicit description or exhibition of sexual subjects or activity ... in a manner intended to stimulate erotic rather than aesthetic feelings," the concept needs to be dismantled to allow for a discussion of medieval art. Indirect representations may have been enticing; explicit representations of sexual organs or acts may have been intended to produce disgust, fear, shame, or laughter. Given the unpredictability of human sexual response, reception must often have been at odds with intention. That sexual and demonic images were sometimes excised from manuscripts, possibly toward the end of the Middle Ages, indicates that medieval responses to them were not uniform.[24] Sexual form, sexual content, and sexual affect so frequently diverge in medieval art that they must be assessed separately. If "pornography came into existence, both as a literary and visual practice and as a category of understanding, at the same time and concomitantly with the long-term emergence of Western modernity," there were, nevertheless, representations of sexual topics prior to modernity.[25] The term "pornography" refers to function and circumstances of consumption as much as it does to content. It was invented in the West to deal with the explicit images discovered to have been on public display in Pompeii. On their excavation in 1748 these were placed in a demarcated zone and made available only to a restricted category of spectators.[26] Augustine and Gerson both describe a pre-pornographic situation, in which explicit images are consumed publicly and collectively. Responses to them are dominated neither by erotic arousal nor by aesthetic appreciation: they are tokens around which families bond and communities are formed. Augustine and Gerson respond by attempting to invent the category of pornography, articulating a deliberately minoritarian reading of the imagery as sexually provocative in order to argue that it should, preferably, be eliminated but at the very least should be removed from the public zone, where it can corrupt Christian families.

Christian values, then, did not keep the Middle Ages sexless. Sex was a central concern of literary genres, including romance, hagiography, fabliaux, riddles, and lyric. Sex was visible. Romances imagined courts that established their glory by displaying beautiful women.[27] Late medieval men's fashions, moralists complained, with their tight hose, short jackets, exaggerated codpieces, and suggestively long shoes, were blatant sexual displays. As Chaucer's Parson memorably put it, they showed "horrible swollen membres, that semeth lik the maladie of hirnia, in the wrappynge of hir hoses; and eek the buttokes of hem faren as it were the hyndre part of a she-ape in the fulle of the moone."[28]

Women's fashions such as low-cut necklines and sideless gowns were likewise denounced as "lascivious and carnal provocation."[29] The erotic glamour of high fashion is evident in an illumination of the dance of Mirth from a *Roman de la rose* manuscript (fig. 9.2). The elegantly clothed figure, indeed, was probably a more enticing image than the naked one until the very end of the period.[30] In the later Middle Ages opportunities to see live erotic or bawdy spectacles were rather plentiful, and though moralists might have disapproved, the majority enjoyed and accepted them. Elements of classical performance may have survived in the twelfth-century Latin comedy *Babio*, which seems to require a performance in which the title character is equipped with an outsize prop-phallus.[31] Professional women dancers performed in inns, courts, and great households: one appears in a margin of the Luttrell Psalter, swaying gracefully as she balances on her partner's shoulders.[32] The pious King Henry VI was shocked at his

FIGURE 9.2: The Dance of Mirth. *Roman de la rose* (mid-fifteenth century). MS Douce 364 fol. 8r. Bodleian Library, University of Oxford. By permission of the Bodleian Library, University of Oxford.

courtiers' choice of a dance by "young ladies with bared bosoms" as Christmas entertainment.[33] Richard Rolle glossed the biblical phrase "vanitates & insanias falsas" in abundant contemporary detail as "vile lustis of this warld, as hoppynge & daunnceynge of tumblers [acrobats] and herlotis [harlots], and other spectakils, that makis men to lose ther wit fra god": the association of tumblers and harlots confirms that there was a sexual element to such performances.[34] More decorously, courtly readers are often depicted gathering to read romances, a form of "erotic reading" that sometimes moved the audience to "imitate immediately the lovers whose story they [had] just read."[35]

The visual arts, however, were often more reticent. Medieval artists used various techniques to connote sexual subject matter in such a way as to reduce the risk of making sex present. The poem *Sir Gawain and the Green Knight*—which would have made an excellent text for courtly erotic reading—offers a set-piece description of the beautiful lady of Hautdesert. The reader is aligned with Gawain's admiring gaze as he takes in

> Kerchofes of that on, with mony cler perlez,
> Hir brest and hir bryght throte bare displayed,
> Schon schyrer then snawe that schedez on hillez
> [shone brighter than snow that falls on hills].[36]

This pleasurable sight, however, is not visualized in the illuminations of the manuscript. When the lady is pictured approaching Gawain in his bed, she wears an elaborate but very demure dress with a high collar that reaches to her chin (fig. 9.3). The picture eliminates not only the lady's breasts but also the poem's witty duplication of them with images of other firm, round, white things, pearls and snowy hillocks. It does not disguise the erotic content of the scene: the lady's seductive intentions are evident in her presence within the curtained enclosure and in the delicate caress of her finger insinuated into Gawain's beard. However, the picture does not itself seduce: it refers to the erotic but does not make it present.

Likewise, illustrations of the *Roman de la rose* attempted various equivalents to the insertion of staff into passageway that ends the poem, ranging from showing the lover picking a flower to showing a couple lying in bed, but none is anywhere near as anatomically specific as the text.[37] The translation from text to image tends to mute sexual explicitness. It can be inferred that most owners and illustrators of romance manuscripts preferred to avoid visual stimulation (at least in the main illustrative cycles) and that they considered visual representations of such scenes to be more inflammatory than their

FIGURE 9.3: The Lady of Hautdesert and Sir Gawain. Gawain-poet (1400–1410). MS Cotton Nero A. X, fol. 129r. British Library, London. © The British Library Board.

textual equivalents. This assessment accords with that of some late medieval writers on devotional art, such as the author of *Dives and Pauper*, who wrote that "often man is more steryd be syghte than be heryng or redyngge."[38]

Sexual content was often concealed within elaborate encodings. The presence of a rabbit may instruct the viewer to read erotic import into an otherwise innocuous scene, because the animal's French name, *con*, puns on the word for female genitals.[39] The impact of the obscene word is thus twice distanced, through the verbal pun and the substitution of image for word. Instead of erotic pleasure, the representation offers the pleasure of disentangling this chain of signification, substituting cerebral for somatic response. The comparable textual genres of romance and lyric, it has been suggested, likewise find "semantic indirection ... more interesting, perhaps more titillating, than outright obscenity."[40] The symbolism of Jan van Eyck's *Arnolfini Portrait* is cryptic because it is, interdependently, Christian and sexual (fig. 9.4). The couple's reflection in the mirror on the back wall is

FIGURE 9.4: *Arnolfini Portrait,* Jan van Eyck (1434).
National Gallery, London. © The National Gallery,
London.

surrounded by scenes of Christ's Passion, thematically appropriate to the
action in the foreground, as the Crucifixion could be imagined as the consummation of Christ's marriage to the church.[41] The Song of Songs, routinely allegorized as referring to the spiritual marriage, is thus a relevant
intertext, in particular its imagery of the female body as domestic architecture: "My beloved put his hand through the key hole, and my bowels were
moved at his touch. I arose up to open to my beloved: my hands dropped
with myrrh."[42] The placing of the two pairs of shoes, matter out of place
in this orderly room, supplies the backstory to the moment depicted. They
show that the man has come into the room, where the woman was waiting:
his discarded shoes in the foreground near the door are outdoor pattens
splashed with mud from the streets, while hers are soft indoor slippers, left
beside the bench in the deep interior of the room at the back of the picture
space. The shoes thus allow the picture to be understood as a cognitive
image of sexual penetration, by an allusion to the bridegroom's entrance
into the chamber, a term used euphemistically, as in the phrase *chambre of*

Venus, for vagina.[43] The shoes are also sexual synecdoches for their owners, his made of hard wood with suggestively extended toes, hers soft and open. The painting's sexual allusion is bound in to Christian marriage theory. It has been persuasively argued that the panel represents a betrothal: if so, the symbolic depiction of the consummation adds the element that, in canon law, would transform the betrothal into a marriage.[44]

While erotic content may be signaled indirectly, an explicitly sexual image, conversely, may convey an anti-erotic impact. Doom and the punishment of sinners in hell were very commonly visible in carving and paint in churches and often included scenes of naked sinners, with their sexual organs attacked by snakes and toads. It is likely that some exhibitionist figures found on churches in the British Isles, western France, and northern Spain were intended to convey similar messages. The best known of these are the female figures known as sheela-na-gigs, but there are also male figures and couples. There is very little evidence to support the persistent popular belief that these are survivals of pre-Christian native religions. More plausible, in view of their location, geographical spread, and date range, is that the iconography is a high medieval innovation that caricatures and admonishes sexual sins: "the function of sexual exhibitionists is not erotic, but rather the reverse. ... They were not intended to inflame the passions but rather to allay them."[45] They are certainly, in Augustine's and Gerson's terms, obscene, but their designers must have come to the conclusion that Christianity could safely appropriate obscenity for its own purposes. The exhibitionists are sexually explicit in their genital display, but their forms are otherwise distorted: they may have contorted bodies or inhuman features and proportions. They display a monstrous sexuality also depicted in creatures such as hypervirile giants and wild men, or dragons with gaping vaginas.[46] The exhibitionists may be personifications of the sexual organs themselves, or parodic representations of humans reduced to sexual urges. Grotesque as their appearance is, they are also recognizable representations of the experience of inhabiting sexual human bodies.

However, exhibitionist figures were probably not invariably intended or read as moralistic instruction, for not all fit the profile of warnings against lust. The distended vulvas of the female figures have connoted childbirth to many observers: the sheelas in the parish church of Kilpeck and the nunnery church of St. Radegund at Poitiers have recently been analyzed as references to the reproductive female body.[47] The pair of figures from Kirknewton, West Lothian (fig. 9.5), has been identified as a birthing woman with midwife, though as no child is visible, the reading remains speculative.[48] However, to identify such an object as a birthing motif is not necessarily to exclude the sexual, or an

FIGURE 9.5: Woman giving birth (?). (1146–1300). National Museum of Scotland, Edinburgh. Previously St. Cuthbert's Church, Kirknewton, West Lothian. Photo © Sarah Salih.

ascetic revulsion from the sexual, from its meanings. The response of nuns was probably not identical to those of villagers: nuns might have allegorized along the lines of the Middle English virginity treatise *Hali Meithhad*, which contrasts the mortal infants conceived in sin and born to pain and death with the virtues, the undying spiritual children born to virgins of God.[49] Alternatively, displays of genitals and buttocks could signify aggression: the *Gesta Herewardi* tells of a witch who participated in a siege by intimidating the defenders "and at the end of her chattering and incantations she bared her arse at them."[50] Some carvings may have been intended to have a similarly aggressive impact: the location of some of the later Irish sheelas on the exterior walls of secular buildings perhaps indicates that they had come to be understood as protective and status enhancing.[51] The bottom-displaying acrobats on the fourteenth-century parclose screen in St. Margaret's Church, Lynn (fig. 9.6), are too small to be threatening, too naturalistically shaped to be grotesque, and too playful to be effective as moral instruction. It is more likely that they were simply comic.

FIGURE 9.6: Exhibitionist. Parclose screen (fourteenth-century). St. Margaret's Church, King's Lynn, Norfolk. Photo © Sarah Salih.

The monumental figures share forms with sexual motifs in other media and locations: either the carvings originated motifs that were later adapted for other purposes and contexts or they are the earliest, being the most robust, survivors of a stock of common imagery. At least one sexual badge replicates a common type of female exhibitionist figure.[52] A distinctively stylized copulation motif appears in male-female versions in stone in Romanesque churches in France and Spain, and in both male-female and male-male versions in the margins of a thirteenth-century French Psalter.[53] Meaning is not inherent in the form but varies according to location. One of the Psalter images is a visual pun on the Latin text of the psalm it accompanies, functioning as an aid to memory and a place marker in the book: mnemonic systems often exploited the impact of sexual, violent, and grotesque imagery.[54] One *Bible moralisée*'s representation of the consequences of the Fall, making the same association of idolatry and sexual transgression as the related image in the Rohan Hours, envisages its sexualizing idol not as a classical or demonic figure, but as an exhibitionist (fig. 9.7).[55] This tends to confirm that the carved figures were interpreted as negative exemplars, but the picture distances and repositions the

FIGURE 9.7: Consequences of the Fall. *Bible moralisée* manuscript (late-fourteenth century). MS Add. 18719, fol. 3v. British Library, London. © The British Library Board.

motif in order to construct an image of historical non-Christian worship. The figure is moved from the relatively inconspicuous locations of the surviving examples to a tabernacle and further emphasized by the gestures of its priest. The exhibitionists of medieval churches may have been intended to disgust, amuse, or shock, but this artist imagined viewing circumstances in which the same object could be sexually stimulating. To use an exhibitionist instead of a classical image type in such a scene is to acknowledge that perverse desires can be stimulated by images of medieval Christianity's own invention.

Judeo-Christian tradition, indeed, supplied explicit material and also pro-hibited looking at it. The biblical narrative of the drunkenness of Noah warns against looking at sexual organs, and depictions of this scene thus often avoid showing them. When they are explicitly represented, the scene possibly func-tions as a guilt-inducing mechanism or even as aversion therapy for those who found themselves fascinated by it and thus found themselves in the position of Ham, cursed for looking, pointing, and laughing at the sight.[56] The carved version on a roof boss in Norwich Cathedral invites determined scrutiny (fig. 9.8). Ham performs the exhibitionist gesture, showing his father's nakedness to the viewer without looking at it himself: the dangerous look is thus ours, not his. Noah's penis is exaggerated in size and distinguished in color from his surrounding garments: these emphases make it just possible to spot the organ from ground level with the naked eye but require the viewer to work hard for the reward. It helps to know which boss to look for: today various guides to the bosses are available, but medieval viewers would have relied on oral guidance. As the Noah boss is placed above the monks' choir, the monks would surely have become the expert viewers. The boss may intend to discourage an all-male community from homoerotic gazing but can do so only by drawing their attention to itself, inviting them to search for and point out to one another a polychrome stone penis rather than a flesh-and-blood organ.

An unusual exhibitionist motif appears on a misericord in Lancaster Priory, in an arrangement that resembles a blasphemous parody of an Annunciation scene (fig. 9.9). Paired roundels contain a naked woman who runs toward a naked,

FIGURE 9.8: Drunkenness of Noah. Roof boss NB7 (1463–1472). Norwich Cathedral. Photo © Julia Hedgecoe 1997.

FIGURE 9.9: Misericord with profane scene. Lancaster Priory (ca. 1340). Photo © Sarah Salih.

apparently masturbating, angel, which raises its left hand, as if to address her. The damaged central scene once showed an elaborately dressed woman with another standing figure. The precise content of this scene is elusive, though some kind of warning against sexual transgression seems the most obvious interpretation.[57] It might have illustrated some fabliau analogue of the tale in Boccaccio's *Decameron*, in which a corrupt friar masquerades as an angel to seduce a vain woman.[58] The central scene then would have shown the characters' social selves, she rejecting his advances, while the roundels showed their sexual selves, his in the angel disguise and hers comically avid. Alternatively, the misericord may refer to St. Paul's instruction to the Corinthians that women should cover their heads in church "because of the angels."[59] Commentators such as Tertullian connected this mysterious command to the narrative in Genesis that "The sons of God seeing the daughters of men, that they were fair, took to themselves wives of all which they chose" to argue that women should veil themselves to avoid presenting a source of temptation.[60] Such fallen angels were identified with the elves of medieval England's woods and hills, who seduced both men and women.[61] The misericord's figures could thus be read as a woman naked but for a matronly headdress, as if in mockery of Paul's instruction, and a tempted angel flanking a central scene that was possibly of sexual encounter. In either interpretation, the misericord constitutes a satire or moralization on the theme of women's frailty and vanity. The misogyny is apt for a monastic church, but the satire, or warning, is directed also at the monks themselves, for it was a commonplace of monastic theory that monasticism was an imitation of the angels.[62] If even an angel could be tempted, then merely human monks should be on guard. But the image exceeds the moral. It is also a celebration of the power of art to represent the impossible, whether that be the hybrid monsters in nearby misericords or a masturbating angel in this one. An angel, an immaterial being "free from all corruption, death, matter, and generation," does not have a body, does not appear naked, does not masturbate—and yet here it is (fig. 9.10).[63] Its form betrays no signs of fall or masquerade. It is not distorted or deformed, nor is it genitally explicit. Its body is smooth and harmoniously proportioned; it is placed in a dignified frontal pose and gestures ceremoniously with its left hand. Though naked, it is unashamed: if it is an image of vice, it is a disturbingly seductive one.

FIGURE 9.10: Masturbating angel (detail of figure 9.9). Lancaster Priory. (ca. 1340). Photo © Dr. S.J.E. Riches.

A varied range of sexual imagery is found in badges, which are further discussed and illustrated by Malcolm Jones in this volume. These are cheap, mass-
produced late medieval items found mainly in the Netherlands and France,
in the same locations and conditions as religious badges and nonsexual secular badges.[64] These circumstances suggest that they were on public display,
pinned onto clothing like any other badge, and that their subject matter did not
constitute them as a distinct class of objects. There are copulation scenes, phalluses, vulvas, and some more elaborate images, such as a vulva-archer on horseback and a vulva carried aloft in procession by phalluses. Other subjects are
derived from classical or romance themes.[65] They share forms with other media;
some look like two-dimensional depictions of the classical three-dimensional
phallic amulets with wings and bells (fig. 9.11); others resemble exhibitionist
figures; motifs such as the phallus-tree are also found in manuscript marginalia and carved caskets.[66] It is hard to imagine that the badges could have been
meant either as warnings against lust or as stimuli to it, but possible that a
determinedly pious or susceptible viewer might have received them in either

FIGURE 9.11: Graeco-Roman phallic amulet.
(100 B.C.E.–C.E. 400). Wellcome Library,
London.

way. The classical amulets are known to have been apotropaic, and though the form cannot be definitely proved to be continuous, it is generally agreed that the badges retained a protective function. However, this does not necessarily exhaust their meanings and functions. These isolated and disembodied organs do not have the architectural or manuscript contexts that might help to make sense of them. As they were portable objects, their meanings quite possibly changed as they moved around the world, comic, perhaps, in one space, but offensive in another. The vulva-pilgrims might be misogynist satires on women's alleged propensity for using pilgrimage as an excuse to wander away from home.[67] The processional version has been read as a parody of the cult of the holy wounds, or of the cult of the Virgin.[68] If the latter, then the misogynist equation of the Virgin and the vagina might have appealed to John Skylan, an English Lollard who surely made the same association in mocking "the Lefdy of Foulpette," though the motif is not known to have circulated in England.[69] The legged, winged, and riding forms of the badges emphasize mobility, and they have been plausibly linked to fabliau narratives about the wanderings of detached genitals and to carnival culture.[70] A sexual organ that rebels against its owner to live an independent life would be a perfect mascot for carnival's licensed misrule and indulgence of the flesh, while the association with carnival would contain the badges within a clearly defined social space. A manuscript marginal drawing of a shapely young woman shooting down a winged and legged phallus closely resembling one badge design surely refers to some narrative in which the woman wishes to curb its mobility or keep it for herself (fig. 9.12). If the badges were worn during carnival periods, they might enable enactments of such stories in capture and ransom games like those played at Hocktide in England.[71]

Early examples of non-monumental exhibitionist figures appear in the margins of the Bayeux Embroidery. In the scene labeled "Ubi unus clericus et Ælfgyva," a sexual encounter of people identifiable to the tapestry's original audience, though unfortunately not to us, is represented with two different strategies of indirection (fig. 9.13). In the main panel we have the euphemistic visual language of gesture. If the common assimilation of female body with enclosing architecture applies, then the thrust of the cleric's arm through the elaborate pillars that fail to protect Ælfgyva is easily legible as sexual violation.[72] The sexual content of the image is also externalized onto the phallic homunculus in the margin, a figure similar to some of the exhibitionist carvings (though earlier than any surviving examples).[73] Here he is a profane and fleshly version of the tiny naked figure that represents the soul, or, in modern terms, a personified projection of the id. The little rude man is not just a sexual image but is also a hermeneutic indicator instructing the viewer to read sexuality into the scene.

FIGURE 9.12: Huntress and winged phallus. *Decretals of Gregory IX* (1392). MS lat 4014, fol. 1r. Bibliothèque nationale de France, Paris. By permission of the Bibliothèque nationale de France.

As the content is not too difficult to decode and there was evidently no absolute prohibition on depicting sexual organs, the reason for the indirection, I would suggest, is social decorum. The tradition of displacing sexuality onto the lower classes was long standing and is visualized in the famous February calendar picture of the duc de Berry's *Très riches heures*, in which a peasant couple, in their innocent animalistic fashion, expose their genitals as they warm themselves before a fire.[74] Identifiable aristocrats, however, even when being publicly slandered, are not to be represented in so explicit a fashion; their sexual bodies are externalized. Similarly, romance marginalia occasionally include sexual images far more explicit than anything in the main picture cycles.[75]

Images of nude, anatomically complete and naturally proportioned adult humans, though they existed, were not common. Both in their innocence and in their shame, Adam and Eve usually conceal their organs, as they do in the Holkham Bible picture book, where Adam's larger size and his facial hair indicate sexual difference (fig. 9.14). They present a facade of unbroken, undifferentiated skin, which makes them the obverse of the exaggeratedly genital exhibitionist figures. However, sexual organs themselves were clearly not taboo, since the detached, exaggerated, or monstrous phalluses and vulvas of the exhibitionist motifs must have been common sights. This disparity implies a perception of sexuality as a large, impersonal force not owned by any

FIGURE 9.13: A cleric and Ælfgyva. Bayeux, Bayeux
Embroidery (ca. 1080). By special permission of the
City of Bayeux.

individual human, and indeed susceptible to capture by others, in motifs such
as a woman harvesting phalluses from a tree.[76] Sex is typically displaced, assigned to other cultures, other classes, or other species. Such a view of sexuality
corresponds with the Augustinian identification of sex, specifically the erect
penis, as the site and sign of human imperfection and the disunity of the self.
It is not, however, limited to the theological or moral register but is expressed
also in popular and comic art and performance. Moralizing, satirical, carni-
valesque, and other instances of sexual imagery may be visually indistinguishable from one another. Though medieval viewers must have been accustomed
to decoding them, slippages of meaning must have been regular occurrences.

   None of the images discussed so far can be demonstrated to have been
intended to arouse: they depict sexuality without themselves being objects of
erotic interest. Arousal may have occurred, of course, but the possibility is not
articulated: hence, perhaps, the absence of any knowledge of erotic imagery in
penitential contexts. Nevertheless, a few images to which an intention to arouse
can more plausibly be attributed are recorded from the fifteenth century. Panel

FIGURE 9.14: Adam and Eve. Holkham Bible picture
book (1320–1330). MS Add. 47682, fol. 3v. British
Library, London. © The British Library Board.

paintings of nude bathing women by the Netherlandish masters Jan van Eyck
and Rogier van der Weyden are known to have existed. One van Eyck nude is
known from an early copy, but opinion is divided as to whether it had an erotic
purpose. Its originality makes its subject difficult to identify, and the numerous
interpretations of it range from simple erotica to an allegorical representation
of Chastity (fig. 9.15).[77] Other images seem to be opportunistic responses to
sexual material. One illuminated canon law text includes "perhaps the most
explicit extant medieval representations of sexual activity" illustrating canons
on impotence and rape (fig. 9.16).[78] These are not gratuitous, for they directly
illustrate the text and would have helped to fix it in readers' memories, but
their treatment of sexual activity is very direct. The sexual pictures are more
mimetic than the stylized gestures of conversation in the same sequences, and
more concerned to convey vigorous activity than other representations of sex.
Stylized depictions could have conveyed the meaning perfectly clearly, so it
seems reasonable to suppose that pleasure in sexual representations is in part
responsible for the nature of the image. These illustrations offer a celibate

FIGURE 9.15: Woman at her Toilet, unidentified artist (early-sixteenth century). Fogg Art Museum, Harvard Art Museum, Cambridge MA. © 2003 The Josef and Anni Albers Foundation/Artists Rights Society, New York. Photo: David Mathews © President and Fellows of Harvard College.

clerical readership a window onto a realm of experience, the sexual lives of the laity, which they were required to regulate without any firsthand knowledge. In a comparable textual instance, it has been suggested that the sexual content of legal proceedings might constitute "voyeuristic erotica" for the celibate court recorders.[79] The book itself does not thereby become a pornographic object, and the vast majority of its illustrations are not sexual. Its function is to teach canon law, but aesthetic and visual pleasures, including those of looking at sexual pictures, are not incompatible with that function.

In some devotional contexts, sexual appeal may be more fundamental to the work of the image. Eros is a central concern of several biblical and hagiographical narratives. The martyrdoms of the saints offer scope for masochistic pleasures, and some visualizations of them seem coded for erotic response.[80]

FIGURE 9.16: Rape narrative. Gratian's *Decretum* (1310–1330). MS 262, fol. 137r. Fitzwilliam Museum, Cambridge. By permission of the Fitzwilliam Museum.

St. Lawrence in the Boucicaut Hours languidly reclines on his griddle, displaying as yet unblemished white flesh, accessorized with silken cords around his ankles and a rather fetching halo (fig. 9.17). A shadow emphasizes the pubic area, inviting the viewer to imagine the concealed genitals pressed firmly against the metal of the griddle. A determined phalanx of torturers advances, staring intensely at his body and wielding phallic weapons, with which one punctures a plump buttock. Lawrence's attention, meanwhile, is directed toward the manuscript's owner, represented by the heraldry carried by angels. Images of Susannah and Bathsheba spied upon as they bathe allow the viewer to identify with the voyeur and thus to re-enact these narratives' sequence of arousal followed by contrition or shame. The lost van Eyck nude may be a version of Bathsheba: if so, it has been detached from its narrative context, presumably for its visual appeal, and would thus represent one of the period's few examples of primarily erotic art in a format that might plausibly be kept in a private chamber (fig. 9.15).[81] Its subject, however, is conspicuously modest: her eyes are downcast as recommended by conduct literature, her loose hair

FIGURE 9.17: Boucicaut Master, St. Lawrence.
Boucicaut Hours (1405–1408). MS 2, fol. 20v.
Musée Jacquemart-André, Institut de France, Paris.

denotes virginity, and her hand covers her genitals. To take erotic pleasure in
beholding her would be violatory, but then perhaps the violation is the pleasure.
A naked Susannah stands out as the only Old Testament figure in a book of
prayers to the saints made for a woman, perhaps Mary of Cleves (fig. 9.18).[82]
Visual pleasure in Susannah's nakedness must have been compatible with emu-
lation of her as a model of female virtue. The figure has a certain ambiguity: her
modest pose and unawareness of the voyeurs behind her speak of her chastity,
but the bath she sits in figures an open vaginal channel. It has been argued that
private reading, an increasingly common practice from the fourteenth century
onward, stimulated the production of such scenes.[83] However, eroticized treatments of these narratives may also occur in illustrated Bibles.[84] And although
most Books of Hours and Psalters were privately owned, they were not secret:
while the books usually belonged to, and were made to suit, a particular owner,
they could be viewed by other household and family members and were dis-
played and bequeathed as prestige objects. The Boucicaut Hours, for example,
was a joint commission from a husband and wife, and its profusion of heraldry

FIGURE 9.18: Susannah bathing. Prayers to the Saints (fifteenth century). MS Egerton 859, fol. 31r. British Library, London. © The British Library Board.

bolstered Marshal Boucicaut's claim to noble status.[85] There is nothing furtive about their eroticism, which is an element of their devotional function.

Eros and religion fuse even more closely, in the visual arts as in literature, in mystical love for God. The Rothschild Canticles image of the spiritual marriage is not in the least explicit, but it is powerfully erotic, "reminiscent of Bernini's St. Teresa or depictions of Zeus descending to Danaë (fig. 9.19)."[86] The sponsa, the figure who stands in for the likely female religious owner of the book, is actively yearning, extending her limbs, wriggling her body and smiling broadly in joyous anticipation of her Bridegroom. Her bedclothes outline her open thighs. A sunburst of divine light energetically penetrates the gap between heaven and bedchamber, reaching out to her with its tendrils. Allegorically, the bed may signify spiritual receptivity, but literalization of the metaphor here produces an image of the kind of somatic mystical experience that Margery Kempe enjoyed with a fully corporeal Jesus, who told her that "most I nedys be homly [intimate] wyth the & lyn in thi bed wyth the."[87] The mystical beguine

FIGURE 9.19: Spiritual marriage. Rothschild
Canticles (ca. 1300). MS 404, fol. 66r. Yale
Collection of American Literature, Beinecke
Rare Book and Manuscript Library, Yale Uni-
versity, New Haven, CT.

Marguerite Porete, adapting the narrative of Candace and Alexander as an
allegory of mystical desire, writes that a princess "had a picture painted to
represent the likeness of the king whom she loved, as near as she could to the
appearance under which she loved him."[88] This makes two significant depar-
tures from its romance source. This image is unambiguously a two-dimensional painting, thus avoiding the appearance of idolatry. And Porete's princess
does not take a likeness but has the picture painted to her own specification.
She generates her own object of desire, which is sufficient in itself, for Porete
omits the scene in which Alexander is brought to face his own image and the
ensuing consummation. The picture, then, is a full substitute for the beloved,
not a temporary representation of him. For God's lovers, as for Pygmalion and
Candace, love of an artifact may be preliminary to love of its referent, but since
consummation of the love of God, except for rare and precious moments of
mystical union, was deferred until the next life, the preliminary stage became

an important cultural formation in its own right. Hence it is love for God that produces the best documented use of erotic imagery in the medieval West.

Modern viewers do not tend to think of a crucifix as an erotic subject: indeed, to sexualize a crucifix is a reliable trigger of outrage.[89] Nevertheless, it was the primary erotic image of the Middle Ages. Crucifix devotion brings to the forefront the erotic layer of the figure by which the Crucifixion was the consummation of Christ's marriage to the church. Pauper, a mendicant priest, instructs Dives, a layman, how to train his emotions onto the image of God incarnate:

> Take heid how naked and pore he hyng vpon the tree for thin synne and thin sake and be thu nought ashamyd to suffryn pouert and myschef for his love. And as Seynt Bernard byddyt [instructs], take heid be the ymage how his heid is bowyd doun to the, redy to kyssyn the and comyn at on wyt [become united with] the. See how hese armys and hese hondys been spred abrod on the tree in tokene that he is redy to fangyn the and halsyn the [take hold of and embrace you] and kyssyn the and takyn the to his mercy. See how his side was openyd and his herte clouyn in too in tokene that his herte is always opyn to the, redy to louyn the and foryeuyn [forgive] the.[90]

Dives is to gaze intensely at the naked body of Christ, focusing on every part of his body (with one exception—the genital region is discreetly passed over), imagining its desire to hold, touch, kiss, unite with him.[91] Christ is his mirror: both the active lover and the beloved object, gazed at and entered into via the hole in his side. This hole, in some images, becomes detached from the body, a free-floating and often distinctly vulval orifice into which the devotee is invited to enter.[92] In the course of this scrutiny, Dives produces Christ's desire for him and comes to know himself as beloved and forgiven. Such an exchange of gazes might itself constitute a form of bodily union, a visual experience that "penetrates, inflames and transforms, leaving an indelible impression on the beholder's soul."[93] No wonder that, as Dives remarks, worshippers showed strong emotion in front of crucifixes: "thei staryn and lokyn on the ymage wyt wepyngge eye. They heldyn vp here hondys, they bunchyn [beat] here brestys."[94] Erotic and spiritual affect here are indistinguishable: to be kissed by Christ is to be forgiven by him. Opportunities to experience such pleasures were plentiful, for every parish church had a life-size rood, and wealthy individuals owned portable images of Christ that could travel with them or be worn as jewelry.[95]

Affection for crucifixes was expressed through touch as well as sight. A Lollard tract deplores the behavior of devotees who could be seen in front of cult images, overcome by the emotions described by Dives, "strokande and kyssand these olde stones and stokkis."[96] Liturgy required priests to kiss the image of the Crucifixion in the Missal: in several extant books the image has been worn away by the repeated touch of lip to skin.[97] It required the laity to kiss Christ's image on paxes. And the crucifixes themselves might be revealed to be not just representations, but active agents that returned their worshippers' affections and caresses. Catherine of Siena's visionary stigmatization was understood and depicted as a penetration by rays emanating from a crucifix, and the crucifix in question remains a cult object to this day (fig. 9.20).[98] In this panel Catherine's outstretched arms imitate those of Christ, and the lines of her clothing form a hollow, ready to receive the figure that leans toward her with such energy that it seems to be about to topple into her arms. Though the actual crucifix was of the two-dimensional iconic type, Giovanni di Paolo represents its uncanny power by showing a naturalistic and three-dimensional figure.[99] The power of Christ's presence was such

FIGURE 9.20: Stigmatization of St. Catherine of Siena, Giovanni di Paolo (ca. 1460–1465). Metropolitan Museum of Art, New York. By permission of the Metropolitan Museum of Art.

that any artifactual image or Eucharistic manifestation of him might convert to the full bodily form. If a crucifix figure might bleed when it was attacked, as occurred in a common miracle story, then it might equally embrace when it was loved.[100] Gazing at an artifact such as the life-sized polychrome Spanish rood figure (fig. 9.21), how easy it would be to see Christ's eyes flickering to open, his limbs trembling with the effort to break free of the crucifix to caress the devotee kneeling at his feet. Indeed, some figures were made with jointed movable limbs, which could be manipulated to provoke just this effect.[101] In Robert Mannyng's *Handlyng Synne*, a knight is rewarded as he prays before a crucifix:

> The crucyfyx, that there was leyd,
> Hys armes fro the cros vpbreyd [raised],
> And clepd the chylde [embraced the knight] hym betwyx,
> And aftyrward kyst hym, that crucyfyx
>
> ....

FIGURE 9.21: Corpus of Christ (thirteenth century). Art Institute of Chicago. Photo © The Art Institute of Chicago.

Of this chylde was grete selkouthe [wonder]
That the crucyfyx kyst wyth mouthe.
Natheles, forsothe and ywys
Y trowe that yn hys herte were moche blys.[102]

Some clerics attempted to draw a line between acceptable and unaccept-
able affections for the crucifix: St. Bernardino of Siena denounced one
devotee who had "sensually and repulsively polluted and defiled himself" in
the course of his worship.[103] Others, however, exploited sensual responses
to Christ's humanity. In the late-fourteenth century the monks of Meaux
Abbey, Yorkshire, correctly calculated that women pilgrims would be attracted to a crucifix with a "beautiful image" of Christ, sculpted from a live
nude model.[104] Love for the crucified Christ was normally bodily, affective,
and erotic, and evidently was also, for an unknown proportion of devotees,
sexual. We have come full circle from fear of idolatry to intense affect and
physical caresses directed at statues of a naked god. Indeed, some cycles of
images acknowledge the formal similarity of idolatry and adoration. The
idol in the Rohan Hours scene (fig. 9.1) shares the fair coloring and elongated proportions of Christ in the same manuscript, and its pointed toes,
useless for standing on a pillar, recall Christ's nailed feet.[105]

The gender asymmetry of modern Western pornography, most of which is
still based on the traditional model of male viewer and female object, does not
apply to medieval erotic art. A few images were restricted to male viewers,
but many more were on public display. Augustine and Gerson's protests indicate a particular anxiety about phallic display, and the viriliphobic strand of
medieval visual culture is evident in treatments of the nakedness of Noah.[106]
However, phalluses could be depicted, male bodies could be eroticized, and
the problems of erotic looking were also explored in depictions of Susannah and Bathsheba. Male bodies were as likely to be eroticized as female,
but the prime site of affective gazing was the body of Christ. The gender of
Christ's exuding, penetrable body is fluid, and it is equally available to male
and female devotees. There was no restricted zone for erotic images: erotic
and non-erotic images coexisted in the same manuscripts and sculptural pro-
grams, and demonstrative affection for devotional images was performed in
public.

Christianity, though it did not govern all forms of erotic art, enabled as
well as inhibited. Some artifacts were experienced as fully present. Thomas
Aquinas's authoritative analysis of religious art argued that "The worship of
religion is paid to images, not as considered in themselves, nor as things, but

as images leading us to God incarnate. Now movement to an image as image does not stop at the image, but goes on to the thing it represents."[107] This belief in the power of the image to access God is evident in the stories of crucifixes embracing their worshippers, but these stories add an engagement with the materiality of the image that Thomas's theory does not anticipate, and that undermines the strict distinction between image and referent on which it depends. When people loved crucifix images, they loved them for being both the absent Christ and the material object that permitted access to him. Medieval erotic art, at its most powerful, enriched the category of Eros and exceeded the category of art.

NOTES

Chapter 1

I would like to thank Matthew Bardowell, Barbara Newman, Julie Peakman, Sarah Salih, Jonathan Sawday, and Damian Smith for their invaluable help.

Quotations from the Bible in this chapter are from the Douay-Rheims translation (1582–1609), which uses St. Jerome's Vulgate chapter and verse numbering and is closest to the (Latin) Bible known to the Middle Ages.

1. Gail Hawkes, *Sex and Pleasure in Western Culture* (Cambridge: Polity Press, 2004), 43.
2. Quoted in Alcuin Blamires, ed., *Woman Defamed and Woman Defended: An Anthology of Medieval Texts,* with Karen Pratt and C. W. Marx (Oxford: Clarendon Press, 1992), 51.
3. The most notable are those of the early humanist Italian writer Christine de Pizan: her riposte to the cleric Matheolus's anti-feminist *Lamentations: The Book of the City of Ladies* (1405) and the letters she exchanged with leading intellectuals of her day between 1400 and 1402 that form part of the so-called *querelle de la rose*: Christine de Pizan, *The Book of the City of Ladies*, trans. Rosalind Brown-Grant (London: Penguin, 1999), xxvi.
4. Augustine of Hippo, *City of God*, trans. Henry Bettenson, ed. David Knowles (London: Penguin, 1980), 584.
5. Ibid., 591.
6. Ibid., 587.
7. Ibid., 522.
8. Augustine of Hippo, *Confessions*, trans. R. S. Pine-Coffin (London: Penguin, 1961), 86.
9. Joseph Bristow, *Sexuality* (London: Routledge, 1997), 171. Anna Clark rather uncritically purveys the view that desire was viewed in the Middle Ages as an "overwhelming force." Anna Clark, *Desire: A History of European Sexuality* (New York: Routledge, 2008), 64.

10. Gratian, *On Marriage*, trans. Paul Hyams (Internet Medieval Sourcebook, 1999), C.32 q.2 c.2, http://www.fordham.edu/halsall/source/gratian1.html (accessed December 30, 2009).

11. Chaucer, *The Riverside Chaucer*, "The Wife of Bath's Prologue," lines 603–623, p. 113.

12. Joan Cadden, *Meanings of Sex Difference in the Middle Ages: Medicine, Science, and Culture* (Cambridge: Cambridge University Press, 1993), 273; Caroline Walker Bynum, "Why All the Fuss about the Body? A Medievalist's Perspective," *Critical Inquiry* 22 (1995): 7. See also Danielle Jacquart and Claude Thomasset, *Sexuality and Medicine in the Middle Ages* (Princeton, NJ: Princeton University Press, 1988), 83–138.

13. Pierre J. Payer, "Sex and Confession in the Thirteenth Century," in *Sex in the Middle Ages: A Book of Essays*, ed. Joyce E. Salisbury (New York: Garland, 1991), 132; Cadden, *Meanings of Sex Difference in the Middle Ages,* 275.

14. Eve Levin, *Sex and Society in the World of the Orthodox Slavs, 900–1700* (Ithaca, NY: Cornell University Press, 1989), 5, 37.

15. Everett Rowson, "Homoerotic Liaisons among the Mamluk Elite in Late Medieval Egypt and Syria," in *Islamicate Sexualities: Translations across Temporal Geographies of Desire*, ed. Kathryn Babayan and Afsaneh Najmabadi, Harvard Middle Eastern Monographs (Cambridge, MA: Harvard University Press, 2008), 205.

16. David M. Halperin, "Is There a History of Sexuality?" in *The Lesbian and Gay Studies Reader*, ed. Henry Abelove, Michèle A. Barale, and David M. Halperin (New York: Routledge, 1993), 420.

17. Robert Padgug, "Sexual Matters: On Conceptualizing Sexuality in History," *Radical History Review* 20 (1979): 16.

18. A point forcibly made by Karma Lochrie, *Heterosyncrasies: Female Sexuality When Normal Wasn't* (Minneapolis: University of Minnesota Press, 2005), 1–25. See also Karma Lochrie, Peggy McCracken, and James A. Schultz, eds., *Constructing Medieval Sexuality* (Minneapolis: University of Minnesota Press, 1997), ix; David M. Halperin, "Forgetting Foucault: Acts, Identities, and the History of Sexuality," *Representations* 63 (1998): 96–97; Ruth Mazo Karras, "Prostitution and the Question of Sexual Identity in Medieval Europe," *Journal of Women's History* 11, no. 2 (1999): 159–77.

19. Pierre J. Payer, *Sex and the Penitentials: The Development of a Sexual Code, 550–1150* (Toronto: University of Toronto Press, 1984), 141.

20. James Schultz, *Courtly Love, the Love of Courtliness, and the History of Sexuality* (Chicago: University of Chicago Press, 2006), 189. For a vigorous defense of modern psychoanalytic approaches to the past, see Nancy F. Partner, "Did Mystics Have Sex?" in *Desire and Discipline: Sex and Sexuality in the Premodern West,* ed. Jacqueline Murray and Konrad Eisenbichler (Toronto: University of Toronto Press, 1996). See also Robert Mills, "A Man Is Being Beaten," *New Medieval Literatures* 5 (2002): 115–53.

21. Michel Foucault, *The History of Sexuality,* vol. 1: *An Introduction*, trans. Robert Hurley (London: Penguin, 1979); Louise Fradenburg and Carla Freccero, eds., *Premodern Sexualities* (New York: Routledge, 1996), vii; Halperin, "Forgetting Foucault."

22. Simon Gaunt, "Straight Minds/'Queer' Wishes in Old French Hagiography: *La vie de Sainte Euphrosine,*" in Fradenburg and Freccero, *Premodern Sexualities,* 157; Sarah Salih, "Sexual Identities: A Medieval Perspective," in *Sodomy in Early Modern Europe,* ed. Tom Betteridge (Manchester, UK: Manchester University Press, 2002), 112–30; Hugh Kennedy, "Al-Jāhiz and the Construction of Homosexuality at the Abbasid Court," in *Medieval Sexuality: A Casebook,* ed. April Harper and Caroline Proctor (London: Routledge, 2008), 186. Karras, "Prostitution and the Question of Sexual Identity in Medieval Europe," argues that the prostitute constituted a medieval sexual identity; for a refutation, see Theo van der Meer, "Medieval Prostitution and the Case of a (Mistaken) Sexual Identity," *Journal of Women's History* 11, no. 2 (1999): 178–85, and for a modification, see Carla Freccero, "Acts, Identities, and Sexuality's (Pre)Modern Regimes," *Journal of Women's History* 11, no. 2 (1999): 186–92.

23. Margery Kempe, *The Book of Margery Kempe,* ed. Sanford Brown Meech and Hope Emily Allen, EETS os 212 (London: Oxford University Press, 1940), 14–15.

24. Kempe's favored self-description.

25. Pierre J. Payer, *Sex and the New Medieval Literature of Confession, 1150–1300* (Toronto: Pontifical Institute of Mediaeval Studies, 2009), 190.

26. Michelle Sauer, "Representing the Negative: Positing the Lesbian Void in Medieval Anchoritism," *Thirdspace* 3, no. 2 (2004), http://www.thirdspace.ca/journal/article/view/sauer/178 (accessed December 31, 2009).

27. Ruth Mazo Karras, *Sexuality in Medieval Europe: Doing unto Others* (New York: Routledge, 2005), 150.

28. Edward Wheatley, "A River Runs through It: Disability, Homosexuality, Queered/Disabled Discourse, and the Isle of Blandie in *Bérinus,*" *Exemplaria* 19, no. 3 (2007): 386–401.

29. Irina Metzler, *Disability in Medieval Europe: Thinking about Physical Impairment in the High Middle Ages, c. 1100–c. 1400* (London: Routledge, 2006), 89, 123.

30. John Baldwin, "Five Discourses on Desire: Sexuality and Gender in Northern France around 1200," *Speculum* 66, no. 4 (1991): 797.

31. This volume, 41. The categories *contiugati, continents,* and *virgins* are taken from ibid., 797.

32. Quoted in Blamires, *Woman Defamed and Woman Defended,* 64–66. See also 1 Cor. 7:25.

33. Dyan Elliott, *Fallen Bodies: Pollution, Sexuality, and Demonology in the Middle Ages* (Philadelphia: University of Pennsylvania Press, 1999), 47.

34. Bella Millett and Jocelyn Wogan-Browne, eds. and trans., *Medieval English Prose for Women from the Katherine Group and Ancrene Wisse* (Oxford: Clarendon Press, 1990), 20.

35. Quoted in Vern L. Bullough, "Medieval Medical and Scientific Views of Women," *Viator* 4 (1973): 499. The same idea was expressed later by St. Ambrose: "She who does not believe is a woman and should be designated by the name of her bodily sex, whereas she who believes progresses to complete manhood." Quoted in ibid.

36. Vern L. Bullough, "Sex Education in Medieval Christianity," *Journal of Sex Research* 13, no. 3 (1977): 190. Other famous bearded female saints are St. Galla and St. Paula. Ibid., 191.

37. Elliott, *Fallen Bodies,* 49.

38. Levin, *Sex and Society in the World of the Orthodox Slavs,* 59.

39. Ibid., 248–49.

40. Gratian, *On Marriage,* C. 32 q. 2 c. 2.

41. Gratian, *Marriage Canons from* The Decretum *of Gratian,* trans. John T. Noonan Jr., ed. Augustine Thompson, 1993, C. 31 q.1 c.10. http://faculty.cua.edu/Pennington/Canon%20Law/marriagelaw.htm (accessed December 30, 2009).

42. Oration 37, in *Cyril of Jerusalem, Gregory Nazianzen,* vol. 7, *Nicene and Post-Nicene Fathers: Second Series,* ed. Philip Schaff and Rev. Henry Wallace (New York: Cosimo, 2007), chap. 8.

43. Anthony Davies, "Sexual Behaviour in Later Anglo-Saxon England," in *This Noble Craft: Proceedings of the Xth Research Symposium of the Dutch and Belgian University Teachers of Old and Middle English and Historical Linguistics, Utrecht, 19–20 January 1989,* ed. E. Kooper (Amsterdam: Rodopi, 1991), 93.

44. Georgina E. Brereton and Janet M. Ferrier, eds., *Le mesnagier de Paris* (Paris: Librairie Générale Française, 1994), 296 (translation mine).

45. Diane Watt, *The Paston Women: Selected Letters* (Cambridge: Brewer, 2004), 113–14. On the role of marriage in cementing the alliances of families, see Christiane Klapisch-Zuber, "Women and the Family," in *The Medieval World,* ed. Jacques Le Goff, trans. Lydia G. Cochrane (London: Collins & Brown, 1990), 287–92.

46. Watt, *The Paston Women,* 96–97.

47. Michael Sheehan, *Marriage, Family, and Law in Medieval Europe: Collected Studies,* ed. James K. Farge (Cardiff: University of Wales Press, 1996), 39–40.

48. Jeremy Goldberg, "Gender and Matrimonial Litigation in the Church Courts in the Later Middle Ages: The Evidence of the Court of York," *Gender & History* 19, no. 1 (2007): 48.

49. Dyan Elliott, *Spiritual Marriage: Sexual Abstinence in Medieval Wedlock* (Princeton, NJ: Princeton University Press, 1993), 4.

50. Ibid., 208–9.

51. Kempe, *The Book of Margery Kempe,* especially 23–25.

52. Elliott, *Spiritual Marriage,* 10.

53. Jerome, *Adversus Jovinianum,* PL 23, 1845, 1.49, 294.

54. Kempe, *The Book of Margery Kempe,* 181.

55. Schultz, *Courtly Love,* 157.

56. Foucault, *The History of Sexuality,* vol. 1, 33.

57. Simon Gaunt, "Marginal Men, Marcabru and Orthodoxy: The Early Troubadours and Adultery," *Medium Ævum* 59 (1990): 55, argues that one context for courtly love is conflicting lay and church models of marriage in the twelfth century.

58. Sarah Kay, *Courtly Contradictions: The Emergence of the Literary Object in the Twelfth Century* (Stanford, CA: Stanford University Press, 2001), 1.

59. Felicity Riddy, "Engendering Pity in the *Franklin's Tale*," in *Feminist Readings in Middle English Literature*, ed. Ruth Evans and Lesley Johnson (London: Routledge, 1994), 59.

60. For a facsimile edition, see Stephanie Viereck Gibbs and Kathryn Karczewska, *The Book of the Love-Smitten Heart* (New York: Routledge, 2001).

61. Carolyn Dinshaw, "'A Kiss Is Just a Kiss': Heterosexuality and Its Consolations in *Sir Gawain and the Green Knight*," *diacritics* 24, no. 2–3 (1994): 205–26; C. Stephen Jaeger, *Ennobling Love: In Search of a Lost Sensibility* (Philadelphia: University of Pennsylvania Press, 1999); Tison Pugh, ed., *Queering Medieval Genres*, The New Middle Ages (New York: Palgrave Macmillan, 2004); William Burgwinkle, *Sodomy, Masculinity, and Law in Medieval Literature: France and England, 1050–1230* (Cambridge: Cambridge University Press, 2004), who also notes the "improper gendering" of the hind in Marie de France's *Guigemar*; Anna Kłosowska, *Queer Love in the Middle Ages*, The New Middle Ages (Basingstoke, UK: Palgrave Macmillan, 2005).

62. Kłosowska, *Queer Love in the Middle Ages,* 133–34.

63. Gayle Margherita, *The Romance of Origins: Language and Sexual Difference in Middle English Literature* (Philadelphia: University of Pennsylvania Press, 1994), 122.

64. Reay Tannahill, *Sex in History* (London: Hamish Hamilton, 1980), 158–59.

65. Mark Jordan, *The Invention of Sodomy in Christian Theology* (Chicago: University of Chicago Press, 1997), 35.

66. Ibid., 29.

67. Peter Damian, *Book of Gomorrah: An Eleventh-century Treatise against Clerical Homosexual Practices*, ed. and trans. Pierre J. Payer (Waterloo, Ont., Canada: Wilfrid Laurier University Press, 1982), 29.

68. Translated by Cary Howie, *Claustrophilia: The Erotics of Enclosure in Medieval Literature* (Basingstoke, UK: Palgrave Macmillan, 2007), 75 with my addition.

69. Burgwinkle, *Sodomy, Masculinity, and Law in Medieval Literature,* 59.

70. Ibid., 51.

71. Thomas Aquinas, *Summa theologica*, 2.2.154.11.

72. Levin, *Sex and Society in the World of the Orthodox Slavs,* 199.

73. Ibid., 16. On the connections between sodomy and heresy, see Carolyn Dinshaw, *Getting Medieval: Sexualities and Communities, Pre- and Postmodern* (Durham, NC: Duke University Press, 1999), 55–99.

74. Fradenburg and Freccero, *Premodern Sexualities,* vii.

75. Karras, *Sexuality in Medieval Europe,* 139.

76. John Boswell, *Christianity, Social Tolerance, and Homosexuality: Gay People in Western Europe from the Beginning of the Christian Era to the Fourteenth Century* (Chicago: University of Chicago Press, 1980), 295.

77. Bruce Holsinger, "Sodomy and Resurrection: The Homoerotic Subject of the *Divine Comedy*," in Fradenburg and Freccero, *Premodern Sexualities*, 247.

78. Jordan, *The Invention of Sodomy in Christian Theology*, 1–9.

79. Kennedy, "Al-Jāhiz and the Construction of Homosexuality," 186.

80. Ibid., 181.

81. Ibid., 186.

82. Diane Watt, *Amoral Gower* (Minneapolis: University of Minnesota Press, 2003), 75.

83. Helmut Puff, "Female Sodomy: The Trial of Katherina Hetzeldorfer (1477)," *Journal of Medieval and Early Modern Studies* 30, no. 1 (2000): 41. Puff coins the term "female sodomy" to fill what he describes as "the terminological void" (41), but his work concerns the period after 1450.

84. For Jacqueline Murray, medieval lesbians are "twice marginal and twice invisible" ("Twice Marginal and Twice Invisible: Lesbians in the Middle Ages," in *Handbook of Medieval Sexuality*, ed. Vern L. Bullough and James A. Brundage [New York: Garland, 1996], 191–221), but the so-called myth of lesbian impunity has been challenged: Carol Lansing, "Donna con Donna? A 1295 Inquest into Female Sodomy," *Studies in Medieval and Renaissance History,* 3rd ser., 2 (2005): 109.

85. Bernadette Brooten, *Love between Women: Early Christian Responses to Female Homoeroticism* (Chicago: University of Chicago Press, 1996), 5.

86. Quoted in Murray, "Twice Marginal and Twice Invisible," 196.

87. Allen Frantzen, *The Literature of Penance in Anglo-Saxon England* (New Brunswick, NJ: Rutgers University Press, 1983), 66–67.

88. Sauer, "Representing the Negative."

89. Levin, *Sex and Society in the World of the Orthodox Slavs,* 203.

90. Lansing, "Donna con Donna?"

91. Judith Bennett, "'Lesbian-Like' and the Social History of Lesbianisms," *Journal of the History of Sexuality* 9 (2000): 3; Cadden, *Meanings of Sex Difference in the Middle Ages,* 224; Edith Benkov, "The Erased Lesbian: Sodomy and the Legal Tradition in Medieval Europe," in *Same Sex Love and Desire among Women in the Middle Ages,* ed. Francesca Canadé Sautman and Pamela Sheingorn (New York: Palgrave, 2001), 101–22. On the trial of Katherina Hetzeldorfer, see Puff, "Female Sodomy."

92. Bennett, "'Lesbian-Like' and the Social History of Lesbianisms," 9–10.

93. Ibid., 20.

94. Mario Sensi, "Anchorites in the Italian Tradition," trans. Ruth Evans, in *Anchoritic Traditions of Medieval Europe*, ed. Liz Herbert McAvoy (Woodbridge, UK: Boydell & Brewer, 2010).

95. Quoted in Jeremy Goldberg, "John Skathelok's Dick: Voyeurism and 'Pornography' in Late Medieval England," in *Medieval Obscenities*, ed. Nicola McDonald (Woodbridge, UK: York Medieval Press, 2006), 115.

96. Sauer, "Representing the Negative." On the erotic possibilities of "claustrophilia" ("a particularly intense and necessarily ambivalent erotic relationship with enclosed space, a relationship that hinges upon the metonymic touching between bodies and the spaces that contain and articulate them"), see Howie, *Claustrophilia,* 40.

97. John Boswell, "Old Habits, New Habits," *New Republic,* January 6, 1986: 36.

98. Caroline Walker Bynum, *Fragmentation and Redemption: Essays on Gender and the Human Body in Medieval Religion* (New York: Zone, 1992), 85–88. On medieval nuns expressing same-sex desire in kissing Christ's wounds, see Karma Lochrie, "Mystical Acts, Queer Tendencies," in Lochrie, McCracken, and Schultz, *Constructing Medieval Sexuality.*

99. E. Ann Matter, "My Sister, My Spouse: Woman-Identified Women in Medieval Christianity," *Journal of Feminist Studies in Religion* 2, no. 1 (1986): 81–93; Kathy Lavezzo, "Sobs and Sighs between Women: The Homoerotics of Compassion in *The Book of Margery Kempe,*" in Fradenburg and Freccero, *Premodern Sexualities*; Ulrike Wiethaus, "Female Homoerotic Discourse and Religion in Medieval Germanic Culture," in *Gender and Difference in the Middle Ages*, ed. Sharon Farmer and Carol Braun Pasternack, Medieval Cultures 32 (Minneapolis: University of Minnesota Press, 2003); Susannah Chewning, ed., *Intersections of Sexuality and the Divine in Medieval Culture: The Word Made Flesh* (Aldershot, UK: Ashgate, 2005); Kłosowska, *Queer Love in the Middle Ages*; Sahar Amer, *Crossing Borders: Love between Women in Medieval French and Arabic Literatures* (Philadelphia: University of Pennsylvania Press, 2008); Sahar Amer, "Cross-Dressing and Female Same-Sex Marriage in Medieval French and Arabic Literatures," in Babayan and Najmabadi, *Islamicate Sexualities*, 114–60. Amer's readings of cross-dressed women marrying women in French literary texts are importantly refracted through the lens of medieval Arabic homoerotic poetry, though her critical framework is not without problems: see Brad Epps, "Comparison, Competition, and Cross-Dressing: Cross-Cultural Analysis in a Contested World," in Babayan and Najmabadi, *Islamicate Sexualities*.

100. *Metamorphoses*, 9:666–797; Watt, *Amoral Gower*, 73–74.

101. Quoted in in Murray, "Twice Marginal and Twice Invisible," 210, trans. Robert L. A. Clark. See also Karras, *Sexuality in Medieval Europe*, 110.

102. Victoria Bonnell, Lynn Avery Hunt, and Richard Biernacki, *Beyond the Cultural Turn: New Directions in the Study of Society and Culture* (Berkeley: University of California Press, 1999), 254.

103. The single most important reason for the rejection of female romantic friendship in the antique and early Christian period: Brooten, *Love between Women*, 359.

104. Quoted in Murray, "Twice Marginal and Twice Invisible," 210, trans. Robert L. A. Clark.

105. Lansing, "Donna con Donna?" 111.

106. Elliott, *Fallen Bodies*, 15.

107. Guibert of Nogent, *Self and Society in Modern France: The Memoirs of Abbot-Guibert of Nogent*, ed. John F. Benton (Toronto: Medieval Academy of America, 2002), bk. 1, chap. 26, 115.

108. Foucault's use of the term "peripheral sexualities" to describe a range of sexual categories that emerged after the eighteenth century seems a more apt, non-pathologizing term for describing medieval sexualities than the clinical word "perversions." Foucault, *The History of Sexuality*, vol. 1, 39.

109. James A. Brundage, *Law, Sex, and Christian Society in Medieval Europe* (Chicago: University of Chicago Press, 1987), 207. For an overview of medieval bestiality, see Joyce E. Salisbury, "Bestiality in the Middle Ages," in Salisbury, *Sex in the Middle Ages*.

110. Salisbury, "Bestiality in the Middle Ages," 178–79.

111. Goldberg, "John Skathelok's Dick," 122.

112. Christiane Klapisch-Zuber, quoted in ibid., 112.

113. Karras, *Sexuality in Medieval Europe*, 111. On medieval cross-dressing, see Valerie Hotchkiss, *Clothes Make the Man: Female Cross Dressing in Medieval Europe* (New York: Garland, 1996).

114. Vern L. Bullough, "Transvestites in the Middle Ages," *American Journal of Sociology* 79, no. 6 (1974): 1390.

115. Rudolf Dekker and Lotte van de Pol, *The Tradition of Female Transvestism in Early Modern Europe* (New York: St. Martin's Press, 1989), 45.

116. The document is translated in Ruth Mazo Karras and David Lorenzo Boyd, "'*Ut cum muliere*': A Male Transvestite Prostitute in Fourteenth-Century London," in Fradenburg and Freccero, *Premodern Sexualities*, 111–12.

117. Ibid., 109.

118. Everett Rowson, "Gender Irregularity as Entertainment: Institutionalized Transvestism at the Caliphal Court in Medieval Baghdad," in Farmer and Pasternack, *Gender and Difference in the Middle Ages.*

119. Bynum, *Fragmentation and Redemption*, 184.

120. Giuseppe Garampi, *Memorie ecclesiastiche appartenenti all'istoria e al culto della B. Chiara di Rimini* (Rome: Palearini, 1755), 44–46, 234–40.

121. Burgwinkle, *Sodomy, Masculinity, and Law in Medieval Literature*, 60.

122. Bynum, *Fragmentation and Redemption*, 184. On women's extravagant ascetic practices, see further Caroline Walker Bynum, *Holy Feast and Holy Fast: The Religious Significance of Food to Medieval Women* (Berkeley: University of California Press, 1987).

123. On medieval scenes of beating, see Robert Mills, *Suspended Animation: Pain, Pleasure and Punishment in Medieval Culture* (London: Reaktion, 2005), 145–76. On martyrdom, pain, and pleasure, see Mills, "A Man Is Being Beaten"; on martyrdom and masochism, see Robert Mills, "'Whatever You Do Is a Delight to Me!' Masculinity, Masochism and Queer Play in Representations of Male Martyrdom," *Exemplaria* 13 (2001): 1–37.

124. William Burgwinkle, "État Présent: Queer Theory and the Middle Ages," *French Studies* 60, no. 1 (2006): 85.

125. See ibid., 63.

126. Ibid.

127. Suzanne Noffke, trans., *Catherine of Siena: The Dialogue*, The Classics of Western Spirituality (New York: Paulist Press, 1980), 30.

128. Ibid.

129. Guibert of Nogent, *Self and Society in Modern France*, 48.

130. Peter Abelard, *Historia Calamitatum*, in *The Letters of Abelard and Heloise*, trans. Betty Radice (Harmondsworth, UK: Penguin, 1974), 66–67.

131. Brian Murdoch, ed. and trans., *The Dedalus Book of Medieval Literature: The Grin of the Gargoyle* (Sawtry, UK: Dedalus, 1995), 82.

132. Ibid., 81.

133. Foucault, *The History of Sexuality*, vol. 1, 40.

134. Murdoch, *The Dedalus Book of Medieval Literature*, 81.

135. Foucault, *The History of Sexuality*, vol. 1, 43.

136. Kiev MS 191, fol. 164r, in Levin, *Sex and Society in the World of the Orthodox Slavs,* 30.

137. Payer, "Sex and Confession in the Thirteenth Century."

138. Frantzen, *The Literature of Penance,* 6, 138.

139. Ibid., 88.

140. See ibid., 56, and Davies, "Sexual Behaviour in Later Anglo-Saxon England," 84.

141. Davies, "Sexual Behaviour in Later Anglo-Saxon England," 92.

142. Frantzen, *The Literature of Penance,* 67.

143. Ibid., 138.

144. Levin, *Sex and Society in the World of the Orthodox Slavs,* 198.

145. Karras, *Sexuality in Medieval Europe,* 125.

146. Guido Ruggiero, *The Boundaries of Eros: Sex Crime and Sexuality in Renaissance Venice* (New York: Oxford University Press, 1985), 19–20.

147. Goldberg, "Gender and Matrimonial Litigation," 48.

148. Karras, *Sexuality in Medieval Europe,* 62. On incest and consanguinity, in law and literature, see Elizabeth Archibald, *Incest and the Medieval Imagination* (Oxford: Clarendon Press, 2001).

149. Davies, "Sexual Behaviour in Later Anglo-Saxon England," 89.

150. Levin, *Sex and Society in the World of the Orthodox Slavs,* 164.

151. Cadden, *Meanings of Sex Difference in the Middle Ages,* 279.

152. Ibid., 273.

153. Bullough, "Medieval Medical and Scientific Views of Women," 496.

154. Cadden, *Meanings of Sex Difference in the Middle Ages,* 97–98.

155. Thomas Laqueur, *Making Sex: Body and Gender from the Greeks to Freud* (Cambridge, MA: Harvard University Press, 1990). But the term has been much contested: see Cadden, *Meanings of Sex Difference in the Middle Ages,* 3.

156. Baldwin, "Five Discourses on Desire," 799; Cadden, *Meanings of Sex Difference in the Middle Ages,* 88–102.

157. Ibid., 70–88.

158. Ibid., 5–6; Roy Porter, *The Greatest Benefit to Mankind* (London: HarperCollins, 1997), 129. On medical literature directed at women, see Monica Green, "From 'Diseases of Women' to 'Secrets of Women': The Transformation of Gynecological Literature in the Later Middle Ages," *Journal of Medieval and Early Modern Studies* 30, no. 1 (2000): 5–39.

159. Cadden, *Meanings of Sex Difference in the Middle Ages,* 20.

160. Jacquart and Thomasset, *Sexuality and Medicine in the Middle Ages,* 44–47.

161. Cadden, *Meanings of Sex Difference in the Middle Ages,* 18.

162. Porter, *The Greatest Benefit to Mankind,* 130.

163. Quoted in Cadden, *Meanings of Sex Difference in the Middle Ages,* 65.

164. Ibid., 93–94.

165. Ibid., 95.

166. Quoted in Davies, "Sexual Behaviour in Later Anglo-Saxon England," 96.

167. Katherine Park, "Medicine and Magic: The Healing Arts," in *Gender and Society in Renaissance Italy*, ed. Judith C. Brown and Robert C. Davis (London: Addison Wesley, 1998).

168. Porter, *The Greatest Benefit to Mankind*, 166. On gonorrhea, see Cadden, *Meanings of Sex Difference in the Middle Ages*, 26–27.

169. Porter, *The Greatest Benefit to Mankind*, 122.

170. Ibid., 130. Sex with a menstruating woman was also thought to result in a still-born, leprous, or disabled child: Carole Rawcliffe, *Medicine and Society in Later Medieval England* (Stroud, UK: Sutton, 1995), 175.

171. J. A. Tasioulas, *The Makars: The Poems of Henryson, Dunbar, and Douglas* (Edinburgh: Canongate, 1999), 204.

172. Bynum, *Fragmentation and Redemption*, 151–65, 200–235.

173. Davies, "Sexual Behaviour in Later Anglo-Saxon England," 90.

174. Richard Kieckhefer, "Erotic Magic in Medieval Europe," in Salisbury, *Sex in the Middle Ages*, 31, 42, 30.

175. Valerie Edden, "Devils, Sermon Stories, and the Problem of Popular Belief in the Middle Ages," *Yearbook of English Studies* 22 (1992): 214.

176. *An Alphabet of Tales: An English 15th Century Translation of the* Alphabetum Narrationum *of Étienne de Besançon from Additional MS. 25,719 of the British Museum*, ed. Mary MacLeod Banks, EETS o.s. 126 and 127 (London: Kegan Paul, 1904), 94–95 (translation mine).

177. Glenn Davis, "The Exeter Book Riddles and the Place of Sexual Idiom in Old English Literature," in McDonald, *Medieval Obscenities*, 44.

178. Chaucer, *The Riverside Chaucer*, "The Parson's Tale," line 839, p. 317.

179. Elliott, *Spiritual Marriage*, 146.

180. Larry Scanlon, "Cultural Studies and Carnal Speech: The Long, Profane Shadow of the Fabliau," in *Medieval Cultural Studies*, ed. Ruth Evans, Helen Fulton, and David Matthews (Cardiff: University of Wales Press, 2006), 33; Baldwin, "Five Discourses on Desire," 799.

181. John Hines, *The Fabliau in English* (London: Longman, 1993), 24.

182. John DuVal, trans., *Fabliaux, Fair and Foul* (Binghamton, NY: Medieval and Renaissance Texts and Studies, 1992), 64.

183. Robert Harrison, trans., *Gothic Salt: Eighteen Fabliaux from the Old French* (Berkeley: University of California Press, 1974), 183.

184. DuVal, *Fabliaux, Fair and Foul*, 185.

185. George Philip Krapp and Elliott V. K. Dobbie, eds., *The Exeter Book*, The Anglo-Saxon Poetic Records 3 (New York: Columbia University Press, 1936). Numbers refer to the riddles in this edition. Translations are mine.

186. Steven F. Kruger, "Conversion and Medieval Sexual, Religious, and Racial Categories," in Lochrie, McCracken, and Schultz, *Constructing Medieval Sexuality*, 159. For a reading of the sexual riddles that emphasizes class, gender, and ethnicity as well as sexuality, see John W. Tanke, "*Wonfeax wale*: Ideology and Figuration in the Sexual Riddles of the Exeter Book," in *Class and Gender in Early English Literature: Intersections*, ed. Britton J. Harwood and Gillian R. Overing (Bloomington: Indiana University Press, 1994).

187. Davis, "The Exeter Book Riddles," 49, 54.

188. Dafydd Johnston, ed. and trans., *Medieval Welsh Erotic Poetry* (Cardiff: Tafol, 1991), 29.

189. Ibid., 37, 41–43.

190. Ibid., 19.

191. For example, Shakespeare's Sonnet 129: "Th'expense of spirit in a waste of shame/Is lust in action …"

192. Chaucer, *The Riverside Chaucer*, "The Shipman's Tale," line 379, p. 207.

193. Goldberg, "John Skathelok's Dick," 119.

194. See Elliott, *Fallen Bodies,* 14–34.

195. Ibid., 153.

196. Ibid., 162.

197. Katherine Crawford, *European Sexualities, 1400–1800* (Cambridge: Cambridge University Press, 2007), 191. For discussion of post-1400 "sodomitical subcultures" and a summary of views on late medieval and early modern identity formations, see 200–206.

198. The Latin anecdote is no. 114, *De Meretrice Conquerente De Tonsoris Maleficio,* in G. Francesco, ed., *The Facetiae or Jocose Tales of Poggio,* vol. 1 (Paris: Isidore Liseux, 1879). For a partial English translation of the *Facetiae* (but not of no. 114), see Edward Storer, trans., *The Facetiae of Poggio and Other Medieval Story-Tellers* (London: Routledge, 1928).

199. Karras, *Sexuality in Medieval Europe,* 106.

200. Cadden, *Meanings of Sex Difference in the Middle Ages,* 247.

201. Payer, *Sex and the Penitentials,* 38 and 60.

202. Karras and Boyd, "*Ut cum muliere,*" 104; Karras, *Sexuality in Medieval Europe,* 104.

203. Karras, *Sexuality in Medieval Europe,* 104; Payer, *Sex and the Penitentials,* 141; Karras and Boyd, "*Ut cum muliere,*" 105.

204. See Karras and Boyd, "*Ut cum muliere.*"

205. Davies, "Sexual Behaviour in Later Anglo-Saxon England," 93.

206. Karras, *Sexuality in Medieval Europe,* 104–5.

207. Davies, "Sexual Behaviour in Later Anglo-Saxon England," 95.

208. Karras, *Sexuality in Medieval Europe,* 106.

209. Ibid., 108.

210. Brundage, *Law, Sex, and Christian Society,* 346, 351–52.

211. Karras, *Sexuality in Medieval Europe,* 107.

212. Goldberg, "Gender and Matrimonial Litigation," 49.

213. Goldberg, "John Skathelok's Dick," 117–19; Ruth Mazo Karras, "'Because the Other Is a Poor Woman She Shall Be Called His Wench': Gender, Sexuality, and Social Status in Late Medieval England," in *Gender and Difference in the Middle Ages,* ed. Sharon Farmer and Carol Braun Pasternack, Medieval Cultures 32 (Minneapolis: University of Minnesota Press, 2003), 221. On impotence in the Middle Ages, see Angus McLaren, *Impotence: A Cultural History* (Chicago: University of Chicago Press, 2007), 25–49.

214. Karras, *Sexuality in Medieval Europe,* 69 and 139.

215. Gratian, *Marriage Canons,* C.32 q.1 c.14.

216. Kempe, *The Book of Margery Kempe,* 49.

217. *Oxford English Dictionary,* 2nd ed., s.v. "erotica": "Matters of love; erotic literature or art (freq. as a heading in catalogues)." The term is first recorded in 1854.

218. Lynn Hunt, "Introduction: Obscenity and the Origins of Modernity, 1500–1800," in *The Invention of Pornography: Obscenity and the Origins of Modernity, 1500–1800,* ed. Lynn Hunt (New York: Zone, 1993), 10–11.

219. Leah Price, "The Tangible Page," *London Review of Books* 24, no. 21 (2002): 38.

220. For important arguments that medieval texts and images either were deliberately erotic or might have been read erotically, see Michael Camille, "Gothic Signs and the Surplus: The Kiss on the Cathedral," *Yale French Studies* 80 (1991): 151–70; Sarah Salih, "When Is a Bosom Not a Bosom? Problems with 'Erotic Mysticism,'" in *Medieval Virginities*, ed. Anke Bernau, Ruth Evans, and Sarah Salih (Cardiff: University of Wales Press, 2003); and Lara Farina, *Erotic Discourse and Early English Religious Writing* (New York: Palgrave Macmillan, 2006).

221. See Anthony Weir and James Jerman, *Images of Lust: Sexual Carvings on Medieval Churches* (London: Routledge, 1999), 11–30. For the Irish sheelas, see Eamonn Kelly, "Irish Sheela-na-gigs and Related Figures with Reference to the Collections of the National Museum of Ireland," in McDonald, *Medieval Obscenities.*

222. Weir and Jerman, *Images of Lust* 17.

223. Ibid., 148.

224. Ibid., 90.

225. Arthur Forgeais, *Notice sur des plombs historiés trouvés dans la Seine* (Paris: Chez l'auteur et chez Dumoulin, 1858). Further finds have emerged from the drowned villages of the Schelde estuary (Netherlands): see Malcolm Jones, "The Secular Badges," in *Heilig en Profaan: 1000 Laatmiddeleeuwse Insignes uit de Collectie H.J.E. van Beuningen*, ed. H.J.E. van Beuningen and A. M. Koldeweij, Rotterdam Papers 8 (Cothen: Stichting Middeleeuwse religieuze en profane insignes, 1993), and *The Secret Middle Ages: Discovering the Real Medieval World* (Stroud, UK: Sutton, 2002), 248; A. M. Koldeweij, "Lifting the Veil on Pilgrim Badges," in *Pilgrimage Explored*, ed. J. Stopford (Woodbridge, UK: York Medieval Press, 1999); Jos Koldeweij, "The Wearing of Significant Badges, Religious and Secular: The Social Meaning of a Behavioural Pattern," in *Showing Status: Representation of Social Positions in the Late Middle Ages*, ed. Wim Blockmans and Antheum Janse (Turnhout: Brepols, 1999). For catalogs of the Dutch badges, see Van Beuningen, Koldeweij, and Kicken, *Heilig en Profaan 1*, and *Heilig en Profaan 2: 1200 Laatmiddeleeuwse insignes uit openbare en particuliere collectives*, Rotterdam Papers 12 (Cothen: Stichting Middeleeuwse religieuze en profane insignes, 2001).

226. Jones, *The Secret Middle Ages,* 256.

227. Ibid., 255.

228. Ibid., 248 and 250. On the lack of consensus of meaning for these badges, see McDonald, *Medieval Obscenities,* 7.

229. Weir and Jerman, *Images of Lust,* 145.

230. Lochrie, "Mystical Acts, Queer Tendencies," 189–94.

231. Lochrie, *Heterosyncrasies,* 96.

232. Percy Reaney and Richard Wilson, *A Dictionary of English Surnames* (London: Routledge, 1991), 353.

233. Simon Gaunt, "Obscene Hermeneutics in Troubadour Lyric," in McDonald, *Medieval Obscenities,* 97.

234. Gaunt, "Obscene Hermeneutics," 95.

235. Foucault, *The History of Sexuality*, vol. 1, 57. On the "cacophony of discourses" that characterized the medieval period, see Bynum, "Why All the Fuss about the Body?" 7.

236. Sarah Salih, Anke Bernau, and Ruth Evans, "Introduction: Virginity and Virginity Studies," in Bernau, Evans, and Salih, *Medieval Virginities*, 3.

237. Lochrie, *Heterosyncrasies*, xxvii. In "Acts, Identities, and Sexuality's (Pre)Modern Regimes," Freccero also questions the view that modern sexuality constitutes a "unitary discursive regime" (187).

238. John Frow, *Time and Commodity Culture: Essays in Cultural Theory and Postmodernity* (Oxford: Oxford University Press, 1997), 229.

Chapter 2

1. Michel Foucault, *The History of Sexuality*, vol. 1, trans. Robert Hurley (London: Penguin, 1979), 43.

2. Ibid., 36–49.

3. Michael Warner, *The Trouble with Normal: Sex, Politics, and the Ethics of Queer Life* (New York: Free Press, 1999), 47.

4. Michael Warner and Lauren Berlant, "Sex in Public," in *Publics and Counterpublics*, ed. Michael Warner (New York: Zone, 2002), 194.

5. Judith Butler, "Gender Regulations," in *Undoing Gender* (New York: Routledge, 2004), 50.

6. Michel Foucault, *Discipline and Punish: The Birth of the Prison*, trans. Alan Sheridan (New York: Vintage, 1977), 182–84.

7. For a history of the ways in which statistical developments in the nineteenth century created epistemological categories like population, see Karma Lochrie, *Heterosyncrasies: Female Sexuality When Normal Wasn't* (Minneapolis: University of Minnesota Press, 2005), 1–11.

8. Ruth Mazo Karras, *Sexuality in Medieval Europe: Doing unto Others* (New York: Routledge, 2005), 17.

9. Joan Cadden, "Trouble in the Earthly Paradise: The Regime of Nature in Late Medieval Christian Culture," in *The Moral Authority of Nature*, ed. Lorraine Daston and Fernando Vidal (Chicago: University of Chicago Press, 2004), 224.

10. Pierre J. Payer, *The Bridling of Desire: Views of Sex in the Later Middle Ages* (Toronto: University of Toronto Press, 1993), 19.

11. For a fuller discussion of the categories of natural and unnatural, see Lochrie, *Heterosyncrasies*, xxii–xxiii, and 23–24.

12. James Schultz, "Heterosexuality as a Threat to Medieval Studies," *Journal of the History of Sexuality* 15, no. 1 (2006): 18.

13. Mark Jordan, *The Invention of Sodomy in Christian Theology* (Chicago: University of Chicago Press, 1997), 70.

14. Alan of Lille, *Plaint of Nature*, trans. James J. Sheridan (Toronto: Pontifical Institute of Mediaeval Studies, 1980), 165.

15. Payer, *The Bridling of Desire*, 54.

16. Quoted in Rebecca Ann Bach, *Shakespeare and Renaissance Literature before Heterosexuality* (New York: Palgrave, 2007), 28.

17. See Chaucer, *The Riverside Chaucer*, "The Knight's Tale," lines 1918–65, p. 51; *The Parliament of Fowls*, lines 218–28, p. 388.

18. Chaucer, *The Riverside Chaucer*, "The Parson's Tale," line 909, p. 320.

19. For an illustration and analysis of the difference between medieval/Renaissance notions of lust and modern sexual desire, see the discussion of Goneril and Regan in Bach, *Shakespeare and Renaissance Literature*, 27–29.

20. Catherine Belsey, "Love as Trompe-l'oeil: Taxonomies of Desire in *Venus and Adonis*," *Shakespeare Quarterly* 46, no. 3 (1995): 267.

21. For more on the gender implications of the highly sexed woman, see Karras, *Sexuality in Medieval Europe*, 3–4.

22. William Peraldus, *Summa de vitiis et virtutibus, tractatus de luxuria* (Venice: Paganinus de Paganinis, 1497), fol. 201vb. For a discussion of William's taxonomy, see Karma Lochrie, *Covert Operations: The Medieval Uses of Secrecy* (Philadelphia: University of Pennsylvania Press, 1999), 183–86.

23. Alan of Lille, *Plaint of Nature*, 68.

24. Ibid., 69.

25. Ibid., 136.

26. For a fuller discussion of homosociality and its relationship to heterosexuality, see Bach, *Shakespeare and Renaissance Literature*, 13–14. The last section of the present chapter also addresses medieval homosociality.

27. Belsey, "Love as Trompe-l'oeil," 271.

28. James Schultz, *Courtly Love, the Love of Courtliness, and the History of Sexuality* (Chicago: University of Chicago Press, 2006), xxii.

29. Malcolm Andrew and Ronald Waldron, eds, *The Poems of the Pearl Manuscript: Pearl, Cleanness, Patience, Sir Gawain and the Green Knight* (Exeter: University of Exeter Press, 1987), lines 697–704 (my translation).

30. For two discussions of this passage, see Carolyn Dinshaw, "'A Kiss Is Just a Kiss': Heterosexuality and Its Consolations in *Sir Gawain and the Green Knight*," *diacritics* 24, no. 2–3 (1994): 217–18, and Elizabeth B. Keiser, *Courtly Desire and Medieval Homophobia: The Legitimation of Sexual Pleasure in* Cleanness *and Its Contexts* (New Haven, CT: Yale University Press, 1997), 65–70.

31. Bach, *Shakespeare and Renaissance Literature*, 12.

32. Schultz, *Courtly Love*, 79–98.

33. For a more extensive discussion of the chaste knight, see Peggy McCracken, "Chaste Subjects: Gender, Heroism, and Desire in the Grail Quest," in *Queering the Middle Ages*, ed. Glenn Burger and Steven F. Kruger, Medieval Cultures 27 (Minneapolis: University of Minnesota Press, 2001), 123–42.

34. Catherine Belsey, "The Serpent in the Garden: Shakespeare, Marriage and Material Culture," *Seventeenth Century* 11, no. 1 (1996): 16.

35. Valerie Traub, *The Renaissance of Lesbianism in Early Modern England* (Cambridge: Cambridge University Press, 2002), 265–66.

36. Foucault, *The History of Sexuality*, vol. 1, 106–14.

37. Ibid., 106.

38. Ibid.

39. Ibid., 108.

40. Dyan Elliott, *Spiritual Marriage: Sexual Abstinence in Medieval Wedlock* (Princeton, NJ: Princeton University Press, 1993), 148.

41. For the development of the marriage debt in theological writings, especially as they drew upon medical theories of women's role in sexual intercourse, see ibid., 148–55.

42. Ibid., 152.

43. Daniel Juan Gil, "Before Intimacy: Modernity and Emotion in the Early Modern Discourse of Sexuality," *ELH* 69, no. 4 (2002): 862. For studies of the role of intimacy in the formation of modern heteronormativity, see Warner and Berlant, "Sex in Public"; Gil, "Before Intimacy"; and Niklas Luhmann, *Love as Passion: The Codification of Intimacy*, trans. Jeremy Gaines and Doris L. Jones (Stanford, CA: Stanford University Press, 1998).

44. Warner and Berlant, "Sex in Public," 194.

45. Ibid., 193.

46. See Traub's discussion of what she chooses to call "domestic heterosexuality" in *The Renaissance of Lesbianism*, 260–62. On the topic of medieval marriage and modernity, see Glenn Burger, *Chaucer's Queer Nation* (Minneapolis: University of Minnesota Press, 2003), 37–118.

47. Traub, *The Renaissance of Lesbianism*, 259.

48. Ibid., 260.

49. Belsey, "Love as Trompe-l'oeil," 272.

50. Quoted in ibid., 273.

51. Chaucer, *The Riverside Chaucer*, "The Wife of Bath's Prologue," line 623, p. 113.

52. Ibid., line 526, p. 112.

53. Ibid., "The Franklin's Tale," line 771, p. 179.

54. Elliott, *Spiritual Marriage*, 3.

55. Ibid., 73.

56. See Eve Kosofky Sedgwick, *Between Men: English Literature and Male Homosocial Desire* (New York: Columbia University Press, 1985).

57. C. Stephen Jaeger, *Ennobling Love: In Search of a Lost Sensibility* (Philadelphia: University of Pennsylvania Press, 1999).

58. Ibid., 6.

59. Ibid., x.

60. William E. Burgwinkle, *Sodomy, Masculinity, and Law in Medieval Literature: France and England, 1050–1230* (Cambridge: Cambridge University Press, 2004), 37–38.

61. Jaeger, *Ennobling Love*, 7.

62. Michel Foucault, *The Care of the Self*, vol. 3, *The History of Sexuality*, trans. Robert Hurley (London: Penguin, 1988), 43–45.

63. Foucault, *The History of Sexuality*, vol. 1, 36–49.

Chapter 3

1. On the motif of spectrality in histories of homosexuality, see Carla Freccero, *Queer/Early/Modern* (Durham, NC: Duke University Press, 2006), 69–104. On the difficulties of reaching beyond the hysteria surrounding sodomy to "objective" social history, see Mark Jordan, *The Silence of Sodom: Homosexuality in Modern Catholicism* (Chicago: University of Chicago Press, 2000), 113–20.

2. James A. Brundage, *Law, Sex, and Christian Society in Medieval Europe* (Chicago: University of Chicago Press, 1987), 589–617.

3. Accounts deploying the image of a premodernity "before" homosexuality and hetero-sexuality, or an era prior to sexual norms, include Khaled El-Rouayheb, *Before Homosexuality in the Arab-Islamic World, 1500–1800* (Chicago: University of Chicago Press, 2005); David M. Halperin, "Forgetting Foucault: Acts, Identities, and the History of Sexuality," *Representations* 63 (1998): 93–119; Karma Lochrie, *Heterosyncrasies: Female Sexuality When Normal Wasn't* (Minneapolis: University of Minnesota Press, 2005); and James Schultz, *Courtly Love, the Love of Courtliness, and the History of Sexuality* (Chicago: University of Chicago Press, 2006).

4. Freccero, *Queer/Early/Modern*, 31–50.

5. Jordan, *The Silence of Sodom*, 108–9.

6. Peter Damian, "Letter 31," in *The Letters of Peter Damian, 31–60*, trans. Otto J. Blum, The Fathers of the Church: Mediaeval Continuation 2 (Washington, DC: Catholic University of America Press, 1990). See Mark Jordan, *The Invention of Sodomy in Christian Theology* (Chicago: University of Chicago Press, 1997), 45–66; William Burgwinkle, *Sodomy, Masculinity, and Law in Medieval Literature: France and England, 1050–1230* (Cambridge: Cambridge University Press, 2004), 53–65.

7. Jordan, *The Invention of Sodomy*, 30–32; Lewis John Eron, "Homosexuality and Judaism," in *Homosexuality and World Religions*, ed. Arlene Swidler (Valley Forge, PA: Trinity Press International, 1993).

8. Jordan, *The Invention of Sodomy*, 34–35.

9. Pierre J. Payer, *Sex and the Penitentials: The Development of a Sexual Code, 550–1150* (Toronto: University of Toronto Press, 1984), 40–43, 135–39; Jordan, *The Invention of Sodomy*, 41–42. For a survey of the various meanings attributed to the story of Sodom in Anglo-Saxon England, see David Clark, *Between Medieval Men: Male Friendship and Desire in Early Medieval English Literature* (Oxford: Oxford University Press, 2009), 68–128.

10. El-Rouayheb, *Before Homosexuality*, 124–27, 136–37; Khalid Dunn, "Homo-sexuality and Islam," in Swidler, *Homosexuality and World Religions*.

11. El-Rouayheb, *Before Homosexuality*, 126; Everett Rowson, "The Categorization of Gender and Sexual Irregularity in Medieval Arabic Vice Lists," in *Body Guards: The Cultural Politics of Gender Ambiguity*, ed. Julia Epstein and Kristina Straub (New York: Routledge, 1991), 63, 68; Sahar Amer, *Crossing Borders: Love between Women in Medieval French and Arabic Literatures* (Philadelphia: University of Pennsylvania Press, 2008), 1–6, 17–18.

12. Karma Lochrie, "Presumptive Sodomy and Its Exclusions." *Textual Practice* 13, no. 2 (1999): 296.

13. Letter 211, in Augustine of Hippo, *Letters, 204–270*, trans. Wilfred Parsons, The Fathers of the Church: A New Translation 32 (Washington, DC: Catholic University of America Press, 1956), 50. See Bernadette Brooten, *Love between Women: Early Christian Responses to Female Homoeroticism* (Chicago: University of Chicago Press, 1996), 350–51.

14. Peter Cantor, *De vitio sodomitico*, in John Boswell, *Christianity, Social Tolerance, and Homosexuality: Gay People in Western Europe from the Beginning of the Christian Era to the Fourteenth Century* (Chicago: University of Chicago Press, 1980), 375–78.

15. Damian, "Letter 31," 31; Lochrie, "Presumptive Sodomy and Its Exclusions," 304–5; Burgwinkle, *Sodomy, Masculinity, and Law,* 57–58.

16. For summaries of ecclesiastical legislation against sodomy, see Michael Goodich, *The Unmentionable Vice: Homosexuality in the Later Medieval Period* (Santa Barbara, CA: Dorset Press, 1979), 23–69; Derrick Sherwin Bailey, *Homosexuality and the Western Christian Tradition* (London: Longmans, Green, 1995).

17. Burchard of Worms, *Decretum, PL* 140, cols. 924, 967–68.

18. Quoted in Bailey, *Homosexuality and the Western Christian Tradition*, 124.

19. Quoted in Boswell, *Christianity, Social Tolerance, and Homosexuality*, 277.

20. Robert Mills, *Suspended Animation: Pain, Pleasure and Punishment in Medieval Culture* (London: Reaktion, 2005), 83–105.

21. The Basel execution is discussed in Helmut Puff, *Sodomy in Reformation Germany and Switzerland, 1400–1600* (Chicago: University of Chicago Press, 2003), 17.

22. Quoted in Bailey, *Homosexuality and the Western Christian Tradition*, 74; Brundage, *Law, Sex, and Christian Society,* 121–23.

23. Bernd-Ulrich Hergemöller, "The Middle Ages," in *Gay Life and Culture: A World History*, ed. Robert Aldrich (London: Thames and Hudson, 2006), 61.

24. Michael Goodich, "Sexual Deviation as Heresy in the XIII–XIVth Centuries," in *Modernité et non-conformisme en France à travers les âges: Actes du colloque organisé par l'Institut d'histoire et de civilisation françaises d l'Université de Haïfa*, ed. Myriam Yardeni (Leiden: Brill, 1983).

25. *Against Arnaud of Verniolle, Son of William of Verniolle of le Mercadal Parish of Pamiers, Concerning the Crime of Heresy and Sodomy*, in Michael Goodich, ed., *Other Middle Ages: Witnesses at the Margins of Medieval Society* (Philadelphia: University of Pennsylvania Press, 1998), 142–43.

26. Puff, *Sodomy in Reformation Germany and Switzerland,* 23–30.

27. Marc Boone, "State Power and Illicit Sexuality: The Persecution of Sodomy in Late Medieval Bruges," *Journal of Medieval History* 22, no. 2 (1996): 135–53.

28. Michael Rocke, *Forbidden Friendships: Homosexuality and Male Culture in Renaissance Florence* (Oxford: Oxford University Press, 1996); Guido Ruggiero, *The Boundaries of Eros: Sex Crime and Sexuality in Renaissance Venice* (New York: Oxford University Press, 1985), 109–45.

29. Rocke, *Forbidden Friendships.*

30. Ruth Mazo Karras, *Sexuality in Medieval Europe: Doing unto Others* (New York: Routledge, 2005), 141–42.

31. Rocke, *Forbidden Friendships*, 46.

32. Edith Benkov, "The Erased Lesbian: Sodomy and the Legal Tradition in Medieval Europe," in *Same Sex Love and Desire among Women in the Middle Ages*, ed. Francesca Canadé Sautman and Pamela Sheingorn (New York: Palgrave, 2001); Jacqueline Murray, "Twice Marginal and Twice Invisible: Lesbians in the Middle Ages," in *Handbook of Medieval Sexuality*, ed. Vern L. Bullough and James A. Brundage (New York: Garland, 1996), 201–2.

33. Puff, *Sodomy in Reformation Germany and Switzerland*, 31–32; Boone, "State Power and Illicit Sexuality," 141.

34. Puff, *Sodomy in Reformation Germany and Switzerland*, 32.

35. El-Rouayheb, *Before Homosexuality*, 123.

36. Jehoeda Sofer, "Sodomy in the Law of Muslim States," in *Sexuality and Eroticism among Males in Moslem Societies*, ed. Arno Schmitt and Jehoeda Sofer (New York: Haworth Press, 1992).

37. Joseph Massad, *Desiring Arabs* (Chicago: University of Chicago Press, 2007); El-Rouayheb, *Before Homosexuality*, 157–61.

38. Justin McCann, trans., *Rule of Saint Benedict in Latin and English* (London: Burns Oates, 1952), e.g., 157, where the desire to avoid "scandals" arising from monks who defend one another is expressed.

39. Brian Patrick McGuire introduces these philosophical and spiritual traditions in *Friendship and Community: The Monastic Experience, 350–1250* (Kalamazoo, MI: Cistercian, 1988).

40. Anselm, *Letters of Saint Anselm of Canterbury*, trans. Walter Fröhlich (Kalamazoo, MI: Cistercian, 1990), letters 4, 130.

41. Boswell, *Christianity, Social Tolerance, and Homosexuality*, 218.

42. Anselm, *Letters of Saint Anselm*, letters 120, 405.

43. J. P. Haseldine, "Love, Separation and Male Friendship: Words and Actions in Saint Anselm's Letters to His Friends," in *Masculinity in Medieval Europe*, ed. D. M. Hadley (Harlow, UK: Longman, 1999).

44. Marbod of Rennes, "A Satire on a Young Boy's Lover," in Thomas Stehling, ed., *Medieval Latin Poems of Male Love and Friendship* (New York: Garland, 1984), 33.

45. "To G., her unique rose," in Stehling, *Medieval Latin Poems*, 105.

46. For examples of these genres, see J. W. Wright and Everett K. Rowson, *Homoeroticism in Classical Arabic Literature* (New York: Columbia University Press, 1997).

47. Boswell, *Christianity, Social Tolerance, and Homosexuality*, 243–66; Franz Rosenthal, "Male and Female: Described and Compared," in Wright and Rowson, *Homoeroticism in Classical Arabic Literature*.

48. Hrotsvit of Gandersheim, *Hrotsvithae Opera*, ed. H. Homeyer (Munich: Ferdinand Schöningh, 1970), 130–46. On the links between Andalusi poetry celebrating beautiful boys and another tenth-century *Life* of St. Pelagius, see Jeffrey A. Bowman, "Beauty and *Passion* in Tenth-Century Córdoba," in *The Boswell Thesis: Essays on Christianity, Social Tolerance, and Homosexuality*, ed. Mathew Kuefler (Chicago: University of Chicago Press, 2006).

49. J. Schirmann, "The Ephebe in Medieval Hebrew Poetry," *Sefarad* 1 (1955): 55–68; Norman Roth, "'Deal Gently with the Young Man': Love of Boys in Medieval Hebrew Poetry of Spain," *Speculum* 57 (1982): 20–51.

50. Massad, *Desiring Arabs*, 51–144.

51. Samia Mehrez, "Take Them out of the Ball Game: Egypt's Cultural Players in Crisis," *Middle East Report* 219 (2001): 12; Massad, *Desiring Arabs*, 181.

52. J. W. Wright, "Masculine Allusion and the Structure of Satire in Early 'Abbāsid Poetry," in Wright and Rowson, *Homoeroticism in Classical Arabic Literature*; El-Rouayheb, *Before Homosexuality*, 79, 95–99; Jim Wafer, "Vision and Passion," in *Islamic Homosexualities: Culture, History, and Literature*, ed. Stephen O. Murray and Will Roscoe (New York: New York University Press, 1997).

53. El-Rouayheb, *Before Homosexuality*, 25–33, 115.

54. Marbod of Rennes, "An Argument Against Copulation between People of Only One Sex" and "An Argument Against Sexual Love," in Stehling, *Medieval Latin Poems*, 35, 37.

55. El-Rouayheb, *Before Homosexuality*, 5–6; Schultz, *Courtly Love*, 51–62.

56. Boswell, *Christianity, Social Tolerance, and Homosexuality*, 251–52; Ilene H. Forsyth, "The Ganymede Capital at Vézelay," *Gesta* 15 (1976): 241–46; V. A. Kolve, "Ganymede/*Son of Getron*: Medieval Monasticism and the Drama of Same-Sex Desire," *Speculum* 73 (1998): 1014–67.

57. Robert Mills, "Male-Male Love and Sex in the Middle Ages, 1000–1500," in *A Gay History of Britain*, ed. Matt Cook, with Robert Mills, Randolph Trumbach, and H. G. Cocks (Oxford: Greenwood, 2007), 14–29, gives an overview of the theme in late medieval England.

58. Ibid., 6–8.

59. Ibid., 8–14; Alan Bray, *The Friend* (Chicago: University of Chicago Press, 2003), 13–41.

60. For general introductions to this literature, see Karma Lochrie, "Between Women," in *The Cambridge Companion to Medieval Women's Writing*, ed. Carolyn Dinshaw and David Wallace (Cambridge: Cambridge University Press, 2003), and Ulrike Wiethaus, "Female Homoerotic Discourse and Religion in Medieval Germanic Culture," in *Gender and Difference in the Middle Ages*, ed. Sharon Farmer and Carol Braun Pasternack, Medieval Cultures 32 (Minneapolis: University of Minnesota Press, 2003).

61. Alan of Lille, *Plaint of Nature*, trans. James J. Sheridan (Toronto: Pontifical Institute of Mediaeval Studies, 1980), 70.

62. Ibid., 200, 204, 214.

63. Valerie Traub, "Friendship's Loss: Alan Bray's Making of History," *GLQ* 10, no. 3 (2004): 350.

64. Bella Millett, trans., *Ancrene Wisse: Guide for Anchoresses* (Exeter: University of Exeter Press, 2009), 79.

65. Lochrie, "Between Women," 78–81.

66. Puff, *Sodomy in Reformation Germany and Switzerland*, 31–35.

67. *Against Arnaud of Verniolle*, in Goodich, *Other Middle Ages*; Francesca Canadé Sautman, "Just Like a Woman': Queer History, Womanizing the Body, and the

Boys in Arnaud's Band," in *Queering the Middle Ages*, ed. Glenn Burger and Steven F. Kruger (Minneapolis: University of Minnesota Press, 2001).

68. David Lorenzo Boyd and Ruth Mazo Karras, "The Interrogation of a Male Transvestite Prostitute in Fourteenth-Century London," *GLQ* 1 (1995): 459–65.

69. Ruggiero, *The Boundaries of Eros*, 136.

70. Alan of Lille, *Plaint of Nature*, 134, 155–56.

71. Hugh of Flavigny, *Chronicon*, PL 154, cols. 390d–91a, discussed in Frank Barlow, *William Rufus* (New Haven, CT: Yale University Press, 2000), 409.

72. Valerie Traub discusses the trope's subsequent development in *The Renaissance of Lesbianism in Early Modern England* (Cambridge: Cambridge University Press, 2002).

73. Robert Easting, ed., *Revelation of the Monk of Eynsham*, EETS os 318 (Oxford: Oxford University Press, 2002), 81 (spelling modernized).

74. Ovid, *The Metamorphoses of Ovid*, trans. William Caxton (New York: George Braziller in association with Magdalene College, Cambridge, 1968), bk. 9, chap. 14 (spelling modernized).

75. El-Rouayheb, *Before Homosexuality*, 126.

76. Rowson, "The Categorization of Gender and Sexual Irregularity," 63, 67–68.

77. El-Rouayheb, *Before Homosexuality*, 25–34.

78. Etymologically, *mukhannath* is related to words signifying bendiness or flexibility. See Rowson, "The Categorization of Gender and Sexual Irregularity," 69–71.

79. Avicenna, *Canon medicinae*, 3.20.40–43, quoted in Jordan, *The Invention of Sodomy*, 119–21.

80. Ibid., 125–35.

81. Petrus de Abano, *Expositio problematum Aristotelis*, part 4, probl. 26, quoted in Joan Cadden, *Meanings of Sex Difference in the Middle Ages: Medicine, Science, and Culture* (Cambridge: Cambridge University Press, 1993), 214–16.

82. Goodich, *Other Middle Ages*, 138.

83. Cadden, *Meanings of Sex Difference*, 273–77.

84. Ibid., 223–24.

85. For an overview of the female-to-male narratives, see Valerie Hotchkiss, *Clothes Make the Man: Female Cross Dressing in Medieval Europe* (New York: Garland, 1996).

86. Lochrie, *Heterosyncrasies*, 76–89.

87. Guilielmus de Saliceto, *Summa conservationis et curationis*, ch. 168, quoted in ibid., 83–84.

88. Michel Foucault, *The History of Sexuality*, vol. 1: *An Introduction*, trans. Robert Hurley (London: Penguin, 1979), 43.

Chapter 4

1. Pierre J. Payer, *The Bridling of Desire: Views of Sex in the Later Middle Ages* (Toronto: University of Toronto Press, 1993), 18–41; James A. Brundage, *Law, Sex, and Christian Society in Medieval Europe* (Chicago: University of Chicago Press, 1987), 58.

2. John Boswell, *Christianity, Social Tolerance, and Homosexuality: Gay People in Western Europe from the Beginning of the Christian Era to the Fourteenth Century* (Chicago: University of Chicago Press, 1980), 93 n. 2.

3. Theresa Tinkle, *Medieval Venuses and Cupids: Sexuality, Hermeneutics, and English Poetry* (Stanford, CA: Stanford University Press, 1996), 9–16.

4. Quoted in ibid., 17.

5. Quoted in ibid., 18.

6. Payer, *The Bridling of Desire*, 9.

7. Michel Foucault, *The History of Sexuality*, vol. 1: *An Introduction*, trans. Robert Hurley (London: Penguin, 1979), 17–19, 156; Carolyn Dinshaw, *Getting Medieval: Sexualities and Communities, Pre- and Postmodern* (Durham, NC: Duke University Press, 1999), 198–200.

8. Peraldus, quoted in Payer, *The Bridling of Desire*, 77.

9. David M. Halperin, *How to Do the History of Homosexuality* (Chicago: University of Chicago Press, 2002), 45.

10. A fine recent discussion of paraphilia is found in Adrian Furnham and Emmy Haraldsen, "Lay Theories of Etiology and 'Cure' for Four Types of Paraphilia: Fetishism, Pedophilia, Sexual Sadism, and Voyeurism," *Journal of Clinical Psychology* 54, no. 5 (1998): 689–700.

11. K. Freund, M. C. Seto, and M. Kuban, "Two Types of Fetishism," *Behaviour Research and Therapy* 34, no. 9 (1996): 687–94.

12. Jacques Le Goff, *The Medieval Imagination*, trans. Arthur Goldhammer (Chicago: University of Chicago Press, 1998), 6.

13. Chrétien de Troyes, *Arthurian Romances*, ed. and trans. D.D.R. Owen (London: Dent, 1993), 247.

14. Ibid., 189–90.

15. Ibid., 245.

16. Jeffrey Jerome Cohen, *Medieval Identity Machines* (Minneapolis: University of Minnesota Press, 2003), 78–115.

17. Chrétien de Troyes, *Arthurian Romances*, 204–5.

18. Ibid., 205.

19. Cohen, *Medieval Identity Machines*, 101.

20. Sheila Delany, *Impolitic Bodies: Poetry, Saints, and Society in Fifteenth-Century England: The Work of Osbern Bokenham* (New York: Oxford University Press, 1998), 73.

21. Sigmund Freud, *On Sexuality*, ed. Angela Richards (Harmondsworth, UK: Penguin, 1977), 352–54.

22. L. F. Lowenstein, "Fetishes and Their Associated Behavior," *Sexuality and Disability* 20, no. 2 (2002): 135.

23. Ibid., 139.

24. Steven F. Kruger, "Fetishism, 1927, 1614, 1461," in *The Postcolonial Middle Ages*, ed. Jeffrey Jerome Cohen (New York: St. Martin's Press, 2000), 197–201.

25. Peter Brown, *The Cult of the Saints: Its Rise and Function in Latin Christianity* (Chicago: University of Chicago Press, 1981), 78–79.

26. Freud, *On Sexuality*, 353.

27. A. J. Giannini, G. Colapietro, A. E. Slaby, S. M. Melemis, and R. K. Bowman, "Sexualization of the Female Foot as a Response to Sexually Transmitted Epidemics: A Preliminary Study," *Psychological Reports* 83, no. 2 (1998): 491–92.

28. Ibid.

29. Freud, *On Sexuality*, 66.

30. Slavoj Žižek, *The Metastases of Enjoyment: On Women and Causality* (London: Verso, 2005), 89–93.

31. Robert Rouse, *The Idea of Anglo-Saxon England in Middle English Romance* (Cambridge: Brewer, 2005), 77.

32. Thomas Malory, *Morte Darthur*, 168.25–36.

33. Ibid., 168.37–38.

34. Mary MacLeod Banks, ed., *An Alphabet of Tales: An English 15th Century Translation of the* Alphabetum Narrationum *of Étienne de Besançon from Additional MS. 25,719 of the British Museum*, vol. 1, EETS o.s. 126 and 127 (London: Kegan Paul, 1904), 93.

35. Leo Bersani, "Sociality and Sexuality," *Critical Inquiry* 26, no. 4 (2000): 645.

36. Vern L. Bullough, *Sexual Practices and the Medieval Church* (Amherst, NY: Prometheus, 1982), 50–52; Alain Boureau, *The Myth of Pope Joan*, trans. Lydia G. Cochrane (Chicago: University of Chicago Press, 2001), passim.

37. Boureau, *The Myth of Pope Joan*, 121–22.

38. Vern L. Bullough, "Cross Dressing and Gender Role Change in the Middle Ages," in *Handbook of Medieval Sexuality*, ed. Vern L. Bullough and James A. Brundage (New York: Garland, 2000), 231–32.

39. Ibid., 234–35.

40. Vern L. Bullough, "Transvestites in the Middle Ages," *American Journal of Sociology* 79, no. 6 (1974): 1389–90.

41. Bullough, "Cross Dressing and Gender Role Change," 231.

42. Corporation of London Records Office, Plea and Memorandum Roll A34, m. 2, in Ruth Mazo Karras and David Lorenzo Boyd, "'Ut cum muliere': A Male Transvestite Prostitute in Fourteenth-Century London," in *Premodern Sexualities*, ed. Louise Fradenburg and Carla Freccero (New York: Routledge, 1996), 111–12.

43. Ibid., 103.

44. Chaucer, *The Riverside Chaucer*, "The General Prologue" to *The Canterbury Tales*, line 691, p. 34.

45. Brigitte Cazelles, *The Lady as Saint* (Philadelphia: University of Pennsylvania Press, 1991), 34, 50–59.

46. Robert Mills, *Suspended Animation: Pain, Pleasure and Punishment in Medieval Culture* (London: Reaktion, 2005), 106–9.

47. Cazelles, *The Lady as Saint*, 50–53.

48. Mills, *Suspended Animation*, 170.

49. Ibid.

50. Translated and discussed in Anne B. Thompson, *Everyday Saints and the Art of Narrative in the* South English Legendary (Aldershot, UK: Ashgate, 2003), 176–77.

51. Gayle Margherita, *The Romance of Origins: Language and Sexual Difference in Middle English Literature* (Philadelphia: University of Pennsylvania Press, 1994), 358.

52. Chaucer, *The Riverside Chaucer*, "The Wife of Bath's Prologue," lines 813–15, p. 116.

53. Leo Bersani, "Is the Rectum a Grave?" *October* 43 (1987): 217–18.

54. Kristina Hildebrand, "Her Desire and His: Letters between Fifteenth-Century Lovers," in *The Erotic in the Literature of Medieval Britain*, ed. Amanda Hopkins and Cory J. Rushton (Cambridge: Brewer, 2007), 137–40.

55. Chaucer, *The Riverside Chaucer*, "The Franklin's Tale," lines 742–50, p. 178.

56. Ibid., lines 764–66, p. 178.

57. Ibid., line 769.

58. *Troilus and Criseyde*, *The Riverside Chaucer*, Book 3, lines 1119–24, p. 529.

59. Ibid., line 1126.

60. Ibid., lines 1200–1201.

61. Ibid., lines 1191–92.

62. Ibid., lines 1205–8.

63. Ibid., lines 1209–11.

64. J.R.R. Tolkien and E. V. Gordon, *Sir Gawain and the Green Knight*, rev. Norman Davis, 2nd ed. (Oxford: Clarendon Press, 1967), Fitt 2, lines 1208–11.

65. Quoted in Virginia Burrus, "Queer Lives of Saints: Jerome's Hagiography," *Journal of the History of Sexuality* 10, no. 3–4 (2001): 450–52.

66. W. L. Marshall and Pamela Kennedy, "Sexual Sadism in Sexual Offenders: An Elusive Diagnosis," *Aggression and Violent Behavior* 8 (2003): 1.

67. Alain Boureau, *The Lord's First Night: The Myth of the* Droit de Cuissage, trans. Lydia G. Cochrane (Chicago: University of Chicago Press, 1998); Albrecht Classen, *The Medieval Chastity Belt: A Myth-Making Process* (Basingstoke, UK: Palgrave Macmillan, 2007), 147–54.

68. Quoted in J. Benedetti, *The Real Bluebeard* (New York: Dorset, 1971), 115. A Lacanian reading of Gilles de Rais can be found in James Penney, *The World of Perversion: Psychoanalysis and the Impossible Absolute of Desire* (New York: State University of New York Press, 2006), and Nicolas Brémaud, "Les crimes de Gilles de Rais. Le sadisme dans la psychose," *L'en-je lacanien* 8, no. 1 (2007): 53–71.

69. Etienne Corillaut, quoted in Benedetti, *The Real Bluebeard*, 113.

70. Ibid., 117.

71. Bersani, "Is the Rectum a Grave?" 214–15.

72. Amanda Hopkins and Cory J. Rushton, "Introduction: The Revel, the Melodye and the Bisynesse of Solas," in Hopkins and Rushton, *The Erotic in the Literature of Medieval Britain*, 9–11.

73. W. W. Allman and D. Thomas Hanks Jr., "Rough Love: Notes toward an Erotics of the *Canterbury Tales*," *Chaucer Review* 38, no. 1 (2003): 53.

Chapter 5

1. Samuel Laeuchli, *Power and Sexuality: The Emergence of Canon Law at the Synod of Elvira* (Philadelphia, PA: Temple University Press, 1972), 88. The full text of the canons is given at 126–35.

2. See J. Oppel, "Saint Jerome and the History of Sex," *Viator* 24 (1993): 1–22.

3. Siegfried Wenzel, ed. and trans., *Fasciculus Morum: A Fourteenth-Century Preacher's Handbook* (University Park: Pennsylvania State University Press, 1989), 681.

4. Women were not allowed to enter a church for forty days after giving birth and then had to participate in a ritual known as churching before they were accepted into the sacred space again. On the forbidden times, places, and situations for having sex according to the penitentials, see the wonderful graphic ("Feeling randy?") of the decision-making process the medieval couple might be faced with in James A. Brundage, *Law, Sex, and Christian Society in Medieval Europe* (Chicago: University of Chicago Press, 1987), 162.

5. James A. Brundage, "Sin, Crime, and the Pleasures of the Flesh: The Medieval Church Judges Sexual Offences," in *The Medieval World*, ed. Peter Linehan and Janet L. Nelson (London: Routledge, 2001), 299.

6. James A. Brundage, *Medieval Canon Law* (London: Longman, 1995), 41.

7. Ruth Mazo Karras, "Sexuality in the Middle Ages," in Linehan and Nelson, *The Medieval World*, 283.

8. Brundage, *Medieval Canon Law*, 90.

9. Ibid., 72.

10. Brundage, "Sin, Crime, and the Pleasures of the Flesh," 296.

11. For an analysis of the proportion of sexual offenses dealt with in a sample of handbooks, see Pierre J. Payer, *Sex and the Penitentials: The Development of a Sexual Code, 550–1150* (Toronto: University of Toronto Press, 1984), 52–53.

12. Brundage, *Medieval Canon Law*, 25.

13. Quoted in John T. McNeill and Helena Gamer, eds., *Medieval Handbooks of Penance: A Translation of the Principal* libri poenitentiales *and Selections from Related Documents* (New York: Columbia University Press, 1938), 94.

14. Karras, "Sexuality in the Middle Ages," 282.

15. For a very readable summary of Burchard's scale of penalties, see Jeffrey Richards, *Sex, Dissidence and Damnation: Minority Groups in the Middle Ages* (London: Routledge, 1990), 29–30.

16. For discussion of this theme, see Hubertus Lutterbach, *Sexualität im Mittelalter: Eine Kulturstudie anhand von Bußbüchern des 6. bis 12. Jahrhunderts*, Beihefte zum Archiv für Kulturgeschichte H. 43 (Cologne: Böhlau, 1999), 240–46.

17. Robert of Flamborough, *Liber Poenitentialis*, ed. J.J.F. Firth (Toronto: Pontifical Institute of Medieval Studies, 1971), 195f., quoted in Michael Goodich, ed., *Other Middle Ages: Witnesses at the Margins of Medieval Society* (Philadelphia: University of Pennsylvania Press, 1998), 112–15.

18. Michael Haren, *Sin and Society in Fourteenth-Century England: A Study of the Memoriale Presbiterorum* (Oxford: Clarendon Press, 2000), 101.

19. Ibid., 183.

20. James A. Brundage, "Playing by the Rules: Sexual Behaviour and Legal Norms in Medieval Europe," in *Desire and Discipline: Sex and Sexuality in the Premodern West*, ed. Jacqueline Murray and Konrad Eisenbichler (Toronto: University of Toronto Press, 1996), 25.

21. *Decretales Gregorii IX*, quoted in Brundage, "Sin, Crime, and the Pleasures of the Flesh," 300. See also Brundage, *Medieval Canon Law,* 93 and 145.

22. *Decretales Gregorii IX*, quoted in Brundage, "Sin, Crime, and the Pleasures of the Flesh," 301.

23. Ibid., 303.

24. Ibid., 303–4.

25. See Brundage, "Playing by the Rules," 33, for examples, notably, the archdeacon in Chaucer's "Friar's Tale."

26. Ruth Mazo Karras, *Sexuality in Medieval Europe: Doing unto Others* (New York: Routledge, 2005), 71.

27. Ibid., 71. See also Jeremy Goldberg, "John Skathelok's Dick: Voyeurism and 'Pornography' in Late Medieval England," in *Medieval Obscenities*, ed. Nicola McDonald (Woodbridge, UK: York Medieval Press, 2006).

28. Karras, *Sexuality in Medieval Europe,* 71.

29. Trevor Dean, *Crime in Medieval Europe, 1200–1550* (Harlow, UK: Longman, 2001), 130.

30. Ibid. He only has a footnote to vols. 8 and 20 of *Ordonnances des rois de France* (Paris, 1723–1849).

31. V. Flint, *The Rise of Magic in Early Medieval Europe* (Oxford: Oxford University Press, 1991), 40–41.

32. See Harald Kleinschmidt, *Understanding the Middle Ages: The Transformation of Ideas and Attitudes in the Medieval World* (Woodbridge, UK: Boydell, 2000) 123. Women of the same kin group (*ingenua*) and other ordinary women were differentiated. The compensation refers to crimes committed by a man of the same kin group (*ingenuus*) against such a woman only; not all women were thus protected from unwanted advances.

33. Karras, "Sexuality in the Middle Ages," 286.

34. Dean, *Crime in Medieval Europe*, 138, source in Matthew Paris's *Chronica Majora*.

35. Ibid., 139.

36. Ibid., 125.

37. Brundage, "Sin, Crime, and the Pleasures of the Flesh," 298. It is debatable how far cases brought before canon lawyers reflect how much or how little "simple fornication" (premarital sex) was actually going on, and we should not from this generalize a modern stereotype of a jolly, sexually unabashed, "popular" Middle Ages contrasting with a restrictive and anti-corporal clerical Middle Ages (see Karras, "Sexuality in the Middle Ages," 280).

38. Wenzel, *Fasciculus Morum,* 669.

39. Ibid., 669.

40. Examples are quoted in Richards, *Sex, Dissidence and Damnation,* 38: the twelfth-century penitential of bishop Bartholomew of Exeter (most people considered fornication to be no sin); bishop Jacques de Vitry of Acre (students especially believed this); the fourteenth-century *Summa* of Thomas of Chobham (complains that many people considered fornication to be a minor sin or no sin at all, so priests must make it clear during confession that it definitely is a sin).

41. Aquinas, *Collationes in decem preceptis*, quoted in Pierre J. Payer, *The Bridling of Desire: Views of Sex in the Later Middle Ages* (Toronto: University of Toronto Press, 1993), 182.

42. Maurice of Sully and Richard of Wetheringsett both made this point. See Pierre J. Payer, "Confession and the Study of Sex in the Middle Ages," in *Handbook of Medieval Sexuality*, ed. Vern L. Bullough and James A. Brundage (New York: Garland, 1996), 14.

43. Karras, *Sexuality in Medieval Europe*, 26.

44. See Kleinschmidt, *Understanding the Middle Ages*, 124–25.

45. James A. Brundage, "Sex and Canon Law," in Bullough and Brundage, *Handbook of Medieval Sexuality*, 38.

46. Kleinschmidt, *Understanding the Middle Ages*, 135. The source is Matthew Paris, *Chronica Majora*.

47. Karras, "Sexuality in the Middle Ages," 283.

48. Wenzel, *Fasciculus Morum*, 683.

49. Quoted in McNeill and Gamer, *Medieval Handbooks of Penance*, 311.

50. A. Lynn Martin, *Alcohol, Sex, and Gender in Late Medieval and Early Modern Europe* (Basingstoke, UK: Palgrave, 2001), 10.

51. Ibid., 45.

52. Ibid., 47.

53. Ibid., 71.

54. Richards, *Sex, Dissidence and Damnation*, 30.

55. Martin, *Alcohol, Sex, and Gender*, 86.

56. Quoted in ibid., 87.

57. A summary of Germanic law codes on rape can be found in Suzanne F. Wemple, "Consent and Dissent to Sexual Intercourse in Germanic Societies from the Fifth to the Tenth Century," in *Consent and Coercion to Sex and Marriage in Ancient and Medieval Societies*, ed. Angeliki E. Laiou (Washington, DC: Dumbarton Oaks Research Library and Collection, 1993), 227–43.

58. Karras, "Sexuality in the Middle Ages," 288.

59. On this definition of rape, see James A. Brundage, "Rape and Seduction in the Medieval Canon Law," in *Sexual Practices and the Medieval Church*, ed. Vern L. Bullough and James A. Brundage (Buffalo, NY: Prometheus, 1982).

60. Quoted in Corinne Saunders, "A Matter of Consent: Middle English Romance and the Law of *Raptus*," in *Medieval Women and the Law*, ed. Noël James Menuge (Woodbridge, UK: Boydell, 2000), 109.

61. Barbara A. Hanawalt, *"Of Good and Ill Repute": Gender and Social Control in Medieval England* (New York: Oxford University Press, 1998), 132, in her analysis of thirteenth-century English rape cases claims that 56 percent of all women dropped charges after the initial appeal.

62. Dean, *Crime in Medieval Europe,* 83–84. See also Christopher Cannon, "The Rights of Medieval English Women: Crime and the Issue of Representation," in *Medieval Crime and Social Control*, ed. Barbara A. Hanawalt and David Wallace, Medieval Cultures 16 (Minneapolis: University of Minnesota Press, 1999), 172–73.

63. Ibid., 85.

64. James A. Brundage, "Implied Consent to Intercourse," in Laiou, *Consent and Coercion*, 255.

65. Payer, *The Bridling of Desire*, 91–2. See also Dyan Elliott, who discusses how Bernardino of Siena challenged the absoluteness of the conjugal debt, allowing for sexual refusal on the part of a wife, in "Bernardino of Siena versus the Marriage Debt," in Murray and Eisenbichler, *Desire and Discipline*.

66. Dean, *Crime in Medieval Europe*, 87–88.

67. Ibid., 89.

68. Richards, *Sex, Dissidence and Damnation*, 119, for more examples.

69. Dean, *Crime in Medieval Europe*, 52. The Pisan legislation of 1286 describes where and when prostitutes are allowed to do certain things; for example, they could only use the bathhouse on Wednesdays (see Goodich, *Other Middle Ages*, 116–17).

70. Hanawalt, "*Of Good and Ill Repute*," 26–27.

71. Richard Holt and Nigel Baker, "Towards a Geography of Sexual Encounter: Prostitution in English Medieval Towns," in *Indecent Exposure: Sexuality, Society and the Archaeological Record*, ed. Lynne Bevan (Glasgow: Cruithne, 2001).

72. Ruth Mazo Karras and David Lorenzo Boyd, "'*Ut cum muliere*': A Male Transvestite Prostitute in Fourteenth-Century London," in *Premodern Sexualities*, ed. Louise Fradenburg and Carla Freccero (New York: Routledge, 1996), 101.

73. Ibid., 110.

74. The *Breviarium practice*, quoted by Peter Lewis Allen, *The Wages of Sin: Sex, Disease, Past and Present* (Chicago: University of Chicago Press, 2000), 15, wrongly attributed to Arnaud of Villanova; the actual author is unknown. See also Karras, *Sexuality in Medieval Europe*, 112.

75. Karras, *Sexuality in Medieval Europe*, 3, where she explains that this is precisely why she subtitled her book *Doing unto Others*, since the Middle Ages "understood sex acts as something that someone did to someone else."

76. Wenzel, *Fasciculus Morum*, 687.

77. Quoted in McNeill and Gamer, *Medieval Handbooks of Penance*, 103.

78. Ibid., 113.

79. James M. Saslow, *Pictures and Passions: A History of Homosexuality in the Visual Arts* (Harmondsworth, UK: Viking, 1999), 60.

80. John Boswell, *Christianity, Social Tolerance, and Homosexuality: Gay People in Western Europe from the Beginning of the Christian Era to the Fourteenth Century* (Chicago: University of Chicago Press, 1980), 176–77.

81. Michael Goodich, *The Unmentionable Vice: Homosexuality in the Later Medieval Period* (Santa Barbara, CA: Dorset Press, 1979), 39.

82. Boswell, *Christianity, Social Tolerance, and Homosexuality*, 291.

83. See the discussion in Dean, *Crime in Medieval Europe*, 59–61.

84. Quoted in Boswell, *Christianity, Social Tolerance, and Homosexuality*, 288.

85. Goodich, *The Unmentionable Vice*, xv.

86. Saslow, *Pictures and Passions*, 76.

87. Ibid., 84.

88. Ibid. See Franco Mormando, *The Preacher's Demons: Bernardino of Siena and the Social Underworld of Early Renaissance Italy* (Chicago: University of Chicago Press, 1999).

89. Mormando, *The Preacher's Demons*, 156.

90. Quoted in Karras, *Sexuality in Medieval Europe*, 111.

91. Richards, *Sex, Dissidence and Damnation*, 106.

92. Ibid., 107.

93. Goodich, *Other Middle Ages*, 108.

94. See ibid., 108 and 118ff.

95. Laeuchli, *Power and Sexuality*, 93.

96. See Lutterbach, *Sexualität im Mittelalter*, on penitential literature reinforcing a paradigm of ritual purity.

97. Karras, *Sexuality in Medieval Europe*, 156.

Chapter 6

1. Chaucer, *The Riverside Chaucer*, "The Wife of Bath's Prologue," lines 115–28, p. 106. Unless otherwise noted, all translations are my own.

2. Thomas Laqueur, *Making Sex: Body and Gender from the Greeks to Freud* (Cambridge, MA: Harvard University Press, 1990), 63–96.

3. For reference to this idea by ancient writers, see Vern L. Bullough, "Medieval Medical and Scientific Views of Women," *Viator* 4 (1973): 492–93.

4. Galen, *Galen on the Usefulness of the Parts of the Body (De usu partium)*, trans. Margaret Tallmadge May (Ithaca, NY: Cornell University Press, 1968), 2:628–30, 14.6.

5. Bartholomaeus Anglicus, *On the Properties of Things: John Trevisa's Translation of Bartholomaeus Anglicus De proprietatibus rerum*, ed. M. C. Seymour et al. (Oxford: Clarendon Press, 1975), 1:294.

6. Aristotle, *Generation of Animals*, ed. A. Peck, Loeb Classical Library (Cambridge, MA: Harvard University Press, 1943), bk. 1, chap. 21, 729b, 113.

7. Erwin Panofsky, *Early Netherlandish Painting: Its Origins and Character*, vol. 1 (1953; repr. New York: Harper and Row, 1971), 143.

8. Isidore of Seville, *Etymologiarum sive originum*, ed. W. Lindsay (Oxford: Oxford University Press, 1911), bk. 9, 5:6.

9. Hildegard of Bingen, *Causae et curae*, ed. P. Kaiser (Leipzig: B. G. Teubner, 1903), 4:60, 76.

10. Constantinus Africanus, *Opera omnia* (Lyon: Andreas Turinus, 1515), fol. 28rb. See Joan Cadden, *Meanings of Sex Difference in the Middle Ages: Medicine, Science, and Culture* (Cambridge: Cambridge University Press, 1993), 65.

11. Brian Lawn, *The Prose Salernitan Questions Edited from a Bodleian Manuscript (Auct.F.3.10)* (London: Oxford University Press, 1979), B10, 6. See Cadden, *Meanings of Sex Difference*, 93–94.

12. Lawn, *The Prose Salernitan Questions*, B11, 7. See Cadden, *Meanings of Sex Difference*, 95.

13. See Danielle Jacquart and Claude Thomasset, *Sexuality and Medicine in the Middle Ages* (Princeton, NJ: Princeton University Press, 1988), 66.

14. Albertus Magnus, *On Animals: A Medieval Summa Zoologica*, ed. K. Kitchell and I. Resnick (Baltimore, MD: Johns Hopkins University Press, 1999), bk. 15, vol. 5, chap. 120, 1139.

15. Anglicus, *On the Properties of Things,* 294.

16. Aristotle, *Generation of Animals*, bk. 4, chap. 3, 767b, 401.

17. Ibid., 737a, 175.

18. Anglicus, *On the Properties of Things,* 294–95, 297.

19. William of Conches, *De philosophia mundi, PL* 172, 89.

20. Oxford, Bodleian Library, MS Douce 37, fol. 3r.

21. Helen Rodnite Lemay, *Women's Secrets: A Translation of Pseudo-Albertus Magnus' De secretis mulierum with Commentaries* (Albany: State University of New York Press, 1992), 117.

22. Ibid.

23. Ibid., 114.

24. Magnus, *On Animals,* bk. 10, vol. 2, chap. 45, 844–45.

25. Lemay, *Women's Secrets,* 114–15.

26. Avicenna, *Liber canonis* (Venice: Pagininis, 1507), bk. 3, fen. 20, tr. 1, chap. 38.

27. Jacquart and Thomasset, *Sexuality and Medicine,* 134.

28. Isidore of Seville, *Etymologiarum sive originum,* bk. 11, 2:24.

29. Lawn, *The Prose Salernitan Questions,* B23, 13–14.

30. Avicenna's *Canon* gives a list of symptoms and considers the various physiological options. See the discussion in Jacquart and Thomasset, *Sexuality and Medicine,* 174–75.

31. Beryl Rowland, *Medieval Woman's Guide to Health: The First English Gynecological Handbook* (London: Croom Helm, 1981), 86–87.

32. Magnus, *On Animals,* bk. 15, vol. 5, chap. 99, 1129–30.

33. Helen Rodnite Lemay, "William of Saliceto on Human Sexuality," *Viator* 12 (1981): 177–78.

34. See I. Veith, *Hysteria: The History of a Disease* (Chicago: University of Chicago Press, 1965), 106.

35. See Jacquart and Thomasset, *Sexuality and Medicine,* 52–55.

36. For an account of Constantine's attempt to reconcile the ancients, see Cadden, *Meanings of Sex Difference,* 60–61.

37. See Jacquart and Thomasset, *Sexuality and Medicine,* 55–56.

38. Quoted in Anthony Preus, "Galen's Criticism of Aristotle's Conception Theory," *Journal of the History of Biology* 10, no. 1 (1977): 70.

39. See Cadden, *Meanings of Sex Difference,* 98.

40. Avicenna, *Liber canonis,* bk. 3, fen. 20, tr. 1, chap. 5.

41. *The Riverside Chaucer,* "The Knight's Tale," lines 1373–76, p. 44.

42. Mary Wack, *Lovesickness in the Middle Ages: The Viaticum and Its Commentaries* (Philadelphia: University of Pennsylvania Press, 1990), 47–48.

43. Ibid., 110–13.

44. Ibid., 142.

45. J. A. Tasioulas, *The Makars: The Poems of Henryson, Dunbar, and Douglas* (Edinburgh: Canongate, 1999), 718.

46. See Carole Rawcliffe, *Leprosy in Medieval England* (Woodbridge, UK: Boydell, 2006), 160–62.

47. Saul Brody, *The Disease of the Soul: Leprosy in Medieval Literature* (Ithaca, NY: Cornell University Press, 1974), 65.

48. Lawn, *The Prose Salernitan Questions*, B33, 8.

49. Lemay, *Women's Secrets*, 130–31.

50. Ibid., 88.

51. William of Conches, *Dragmaticon*, ed. G. Gratarolus (Frankfurt: Minerva, 1967), 243–44.

52. Jacquart and Thomasset, *Sexuality and Medicine,* 187, 190.

53. Lemay, "William of Saliceto," 28–30.

54. See Tasioulas, *The Makars,* 187–214.

55. Ibid., 553–54, ll. 175–92.

56. Decima Douie and Hugh Farmer, *The Life of St. Hugh of Lincoln* (London: Nelson, 1962), 2:7–10. See Stanley Rubin, *Medieval English Medicine* (New York: Barnes and Noble, 1974), 93.

57. Tasioulas, *The Makars,* 549, l.96.

58. Hildegard of Bingen, *Causae et curae*, 2:139.

59. John Lydgate, *The Minor Poems of John Lydgate*, ed. H. N. MacCracken, EETS os 192 (London: Oxford University Press, 1939), 704.

60. For Trotula, see Jacquart and Thomasset, *Sexuality and Medicine,* 121–22.

61. Paul Delaney, "Constantinus Africanus' *De coitu*: A Translation," *Chaucer Review* 4 (1969): 64. Jacquart and Thomasset, in *Sexuality and Medicine*, also discuss a twelfth-century treatise by Maimonides that contains a recipe for an ointment "with which one smears the … penis three hours before coitus and which enables an erection to be maintained after a first ejaculation. One can thus satisfy a partner who takes a long time to be stimulated, or even several women" (120).

62. Jacquart and Thomasset, *Sexuality and Medicine,* 91.

63. For a discussion of such disclaimers in the Arabic source material, see Monica Green, "Constantinus Africanus and the Conflict between Religion and Science," in *The Human Embryo: Aristotle and the Arabic and European Traditions*, ed. G. Dunstan (Exeter: University of Exeter Press, 1990), 50–51. For Peter of Spain, see J. M. Riddle, *Contraception and Abortion from the Ancient World to the Renaissance* (Cambridge, MA: Harvard University Press, 1992), 138.

64. See Riddle, *Contraception and Abortion,* 116–17.

Chapter 7

1. John J. O'Meara, trans. and ed., *The History and Topography of Ireland by Gerald of Wales: Topographia Hiberniae* (Harmondsworth, UK: Penguin, 1982), 110.

2. Sigurður Nordal et al., eds., *Flateyjarbók*, 4 vols. (Akranes: Flateyjarútgáfan, 1944–1945).

3. Translation by Eysteinn Björnsson, at http://www3.hi.is/~eybjorn/ugm/volsi.html (accessed August 4, 2009).

4. Adam of Bremen, *Gesta Hammaburgensis ecclesiae pontificum,* ed. G. Waitz (Berlin: Hahn, 1876), bk. 4, sections 26–27.

5. J. Stevenson, *Chronicon de Lanercost* (Edinburgh: Bannatyne and Maitland Clubs, 1839), 85 (translation mine).

6. Ibid.

7. *The Oxford English Dictionary,* 2nd ed., s.v., "needfire," has a very pertinent, though much later, quotation from the Presbytery Book of Strathbogie (1644): "It was regraited by Mr. Robert Watsone that ther vas neid fyre raysed vithin his parochin [parish] for the curing of cattell."

8. William Hamilton, Richard Payne Knight, and Thomas Wright, *A Discourse on the Worship of Priapus, and Its Connection with the Mystic Theology of the Ancients . . . (a New Edition). To Which Is Added Essay on the Worship on the Worship of the Generative Powers during the Middle Ages of Western Europe* (1865; repr. New York: Dorset Press, 1992), 32–33.

9. Burchard of Worms, *Decretum, PL* 140, cols. 1012 ff.

10. Johannes Goropius Becanus, *Origines Antwerpianae, siue Cimmeriorum Becceselana nouem libros complexa* (Antwerp: Plantini, 1569), lib. 1, 26, 101.

11. Richard N. Bailey, "Apotropaic Figures in Milan and North-West England," *Folklore* 94, no. 1 (1983): 114.

12. See Malcolm Jones, "Folklore Motifs in Late Medieval Art III: Erotic Animal Imagery," *Folklore* 102, no. 2 (1991): 192–219. In *Humour and Folly in Secular and Profane Prints of Northern Europe, 1430–1540* (London: Harvey Miller, 2002), Christa Grössinger labels the image "Woman cutting her chastity-belt" (200).

13. For Zoan Andrea's engraving *Due donne,* see http://commons.wikimedia.org/wiki/File:Zoan-Andrea_%281464-1526%29_-_Due_donne.jpg (accessed October 12, 2009).

14. David Landau and Peter Parshall, *The Renaissance Print: 1470–1550* (New Haven, CT: Yale University Press, 1994), 296, ill. 313.

15. Arthur Forgeais, *Notice sur des plombs historiés trouvés dans la Seine* (Paris: Chez l'auteur et chez Dumoulin, 1858).

16. Plutarch, *Quaestiones Conviviales: Plutarch's Moralia VIII,* trans. Paul A. Clement and H. B. Hoffleit, Loeb Classical Library (Cambridge, MA: Harvard University Press, 1969), bk. 5, chap. 7, 3.

17. In a letter of Sir William Hamilton: see Catherine Johns, *Sex or Symbol? Erotic Images of Greece and Rome* (London: Routledge, 1999), 24f. See also K. Sudhoff, "Antike Votivgaben, die weiblichen Genitalorgane darstellend," *Monatsschrift für Geburtshilfe und Gynäkologie* 38 (1914): 185–99.

18. Sir Thomas More, *A Dialogue Concerning Heresies,* vol. 6, *The Complete Works of Sir Thomas More,* ed. T.M.C. Lawler, Germain Marc'hadour, and Richard C. Marius (New Haven, CT: Yale University Press, 1981), 228, lines 10–13. I owe this reference to Dr. Richard Axton.

19. Pietro Aretino, *Lettere sull'arte,* ed. F. Pertile and E. Camesasca, 4 vols. (Milan: Milione, 1957–60), 2:110f., no. 68; translation adapted from T. C. Chubb, *The*

Letters of Pietro Aretino (New Haven, CT: Yale University Press, 1967), 124, no. 58, *To Messer Battista Zatti of Brescia*, December 11, 1537.

20. See Old English *pintel*, Danish dialect *pint*, *pintel*, Dutch *pint*. The wild flower now known as the cuckoopint (*Arum maculatum*) was earlier *cokku-pyntel* and *gauk pyntill* (fifteenth century) (and once *hoggspyntyl*), so called from its characteristic erect spadix. In the late Middle Ages the word was also a component of English nicknames of both simplex (Robert *Pintel*, 1187) and compound form (John *Swet-pintel*, 1275; Joh. *Wytepintell*, 1313; William *Doggepintel*, 1361).

21. H.J.E. van Beuningen, A. M. Koldeweij, and D. Kicken, eds., *Heilig en Profaan 1: 1200 Laatmiddeleeuwse insignes uit openbare en particuliere collectives*, Rotterdam Papers 8 (Cothen: Stichting Middeleeuwse religieuze en profane insignes, 1993), afb. 641.

22. Ibid. and H.J.E. Van Beuningen, A. M. Koldeweij, and D. Kicken, eds., *Heilig en Profaan 2: 1200 Laatmiddeleeuwse insignes uit openbare en particuliere collectives*, Rotterdam Papers 12 (Cothen: Stichting Middeleeuwse religieuze en profane insignes, 2001).

23. Jan Smeken, *Dwonder van Claren ijse en snee: Een verloren en teruggevonden gedicht*, ed. Rena Pennink and Dirk Enklaar (Gravenhage: Martinus Nijhoff, 1946), my translation.

24. N. Dupire, ed., *Les faictz et dictz de J. Molinet* (Paris: Société des Anciens textes français, 1937), 2:540ff.

25. I thank Prof. Kurt Baldinger for a copy of his highly informative study of obscene punning in the late Middle French riddles. Kurt Baldinger, "Homonymie- und Polysemiespiele im Mittelfranzösischen," *Zeitschrift für Romanische Philologie* 100 (1984): 241–81. See also Kurt Baldinger, "Zum Wortschatz der Rätselfragen im 15.Jahrhundert," *Zeitschrift für Romanische Philologie* 100 (1984): 282–305.

26. See J. C. Margolin and J. Céard, *Rébus de la Renaissance* (Paris: Maisonneuve & Larose, 1986).

27. *Kryptadia: Recueil de documents pour servir à l'étude des traditions populaires*, vol. 3 (Heilbronn: Henninger Frères, 1886), 395.

28. The episode "Come Renart parfist le con" is in Mario Roques, ed., *Le roman de Renart*, 6 vols. (Paris: Champion, 1951–1963), 25, line 13, 775ff.

29. The drawings belong to Jose Mindlin, a private collector in São Paulo, Brazil. See Malcolm Jones, *The Secret Middle Ages: Discovering the Real Medieval World* (Stroud, UK: Sutton, 2002), plates 22–24, and 257–58 and 266.

30. A. G. Rigg, ed. and trans., *Gawain on Marriage: The Textual Tradition of the* De Coniuge Non Ducenda (Toronto: Pontifical Institute of Mediaeval Studies, 1986).

31. John Lydgate, *The Minor Poems of John Lydgate*, ed. H. N. MacCracken, EETS os 192 (London: Oxford University Press, 1939), 2:459, line 78.

32. John Skelton, *The Bowge of Courte*, in *John Skelton: The Complete English Poems*, ed. J. Scattergood (Harmondsworth, UK: Penguin, 1983), 57, line 410. The identical idiom also exists in Middle French: *rompre une lance*.

33. See J. O. Halliwell, ed., *A Selection from the Minor Poems of Dan John Lydgate* (London: Percy Society, 1840), 204. The thirteenth-century German romance *Der Vrouwen Turnei* describes a group of women dressing up as men in order to

participate in a joust and ends with an elaborate sexual innuendo: F. H. von der Hagen, *Gesamtabenteuer: Hundert altdeutsche Erzählungen* (Darmstadt: Wissenschaftliche Buchgesellschaft, 1961), 1:371–82.

34. See n. 29.

35. The second edition of *The Oxford English Dictionary* cites "unum dagar ballokhefted" from a York will of 1438. The *Middle English Dictionary* (hereafter *MED)*, s.v., "ballok" (2a), adds citations from 1423 and 1442.

36. A.V.C. Schmidt, *The Vision of Piers Plowman: A Critical Edition of the B-tRext* (London: Dent, 1978), Passus 15, line 124. See also the fifteenth-century carol entitled by its editor "The Braggart and His Baselard" in R. L. Green, *The Early English Carols*, 2nd ed. (Oxford: Clarendon Press, 1977), no. 417.

37. See *OED*, "bollock knife" s.v. "bollock" (*n.* and *adj.*).

38. J. B. Ward-Perkins, *London Museum Medieval Catalogue* (London: HMSO, 1940), 47 and pl. 9, no. 1.

39. Schmidt, *The Vision of Piers Plowman*, 344.

40. BL MS Egerton 1894, fol. 17r, redrawn as fig. 38 in J. Cowgill, M. de Neergaard, and N. Griffiths, *Knives and Scabbards*, Medieval Finds from Excavations in London l (London: HMSO, 1987).

41. A. von Keller, *Fastnachtspiele aus dem fünfzehnten Jahrhundert* (Stuttgart: Anton Hiersemann, 1853), 2:717, line 17.

42. A. Bodtker, ed., *Partonope of Blois*, EETS es 109 (London: Oxford University Press, 1912), line 1772f. Compare the practice recorded by J.-B. Thiers in his *Traité des superstitions* of 1679, in which the newly wed husband would urinate into the keyhole of the church in which he had just been married, in order to counteract any spell put on him to prevent him from fulfilling his conjugal duties: see Robert Muchembled, "The Order of Gestures: A Social History of Sensibilities under the Ancien Régime in France," in *A Cultural History of Gesture from Antiquity to the Present Day*, ed. Jan Bremmer and Herman Roodenburg (Oxford: Polity Press, 1991), 139f.

43. J. D. Gordon, ed., *The Epistle of Othea to Hector* (Philadelphia: University of Pennsylvania Press, 1942), 136.

44. Chaucer, *The Riverside Chaucer*, "The General Prologue" to the *Canterbury Tales*, line 618, p. 33. See further B. Moore, "The Reeve's 'Rusty Blade,'" *Medium Ævum* 58 (1959): 304–12.

45. Femke Speelberg and Jacoline Zilverschoon, *"Zotheid" in de duisternis: Middeleeuwse tekeneingen in de Sint-Pietersberg* (Rotterdam: Nijmegen University Press, 2007), cat. no. 13.

46. Beryl Rowland, *Medieval Woman's Guide to Health: The First English Gynecological Handbook* (London: Croom Helm, 1981), 168 and 94.

47. A. H. Thomas, ed., *Calendar of Plea and Memoranda Rolls ... of the ... City of London*, 3 vols. (Cambridge: Cambridge University Press, 1926–32), 1:125.

48. MS Wel. 564, fol. 45r, col. 1. According to *MED*, s.v., "osse," (*n.*), the text reads "the cheste or the purs of the cod or ballokis." I suggest the scribe has mistakenly transposed the "of" and second "or."

49. John Russell, *Book of Carving and Nurture*, in *Early English Meals and Manners*, ed. Frederick J. Furnivall, EETS os 32 (Oxford: Oxford University Press, 1868), 286.

50. The first element is perhaps "sharp" rather than "share" (pubic region, groin).
51. John Insley, review of Ingrid Hjertstedt, *Middle English Nicknames in the Lay Subsidy Rolls for Warwickshire, Studia Neophilologica* 62, no.1 (1990): 118.
52. Adolf Socin, *Mittelhochdeutsches Namenbuch: Nach oberrheinischen Quellen des 12. und 13. Jahrhunderts* (Basel: Helbing & Lichtenhahn, 1903), 427.
53. "A Talk of Ten Wives on Their Husbands' Ware," in *The Trials and Joys of Marriage*, ed. Eve Salisbury (Kalamazoo, MI: Medieval Institute, 2002), lines 35–36.
54. David Postles, *Talking Ballocs: Nicknames and English Medieval Sociolinguistics* (Leicester: University of Leicester, Centre for English Local History, 2003), 14.
55. See Tony Hunt, *The Plant Names of Medieval England* (Cambridge: Brewer, 1989).
56. Ibid.
57. Johns, *Sex or Symbol?* 43.
58. I am not aware of any unequivocal examples of "prick" signifying "penis" in Middle English, but note the game called "fart prick in cule" in the play *Fulgens and Lucrece* (ca. 1497), and in John Palgrave's *Acolastus* (1540) the word is used to translate Latin *mentula* ("little prick"). The verb *priken* is attested in the sense "copulate" from the time of Chaucer ("Reeve's Tale," l. 4231), however, so it is always possible that the nickname could denote a man proud of his sexual performance and be construed as "[who] pricks proudly."
59. "A Talk of Ten Wives," line 23. The name Roger Prikeproud (1332) is attested in *MED*, s.v., "priken."
60. Ernest Weekley, *Surnames* (New York: Dutton, 1916), 273.
61. Richard Coates, "*Fockynggroue* in Bristol," *Notes and Queries* 252, no. 4 (2007): 373–76.
62. *OED*, 2nd ed., s.v., "fuck" (*v.*).
63. The full inscription reads "ɪᴏʜ ɢʀᴠɴᴀʀᴅ ꜰᴏᴄᴀᴛᴏᴠᴛ." *Grunard* is itself a nickname meaning "grumbler, grunter." It is possible that the final word is not Jean's second byname but merely a facetious (boastful?) comment on his sexual behavior. The matrix is British Museum reg. no. 1856,0627.138.
64. The same name, though no longer extant, is attested in the form *Cunteclyf* in 1358: J. McN. Dodgson, *The Place-Names of Cheshire*, 5 vols., EPNS 44–48, 54, 74 (Cambridge: Cambridge University Press, 1970–97), 2:76.
65. J. Buchanan-Brown, ed., *John Aubrey: Three Prose Works* (Fontwell, UK: Centaur, 1972), 254–55.
66. See S. R. Fischer, *The Complete Medieval Dreambook: A Multilingual, Alphabetical "Somnia Danielis" Collation* (Bern: Peter Lang, 1982), 150; *MED*, s.v., "twig" (*n.*) (c), as the author has not understood that in this combination (i.e., with *virilis*), *virga* means "penis."
67. On the fabliau *Trubert*, see Kathryn Gravdal, *Vilain and Courtois: Transgressive Parody in French Literature of the Twelfth and Thirteenth Century* (Lincoln: University of Nebraska Press, 1989), 134.
68. Heinrich Kramer and Jakob Sprenger, *Malleus Maleficarum*, trans. M. Summers (London: Arrow, 1971), pt. 2, Q. 1, ch. 7, ll. 267f.
69. Han Bos and Gerrit Groeneweg, *Schatten uit de Schelde: Gebruiks- en Sierwoorwerpen uit de Verdronken Plaatsen in de Oosterschelde: Markiezenhof*

Gemeente–Museum Bergen op Zoom, 14 maart–27 april 1987 (Bergen op Zoom: Gemeentemuseum Bergen op Zoom, 1987).

70. Hans Vintler, *Blumen der Tugend*, ed. Ignaz von Zingerle (Innsbrück: Wagner'sche Universitäts-Buchhandlung, 1874), 268, ll. 799 ff.

71. Barisa Krekic, "*Abominandum Crimen:* Punishment of Homosexuals in Renaissance Dubrovnik," *Viator* 18 (1987): 342, n. 24.

72. Illustrated in a miniature reproduced (unfortunately, without provenance) by Eduard Fuchs in *Illustrierte Sittengeschichte vom Mittelalter bis zur Gegenwart I: Renaissance (mit Ergänzungsband)* (Munich: Albert Langen, 1928), abb. l6, with the caption "Women mock their fleeing menfolk."

73. E. Kislinger, "Anasyrma. Notizen zur Geste des Schamwesens," in *Symbole des Alltags, Alltag der Symbole: Festschrift für Harry Kühnel zum 65. Geburtstag,* ed. G. Blaschitz, H. Hundsbichler, G. Jaritz, and E. Vavra (Graz: ADEVA, 1992), 377–94, supersedes all other discussions of this motif. To his examples may be added the episode recorded in the third-century apocryphal *Acts of Paul and Thecla,* in which the virgin St. Thecla of Iconium, sentenced to be killed by wild beasts in the Coliseum, repulsed a lion by exposing her vagina, an incident alluded to by St. Ambrose in his *De Virginibus* (377), vol. 3, chap. 19: *Ambrose: Select Works and Letters.* vol. 10 of *Nicene and Post-Nicene Fathers: Second Series*, ed. Philip Schaff and Rev. Henry Wallace (New York: Cosimo, 2007).

74. See Hans-Jörg Uther, *The Types of International Folktales: A Classification and Bibliography* (Helsinki: Suomalainen Tiedeakatemia, 2004), ATU 1153.

75. From Trevisa's 1398 translation of Bartholomaeus Anglicus's *De Proprietatibus Rerum* (*On the Nature of Things*), 5:xlviii, in Bodleian MS e Mus 16.

76. S. E. Roberts, *The Legal Triads of Medieval Wales* (Cardiff: University of Wales Press, 2007), 145. I have paraphrased the "false virgin" of Roberts's translation as "bride who falsely claims to be a virgin."

Chapter 8

I would like to thank Ruth Mazo Karras for helping to supervise the writing of this chapter, and for her expertise, her keen editorial eye, and her generosity.

1. E. P. Thompson, "The Moral Economy of the English Crowd in the Eighteenth Century" and "The Moral Economy Reviewed," in *Customs in Common* (New York: Norton, 1991), 285–351.

2. D. Nirenberg, *Communities of Violence: Persecution of Minorities in the Middle Ages* (Princeton, NJ: Princeton University Press, 1996), 56. The metaphor of the moral economy has been employed in a variety of disciplines and contexts, including economics and political science.

3. For Louis IX, see B. Geremek, *The Margins of Society in Late Medieval Paris* (Cambridge: Cambridge University Press, 1987), 212–13. For prostitution and the Crusades, see James A. Brundage, "Prostitution, Miscegenation and Sexual Purity in the First Crusade," in *Crusade and Settlement*, ed. Peter W. Edbury (Cardiff: University College Cardiff Press, 1985), 57–65.

4. Prostitution was not an exclusively female practice in the medieval period. See Ruth Mazo Karras and David Lorenzo Boyd, "'*Ut cum muliere*': A Male Transvestite Prostitute in Fourteenth-Century London," in *Premodern Sexualities*, ed. Louise Fradenburg and Carla Freccero (New York: Routledge, 1996), 99–116.

5. For a good discussion of the relationship of traveling merchants and prostitutes, see J. Murray, *Bruges, Cradle of Capitalism, 1280–1390* (Cambridge: Cambridge University Press, 2005), 326–43.

6. For Mallorca, see M. Bernat Roca and J. Serra-Barceló, "Folles fembres bordelleres: La prostitució femenina al tombant de l'Edat Mitjana (Ciutat de Mallorca). Segles XIV–XVI," in *Al tombant de l'Edat Mitjana*, ed. Maria Barceló Crespi, Tradició medieval i cultural humanista XVIII Jornades d'Estudis Històrics Locals (Palma de Mallorca: Institut d'Estudis Baleàrics, 2000), 213–49. For England, see Ruth Karras, *Common Women: Prostitution and Sexuality in Medieval England* (Oxford: Oxford University Press, 1996).

7. For a general overview of the power of *fama*, see T. Fenster and D. C. Smail, eds., *Fama: The Politics of Talk and Reputation in Medieval Europe* (Ithaca, NY: Cornell University Press, 2003).

8. James A. Brundage, *Law, Sex, and Christian Society in Medieval Europe* (Chicago: University of Chicago Press, 1987), 120–21.

9. M. McCormick, *Origins of the European Economy: Communications and Commerce, AD 300–900* (Cambridge: Cambridge University Press, 2001).

10. Suzanne F. Wemple, *Women in Frankish Society: Marriage and the Cloister, 500–900* (Philadelphia: University of Pennsylvania Press, 1981), 66–67.

11. Brundage, *Law, Sex, and Christian Society*, 147.

12. Ibid., 133.

13. Ibid., 389–96.

14. For an excellent discussion of repentant houses, see J. Rollo-Koster, "From Prostitutes to Brides of Christ: The Avignonese *Repenties* in the Late Middle Ages," *Journal of Medieval and Early Modern Studies* 32, no. 1 (2002): 109–44. For German prostitution, see Peter Schuster, *Das Frauenhaus: Städtische Bordelle in Deutschland (1350–1600)* (Paderborn: Ferdinand Schöningh, 1992).

15. A phrase originally used by Iwan Bloch, noted by Schuster, *Das Frauenhaus*, 57. For prostitution in fifteenth-century Germany, see 57–133.

16. Karras, *Common Women*, 45.

17. Murray, *Bruges, Cradle of Capitalism*, 326–43; G. Dupond, *Maagdenverleisters, hoeren en speculanten: Prostitutie in Brugge tijdens de Bourgondische periode (1385–1515)* (Bruges: Uitgeverij Marc Van de Wiele, 1996), 233.

18. J. Bennett, *History Matters: Patriarchy and the Challenge of Feminism* (Philadelphia: University of Pennsylvania Press, 2006), chap. 5.

19. Diane Ghirardo has pointed out that the city fathers of Ferrara were not concerned with the immoral activities of prostitutes, but with the locations of prostitutes and pimps, or what she has aptly called "the conjunction of space and sex." Diane Ghirardo, "The Topography of Prostitution in Renaissance Ferrara," *Journal of the Society of Architectural Historians* 60, no. 4 (2001): 402.

20. Leah Otis, *Prostitution in Medieval Society* (Chicago: University of Chicago Press, 1985), 162 n. 24.

21. Geremek, *The Margins of Society,* 212–13.

22. Brundage, *Law, Sex, and Christian Society,* 463; S. R. Blanshei, "Crime and Law Enforcement in Medieval Bologna," *Journal of Social History* 16, no. 1 (1982): 121.

23. Beate Schuster, "L'imaginaire de la prostitution et la société urbaine en Allemagne (XIII–XVIe siècles)," *Médiévales: Langue, textes, histoire* 27 (1994): 79.

24. John K. Brackett, "The Florentine Onestá and the Control of Prostitution, 1403–1680," *Sixteenth Century Journal* 24, no. 2 (1993): 279 n. 20, citing Maria Mazzi's claim that bordello prostitutes were only "the tip of the iceberg" of those practicing illicit sex in Florence.

25. Jeremy Goldberg, "Pigs and Prostitutes: Streetwalking in Comparative Perspective," in *Young Medieval Women,* ed. Katherine Lewis, Noël Menuge, and Kim M. Phillips (Gloucester, UK: Sutton, 1999), 172.

26. Most notably Richard C. Trexler, "Florentine Prostitution in the Fifteenth Century," in *The Women of Renaissance Florence* (Binghamton, NY: Medieval and Renaissance Texts and Studies, 1993), 32ff. See also the discussion in Otis, *Prostitution in Medieval Society,* esp. 100–102.

27. Schuster, *Das Frauenhaus,* 49–51. Also see D. Mengel, "From Venice to Jerusalem and Beyond: Milíč of Kroměříž and the Topography of Prostitution in Fourteenth-Century Prague," *Speculum* 79, no. 2 (2004): 427.

28. Mengel, "From Venice to Jerusalem and Beyond," 427–28.

29. For the development of late medieval administration, see D. Nicholas, *The Later Medieval City* (London: Longman, 1997), esp. chap. 5.

30. Pavan, "Police des moeurs, société et politique," 245.

31. Schuster, *Das Frauenhaus,* 41.

32. Otis, *Prostitution in Medieval Society,* 116.

33. I. Bazn-Daz, F. Garca, and A. Mengibar, "La prostitution au pays Basque entre XIVe et XVIIe siècles," *Annales Histoire* 55, no. 6 (2000): 1258.

34. For tenant farming, see the work of Leah Otis-Cour on Millau (present-day France), where the operation of the municipal brothel was rented out to private individuals (*tenanciers* and *tenancières*) on a yearly basis. Leah Otis-Cour, "La tenancière de la maison publique de Millau au XVe siècle," in *La femme dans l'histoire et la société méridionales (IX–XIX s.)* (Montpellier: Fédération historique du Languedoc méditerranéen, 1995), 219–29.

35. Geremek, *The Margins of Society,* 212–15.

36. Rollo-Koster, "From Prostitutes to Brides of Christ," 111–13.

37. See Otis, *Prostitution in Medieval Society,* 78 and 197 n. 2, for the movement of the red-light district from the suburb of Villanova to the suburb of Lattes in the fourteenth century.

38. M. A. Esteban Recio and M. J. Izquierdo García, "Pescado y marginación. Mujeres públicas en Valladolid y Palencia durante los siglos XV y XVI," in *La ciudad medieval: Aspectos de la vida urbana en la Castilla Bajo-medieval*, ed. Juan Antonio Bonachía Hernando (Valladolid: Secretariado de Publicaciones e Intercambio Cientifico, Universidad de Valladolid, 1996), 131–68, esp. 145–146.

39. Schuster, *Das Frauenhaus*, 44–45. The location of public bordellos near a river, while not exactly cordoning them off, may have to do with moral hygiene, in much the same way that cities pushed their waste into the river. More practically, houses of prostitution on waterways would make them more accessible to merchants and travelers.

40. Mengel, "From Venice to Jerusalem and Beyond," 414.

41. Dupond, *Maagdenverleisters, hoeren en speculanten*, esp. maps illustrating the topography of prostitution on 152–56.

42. L. Roper, "Discipline and Respectability: Prostitution and the Reformation in Augsburg," *History Workshop* 19 (1985): 8.

43. Pavan, "Police des moeurs, société et politique," 245.

44. P. Labalme, "Sodomy and Venetian Justice in the Renaissance," *Revue d'histoire de droit* 52 (1984): 247.

45. Jacques Rossiaud, *Medieval Prostitution*, trans. Lydia G. Cochrane (New York: Barnes and Noble, 1996), 7.

46. Murray, *Bruges, Cradle of Capitalism*, 340 and 340 n. 161.

47. H. A. Kelly, "Bishop, Prioress, and Baud in the Stews of Southwark," *Speculum* 75, no. 2 (2000): 3350 ff. The accepted work on Southwark is M. Carlin, *Medieval Southwark* (London: Hambledon, 1996).

48. Karras, *Common Women*, 41; J. Post, "A Fifteenth-Century Customary of the Southwark Stews," *Journal of the Society of Archivists* 5 (1977): 418–28.

49. Otis, *Prostitution in Medieval Society*, 33.

50. Rollo-Koster, "From Prostitutes to Brides of Christ," 111.

51. Schuster, "L'imaginaire de la prostitution," 80.

52. Rossiaud, *Medieval Prostitution*, 41.

53. Ghirardo, "The Topography of Prostitution," 414.

54. Pavan, "Police des moeurs, société et politique," 246.

55. M. T. López-Beltrán, "Las transgresiones a la ideología del honor y la prostitución en Málaga a fi nales de la edad media, in *Las Mujeres en Andalucía*, ed. M. T. López-Beltrán (Malaga: Servicio de Publicaciones Diputación Provincial de Málaga, 1993), 145.

56. Esteban-Recio and Izquierdo García, "Pescado y marginación," 144.

57. A. L. Molina, "Notas para el estudio de los grupos sociales marginados: La prostitucion en Albacete a finales de La Edad Media," *Congreso de Historia de Albacete* 2 (1984): 217.

58. Otis-Cour, "La tenancière de la maison publique," 221.

59. Diane Ghirardo has suggested that immigration, that is, leaving home, was "the first spatial consequence of prostitution." Ghirardo, "The Topography of Prostitution," 405.

60. Rossiaud, *Medieval Prostitution*, 32.

61. M. Guénette, "Errance et solitude féminines à Manosque (1314–1358)," in *Vie priveé et ordre public a la fin du Moyen-Age*, ed. Michel Hébert (Aix-en Provence: Université de Provence, Service des Publications, 1987), 33–35. Guénette's figures are for all single women, though her data suggest that many immigrants practiced prostitution, and that few prostitutes came from Manosque. The largest influx of

women practicing prostitution came during three famine periods: 1314–1316, the early 1320s (1320, 1321, 1323), and 1341–1343.

62. Trexler, "Florentine Prostitution," 35–39.

63. Karras, *Common Women*, 56–57.

64. M. Carmen-Peris, "La prostitución Valenciana en la segunda mitad del siglo XIV," *Revista d'història medieval* 1 (1990): 190, 191. Only 12.27 percent of the 676 women registered for violating prostitution codes between 1367 and 1399 had their place of origin recorded.

65. López-Beltrán, "Las transgresiones," 160.

66. For Exeter, see M. Kowaleski, "Women's Work in a Market Town: Exeter in the Late Fourteenth Century," in *Women and Work in Preindustrial Europe*, ed. Barbara Hanawalt (Bloomington: Indiana University Press, 1986), 154.

67. For Clarice, see Karras, *Common Women*, 56. For Guillemette, see M. Guénette, "Errance et solitude féminines," 28.

68. K. Reyerson, "Prostitution in Medieval Montpelier: The Ladies of Campus Polverel," *Medieval Prosopography* 18 (1997): 211 n. 19.

69. M. Meyerson, "Prostitution of Muslim Women in the Kingdom of Valencia: Religious and Sexual Discrimination in a Medieval Plural Society," in *The Medieval Mediterranean: Cross-Cultural Contacts*, ed. M. Chiat and Katherine Reyerson (St. Cloud, MN: North Star Press of St. Cloud, 1988), 88.

70. Bernat Roca and Serra-Barceló, "Folles fembres bordelleres," 221–22.

71. Geremek, *The Margins of Society*, 218.

72. Reyerson, "Prostitution in Medieval Montpelier," 221–22.

73. For Paris, see Geremek, *The Margins of Society*, 218–19. For Florence, see Trexler, "Florentine Prostitution," 39–40. For Venice, see E. Pavan, "Police des moeurs, société et politique à Venise à la fin du Moyen Age," *Revue Historique* 264, no. 2 (1980): 262–63. Some prostitutes were better off than others, of course, but the point here is that of the countless thousands of women who provided illicit sex, only a few show up in the record as holding property, running bordellos of their own, leading sumptuous lives, and so forth. As with other issues that deal with the relative victimhood and agency of medieval women, there is not a clear consensus on this point, and more detailed searches of local records need to be done.

74. Karras, *Common Women*, 60–61.

75. Carmen-Peris, "La prostitución Valenciana," 190–91.

76. The *rei d'Arlots*, or king of the ribalds, was allegedly the person in charge of debauchery before prostitution became the concern of public courts. In the area from Lyons to Artois there existed a *roi des ribauds* who had some authority over prostitutes, and this office also existed in the royal palace. The office was abolished in Lille in 1364, in Lyon around 1400, and in the royal court in 1449: Rossiaud, *Medieval Prostitution*, 57, 65.

77. Ibid., 198.

78. Carlin, *Medieval Southwark*, 217. The only surviving court roll of the bishop's manor before 1550 is that of 1505–1506, but brothels had been operating in Stewside since at least the mid-fourteenth century, and there is no evidence that ordinances were followed any more closely in that period than in the later.

79. D. Menjot, "Prostitutas y rufianes en las ciudades castellanas a fines de la Edad Media," *Temas medievales* 4 (1994): 202.

80. Otis, *Prostitution in Medieval Society,* 137.

81. Carmen-Peris, "La prostitución Valenciana," 181.

82. Karras, *Common Women,* 68.

83. Geremek, *The Margins of Society,* 228.

84. Rossiaud, *Medieval Prostitution,* 30–31.

85. Karras, *Common Women,* 60.

86. Schuster, *Das Frauenhaus,* 36–39, contains a comprehensive listing of the opening of civic bordellos in Germany.

87. M. Wiesner, *Working Women in Renaissance Germany* (New Brunswick, NJ: Rutgers University Press, 1986), 104.

88. Mary Elizabeth Perry, *Gender and Disorder in Early Modern Seville* (Princeton, NJ: Princeton University Press, 1990), 137.

Chapter 9

I am grateful to Ruth Evans, Shari Lindquist, Bob Mills, and Sam Riches for their comments on drafts of this chapter and to Shari Lindquist and Paul Hardwick for pre-publication access to their current work.

1. Barbican Art Gallery Events Details, http://www.barbican.org.uk/artgallery/event-detail.asp?ID=5625 (accessed November 2, 2007).

2. Peter Webb, *The Erotic Arts* (London: Secker and Warburg, 1975), 104.

3. Bruce Holsinger, *The Premodern Condition: Medievalism and the Making of Theory* (Chicago: University of Chicago Press, 2005), 13.

4. Andreas Capellanus, *Andreas Capellanus on Love,* ed. and trans. P. G. Walsh (London: Duckworth, 1982), 33.

5. Suzannah Biernoff, *Sight and Embodiment in the Middle Ages* (Basingstoke, UK: Palgrave Macmillan, 2002), 58.

6. John T. McNeill and Helena M. Garner, eds., *Medieval Handbooks of Penance: A Translation of the Principal* libri poenitentiales *and Selections from Related Documents* (New York: Columbia University Press, 1938).

7. W. Nelson Francis, ed., *The Book of Vices and Virtues: A Fourteenth Century English Translation of the* Somme le Roi *of Lorens d'Orleans,* EETS os 217 (London: Oxford University Press, 1942), 43–44.

8. Master Gregorius, *The Marvels of Rome,* trans. John Osborne (Toronto: Pontifical Institute of Mediaeval Studies, 1987), 26.

9. David Freedberg, *The Power of Images: Studies in the History and Theory of Response* (Chicago: University of Chicago Press, 1989), 330–31.

10. Michael Camille, "Obscenity under Erasure: Censorship in Medieval Illuminated Manuscripts," in *Obscenity: Social Control and Artistic Creation in the European Middle Ages,* ed. Jan M. Ziolkowski (Leiden: Brill, 1998), 148–50.

11. G. V. Smithies, ed., *Kyng Alisaunder,* EETS os 227 (London: Oxford University Press, 1952), 359.

12. D.J.A. Ross, *Illustrated Medieval Alexander Books in Germany and the Netherlands* (Cambridge: MHRA, 1971), figs. 195, 325, 420.

13. Guillaume de Lorris and Jean de Meun, *The Romance of the Rose*, trans. Frances Horgan (Oxford: Oxford University Press, 1994), 323.

14. See Richard Kieckhefer, "Erotic Magic in Medieval Europe," in *Sex in the Middle Ages: A Book of Essays*, ed. Joyce E. Salisbury (New York: Garland, 1991), 38–41, on the use of images in erotic magic.

15. James A. Brundage, *Law, Sex, and Christian Society in Medieval Europe* (Chicago: University of Chicago Press, 1987), 110.

16. Michael Camille, *The Gothic Idol: Ideology and Image-Making in Medieval Art* (Cambridge: Cambridge University Press, 1989), 87.

17. Catherine Johns, *Sex or Symbol? Erotic Images of Greece and Rome* (London: Routledge, 1999), 56.

18. Augustine of Hippo, *City of God*, trans. Henry Bettenson, ed. David Knowles (London: Penguin, 1980), 523.

19. Ibid., 279.

20. Jean Gerson, *Oeuvres Complètes*, ed. Palémon Glorieux, 10 vols. (Paris: Desclée, 1960–73), 10:28, trans. D. Catherine Brown, *Pastor and Laity in the Theology of Jean Gerson* (Cambridge: Cambridge University Press, 1987), 242.

21. Jos Koldeweij, "'Shameless and Naked Images': Obscene Badges as Parodies of Popular Devotion," in *Art and Architecture of Late Medieval Pilgrimage in Northern Europe and the British Isles*, ed. Sarah Blick and Rita Tekippe (Leiden: Brill, 2005), 499.

22. John Day, *Yahweh and the Gods and Goddesses of Canaan* (New York: Sheffield Academic Press, 2000), 73; Numbers 25:1–8.

23. Walter Kendrick, *The Secret Museum: Pornography in Modern Culture* (Berkeley: University of California Press, 1987), 35–40.

24. Michael Camille, *The Medieval Art of Love: Objects and Subjects of Desire* (New York: Harry N. Abrams, 1998), 147–53.

25. Lynn Hunt, "Introduction: Obscenity and the Origins of Modernity, 1500–1800," in *The Invention of Pornography: Obscenity and the Origins of Modernity, 1500–1800,* ed. Lynn Hunt (New York: Zone, 1993), 10–11.

26. Kendrick, *The Secret Museum,* 11.

27. James Schultz, *Courtly Love, the Love of Courtliness, and the History of Sexuality* (Chicago: University of Chicago Press, 2006), 38.

28. *The Riverside Chaucer*, "The Parson's Tale," lines 422–23, p. 301.

29. G. R. Owst, *Literature and Pulpit in Medieval England* (Oxford: Blackwell, 1961), 397.

30. Brigitte Buettner, "Dressing and Undressing Bodies in Late Medieval Images," in *Artistic Exchange: 28th Internationalen Kongresses für Kunstgeschichte*, ed. Thomas W. Gaehtgens (Berlin: Akademic Verlag, 1993), 383.

31. Martin W. Walsh, "*Babio*: Towards a Performance Reconstruction of Secular Farce in Twelfth-Century England," in *England in the Twelfth Century: Proceedings of the 1988 Harlaxton Symposium*, ed. Daniel Williams (Woodbridge, UK: Boydell, 1990), 232.

32. Michael Camille, *Image on the Edge: The Margins of Medieval Art* (London: Reaktion, 1992), 116; British Library MS Add. 42130, fol. 68r.

33. John Blacman, *Henry VI: A Reprint of John Blacman's Memoir*, trans. M. R. James (Cambridge: Cambridge University Press, 1919), 30.

34. Psalm 39:6; Richard Rolle, *The Psalter, or Psalms of David and Certain Canticles with a Translation and Exposition in English by Richard Rolle of Hampole*, ed. H. R. Bramley (Oxford: Clarendon Press, 1884), 147.

35. Evelyn Birge Vitz, "Erotic Reading in the Middle Ages: Performance and the Re-performance of Romance," in *Performing Medieval Narrative*, ed. Evelyn Birge Vitz, Nancy Freeman Regalado, and Marilyn Lawrence (Cambridge: Brewer, 2005), 73.

36. J.R.R. Tolkien and E. V. Gordon, ed. and trans., *Sir Gawain and the Green Knight,* rev. Norman Davis, 2nd ed. (Oxford: Clarendon Press, 1967), Fitt 2, lines 954–96.

37. Suzanne Lewis, "Images of Opening, Penetration and Closure in the *Roman de la Rose*," *Word and Image* 8, no. 3 (1992): 239.

38. Priscilla Heath Barnum, ed., *Dives and Pauper*, vol. 1, EETS os 275 (London: Oxford University Press, 1976), 82.

39. Camille, "Obscenity under Erasure," 96.

40. Simon Gaunt, "Obscene Hermeneutics in Troubadour Lyric," in *Medieval Obscenities*, ed. Nicola McDonald (Woodbridge, UK: York Medieval Press, 2006), 94.

41. Robert Baldwin, "Marriage as a Sacramental Reflection of the Passion: The Mirror in Jan van Eyck's *Arnolfini Wedding*," *Oud Holland* 98, no. 2 (1984): 59–63.

42. Song of Songs 5:4–5.

43. *The Riverside Chaucer*, "The Wife of Bath's Prologue," line 618, p. 113.

44. Edwin Hall, *The Arnolfini Betrothal: Medieval Marriage and the Enigma of Van Eyck's Double Portrait* (Berkeley: University of California Press, 1994), 49–94.

45. Anthony Weir and James Jerman, *Images of Lust: Sexual Carvings on Medieval Churches* (London: Routledge, 1999), 11.

46. Camille, "Obscenity under Erasure," 66–67; Samantha Riches, *St. George: Hero, Martyr and Myth* (Stroud, UK: Sutton, 2000), 158–77.

47. Marian Bleeke, "Sheelas, Sex, and Significance in Romanesque Sculpture: The Kilpeck Corbel Series," *Studies in Iconography* 26 (2005): 21; Madeline H. Caviness, "Obscenity and Alterity: Images that Shock and Offend Us/Them, Now/Then?" in *Obscenity: Social Control and Artistic Creation in the European Middle Ages*, ed. Jan M. Ziolkowski (Leiden: Brill, 1998), 164.

48. Barbara Freitag, *Sheela-na-gigs: Unravelling an Enigma* (London: Routledge, 2004), 156.

49. Bella Millett and Jocelyn Wogan-Browne, eds. and trans., *Medieval English Prose for Women from the Katherine Group and Ancrene Wisse* (Oxford: Clarendon Press, 1990), 37.

50. Michael Swanton, trans., "The Deeds of Hereward," in *Medieval Outlaws: Ten Tales in Modern English*, ed. Thomas H. Ohlgren (Stroud, UK: Sutton, 1998), 50.

51. Eamonn Kelly, "Irish Sheela-na-gigs and Related Figures with Reference to the Collections of the National Museum of Ireland," in McDonald, *Medieval Obscenities*, 131–33.

52. Ruth Mellinkoff, *Averting Demons: The Protective Power of Medieval Visual Motifs and Themes*, 2 vols. (Los Angeles, CA: Ruth Mellinkoff, 2004), vol. 2, figs. 6.98–99.

53. Ibid., 2:138, figs. 6.19–21, 7.77–8.

54. Paula Gerson, "Margins for Eros," *Romance Languages Annual* 5 (1993): 50; Mary Carruthers, *The Book of Memory: A Study of Memory in Medieval Culture* (Cambridge: Cambridge University Press, 1990), 228.

55. See Weir and Jarman, *Images of Lust*, 13, type III.

56. Madeline H. Caviness, "A Son's Gaze on Noah: Cause or Case of Viriliphobia?" in *Compartamenti e Immaginario della Sessualita Nell'Alto Medioevo* 53 (2006): 996–1002.

57. John Dickinson, *Misericords of North West England: Their Nature and Significance* (Lancaster: Centre for North-West Regional Studies, University of Lancaster, 2008), 22; Paul Hardwick, *English Misericords and the Margins of the Sacred* (Woodbridge, UK: Boydell and Brewer, forthcoming).

58. Giovanni Boccaccio, *The Decameron*, trans. Mark Musa and Peter Bondanella (New York: Norton, 1983), fourth day, second tale.

59. 1 Cor. 11:10.

60. Tertullian, *The Writings of Tertullian*, vol. 3, trans. S. Thelwell (Edinburgh: T. and T. Clark, 1895), 165–66; Gen. 6:2.

61. Alaric Hall, *Elves in Anglo-Saxon England: Matters of Belief, Health, Gender and Identity* (Woodbridge, UK: Boydell, 2007), 142.

62. David Keck, *Angels and Angelology in the Middle Ages* (Oxford: Oxford University Press, 1998), 117–23.

63. Thomas Aquinas, *Summa theologica*, 1.1.50.5.

64. A. M. Koldeweij, "Lifting the Veil on Pilgrim Badges," in *Pilgrimage Explored*, ed. J. Stopford (Woodbridge, UK: York Medieval Press, 1999), 164.

65. Jos Koldeweij, "The Wearing of Significant Badges, Religious and Secular: The Social Meaning of a Behavioural Pattern," in *Showing Status: Representation of Social Positions in the Late Middle Ages*, ed. Wim Blockmans and Antheum Janse (Turnhout: Brepols, 1999), 323.

66. Malcolm Jones, "The Secular Badges," in *Heilig en Profaan: 1000 Laatmiddeleeuwse Insignes uit de Collectie H.J.E. van Beuningen*, ed. H.J.E. van Beuningen and A. M. Koldeweij, Rotterdam Papers 8 (Cothen: Stichting Middeleeuwse religieuze en profane insignes, 1993), 104.

67. Malcolm Jones, *The Secret Middle Ages: Discovering the Real Medieval World* (Stroud, UK: Sutton, 2002), 256; Susan Signe Morrison, *Women Pilgrims in Late Medieval England: Private Piety as Public Performance* (London: Routledge, 2000), 107–19.

68. Caviness, "A Son's Gaze," 1008; Jones, *The Secret Middle Ages,* 255.

69. Norman P. Tanner, ed., *Heresy Trials in the Diocese of Norwich, 1428–31*, Camden Society 4.20 (London: Royal Historical Society, 1977). 148.

70. Anne Marie Rasmussen, *Wandering Genitalia: Sexuality and the Body in German Culture Between the Late Middle Ages and Early Modernity*, King's College London Medieval Studies (London: Centre for Late Antique and Medieval Studies, 2009).

71. Ronald Hutton, *The Rise and Fall of Merry England: The Ritual Year, 1400–1700* (Oxford: Oxford University Press, 1994), 59–60.

72. Sarah Salih, *Versions of Virginity in Late Medieval England* (Cambridge: Brewer, 2001), 145–46.

73. See Weir and Jarman, *Images of Lust*, 13, type IV.

74. Caviness, "A Son's Gaze," 1018–19; Jonathan Alexander, "*Labeur* and *Paresse*: Ideological Representations of Medieval Peasant Labor," *Art Bulletin* 72, no. 3 (1990): 439.

75. See, e.g., Sylvia Huot, *The* Romance of the Rose *and Its Medieval Readers* (Cambridge: Cambridge University Press, 1993), 273–322.

76. See, e.g., Michael Camille, *The Medieval Art of Love*, fig. 95.

77. Ludwig Baldass, *Jan van Eyck* (London: Phaidon, 1952), 83–86; Lucy Freeman Sandler, "The Handclasp in the *Arnolfini Wedding*: A Manuscript Precedent," *Art Bulletin* 66, no. 3 (1984): 491.

78. Susan L'Engle and Robert Gibbs, *Illuminating the Law: Legal Manuscripts in Cambridge Collections* (London: Harvey Miller, 2001), 89.

79. Jeremy Goldberg, "John Skathelock's Dick: Voyeurism and 'Pornography' in Late Medieval England," in McDonald, *Medieval Obscenities*, 122.

80. Madeline H. Caviness, *Visualizing Women in the Middle Ages: Sight, Spectacle and Scopic Economy* (Philadelphia: University of Pennsylvania Press, 2001), 128; Robert Mills, "A Man Is Being Beaten," *New Medieval Literatures* 5 (2002): 115–53.

81. Bernhard Ridderbos, "Objects and Questions," in *Early Netherlandish Paintings: Rediscovery, Reception, and Research*, ed. Anne van Buren Ridderbos and Henk van Veen (Los Angeles, CA: J. Paul Getty Museum, 2005), 70–71.

82. Erwin Panofsky, *Early Netherlandish Painting: Its Origins and Character*, vol. 1 (1953; repr. New York: Harper and Row, 1971), 106.

83. Paul Saenger, "Silent Reading: Its Impact on Late Medieval Script and Society," *Viator* 13 (1982): 412.

84. See discussion of the Crusader Bible's Bathsheba sequence in Caviness, *Visualizing Women*, 96–99.

85. Millard Meiss, *French Painting in the Time of Jean de Berry: The Boucicaut Master*, with the assistance of Kathleen Morand and Edith W. Kirsch (New York: Phaidon, 1968), 7–8.

86. Jeffrey F. Hamburger, *The Rothschild Canticles: Art and Mysticism in Flanders and the Rhineland, c. 1300* (New Haven, CT: Yale University Press, 1990), 106.

87. Margery Kempe, *The Book of Margery Kempe*, ed. Sanford Brown Meech and Hope Emily Allen, EETS os 212 (London: Oxford University Press, 1940), 90.

88. Margaret Porette, *The Mirror of Simple Souls*, trans. Edmund College, J. C. Marler, and Judith Grant (Notre Dame, IN: University of Notre Dame Press, 1999), 11.

89. For example, in Madonna's 2006 "Confessions" tour: BBC News, "Rome 'unites to condemn Madonna,'" August 3, 2006, http://news.bbc.co.uk/1/hi/entertainment/5242638.stm (accessed September 10, 2008).

90. *Dives and Pauper*, 84–85.

91. See Richard C. Trexler, "Gendering Jesus Crucified," in *Iconography at the Crossroads*, ed. Brendan Cassidy (Princeton, NJ: Princeton University, 1993), 107–20, on the invisibility of Christ's groin in medieval art.

92. Karma Lochrie, *Covert Operations: The Medieval Uses of Secrecy* (Philadelphia: University of Pennsylvania Press, 1999), 188–94.

93. Suzannah Biernoff, *Sight and Embodiment in the Middle Ages* (Basingstoke, UK: Palgrave Macmillan, 2002), 139.

94. *Dives and Pauper*, 86.

95. Eugène Honée, "Image and Imagination in the Medieval Culture of Prayer: A Historical Perspective," in *The Art of Devotion in the Late Middle Ages in Europe, 1300–1500*, ed. Henk van Os, with Eugène Honée, Hans Nieuwdorp, and Bernhard Ridderbos (London: Merrell Holberton, 1994), 163 and fig. 74.

96. Anne Hudson, ed., *Selections from English Wycliffite Writings* (Toronto: University of Toronto Press, 1997), 87.

97. Michael Camille, "Gothic Signs and the Surplus: The Kiss on the Cathedral," *Yale French Studies* 80 (1991): 160.

98. Siena Online, "St. Catherine Sanctuary," http://www.sienaonline.com/st_catherine_sanctuary.html (accessed September 10, 2008).

99. The original crucifix is shown in Raymond of Capua (1960), frontispiece verso.

100. See John Mirk, *Mirk's Festial: A Collection of Homilies*, ed. Theodore Erbe, EETS es 96 (London: Kegan Paul, Trench, Trübner, 1905), 252, for a bleeding crucifix.

101. Freedberg, *The Power of Images*, 286–87.

102. Robert Mannyng, *Robert of Brunne's "Handlyng Synne,"* ed. Frederick J. Furnivall, EETS os 119 (London: Kegan Paul, Trench, Trübner, 1901), 132.

103. Quoted in Robert Mills, *Suspended Animation: Pain, Pleasure and Punishment in Medieval Culture* (London: Reaktion, 2005), 193.

104. Kathleen Kamerick, *Popular Piety and Art in the Late Middle Ages: Image Worship and Idolatry in England, 1350–1500* (New York: Palgrave, 2002), 122.

105. See *The Rohan Book of Hours: Bibliothèque Nationale, Paris (MS Latin 9471)*, intr. Millard Meiss, intr. and commentaries Marcel Thomas (London: Thames and Hudson, 1973), fol. 10r, plate 13.

106. Caviness, "A Son's Gaze."

107. Aquinas, *Summa theologica*, 2.2.81.3.3.

BIBLIOGRAPHY

Abbreviations

EETS Early English Text Society
PL   *Patrologia Latina*. Ed. J. P. Migne. 221 vols. Paris, 1844–64.

Abelard, Peter. *Historia Calamitatum*. In *The Letters of Abelard and Heloise*. Translated by Betty Radice. Harmondsworth, UK: Penguin, 1974.
Adam of Bremen. *Gesta Hammaburgensis ecclesiae pontificum*. Edited by G. Waitz. Berlin: Hahn, 1876.
Alan of Lille. *Plaint of Nature*. Translated by James J. Sheridan. Toronto: Pontifical Institute of Mediaeval Studies, 1980.
Alexander, Jonathan. "*Labeur* and *Paresse*: Ideological Representations of Medieval Peasant Labor." *Art Bulletin* 72, no. 3 (1990): 436–52.
Allen, Peter Lewis. *The Wages of Sin: Sex, Disease, Past and Present*. Chicago: University of Chicago Press, 2000.
Allman, W. W., and D. Thomas Hanks Jr. "Rough Love: Notes toward an Erotics of the *Canterbury Tales*." *Chaucer Review* 38, no. 1 (2003): 36–65.
Ambrose: Select Works and Letters. Vol. 10 of *Nicene and Post-Nicene Fathers: Second Series*. Edited by Philip Schaff and Rev. Henry Wallace. New York: Cosimo, 2007.
Amer, Sahar. *Crossing Borders: Love between Women in Medieval French and Arabic Literatures*. Philadelphia: University of Pennsylvania Press, 2008.
Amer, Sahar. "Cross-Dressing and Female Same-Sex Marriage in Medieval French and Arabic Literatures." In *Islamicate Sexualities: Translations across Temporal Geographies of Desire*, edited by Kathryn Babayan and Afsaneh Najmabadi. Harvard Middle Eastern Monographs. Cambridge, MA: Harvard University Press, 2008.
Andrew, Malcolm, and Ronald Waldron, eds. *The Poems of the Pearl Manuscript: Pearl, Cleanness, Patience, Sir Gawain and the Green Knight*. Exeter: University of Exeter Press, 1987.

Anselm. *Letters of Saint Anselm of Canterbury*. Translated by Walter Fröhlich. Kalamazoo, MI: Cistercian, 1990.

Aquinas, Thomas. *Summa theologica*. Translated by Fathers of the English Dominican Province. 2nd and revised ed. New Advent, 1920. http://www.newadvent.org/summa/ (accessed December 30, 2009).

Archibald, Elizabeth. *Incest and the Medieval Imagination*. Oxford: Clarendon Press, 2001.

Aretino, Pietro. *Lettere sull'arte*. Edited by F. Pertile and E. Camesasca. 4 vols. Milan: Milione, 1957–1960.

Aristotle. *Generation of Animals*. Edited by A. Peck. Loeb Classical Library. Cambridge, MA: Harvard University Press, 1943.

Augustine of Hippo. *City of God*. Translated by Henry Bettenson. Edited by David Knowles. London: Penguin, 1980.

Augustine of Hippo. *Concerning the City of God against the Pagans*. Translated by Henry Bettenson. Harmondsworth, UK: Penguin, 1972.

Augustine of Hippo. *Confessions*. Translated by R. S. Pine-Coffin. London: Penguin, 1961.

Augustine of Hippo. *Letters, 204–270*. Translated by Wilfred Parsons. The Fathers of the Church: A New Translation 32. Washington, DC: Catholic University of America Press, 1956.

Avicenna. *Liber canonis*. Venice: Pagininis, 1507.

Bach, Rebecca Ann. *Shakespeare and Renaissance Literature before Heterosexuality*. New York: Palgrave, 2007.

Bailey, Derrick Sherwin. *Homosexuality and the Western Christian Tradition*. London: Longmans, Green, 1955.

Bailey, Richard N. "Apotropaic Figures in Milan and North-West England." *Folklore* 94, no. 1 (1983): 113–17.

Baldass, Ludwig. *Jan van Eyck*. London: Phaidon, 1952.

Baldinger, Kurt. "Homonymie- und Polysemiespiele im Mittelfranzösischen." *Zeitschrift für Romanische Philologie* 100 (1984): 241–81.

Baldinger, Kurt. "Zum Wortschatz der Rätselfragen im 15.Jahrhundert." *Zeitschrift für Romanische Philologie* 100 (1984): 282–305.

Baldwin, John. "Five Discourses on Desire: Sexuality and Gender in Northern France around 1200." *Speculum* 66, no. 4 (1991): 797–819.

Baldwin, Robert. "Marriage as a Sacramental Reflection of the Passion: The Mirror in Jan van Eyck's *Arnolfini Wedding*." *Oud Holland* 98, no. 2 (1984): 57–75.

Banks, Mary MacLeod, ed. *An Alphabet of Tales: An English 15th Century Translation of the* Alphabetum Narrationum *of Étienne de Besançon*. EETS o.s. 126 and 127, London: Kegan Paul, 1904.

Barlow, Frank. *William Rufus*. New Haven, CT: Yale University Press, 2000.

Barnum, Priscilla Heath, ed. *Dives and Pauper*. Vol. 1. EETS os 275. London: Oxford University Press, 1976.

Bartholomaeus Anglicus. *On the Properties of Things: John Trevisa's Translation of Bartholomaeus Anglicus De proprietatibus rerum*. Edited by M. C. Seymour et al. Oxford: Clarendon Press, 1975.

Bazn-Daz, I., F. Garca, and A. Mengibar. "La prostitution au pays Basque entre XIVe et XVIIe siècles." *Annales Histoire 55*, no. 6 (2000): 1255–82.

Becanus, Johannes Goropius. *Origines Antwerpianae, siue Cimmeriorum Becceselana nouem libros complexa*. Antwerp: Plantini, 1569.

Belsey, Catherine. "Love as Trompe-l'oeil: Taxonomies of Desire in *Venus and Adonis*." *Shakespeare Quarterly* 46, no. 3 (1995): 257–76.

Belsey, Catherine. "The Serpent in the Garden: Shakespeare, Marriage and Material Culture." *Seventeenth Century* 11, no. 1 (1996): 1–20.

Benedetti, J. *The Real Bluebeard*. New York: Dorset, 1971.

Benkov, Edith. "The Erased Lesbian: Sodomy and the Legal Tradition in Medieval Europe." In *Same Sex Love and Desire among Women in the Middle Ages*, edited by Francesca Canadé Sautman and Pamela Sheingorn. New York: Palgrave, 2001.

Bennett, Judith M. *History Matters: Patriarchy and the Challenge of Feminism*. Philadelphia: University of Pennsylvania Press, 2006.

Bennett, Judith M. "'Lesbian-Like' and the Social History of Lesbianisms." *Journal of the History of Sexuality* 9 (2000): 1–24.

Bernat Roca, M., and J. Serra-Barceló. "Folles fembres bordelleres: La prostitució femenina al tombant de l'Edat Mitjana (Ciutat de Mallorca). Segles XIV–XVI." In *Al tombant de l'Edat Mitjana*, edited by Maria Barceló Crespi. Tradició medieval i cultural humanista XVIII Jornades d'Estudis Històrics Locals. Palma de Mallorca: Institut d'Estudis Baleárics, 2000.

Bersani, Leo. "Is the Rectum a Grave?" *October* 43 (1987): 197–222.

Bersani, Leo. "Sociality and Sexuality." *Critical Inquiry* 26, no. 4 (2000): 641–56.

Biernoff, Suzannah. *Sight and Embodiment in the Middle Ages*. Basingstoke, UK: Palgrave Macmillan, 2002.

Blacman, John. *Henry VI: A Reprint of John Blacman's Memoir*. Translated by M. R. James. Cambridge: Cambridge University Press, 1919.

Blamires, Alcuin, ed. *Woman Defamed and Woman Defended: An Anthology of Medieval Texts*. With Karen Pratt and C. W. Marx. Oxford: Clarendon Press, 1992.

Blanshei, S. R. "Crime and Law Enforcement in Medieval Bologna." *Journal of Social History* 16, no. 1 (1982): 121–38.

Bleeke, Marian. "Sheelas, Sex, and Significance in Romanesque Sculpture: The Kilpeck Corbel Series." *Studies in Iconography* 26 (2005): 1–26.

Boccaccio, Giovanni. *The Decameron*. Translated by Mark Musa and Peter Bondanella. New York: Norton, 1983.

Bodtker, A., ed. *Partonope of Blois*. EETS es 109. London: Oxford University Press, 1912.

Bonnell, Victoria, Lynn Avery Hunt, and Richard Biernacki. *Beyond the Cultural Turn: New Directions in the Study of Society and Culture*. Berkeley: University of California Press, 1999.

Boone, Marc. "State Power and Illicit Sexuality: The Persecution of Sodomy in Late Medieval Bruges." *Journal of Medieval History* 22, no. 2 (1996): 135–53.

Bos, Han, and Gerrit Groeneweg. *Schatten uit de Schelde: Gebruiks- en Sierwoorwerpen uit de Verdronken Plaatsen in de Oosterschelde: Markiezenhof Gemeente–Museum*

Bergen op Zoom, 14 maart–27 april 1987. Bergen op Zoom: Gemeentemuseum Bergen op Zoom, 1987.

Boswell, John. *Christianity, Social Tolerance, and Homosexuality: Gay People in Western Europe from the Beginning of the Christian Era to the Fourteenth Century.* Chicago: University of Chicago Press, 1980.

Boswell, John. "Old Habits, New Habits." *New Republic,* January 6, 1986: 36–39.

Boureau, Alain. *The Lord's First Night: The Myth of the Droit de Cuissage.* Translated by Lydia G. Cochrane. Chicago: University of Chicago Press, 1998.

Boureau, Alain. *The Myth of Pope Joan.* Translated by Lydia G. Cochrane. Chicago: University of Chicago Press, 2001.

Bowman, Jeffrey A. "Beauty and *Passion* in Tenth-Century Córdoba." In *The Boswell Thesis: Essays on Christianity, Social Tolerance, and Homosexuality,* edited by Mathew Kuefler. Chicago: University of Chicago Press, 2006.

Boyd, David Lorenzo, and Ruth Mazo Karras. "The Interrogation of a Male Transvestite Prostitute in Fourteenth-Century London." *GLQ* 1 (1995): 459–65.

Brackett, John K. "The Florentine Onestá and the Control of Prostitution, 1403–1680." *Sixteenth Century Journal* 24, no. 2 (1993): 273–300.

Bray, Alan. *The Friend.* Chicago: University of Chicago Press, 2003.

Brémaud, Nicolas. "Les crimes de Gilles de Rais: Le sadisme dans la psychose." *L'en-je lacanien* 8, no. 1 (2007): 53–71.

Brereton, Georgina E., and Janet M. Ferrier, eds. *Le mesnagier de Paris.* Paris: Librairie Générale Française, 1994.

Bristow, Joseph. *Sexuality.* London: Routledge, 1997.

Brody, Saul. *The Disease of the Soul: Leprosy in Medieval Literature.* Ithaca, NY: Cornell University Press, 1974.

Brooten, Bernadette. *Love Between Women: Early Christian Responses to Female Homoeroticism.* Chicago: University of Chicago Press, 1996.

Brown, D. Catherine. *Pastor and Laity in the Theology of Jean Gerson.* Cambridge: Cambridge University Press, 1987.

Brown, Peter. *The Cult of the Saints: Its Rise and Function in Latin Christianity.* Chicago: University of Chicago Press, 1981.

Brundage, James A. "Implied Consent to Intercourse." In *Consent and Coercion to Sex and Marriage in Ancient and Medieval Societies,* edited by Angeliki E. Laiou. Washington, DC: Dumbarton Oaks Research Library and Collection, 1993.

Brundage, James A. *Law, Sex, and Christian Society in Medieval Europe.* Chicago: University of Chicago Press, 1987.

Brundage, James A. *Medieval Canon Law.* London: Longman, 1995.

Brundage, James A. "Playing by the Rules: Sexual Behaviour and Legal Norms in Medieval Europe." In *Desire and Discipline: Sex and Sexuality in the Premodern West,* edited by Jacqueline Murray and Konrad Eisenbichler. Toronto: University of Toronto Press, 1996.

Brundage, James A. "Prostitution, Miscegenation and Sexual Purity in the First Crusade." In *Crusade and Settlement,* edited by Peter W. Edbury. Cardiff: University College Cardiff Press, 1985.

Brundage, James A. "Rape and Seduction in the Medieval Canon Law." In *Sexual Practices and the Medieval Church*, edited by Vern L. Bullough and James A. Brundage. Buffalo, NY: Prometheus, 1982.

Brundage, James A. "Sex and Canon Law." In *Handbook of Medieval Sexuality*, edited by Vern L. Bullough and James A. Brundage. New York: Garland, 1996.

Brundage, James A. "Sin, Crime, and the Pleasures of the Flesh: The Medieval Church Judges Sexual Offences." In *The Medieval World*, edited by Peter Linehan and Janet L. Nelson. London: Routledge, 2001.

Buchanan-Brown, J., ed. *John Aubrey: Three Prose Works*. Fontwell, UK: Centaur, 1972.

Buettner, Brigitte. "Dressing and Undressing Bodies in Late Medieval Images." In *Artistic Exchange: 28th Internationalen Kongresses für Kunstgeschichte*, edited by Thomas W. Gaehtgens. Berlin: Akademic Verlag, 1993.

Bullough, Vern L. "Cross Dressing and Gender Role Change in the Middle Ages." In *Handbook of Medieval Sexuality*, edited by Vern L. Bullough and James A. Brundage. New York: Garland, 2000.

Bullough, Vern L. "Medieval Medical and Scientific Views of Women." *Viator* 4 (1973): 485–501.

Bullough, Vern L. "Sex Education in Medieval Christianity." *Journal of Sex Research* 13, no. 3 (1977): 185–96.

Bullough, Vern L. *Sexual Practices and the Medieval Church*. Amherst, NY: Prometheus, 1982.

Bullough, Vern L. "Transvestites in the Middle Ages." *American Journal of Sociology* 79, no. 6 (1974): 1381–94.

Burchard of Worms. *Decretum*. PL 140.

Burger, Glenn. *Chaucer's Queer Nation*. Minneapolis: University of Minnesota Press, 2003.

Burgwinkle, William. "État Présent: Queer Theory and the Middle Ages." *French Studies* 60, no. 1 (2006): 79–88.

Burgwinkle, William. *Sodomy, Masculinity, and Law in Medieval Literature: France and England, 1050–1230*. Cambridge: Cambridge University Press, 2004.

Burrus, Virginia. "Queer Lives of Saints: Jerome's Hagiography." *Journal of the History of Sexuality* 10, no. 3–4 (2001): 442–79.

Butler, Judith. "Gender Regulations." In *Undoing Gender*. New York: Routledge, 2004.

Bynum, Caroline Walker. *Fragmentation and Redemption: Essays on Gender and the Human Body in Medieval Religion*. New York: Zone, 1992.

Bynum, Caroline Walker. *Holy Feast and Holy Fast: The Religious Significance of Food to Medieval Women*. Berkeley: University of California Press, 1987.

Bynum, Caroline Walker. "Why All the Fuss about the Body? A Medievalist's Perspective." *Critical Inquiry* 22 (1995): 1–33.

Cadden, Joan. *Meanings of Sex Difference in the Middle Ages: Medicine, Science, and Culture*. Cambridge: Cambridge University Press, 1993.

Cadden, Joan. "Trouble in the Earthly Paradise: The Regime of Nature in Late Medieval Christian Culture." In *The Moral Authority of Nature*, edited by Lorraine Daston and Fernando Vidal. Chicago: University of Chicago Press, 2004.

Camille, Michael. *The Gothic Idol: Ideology and Image-Making in Medieval Art.* Cambridge: Cambridge University Press, 1989.

Camille, Michael. "Gothic Signs and the Surplus: The Kiss on the Cathedral." *Yale French Studies* 80 (1991): 151–70.

Camille, Michael. *Image on the Edge: The Margins of Medieval Art.* London: Reaktion, 1992.

Camille, Michael. *The Medieval Art of Love: Objects and Subjects of Desire.* New York: Harry N. Abrams, 1998.

Camille, Michael. "Obscenity under Erasure: Censorship in Medieval Illuminated Manuscripts." In *Obscenity: Social Control and Artistic Creation in the European Middle Ages,* edited by Jan M. Ziolkowski. Leiden: Brill, 1998.

Cannon, Christopher. "The Rights of Medieval English Women: Crime and the Issue of Representation." In *Medieval Crime and Social Control,* edited by Barbara A. Hanawalt and David Wallace. Medieval Cultures 16. Minneapolis: University of Minnesota Press, 1999.

Capellanus, Andreas. *Andreas Capellanus on Love.* Edited and translated by P. G. Walsh. London: Duckworth, 1982.

Carlin, M. *Medieval Southwark.* London: Hambledon, 1996.

Carmen-Peris, M. "La prostitución Valenciana en la segunda mitad del siglo XIV." *Revista d'història medieval* 1 (1990): 179–99.

Carruthers, Mary. *The Book of Memory: A Study of Memory in Medieval Culture.* Cambridge: Cambridge University Press, 1990.

Carter, John Marshall. *Rape in Medieval England: An Historical and Sociological Study.* Lanham, MD: University Press of America, 1985.

Carton, E. "Complicity and Responsibility in Pandarus' Bed and Chaucer's Art." *PMLA* 94, no. 1 (1979): 47–61.

Caviness, Madeline H. "Obscenity and Alterity: Images that Shock and Offend Us/Them, Now/Then?" In *Obscenity: Social Control and Artistic Creation in the European Middle Ages,* edited by Jan M. Ziolkowski. Leiden: Brill, 1998.

Caviness, Madeline H. "A Son's Gaze on Noah: Cause or Case of Viriliphobia?" *Compartamenti e Immaginario della Sessualita Nell'Alto Medioevo* 53 (2006): 981–1024.

Caviness, Madeline H. *Visualizing Women in the Middle Ages: Sight, Spectacle and Scopic Economy.* Philadelphia: University of Pennsylvania Press, 2001.

Cazelles, Brigitte. *The Lady as Saint.* Philadelphia: University of Pennsylvania Press, 1991.

Chaucer, Geoffrey. *The Riverside Chaucer.* Edited by Larry D. Benson. 3rd ed. Oxford: Oxford University Press, 1988.

Chewning, Susannah, ed. *Intersections of Sexuality and the Divine in Medieval Culture: The Word Made Flesh.* Aldershot, UK: Ashgate, 2005.

Chubb, T. C. *The Letters of Pietro Aretino.* New Haven, CT: Yale University Press, 1967.

Clark, Anna. *Desire: A History of European Sexuality.* New York: Routledge, 2008.

Clark, David. *Between Medieval Men: Male Friendship and Desire in Early Medieval English Literature.* Oxford: Oxford University Press, 2009.

Classen, Albrecht. *The Medieval Chastity Belt: A Myth-Making Process.* Basingstoke, UK: Palgrave Macmillan, 2007.

Coates, Richard. "*Fockynggroue* in Bristol." *Notes and Queries* 252, no. 4 (2007): 373–76.

Cohen, Jeffrey Jerome. *Medieval Identity Machines*. Minneapolis: University of Minnesota Press, 2003.

Constantinus Africanus. *Opera omnia*. Lyon: Andreas Turinus, 1515.

Cowgill, J., M. de Neergaard, and N. Griffiths. *Knives and Scabbards*. Medieval Finds from Excavations in London l. London: HMSO, 1987.

Crawford, Katherine. *European Sexualities, 1400–1800*. Cambridge: Cambridge University Press, 2007.

Cyril of Jerusalem, Gregory Nazianzen. Vol. 7 of *Nicene and Post-Nicene Fathers: Second Series*. Edited by Philip Schaff and Rev. Henry Wallace. New York: Cosimo, 2007.

Daichman, Graciela S. *Wayward Nuns in Medieval Literature*. Syracuse, NY: Syracuse University Press, 1986.

Damian, Peter. *Book of Gomorrah: An Eleventh-Century Treatise against Clerical Homosexual Practices*. Edited and translated by Pierre J. Payer. Waterloo, Ont., Canada: Wilfrid Laurier University Press, 1982.

Damian, Peter. *The Letters of Peter Damian, 31–60*. Translated by Otto J. Blum. The Fathers of the Church: Mediaeval Continuation 2. Washington, DC: Catholic University of America Press, 1990.

Davies, Anthony. "Sexual Behaviour in Later Anglo-Saxon England." In *This Noble Craft: Proceedings of the Xth Research Symposium of the Dutch and Belgian University Teachers of Old and Middle English and Historical Linguistics, Utrecht, 19–20 January 1989*, edited by E. Kooper. Amsterdam: Rodopi, 1991.

Davis, Glenn. "The Exeter Book Riddles and the Place of Sexual Idiom in Old English Literature." In *Medieval Obscenities*, edited by Nicola McDonald. Woodbridge, UK: York Medieval Press, 2006.

Day, John. *Yahweh and the Gods and Goddesses of Canaan*. New York: Sheffield Academic Press, 2000.

Dean, Trevor. *Crime in Medieval Europe, 1200–1550*. Harlow, UK: Longman, 2001.

Dekker, Rudolf, and Lotte van de Pol. *The Tradition of Female Transvestism in Early Modern Europe*. New York: St. Martin's Press, 1989.

Delaney, Paul. "Constantinus Africanus' *De coitu*: A Translation." *Chaucer Review* 4 (1969): 55–65.

Delany, Sheila. *Impolitic Bodies: Poetry, Saints, and Society in Fifteenth-Century England: The Work of Osbern Bokenham*. New York: Oxford University Press, 1998.

De Lorris, Guillaume, and Jean de Meun. *The Romance of the Rose*. Translated by Frances Horgan. Oxford: Oxford University Press, 1994.

De Pizan, Christine. *The Book of the City of Ladies*. Translated by Rosalind Brown-Grant. London: Penguin, 1999.

De Troyes, Chrétien. *Arthurian Romances*. Edited and translated by D.D.R. Owen. London: Dent, 1993.

Dickinson, John. *Misericords of North West England: Their Nature and Significance*. Lancaster: Centre for North-West Regional Studies, University of Lancaster, 2008.

Dinshaw, Carolyn. *Getting Medieval: Sexualities and Communities, Pre- and Post-modern*. Durham, NC: Duke University Press, 1999.

Dinshaw, Carolyn. "'A Kiss Is Just a Kiss': Heterosexuality and Its Consolations in *Sir Gawain and the Green Knight*." *diacritics* 24, no. 2–3 (1994): 205–26.

Dodgson, J. McN. *The Place-Names of Cheshire*. 5 vols. EPNS 44–48, 54, 74. Cambridge: Cambridge University Press, 1970–1997.

Douie, Decima, and Hugh Farmer. *The Life of St. Hugh of Lincoln*. London: Nelson, 1962.

Dunn, Khalid. "Homosexuality and Islam." In *Homosexuality and World Religions*, edited by Arlene Swidler. Valley Forge, PA: Trinity Press International, 1993.

Dupire, N., ed. *Les faictz et dictz de J. Molinet*. Paris: Société des anciens textes français, 1937.

Dupond, Guy. *Maagdenverleisters, hoeren en speculanten: Prostitutie in Brugge tijdens de Bourgondische periode (1385–1515)*. Bruges: Uitgeverij Marc Van de Wiele, 1996.

DuVal, John, trans. *Fabliaux, Fair and Foul*. Binghamton, NY: Medieval & Renaissance Texts & Studies, 1992.

Easting, Robert, ed. *Revelation of the Monk of Eynsham*. EETS os 318. Oxford: Oxford University Press, 2002.

Edden, Valerie. "Devils, Sermon Stories, and the Problem of Popular Belief in the Middle Ages." *Yearbook of English Studies* 22 (1992): 213–25.

Elliott, Dyan. "Bernardino of Siena versus the Marriage Debt." In *Desire and Discipline: Sex and Sexuality in the Premodern West*, edited by Jacqueline Murray and Konrad Eisenbichler. Toronto: University of Toronto Press, 1996.

Elliot, Dyan. *Fallen Bodies: Pollution, Sexuality, and Demonology in the Middle Ages*. Philadelphia: University of Pennsylvania Press, 1999.

Elliott, Dyan. *Spiritual Marriage: Sexual Abstinence in Medieval Wedlock*. Princeton, NJ: Princeton University Press, 1993.

El-Rouayheb, Khaled. *Before Homosexuality in the Arab-Islamic World, 1500–1800*. Chicago: University of Chicago Press, 2005.

Epps, Brad. "Comparison, Competition, and Cross-Dressing: Cross-Cultural Analysis in a Contested World." In *Islamicate Sexualities: Translations across Temporal Geographies of Desire*, edited by Kathryn Babayan and Afsaneh Najmabadi. Harvard Middle Eastern Monographs. Cambridge, MA: Harvard University Press, 2008.

Eron, Lewis John. "Homosexuality and Judaism." In *Homosexuality and World Religions*, edited by Arlene Swidler. Valley Forge, PA: Trinity Press International, 1993.

Esteban Recio, M. A., and M. J. Izquierdo García. "Pescado y marginación. Mujeres públicas en Valladolid y Palencia durante los siglos XV y XVI." In *La ciudad medieval: Aspectos de la vida urbana en la Castilla Bajo-medieval*, edited by Juan Antonio Bonachía Hernando. Valladolid: Secretariado de Publicaciones e Intercambio Científico, Universidad de Valladolid, 1996.

Farina, Lara. *Erotic Discourse and Early English Religious Writing*. New York: Palgrave Macmillan, 2006.

Fenster, T., and D. C. Smail, eds. *Fama: The Politics of Talk and Reputation in Medieval Europe*. Ithaca, NY: Cornell University Press, 2003.

Fischer, S. R. *The Complete Medieval Dreambook: A Multilingual, Alphabetical "Somnia Danielis" Collation*. Bern: Peter Lang, 1982.

Flint, V. *The Rise of Magic in Early Medieval Europe*. Oxford: Oxford University Press, 1991.

Forgeais, Arthur. *Notice sur des plombs historiés trouvés dans la Seine*. Paris: Chez l'auteur et chez Dumoulin, 1858.

Forsyth, Ilene H. "The Ganymede Capital at Vézelay." *Gesta* 15 (1976): 241–46.

Foucault, Michel. *Discipline and Punish: The Birth of the Prison*. Translated by Alan Sheridan. New York: Vintage, 1977.

Foucault, Michel. *The History of Sexuality*, Vol. 1: *An Introduction*. Translated by Robert Hurley. London: Penguin, 1979.

Foucault, Michel. *The Use of Pleasure*, Vol. 2 of *The History of Sexuality*. Translated by Robert Hurley. London: Penguin, 1987.

Foucault, Michel. *The Care of the Self*. Vol. 3 of *The History of Sexuality*. Translated by Robert Hurley. London: Penguin, 1988.

Fradenburg, Louise, and Carla Freccero, eds. *Premodern Sexualities*. New York: Routledge, 1996.

Francesco, G., ed. *The Facetiae or Jocose Tales of Poggio*. Vol. 1. Paris: Isidore Liseux, 1879.

Francis, W. Nelson, ed. *The Book of Vices and Virtues: A Fourteenth Century English Translation of the* Somme le Roi *of Lorens d'Orleans*. EETS os 217. London: Oxford University Press, 1942.

Frantzen, Allen. *The Literature of Penance in Anglo-Saxon England*. New Brunswick, NJ: Rutgers University Press, 1983.

Freccero, Carla. "Acts, Identities, and Sexuality's (Pre)Modern Regimes." *Journal of Women's History* 11, no. 2 (1999): 186–92.

Freccero, Carla. *Queer/Early/Modern*. Durham, NC: Duke University Press, 2006.

Freedberg, David. *The Power of Images: Studies in the History and Theory of Response*. Chicago: University of Chicago Press, 1989.

Freitag, Barbara. *Sheela-na-gigs: Unravelling an Enigma*. London: Routledge, 2004.

Freud, Sigmund. *On Sexuality*. Edited by Angela Richards. Harmondsworth, UK: Penguin, 1977.

Freund, K., M. C. Seto, and M. Kuban. "Two Types of Fetishism." *Behaviour Research and Therapy* 34, no. 9 (1996): 687–94.

Frow, John. *Time and Commodity Culture: Essays in Cultural Theory and Postmodernity*. Oxford: Oxford University Press, 1997.

Fuchs, Eduard. *Illustrierte Sittengeschichte vom Mittelalter bis zur Gegenwart I: Renaissance (mit Ergänzungsband)*. Munich: Albert Langen, 1928.

Furnham, Adrian, and Haraldsen, Emmy. "Lay Theories of Etiology and 'Cure' for Four Types of Paraphilia: Fetishism, Pedophilia, Sexual Sadism, and Voyeurism." *Journal of Clinical Psychology* 54, no. 5 (1998): 689–700.

Galen. *Galen on the Usefulness of the Parts of the Body (De usu partium)*. Translated by Margaret Tallmadge May. 2 vols. Ithaca, NY: Cornell University Press, 1968.

Garampi, Giuseppe. *Memorie ecclesiastiche appartenenti all'istoria e al culto della B. Chiara di Rimini*. Rome: Palearini, 1755.

Gaunt, Simon. "Marginal Men, Marcabru and Orthodoxy: The Early Troubadours and Adultery." *Medium Ævum* 59 (1990): 55–72.

Gaunt, Simon. "Obscene Hermeneutics in Troubadour Lyric." In *Medieval Obscenities*, edited by Nicola McDonald. Woodbridge, UK: York Medieval Press, 2006.

Gaunt, Simon. "Straight Minds/'Queer' Wishes in Old French Hagiography: *La vie de Sainte Euphrosine*." In *Premodern Sexualities*, edited by Louise Fradenburg and Carla Freccero. New York: Routledge, 1996.

Geremek, B. *The Margins of Society in Late Medieval Paris*. Cambridge: Cambridge University Press, 1987.

Gerson, Jean. *Oeuvres Complètes*. Edited by Palémon Glorieux. 10 vols. Paris: Desclée, 1960–1973.

Gerson, Paula. "Margins for Eros." *Romance Languages Annual* 5 (1993): 47–53.

Ghirardo, Diane. "The Topography of Prostitution in Renaissance Ferrara." *Journal of the Society of Architectural Historians* 60, no. 4 (2001): 402–431.

Giannini, A. J., G. Colapietro, A. E. Slaby, S. M. Melemis, and R. K. Bowman. "Sexualization of the Female Foot as a Response to Sexually Transmitted Epidemics: A Preliminary Study." *Psychological Reports* 83, no. 2 (1998): 491–98.

Gibbs, Stephanie Viereck, and Kathryn Karczewska. *The Book of the Love-Smitten Heart*. New York: Routledge, 2001.

Gil, Daniel Juan. "Before Intimacy: Modernity and Emotion in the Early Modern Discourse of Sexuality." *ELH* 69, no. 4 (2002): 861–87.

Goldberg, Jeremy. "John Skathelok's Dick: Voyeurism and 'Pornography' in Late Medieval England." In *Medieval Obscenities*, edited by Nicola McDonald. Woodbridge, UK: York Medieval Press, 2006.

Goldberg, P. J. P. "Gender and Matrimonial Litigation in the Church Courts in the Later Middle Ages: The Evidence of the Court of York." *Gender & History* 19, no. 1 (2007): 43–59.

Goldberg, P. J. P. "Pigs and Prostitutes: Streetwalking in Comparative Perspective." In *Young Medieval Women*, edited by Katherine Lewis, Noël Menuge, and Kim M. Phillips. Gloucester, UK: Sutton, 1999.

Goodich, Michael. "Sexual Deviation as Heresy in the XIII–XIVth Centuries." In *Modernité et non-conformisme en France à travers les âges: Actes du colloque organisé par l'Institut d'histoire et de civilisation françaises d l'Université de Haïfa*, edited by Myriam Yardeni. Leiden: Brill, 1983.

Goodich, Michael, ed. *Other Middle Ages: Witnesses at the Margins of Medieval Society*. Philadelphia: University of Pennsylvania Press, 1998.

Goodich, Michael. *The Unmentionable Vice: Homosexuality in the Later Medieval Period*. Santa Barbara, CA: Dorset Press, 1979.

Gordon, J. D., ed. *The Epistle of Othea to Hector*. Philadelphia: University of Pennsylvania Press, 1942.

Gratian. *Marriage Canons from* The Decretum *of Gratian*. Translated by John T. Noonan Jr. Edited by Augustine Thompson. 1993. http://faculty.cua.edu/Pennington/Canon%20Law/marriagelaw.htm (accessed December 30, 2009).

Gratian. *On Marriage*. Translated by Paul Hyams, Internet Medieval Sourcebook, 1999. http://www.fordham.edu/halsall/source/gratian1.html (accessed December 30, 2009).

Gravdal, Kathryn. *Vilain and Courtois: Transgressive Parody in French Literature of the Twelfth and Thirteenth Century*. Lincoln: University of Nebraska Press, 1989.

Gravdal, Kathryn. *Ravishing Maidens: Writing Rape in Medieval French Literature and Law*. Philadelphia: University of Pennsylvania Press, 1991.

Green, Monica. "Constantinus Africanus and the Conflict between Religion and Science." In *The Human Embryo: Aristotle and the Arabic and European Traditions*, edited by G. Dunstan. Exeter: University of Exeter Press, 1990.

Green, Monica. "From 'Diseases of Women' to 'Secrets of Women': The Transformation of Gynecological Literature in the Later Middle Ages." *Journal of Medieval and Early Modern Studies* 30, no. 1 (2000): 5–39.

Green, R. L. *The Early English Carols*. 2nd ed. Oxford: Clarendon Press, 1977.

Grössinger, Christa. *Humour and Folly in Secular and Profane Prints of Northern Europe, 1430–1540*. London: Harvey Miller, 2002.

Guénette, M. "Errance et solitude féminines à Manosque (1314–1358)." In *Vie privée et ordre public a la fin du Moyen-Age*, edited by Michel Hébert. Aix-en-Provence: Université de Provence, Service des Publications, 1987.

Guibert of Nogent. *Self and Society in Modern France: The Memoirs of Abbot Guibert of Nogent*. Edited by John F. Benton. Toronto: Medieval Academy of America, 2002.

Hall, Alaric. *Elves in Anglo-Saxon England: Matters of Belief, Health, Gender and Identity*. Woodbridge, UK: Boydell, 2007.

Hall, Edwin. *The Arnolfini Betrothal: Medieval Marriage and the Enigma of Van Eyck's Double Portrait*. Berkeley: University of California Press, 1994.

Halliwell, J. O., ed. *A Selection from the Minor Poems of Dan John Lydgate*. London: Percy Society, 1840.

Halperin, David M. "Forgetting Foucault: Acts, Identities, and the History of Sexuality." *Representations* 63 (1998): 93–119.

Halperin, David M. *How to Do the History of Homosexuality*. Chicago: University of Chicago Press, 2002.

Halperin, David M. "Is There a History of Sexuality?" In *The Lesbian and Gay Studies Reader*, edited by Henry Abelove, Michèle A. Barale, and David M. Halperin. New York: Routledge, 1993.

Hamburger, Jeffrey F. *The Rothschild Canticles: Art and Mysticism in Flanders and the Rhineland, c. 1300*. New Haven, CT: Yale University Press, 1990.

Hamilton, William, Richard Payne Knight, and Thomas Wright. *A Discourse on the Worship of Priapus, and Its Connection with the Mystic Theology of the Ancients ... (a New Edition). To Which Is Added Essay on the Worship on the Worship of the Generative Powers during the Middle Ages of Western Europe*. 1865. Reprint, New York: Dorset Press, 1992.

Hanawalt, Barbara A. *"Of Good and Ill Repute": Gender and Social Control in Medieval England*. New York: Oxford University Press, 1998.

Hardwick, Paul. *English Misericords and the Margins of the Sacred*. Woodbridge, UK: Boydell and Brewer, forthcoming.

Haren, Michael. *Sin and Society in Fourteenth-Century England: A Study of the* Memoriale Presbiterorum. Oxford: Clarendon Press, 2000.

Harrison, Robert, trans. *Gothic Salt: Eighteen Fabliaux from the Old French*. Berkeley: University of California Press, 1974.

Haseldine, J. P. "Love, Separation and Male Friendship: Words and Actions in Saint Anselm's Letters to His Friends." In *Masculinity in Medieval Europe*, edited by D. M. Hadley. Harlow, UK: Longman, 1999.

Hawkes, Gail. *Sex and Pleasure in Western Culture*. Cambridge: Polity Press, 2004.

Hergemöller, Bernd-Ulrich. "The Middle Ages." In *Gay Life and Culture: A World History*, edited by Robert Aldrich. London: Thames and Hudson, 2006.

Hildebrand, Kristina. "Her Desire and His: Letters between Fifteenth-Century Lovers." In *The Erotic in the Literature of Medieval Britain*, edited by Amanda Hopkins and Cory J. Rushton. Cambridge: Brewer, 2007.

Hildegard of Bingen. *Causae et curae*. Edited by P. Kaiser. Leipzig: B. G. Teubner, 1903.

Hines, John. *The Fabliau in English*. London: Longman, 1993.

Holsinger, Bruce. *The Premodern Condition: Medievalism and the Making of Theory*. Chicago: University of Chicago Press, 2005.

Holsinger, Bruce. "Sodomy and Resurrection: The Homoerotic Subject of the *Divine Comedy*." In *Premodern Sexualities*, edited by Louise Fradenburg and Carla Freccero. New York: Routledge, 1996.

Holt, Richard, and Nigel Baker. "Towards a Geography of Sexual Encounter: Prostitution in English Medieval Towns." In *Indecent Exposure: Sexuality, Society and the Archaeological Record*, edited by Lynne Bevan. Glasgow: Cruithne, 2001.

Honée, Eugène. "Image and Imagination in the Medieval Culture of Prayer: A Historical Perspective." In *The Art of Devotion in the Late Middle Ages in Europe, 1300–1500*, edited by Henk van Os, with Eugène Honée, Hans Nieuwdorp, and Bernhard Ridderbos. London: Merrell Holberton, 1994.

Hopkins, Amanda, and Cory J. Rushton. "Introduction: The Revel, the Melodye and the Bisynesse of Solas." In *The Erotic in the Literature of Medieval Britain*, edited by Amanda Hopkins and Cory J. Rushton. Cambridge: Brewer, 2007.

Hotchkiss, Valerie. *Clothes Make the Man: Female Cross Dressing in Medieval Europe*. New York: Garland, 1996.

Howie, Cary. *Claustrophilia: The Erotics of Enclosure in Medieval Literature*. Basingstoke, UK: Palgrave Macmillan, 2007.

Hrotsvit of Gandersheim. *Hrotsvithae Opera*. Edited by H. Homeyer. Munich: Ferdinand Schöningh, 1970.

Hudson, Anne, ed. *Selections from English Wycliffite Writings*. Toronto: University of Toronto Press, 1997.

Hugh of Flavigny. *Chronicon*. PL 154.

Hunt, Lynn. "Introduction: Obscenity and the Origins of Modernity, 1500–1800." In *The Invention of Pornography: Obscenity and the Origins of Modernity, 1500–1800*, edited by Lynn Hunt. New York: Zone, 1993.

Hunt, Tony. *The Plant Names of Medieval England*. Cambridge: Brewer, 1989.

Huot, Sylvia. *The* Romance of the Rose *and Its Medieval Readers*. Cambridge: Cambridge University Press, 1993.

Hutton, Ronald. *The Rise and Fall of Merry England: The Ritual Year, 1400–1700.* Oxford: Oxford University Press, 1994.

Insley, John. Review of Ingrid Hjertstedt, *Middle English Nicknames in the Lay Subsidy Rolls for Warwickshire. Studia Neophilologica* 62, no. 1 (1990): 115–19.

Isidore of Seville. *Etymologiarum sive originum.* Edited by W. Lindsay. Oxford: Oxford University Press, 1911.

Jacquart, Danielle, and Claude Thomasset. *Sexuality and Medicine in the Middle Ages.* Princeton, NJ: Princeton University Press, 1988.

Jaeger, C. Stephen. *Ennobling Love: In Search of a Lost Sensibility.* Philadelphia: University of Pennsylvania Press, 1999.

Jerome. *Adversus Jovinianum. PL* 23.

Johns, Catherine. *Sex or Symbol? Erotic Images of Greece and Rome.* London: Routledge, 1999.

Johnston, Dafydd, ed. and trans. *Medieval Welsh Erotic Poetry.* Cardiff: Tafol, 1991.

Jones, Malcolm. "Folklore Motifs in Late Medieval Art III: Erotic Animal Imagery." *Folklore* 102, no. 2 (1991): 192–219.

Jones, Malcolm. *The Secret Middle Ages: Discovering the Real Medieval World.* Stroud, UK: Sutton, 2002.

Jones, Malcolm. "The Secular Badges." In *Heilig en Profaan: 1000 Laatmiddeleeuwse Insignes uit de Collectie H.J.E. van Beuningen,* edited by H.J.E. van Beuningen and A. M. Koldeweij. Rotterdam Papers 8. Cothen: Stichting Middeleeuwse religieuze en profane insignes, 1993.

Jordan, Mark. *The Invention of Sodomy in Christian Theology.* Chicago: University of Chicago Press, 1997.

Jordan, Mark. *The Silence of Sodom: Homosexuality in Modern Catholicism.* Chicago: University of Chicago Press, 2000.

Kamerick, Kathleen. *Popular Piety and Art in the Late Middle Ages: Image Worship and Idolatry in England, 1350–1500.* New York: Palgrave, 2002.

Kane, George, and E. Talbot Donaldson. *Piers Plowman: The B-Version.* London: Athlone Press, 1975.

Karras, Ruth Mazo. "'Because the Other Is a Poor Woman She Shall Be Called His Wench': Gender, Sexuality, and Social Status in Late Medieval England." In *Gender and Difference in the Middle Ages,* edited by Sharon Farmer and Carol Braun Pasternack. Medieval Cultures 32. Minneapolis: University of Minnesota Press, 2003.

Karras, Ruth Mazo. *Common Women: Prostitution and Sexuality in Medieval England.* Oxford: Oxford University Press, 1996.

Karras, Ruth Mazo. "Prostitution and the Question of Sexual Identity in Medieval Europe." *Journal of Women's History* 11, no. 2 (1999): 159–77.

Karras, Ruth Mazo. *Sexuality in Medieval Europe: Doing unto Others.* New York: Routledge, 2005.

Karras, Ruth Mazo. "Sexuality in the Middle Ages." In *The Medieval World,* edited by Peter Linehan and Janet L. Nelson. London: Routledge, 2001.

Karras, Ruth Mazo, and David Lorenzo Boyd. "'Ut cum muliere': A Male Transvestite Prostitute in Fourteenth-Century London." In *Premodern Sexualities,* edited by Louise Fradenburg and Carla Freccero. New York: Routledge, 1996.

Kay, Sarah. *Courtly Contradictions: The Emergence of the Literary Object in the Twelfth Century*. Stanford, CA: Stanford University Press, 2001.

Keck, David. *Angels and Angelology in the Middle Ages*. Oxford: Oxford University Press, 1998.

Keiser, Elizabeth B. *Courtly Desire and Medieval Homophobia: The Legitimation of Sexual Pleasure in* Cleanness *and Its Contexts*. New Haven, CT: Yale University Press, 1997.

Kelly, Eamonn. "Irish Sheela-na-gigs and Related Figures with Reference to the Collections of the National Museum of Ireland." In *Medieval Obscenities*, edited by Nicola McDonald. Woodbridge, UK: York Medieval Press, 2006.

Kelly, H. A. "Bishop, Prioress, and Baud in the Stews of Southwark." *Speculum* 75, no. 2 (2000): 342–88.

Kempe, Margery. *The Book of Margery Kempe*. Edited by Sanford Brown Meech and Hope Emily Allen. EETS os 212. London: Oxford University Press, 1940.

Kendrick, Walter. *The Secret Museum: Pornography in Modern Culture*. Berkeley: University of California Press, 1987.

Kennedy, Hugh. "Al-Jāhiz and the Construction of Homosexuality at the Abbasid Court." In *Medieval Sexuality: A Casebook*, edited by April Harper and Caroline Proctor. London: Routledge, 2008.

Kieckhefer, Richard. "Erotic Magic in Medieval Europe." In *Sex in the Middle Ages: A Book of Essays*, edited by Joyce E. Salisbury. New York: Garland, 1991.

Kislinger, E. "Anasyrma. Notizen zur Geste des Schamwesens." In *Symbole des Alltags, Alltag der Symbole: Festschrift für Harry Kühnel zum 65. Geburtstag*, edited by G. Blaschitz, H. Hundsbichler, G. Jaritz, and E. Vavra. Graz: ADEVA, 1992.

Klapisch-Zuber, Christiane. "Women and the Family." In *The Medieval World*, edited by Jacques Le Goff. Translated by Lydia G. Cochrane. London: Collins & Brown, 1990.

Kleinschmidt, Harald. *Understanding the Middle Ages: The Transformation of Ideas and Attitudes in the Medieval World*. Woodbridge, UK: Boydell, 2000.

Kłosowska, Anna. *Queer Love in the Middle Ages*. The New Middle Ages. Basingstoke, UK: Palgrave Macmillan, 2005.

Koldeweij, A. M. *Foi et bonne fortune: Parure et dévotion en Flandre médiévale*. Arnhem: Terra Lannoo, 2006.

Koldeweij, A. M. "Lifting the Veil on Pilgrim Badges." In *Pilgrimage Explored*, edited by J. Stopford. Woodbridge, UK: York Medieval Press, 1999.

Koldeweij, Jos. "'Shameless and Naked Images': Obscene Badges as Parodies of Popular Devotion." In *Art and Architecture of Late Medieval Pilgrimage in Northern Europe and the British Isles*, edited by Sarah Blick and Rita Tekippe. Leiden: Brill, 2005.

Koldeweij, Jos. "The Wearing of Significant Badges, Religious and Secular: The Social Meaning of a Behavioural Pattern." In *Showing Status: Representation of Social Positions in the Late Middle Ages*, edited by Wim Blockmans and Antheum Janse. Turnhout: Brepols, 1999.

Kolve, V. A. "Ganymede/*Son of Getron*: Medieval Monasticism and the Drama of Same-Sex Desire." *Speculum* 73 (1998): 1014–67.

Kowaleski, M. "Women's Work in a Market Town: Exeter in the Late Fourteenth Century." In *Women and Work in Preindustrial Europe*, edited by Barbara Hanawalt. Bloomington: Indiana University Press, 1986.

Krafft-Ebbing, R. Psychopathia Sexualis, *with Especial Reference to the Antipathic Sexual Instinct: A Medico-Forensic Study*. Translated by Franklin S. Klaf. New York: Stein and Day, 1965.

Kramer, Heinrich, and Jakob Sprenger. *Malleus Maleficarum*. Translated by M. Summers. London: Arrow, 1971.

Krapp, George Philip, and Elliott V. K. Dobbie, eds. *The Exeter Book*. The Anglo-Saxon Poetic Records 3. New York: Columbia University Press, 1936.

Krekic, Barisa. "*Abominandum Crimen*: Punishment of Homosexuals in Renaissance Dubrovnik." *Viator* 18 (1987): 337–46.

Kruger, Steven F. "Conversion and Medieval Sexual, Religious, and Racial Categories." In *Constructing Medieval Sexuality*, edited by Karma Lochrie, Peggy McCracken, and James A. Schultz. Minneapolis: University of Minnesota Press, 1997.

Kruger, Steven F. "Fetishism, 1927, 1614, 1461." In *The Postcolonial Middle Ages*, edited by Jeffrey Jerome Cohen. New York: St. Martin's Press, 2000.

Kryptadia: Recueil de documents pour servir à l'étude des traditions populaires. Vol. 3. Heilbronn: Henninger Frères, 1886.

Labalme, P. "Sodomy and Venetian Justice in the Renaissance." *Revue d'histoire de droit* 52 (1984): 217–54.

Laeuchli, Samuel. *Power and Sexuality: The Emergence of Canon Law at the Synod of Elvira*. Philadelphia, PA: Temple University Press, 1972.

Landau, David, and Peter Parshall. *The Renaissance Print: 1470–1550*. New Haven, CT: Yale University Press, 1994.

Lansing, Carol. "Donna con Donna? A 1295 Inquest into Female Sodomy." *Studies in Medieval and Renaissance History*, 3rd ser., 2 (2005): 109.

Laqueur, Thomas. *Making Sex: Body and Gender from the Greeks to Freud*. Cambridge, MA: Harvard University Press, 1990.

Lavezzo, Kathy. "Sobs and Sighs between Women: The Homoerotics of Compassion in *The Book of Margery Kempe*." In *Premodern Sexualities*, edited by Louise Fradenburg and Carla Freccero. London: Routledge, 1996.

Lawn, Brian, ed. *The Prose Salernitan Questions Edited from a Bodleian Manuscript (Auct.F.3.10)*. London: Oxford University Press, 1979.

Le Goff, Jacques. *The Medieval Imagination*. Translated by Arthur Goldhammer. Chicago: University of Chicago Press, 1998.

Lemay, Helen Rodnite. "William of Saliceto on Human Sexuality." *Viator* 12 (1981): 165–81.

Lemay, Helen Rodnite. *Women's Secrets: A Translation of Pseudo-Albertus Magnus'* De secretis mulierum *with Commentaries*. Albany: State University of New York Press, 1992.

L'Engle, Susan, and Robert Gibbs. *Illuminating the Law: Legal Manuscripts in Cambridge Collections*. London: Harvey Miller, 2001.

Levin, Eve. *Sex and Society in the World of the Orthodox Slavs, 900–1700*. Ithaca, NY: Cornell University Press, 1989.

Lewis, Suzanne. "Images of Opening, Penetration and Closure in the *Roman de la Rose*." *Word and Image* 8, no. 3 (1992): 215–42.

Lochrie, Karma. "Between Women." In *The Cambridge Companion to Medieval Women's Writing*, edited by Carolyn Dinshaw and David Wallace. Cambridge: Cambridge University Press, 2003.

Lochrie, Karma. *Covert Operations: The Medieval Uses of Secrecy*. Philadelphia: University of Pennsylvania Press, 1999.

Lochrie, Karma. *Heterosyncrasies: Female Sexuality When Normal Wasn't*. Minneapolis: University of Minnesota Press, 2005.

Lochrie, Karma. "Mystical Acts, Queer Tendencies." In *Constructing Medieval Sexuality*, edited by Karma Lochrie, Peggy McCracken, and James A. Schultz. Minneapolis: University of Minnesota Press, 1997.

Lochrie, Karma. "Presumptive Sodomy and Its Exclusions." *Textual Practice* 13, no. 2 (1999): 295–310.

Lochrie, Karma, Peggy McCracken, and James A. Schultz, eds. *Constructing Medieval Sexuality*. Minneapolis: University of Minnesota Press, 1997.

López-Beltrán, M. T. "Las transgresiones a la ideología del honor y la prostitución en Málaga a finales de la edad media." In *Las Mujeres en Andalucía*, edited by M. T. López-Beltrán. Málaga: Servicio de Publicaciones Diputación Provincial de Málaga, 1993.

Lowenstein, L. F. "Fetishes and Their Associated Behavior." *Sexuality and Disability* 20, no. 2 (2002): 135–47.

Luhmann, Niklas. *Love as Passion: The Codification of Intimacy*. Translated by Jeremy Gaines and Doris L. Jones. Stanford, CA: Stanford University Press, 1998.

Lutterbach, Hubertus. *Sexualität im Mittelalter: Eine Kulturstudie anhand von Bußbüchern des 6. bis 12. Jahrhunderts*. Beihefte zum Archiv für Kulturgeschichte H. 43. Cologne: Böhlau, 1999.

Lydgate, John. *The Minor Poems of John Lydgate*. Edited by H. N. MacCracken. EETS os 192. London: Oxford University Press, 1939.

Magnus, Albertus. *On Animals: A Medieval Summa Zoologica*. Edited by K. Kitchell and I. Resnick. Baltimore, MD: Johns Hopkins University Press, 1999.

Mannyng, Robert. *Robert of Brunne's "Handlyng Synne."* Edited by Frederick J. Furnivall. EETS os 119. London: Kegan Paul, Trench, Trübner, 1901.

Margherita, Gayle. *The Romance of Origins: Language and Sexual Difference in Middle English Literature*. Philadelphia: University of Pennsylvania Press, 1994.

Margolin, J. C., and J. Céard. *Rébus de la Renaissance*. Paris: Maisonneuve & Larose, 1986.

Marshall, W. L., and Pamela Kennedy. "Sexual Sadism in Sexual Offenders: An Elusive Diagnosis." *Aggression and Violent Behavior* 8 (2003): 1–22.

Martin, A. Lynn. *Alcohol, Sex, and Gender in Late Medieval and Early Modern Europe*. Basingstoke, UK: Palgrave, 2001.

Massad, Joseph A. *Desiring Arabs*. Chicago: University of Chicago Press, 2007.

Master Gregorius. *The Marvels of Rome*. Translated by John Osborne. Toronto: Pontifical Institute of Mediaeval Studies, 1987.

Matter, E. Ann. "My Sister, My Spouse: Woman-Identified Women in Medieval Christianity." *Journal of Feminist Studies in Religion* 2, no. 1 (1986): 81–93.

McCann, Julius, trans. *Rule of Saint Benedict in Latin and English*. London: Burns Oates, 1952.

McCormick, M. *Origins of the European Economy: Communications and Commerce, AD 300–900*. Cambridge: Cambridge University Press, 2001.

McCracken, Peggy. "Chaste Subjects: Gender, Heroism, and Desire in the Grail Quest." In *Queering the Middle Ages*, edited by Glenn Burger and Steven F. Kruger. Medieval Cultures 27. Minneapolis: University of Minnesota Press, 2001.

McDonald, Nicola, ed. *Medieval Obscenities*. Woodbridge, UK: York Medieval Press, 2006

McGuire, Brian Patrick. *Friendship and Community: The Monastic Experience, 350–1250*. Kalamazoo, MI: Cistercian, 1988.

McLaren, Angus. *Impotence: A Cultural History*. Chicago: University of Chicago Press, 2007.

McNeill, John T., and Helena M. Gamer, eds. *Medieval Handbooks of Penance: A Translation of the Principal* libri poenitentiales *and Selections from Related Documents*. New York: Columbia University Press, 1938.

Mehrez, Samia. "Take Them out of the Ball Game: Egypt's Cultural Players in Crisis." *Middle East Report* 219 (2001): 10–15.

Meiss, Millard. *French Painting in the Time of Jean de Berry: The Boucicaut Master*. With the assistance of Kathleen Morand and Edith W. Kirsch. New York: Phaidon, 1968.

Mellinkoff, Ruth. *Averting Demons: The Protective Power of Medieval Visual Motifs and Themes*. 2 vols. Los Angeles, CA: Ruth Mellinkoff, 2004.

Mengel, D. "From Venice to Jerusalem and Beyond: Milíč of Kroměříž and the Topography of Prostitution in Fourteenth-Century Prague." *Speculum* 79, no. 2 (2004): 407–42.

Menjot, D. "Prostitutas y rufianes en las ciudades castellanas a fines de la Edad Media." *Temas medievales* 4 (1994): 189–204.

Metzler, Irina. *Disability in Medieval Europe: Thinking about Physical Impairment in the High Middle Ages, c. 1100–c. 1400*. London: Routledge, 2006.

Meyerson, M. "Prostitution of Muslim Women in the Kingdom of Valencia: Religious and Sexual Discrimination in a Medieval Plural Society." In *The Medieval Mediterranean: Cross-Cultural Contacts*, edited by M. Chiat and Katherine Reyerson. St. Cloud, MN: North Star Press of St. Cloud, 1988.

Millett, Bella, trans. *Ancrene Wisse: Guide for Anchoresses*. Exeter: University of Exeter Press, 2009.

Millett, Bella, and Jocelyn Wogan-Browne, eds. and trans. *Medieval English Prose for Women from the Katherine Group and* Ancrene Wisse. Oxford: Clarendon Press, 1990.

Mills, Robert. "A Man Is Being Beaten." *New Medieval Literatures* 5 (2002): 115–53.

Mills, Robert. "Male-Male Love and Sex in the Middle Ages, 1000–1500." In *A Gay History of Britain*, edited by Matt Cook, with Robert Mills, Randolph Trumbach, and H. G. Cocks. Oxford: Greenwood, 2007.

Mills, Robert. *Suspended Animation: Pain, Pleasure and Punishment in Medieval Culture*. London: Reaktion, 2005.

Mills, Robert. "'Whatever You Do Is a Delight to Me!' Masculinity, Masochism and Queer Play in Representations of Male Martyrdom." *Exemplaria* 13 (2001): 1–37.

Mirk, John. *Mirk's Festial: A Collection of Homilies*. Edited by Theodore Erbe. EETS es 96. London: Kegan Paul, Trench, Trübner, 1905.

Molina, A. L. "Notas para el estudio de los grupos sociales marginados: La prostitucion en Albacete a finales de La Edad Media." *Congreso de Historia de Albacete* 2 (1984): 1215–22.

Moore, B. "The Reeve's 'Rusty Blade.'" *Medium Ævum* 58 (1959): 304–12.

More, Sir Thomas. *A Dialogue Concerning Heresies*. Vol. 6 of *The Complete Works of Sir Thomas More*. Edited by T.M.C. Lawler, Germain Marc'hadour, and Richard C. Marius. New Haven, CT: Yale University Press, 1981.

Mormando, Franco. *The Preacher's Demons: Bernardino of Siena and the Social Underworld of Early Renaissance Italy*. Chicago: University of Chicago Press, 1999.

Morrison, Susan Signe. *Women Pilgrims in Late Medieval England: Private Piety as Public Performance*. London: Routledge, 2000.

Muchembled, Robert. "The Order of Gestures: A Social History of Sensibilities under the Ancien Régime in France." In *A Cultural History of Gesture from Antiquity to the Present Day*, edited by Jan Bremmer and Herman Roodenburg. Oxford: Polity Press, 1991.

Murdoch, Brian, ed. and trans. *The Dedalus Book of Medieval Literature: The Grin of the Gargoyle*. Sawtry, UK: Dedalus, 1995.

Murray, Jacqueline. "Twice Marginal and Twice Invisible: Lesbians in the Middle Ages." In *Handbook of Medieval Sexuality*, edited by Vern L. Bullough and James A. Brundage. New York: Garland, 1996.

Murray, James M. *Bruges, Cradle of Capitalism, 1280–1390*. Cambridge: Cambridge University Press, 2005.

Nicholas, D. *The Later Medieval City*. London: Longman, 1997.

Nirenberg, D. *Communities of Violence: Persecution of Minorities in the Middle Ages*. Princeton, NJ: Princeton University Press, 1996.

Noffke, Suzanne, trans. *Catherine of Siena: The Dialogue*. The Classics of Western Spirituality. New York: Paulist Press, 1980.

Nordal, Sigurður, et al., eds. *Flateyjarbók*. 4 vols. Akranes: Flateyjarútgáfan, 1944–1945.

O'Meara, John J., trans. and ed. *The History and Topography of Ireland by Gerald of Wales: Topographia Hiberniae*. Harmondsworth, UK: Penguin, 1982.

Oppel, J. "Saint Jerome and the History of Sex." *Viator* 24 (1993): 1–22.

Otis, Leah. "Prostitution and Repentance in Late Medieval Perpignan." In *Women of the Medieval World: Essays in Honor of John H. Mundy*, edited by Julius Kirshner and Suzanne Wemple. Oxford: Blackwell, 1985.

Otis, Leah. *Prostitution in Medieval Society*. Chicago: University of Chicago Press, 1985.

Otis-Cour, Leah. "La tenancière de la maison publique de Millau au XVe siècle." In *La femme dans l'histoire et la société méridionales (IX–XIX s.)*. Montpellier: Fédération historique du Languedoc méditerranéen, 1995.

Ovid. *The Metamorphoses of Ovid.* Translated by William Caxton. New York: George
  Braziller in association with Magdalene College, Cambridge, 1968.
Owst, G. R. *Literature and Pulpit in Medieval England.* Oxford: Blackwell, 1961.
Padgug, Robert. "Sexual Matters: On Conceptualizing Sexuality in History." *Radical
  History Review* 20 (1979): 3–23.
Panofsky, Erwin. *Early Netherlandish Painting: Its Origins and Character.* Vol. 1. 1953.
  Reprint, New York: Harper and Row, 1971.
Park, Katharine. "Medicine and Magic: The Healing Arts." In *Gender and Society
  in Renaissance Italy,* edited by Judith C. Brown and Robert C. Davis. London:
  Addison Wesley, 1998.
Partner, Nancy F. "Did Mystics Have Sex?" In *Desire and Discipline: Sex and Sexual-
  ity in the Premodern West,* edited by Jacqueline Murray and Konrad Eisenbichler.
  Toronto: University of Toronto Press, 1996.
Pavan, E. "Police des moeurs, société et politique à Venise à la fin du Moyen Age."
  Revue Historique 264, no. 2 (1980): 241–88.
Payer, Pierre J. *The Bridling of Desire: Views of Sex in the Later Middle Ages.* Toronto:
  University of Toronto Press, 1993.
Payer, Pierre J. "Confession and the Study of Sex in the Middle Ages." In *Handbook of
  Medieval Sexuality,* edited by Vern L. Bullough and James A. Brundage. New York:
  Garland, 1996.
Payer, Pierre J. "Sex and Confession in the Thirteenth Century." In *Sex in the Middle
  Ages: A Book of Essays,* edited by Joyce E. Salisbury. New York: Garland, 1991.
Payer, Pierre J. *Sex and the New Medieval Literature of Confession, 1150–1300.*
  Toronto: Pontifical Institute of Mediaeval Studies, 2009.
Payer, Pierre J. *Sex and the Penitentials: The Development of a Sexual Code, 550–1150.*
  Toronto: University of Toronto Press, 1984.
Penney, James. *The World of Perversion: Psychoanalysis and the Impossible Absolute
  of Desire.* New York: State University of New York Press, 2006.
Peraldus, William. *Summa de vitiis et virtutibus, tractatus de luxuria.* Venice: Paganinus
  de Paganinis, 1497.
Perry, Mary Elizabeth. *Gender and Disorder in Early Modern Seville.* Princeton, NJ:
  Princeton University Press, 1990.
Plutarch. *Quaestiones Convivales: Plutarch's Moralia VIII.* Translated by Paul A.
  Clement and H. B. Hoffleit. Loeb Classical Library. Cambridge, MA: Harvard
  University Press, 1969.
Porette, Margaret. *The Mirror of Simple Souls.* Translated by Edmund College, J. C. Mar-
  ler, and Judith Grant. Notre Dame, IN: University of Notre Dame Press, 1999.
Porter, Roy. *The Greatest Benefit to Mankind.* London: HarperCollins, 1997.
Post, J. "A Fifteenth-Century Customary of the Southwark Stews." *Journal of the
  Society of Archivists* 5 (1977): 418–28.
Postles, David. *Talking Ballocs: Nicknames and English Medieval Sociolinguistics.*
  Leicester: University of Leicester, Centre for English Local History, 2003.
Preus, Anthony. "Galen's Criticism of Aristotle's Conception Theory." *Journal of the
  History of Biology* 10, no. 1 (1977): 65–85.
Price, Leah. "The Tangible Page." *London Review of Books* 24, no. 21 (2002): 36–39.

Puff, Helmut. "Female Sodomy: The Trial of Katherina Hetzeldorfer (1477)." *Journal of Medieval and Early Modern Studies* 30, no. 1 (2000): 41–61.

Puff, Helmut. *Sodomy in Reformation Germany and Switzerland, 1400–1600.* Chicago: University of Chicago Press, 2003.

Pugh, Tison, ed. *Queering Medieval Genres.* The New Middle Ages. New York: Palgrave Macmillan, 2004.

Rasmussen, Anne Marie. *Wandering Genitalia: Sexuality and the Body in German Culture between the Late Middle Ages and Early Modernity.* King's College London Medieval Studies. London: Centre for Late Antique and Medieval Studies, 2009.

Raymond of Capua. *The Life of St. Catherine of Siena.* Trans. George Lamb. New York: P. J. Kenedy.

Rawcliffe, Carole. *Leprosy in Medieval England.* Woodbridge, UK: Boydell, 2006.

Rawcliffe, Carole. *Medicine and Society in Later Medieval England.* Stroud, UK: Sutton, 1995.

Reaney, Percy Hide, and Richard Middlewood Wilson. *A Dictionary of English Surnames.* London: Routledge, 1991.

Reyerson, K. "Prostitution in Medieval Montpelier: The Ladies of Campus Polverel." *Medieval Prosopography* 18 (1997): 209–28.

Richards, Jeffrey. *Sex, Dissidence and Damnation: Minority Groups in the Middle Ages.* London: Routledge, 1990.

Riches, Samantha. *St. George: Hero, Martyr and Myth.* Stroud, UK: Sutton, 2000.

Ridderbos, Barnhard. "Objects and Questions." In *Early Netherlandish Paintings: Rediscovery, Reception, and Research*, edited by Anne van Buren Ridderbos and Henk van Veen. Los Angeles, CA: J. Paul Getty Museum, 2005.

Riddle, J. M. *Contraception and Abortion from the Ancient World to the Renaissance.* Cambridge, MA: Harvard University Press, 1992.

Riddy, Felicity. "Engendering Pity in the *Franklin's Tale*." In *Feminist Readings in Middle English Literature*, edited by Ruth Evans and Lesley Johnson. London: Routledge, 1994.

Rigg, A. G., ed. and trans. *Gawain on Marriage: The Textual Tradition of the* De Coniuge Non Ducenda. Toronto: Pontifical Institute of Mediaeval Studies, 1986.

Roberts, S. E. *The Legal Triads of Medieval Wales.* Cardiff: University of Wales Press, 2007.

Rocke, Michael. *Forbidden Friendships: Homosexuality and Male Culture in Renaissance Florence.* Oxford: Oxford University Press, 1996.

The Rohan Book of Hours: Bibliothèque Nationale, Paris (MS Latin 9471). Introduction by Millard Meiss. Introduction and commentaries by Marcel Thomas. London: Thames and Hudson, 1973.

Rolle, Richard. *The Psalter, or Psalms of David and Certain Canticles with a Translation and Exposition in English by Richard Rolle of Hampole*, edited by H. R. Bramley. Oxford: Clarendon Press, 1884.

Rollo-Koster, J. "From Prostitutes to Brides of Christ: The Avignonese *Repenties* in the Late Middle Ages." *Journal of Medieval and Early Modern Studies* 32, no. 1 (2002): 109–44.

Roper, L. "Discipline and Respectability: Prostitution and the Reformation in Augsburg." *History Workshop* 19 (1985): 3–28.

Roques, Mario, ed. *Le roman de Renart*. 6 vols. Paris: Champion, 1951–1963.

Rosenthal, Franz. "Male and Female: Described and Compared." In *Homoeroticism in Classical Arabic Literature*, edited by J. W. Wright and Everett Rowson. New York: Columbia University Press, 1997.

Rossiaud, Jacques. *Medieval Prostitution*. Translated by Lydia G. Cochrane. New York: Barnes and Noble, 1996.

Ross, D.J.A. *Illustrated Medieval Alexander Books in Germany and the Netherlands*. Cambridge: MHRA, 1971.

Roth, Norman. "'Deal Gently with the Young Man': Love of Boys in Medieval Hebrew Poetry of Spain." *Speculum* 57 (1982): 20–51.

Rouse, Robert. *The Idea of Anglo-Saxon England in Middle English Romance*. Cambridge: Brewer, 2005.

Rowland, Beryl. *Medieval Woman's Guide to Health: The First English Gynecological Handbook*. London: Croom Helm, 1981.

Rowson, Everett. "The Categorization of Gender and Sexual Irregularity in Medieval Arabic Vice Lists." In *Body Guards: The Cultural Politics of Gender Ambiguity*, edited by Julia Epstein and Kristina Straub. New York: Routledge, 1991.

Rowson, Everett. "Gender Irregularity as Entertainment: Institutionalized Transvestism at the Caliphal Court in Medieval Baghdad." In *Gender and Difference in the Middle Ages*, edited by Sharon Farmer and Carol Braun Pasternack. Minneapolis: University of Minnesota Press, 2003.

Rowson, Everett. "Homoerotic Liaisons among the Mamluk Elite in Late Medieval Egypt and Syria." In *Islamicate Sexualities: Translations across Temporal Geographies of Desire*, edited by Kathryn Babayan and Afsaneh Najmabadi. Harvard Middle Eastern Monographs. Cambridge, MA: Harvard University Press, 2008.

Rubin, Stanley. *Medieval English Medicine*. New York: Barnes and Noble, 1974.

Ruggiero, Guido. *The Boundaries of Eros: Sex Crime and Sexuality in Renaissance Venice*. New York: Oxford University Press, 1985.

Russell, John. *Book of Carving and Nurture*. In *Early English Meals and Manners*. Edited by Frederick J. Furnivall. EETS os 32. Oxford: Oxford University Press, 1868.

Saenger, Paul. "Silent Reading: Its Impact on Late Medieval Script and Society." *Viator* 13 (1982): 367–414.

Salih, Sarah. "Sexual Identities: A Medieval Perspective." In *Sodomy in Early Modern Europe*, edited by Tom Betteridge. Manchester: Manchester University Press, 2002.

Salih, Sarah. *Versions of Virginity in Late Medieval England*. Cambridge: Brewer, 2001.

Salih, Sarah. "When Is a Bosom Not a Bosom? Problems with 'Erotic Mysticism.'" In *Medieval Virginities*, edited by Anke Bernau, Ruth Evans, and Sarah Salih. Cardiff: University of Wales Press, 2003.

Salih, Sarah, Anke Bernau, and Ruth Evans. "Introduction: Virginity and Virginity Studies." In *Medieval Virginities*, edited by Anke Bernau, Ruth Evans, and Sarah Salih. Cardiff: University of Wales Press, 2003.

Salisbury, Joyce E. "Bestiality in the Middle Ages." In *Sex in the Middle Ages: A Book of Essays*, Joyce E. Salisbury 173–86. New York: Garland, 1991.

Sandler, Lucy Freeman. "The Handclasp in the *Arnolfini Wedding*: A Manuscript Precedent." *Art Bulletin* 66, no. 3 (1984): 488–91.

Saslow, James M. *Pictures and Passions: A History of Homosexuality in the Visual Arts*. Harmondsworth, UK: Viking, 1999.

Sauer, Michelle. "Representing the Negative: Positing the Lesbian Void in Medieval Anchoritism." *Thirdspace* 3, no. 2 (2004), http://www.thirdspace.ca/journal/article/view/sauer/178 (accessed December 31, 2009).

Saunders, Corinne. "A Matter of Consent: Middle English Romance and the Law of *Raptus*." In *Medieval Women and the Law*, edited by Noël James Menuge. Woodbridge, UK: Boydell, 2000.

Sautman, Francesca Canadé. "Just Like a Woman': Queer History, Womanizing the Body, and the Boys in Arnaud's Band." In *Queering the Middle Ages*, edited by Glenn Burger and Steven F. Kruger. Minneapolis: University of Minnesota Press, 2001.

Scanlon, Larry. "Cultural Studies and Carnal Speech: The Long, Profane Shadow of the Fabliau." In *Medieval Cultural Studies*, edited by Ruth Evans, Helen Fulton, and David Matthews. Cardiff: University of Wales Press, 2006.

Schirmann, J. "The Ephebe in Medieval Hebrew Poetry." *Sefarad* 1 (1955): 55–68.

Schmidt, A.V.C., ed. *The Vision of Piers Plowman: A Critical Edition of the B-Text*. London: Dent, 1978.

Schultz, James. *Courtly Love, the Love of Courtliness, and the History of Sexuality*. Chicago: University of Chicago Press, 2006.

Schultz, James. "Heterosexuality as a Threat to Medieval Studies." *Journal of the History of Sexuality* 15, no. 1 (2006): 14–29.

Schuster, Beate. "L'imaginaire de la prostitution et la société urbaine en Allemagne (XIII–XVIe siècles)." *Médiévales: Langue, textes, histoire* 27 (1994): 75–93.

Schuster, Peter. *Das Frauenhaus: Städtische Bordelle in Deutschland (1350–1600)*. Paderborn: Ferdinand Schöningh, 1992.

Sedgwick, Eve Kosofsky. *Between Men: English Literature and Male Homosocial Desire*. New York: Columbia University Press, 1985.

Sensi, Mario. "Anchorites in the Italian Tradition." Translated by Ruth Evans. In *Anchoritic Traditions of Medieval Europe*, edited by Liz Herbert McAvoy. Woodbridge, UK: Boydell & Brewer, 2010.

Sheehan, Michael. *Marriage, Family, and Law in Medieval Europe: Collected Studies*, edited by James K. Farge. Cardiff: University of Wales Press, 1996.

Skelton, John. *The Bowge of Courte*. in *John Skelton: The Complete English Poems*. Edited by J. Scattergood. Harmondsworth, UK: Penguin, 1983.

Smeken, Jan. *Dwonder van Claren ijse en snee: Een verloren en teruggevonden gedicht*. Edited by Rena Pennink and Dirk Enklaar. Gravenhage: Martinus Nijhoff, 1946.

Smithies, G. V., ed. *Kyng Alisaunder*. EETS os 227. London: Oxford University Press, 1952.

Socin, Adolf. *Mittelhochdeutsches Namenbuch: Nach oberrheinischen Quellen des 12. und 13. Jahrhunderts*. Basel: Helbing & Lichtenhahn, 1903.

Sofer, Jehoeda. "Sodomy in the Law of Muslim States." In *Sexuality and Eroticism among Males in Moslem Societies*, edited by Arno Schmitt and Jehoeda Sofer. New York: Haworth Press, 1992.

Speelberg, Femke, and Jacoline Zilverschoon. *"Zotheid" in de duisternis: Middeleeu-wse tekeneingen in de Sint-Pietersberg*. Rotterdam: Nijmegen University Press, 2007.

Stehling, Thomas, ed. *Medieval Latin Poems of Male Love and Friendship*. New York: Garland, 1984.

Stevenson, J. *Chronicon de Lanercost*. Edinburgh: Bannatyne and Maitland Clubs, 1839.

Storer, Edward, trans. *The Facetiae of Poggio and Other Medieval Story-Tellers*. London: Routledge, 1928.

Sudhoff, K. "Antike Votivgaben, die weiblichen Genitalorgane darstellend." *Monats-schrift für Geburtshilfe und Gynäkologie* 38 (1914): 185–199.

Swanton, Michael, trans. "The Deeds of Hereward." In *Medieval Outlaws: Ten Tales in Modern English*, edited by Thomas H. Ohlgren. Stroud, UK: Sutton, 1998.

"A Talk of Ten Wives on Their Husbands' Ware." In *The Trials and Joys of Marriage*, ed. Eve Salisbury. Kalamazoo, MI: Medieval Institute, 2002.

Tanke, John W. "*Wonfeax wale*: Ideology and Figuration in the Sexual Riddles of the Exeter Book." In *Class and Gender in Early English Literature: Intersections*, edited by Britton J. Harwood and Gillian R. Overing. Bloomington: Indiana University Press, 1994.

Tannahill, Reay. *Sex in History*. London: Hamish Hamilton, 1980.

Tanner, Norman P., ed. *Heresy Trials in the Diocese of Norwich, 1428–31*. Camden Society 4.20. London: Royal Historical Society, 1977.

Tasioulas, J. A. *The Makars: The Poems of Henryson, Dunbar, and Douglas*. Edinburgh: Canongate, 1999.

Taylor, A. "Reading the Dirty Bits." In *Desire and Discipline: Sex and Sexuality in the Premodern West*, edited by Jacqueline Murray and Konrad Eisenbichler. Toronto: University of Toronto Press, 1996.

Tertullian. *The Writings of Tertullian*. Vol. 3. Translated by S. Thelwell. Edinburgh: T. and T. Clark, 1895.

Thomas, A. H., ed. *Calendar of Plea and Memoranda Rolls ... of the ... City of London*. 3 vols. Cambridge: Cambridge University Press, 1926–1932.

Thompson, Anne B. *Everyday Saints and the Art of Narrative in the South English Legendary*. Aldershot, UK: Ashgate, 2003.

Thompson, E. P. *Customs in Common*. New York: Norton, 1991.

Tinkle, Theresa. *Medieval Venuses and Cupids: Sexuality, Hermeneutics, and English Poetry*. Stanford, CA: Stanford University Press, 1996.

Tolkien, J.R.R., and E. V. Gordon, ed. and trans. *Sir Gawain and the Green Knight*. Revised by Norman Davis. 2nd ed. Oxford: Clarendon Press, 1967.

Traub, Valerie. "Friendship's Loss: Alan Bray's Making of History." *GLQ* 10, no. 3 (2004): 339–65.

Traub, Valerie. *The Renaissance of Lesbianism in Early Modern England*. Cambridge: Cambridge University Press, 2002.

Trexler, Richard C. "Florentine Prostitution in the Fifteenth Century." In *The Women of Renaissance Florence*. Binghamton, NY: Medieval and Renaissance Texts and Studies, 1993.

Trexler, Richard C. "Gendering Jesus Crucified." In *Iconography at the Crossroads*, edited by Brendan Cassidy. Princeton, NJ: Princeton University, 1993.

Uebel, Michael. "The Pathogenesis of Medieval History." *Texas Studies in Language and Literature* 44, no. 1 (2002): 47–65.

Uther, Hans-Jörg. *The Types of International Folktales: A Classification and Bibliography*. Helsinki: Suomalainen Tiedeakatemia, 2004.

Van Beuningen, H.J.E., A. M. Koldeweij, and D. Kicken, eds. *Heilig en Profaan 1: 1200 Laatmiddeleeuwse insignes uit openbare en particuliere collectives*. Rotterdam Papers 8. Cothen: Stichting Middeleeuwse religieuze en profane insignes, 1993.

Van Beuningen, H.J.E., A. M. Koldeweij, and D. Kicken, eds. *Heilig en Profaan 2: 1200 Laatmiddeleeuwse insignes uit openbare en particuliere collectives*. Rotterdam Papers 12. Cothen: Stichting Middeleeuwse religieuze en profane insignes, 2001.

Van der Meer, Theo. "Medieval Prostitution and the Case of a (Mistaken) Sexual Identity." *Journal of Women's History* 11, no. 2 (1999): 178–85.

Veith, I. *Hysteria: The History of a Disease*. Chicago: University of Chicago Press, 1965.

Vintler, Hans. *Blumen der Tugend*. Edited by Ignaz von Zingerle. Innsbrück: Wagner'sche Universitäts-Buchhandlung, 1874.

Vitz, Evelyn Birge. "Erotic Reading in the Middle Ages: Performance and the Re-performance of Romance." In *Performing Medieval Narrative*, edited by Evelyn Birge Vitz, Nancy Freeman Regalado, and Marilyn Lawrence. Cambridge: Brewer, 2005.

Von der Hagen, F. H. *Gesamtabenteuer: Hundert altdeutsche Erzählungen*. Darmstadt: Wissenschaftliche Buchgesellschaft, 1961.

Von Keller, A., ed. *Fastnachtspiele aus dem fünfzehnten Jahrhundert*. Stuttgart: Anton Hiersemann, 1853.

Wack, M. *Lovesickness in the Middle Ages: The Viaticum and Its Commentaries*. Philadelphia: University of Pennsylvania Press, 1990.

Wafer, Jim. "Vision and Passion." In *Islamic Homosexualities: Culture, History, and Literature*, edited by Stephen O. Murray and Will Roscoe. New York: New York University Press, 1997.

Walsh, Martin W. "*Babio:* Towards a Performance Reconstruction of Secular Farce in Twelfth-Century England." In *England in the Twelfth Century: Proceedings of the 1988 Harlaxton Symposium*, edited by Daniel Williams. Woodbridge, UK: Boydell, 1990.

Ward-Perkins, J. B. *London Museum Medieval Catalogue*. London: HMSO, 1940.

Warner, Michael. *The Trouble with Normal: Sex, Politics, and the Ethics of Queer Life*. New York: Free Press, 1999.

Warner, Michael, and Lauren Berlant. "Sex in Public." In *Publics and Counterpublics*, edited by Michael Warner. New York: Zone, 2002.

Watt, Diane. *Amoral Gower*. Minneapolis: University of Minnesota Press, 2003.

Watt, Diane. *The Paston Women: Selected Letters*. Cambridge: Brewer, 2004.

Webb, Peter. *The Erotic Arts*. London: Secker and Warburg, 1975.

Weekley, Ernest. *Surnames*. New York: Dutton, 1916.

Weir, Anthony, and James Jerman. *Images of Lust: Sexual Carvings on Medieval Churches.* London: Routledge, 1999.

Wemple, Suzanne F. "Consent and Dissent to Sexual Intercourse in Germanic Societies from the Fifth to the Tenth Century." In *Consent and Coercion to Sex and Marriage in Ancient and Medieval Societies,* edited by Angeliki E. Laiou. Washington, DC: Dumbarton Oaks Research Library and Collection, 1993.

Wemple, Suzanne F. *Women in Frankish Society: Marriage and the Cloister, 500–900.* Philadelphia: University of Pennsylvania Press, 1981.

Wenzel, Siegfried, ed. and trans. *Fasciculus Morum: A Fourteenth-Century Preacher's Handbook.* University Park: Pennsylvania State University Press, 1989.

Wheatley, Edward. "A River Runs through It: Disability, Homosexuality, Queered/ Disabled Discourse, and the Isle of Blandie in *Bérinus.*" *Exemplaria* 19, no. 3 (2007): 386–401.

Wiesner, M. *Working Women in Renaissance Germany.* New Brunswick, NJ: Rutgers University Press, 1986.

Wiethaus, Ulrike. "Female Homoerotic Discourse and Religion in Medieval Germanic Culture." In *Gender and Difference in the Middle Ages,* edited by Sharon Farmer and Carol Braun Pasternack. Medieval Cultures 32. Minneapolis: University of Minnesota Press, 2003.

William of Conches. *De philosophia mundi. PL* 172.

William of Conches. *Dragmaticon.* Edited by G. Gratarolus. Frankfurt: Minerva, 1967.

Williams, Linda. *Hard Core: Power, Pleasure, and the "Frenzy of the Visible."* Berkeley: University of California Press, 1989.

Wright, J. W. "Masculine Allusion and the Structure of Satire in Early 'Abbāsid Poetry." In *Homoeroticism in Classical Arabic Literature,* edited by J. W. Wright and Everett Rowson. New York: Columbia University Press, 1997.

Wright, J. W., and Everett K. Rowson, eds. *Homoeroticism in Classical Arabic Literature.* New York: Columbia University Press, 1997.

Žižek, Slavoj. *The Metastases of Enjoyment: On Women and Causality.* London: Verso, 2005.

CONTRIBUTORS

Ruth Evans is Dorothy McBride Orthwein Chair of English at Saint Louis University. She is a fellow of the English Association and sits on the advisory boards of *Exemplaria* and *Social Semiotics*, and on the editorial boards of *Literature Compass* and Manchester University Press Medieval Literature Series. She is the co-editor (with Anke Bernau and Sarah Salih) of *Medieval Virginities*, (with Helen Fulton and David Matthews) of *Medieval Cultural Studies* and (with Terence Hughes and Georges Letissier) *Secrets, Mysteries and Silences*. She is currently finishing a book on Chaucer and memory.

Malcolm Jones is a leading authority on medieval folklore and folk customs. Until recently, he was a lecturer in folklore and folklife studies at the University of Sheffield. He is the author of *The Secret Middle Ages: Discovering the Real Medieval World*. He is currently completing a book on English sixteenth- and seventeenth-century prints for Yale University Press.

Karma Lochrie is Ruth N. Halls Professor of English and chair of the Department of Gender Studies at Indiana University. She is the author of *Heterosyncrasies: Female Sexuality When Normal Wasn't* and *Covert Operations: The Medieval Uses of Secrecy*, and she is co-editor, with James Schultz and Peggy McCracken, of *Constructing Medieval Sexuality*.

Irina Metzler is research fellow in the Department of History, University of Swansea, and was previously an independent scholar based in Bristol. She has written on medieval hermaphrodites and intersex in the European Middle Ages and is the author of *Disability in Medieval Europe Thinking about Physical Impairment in the High Middle Ages, c.1100–c.1400*.

Robert Mills is senior lecturer in the Department of English, King's College London. He is the author of *Suspended Animation: Pain, Pleasure and Punishment in Medieval Culture*, and the co-editor of *Troubled Vision: Gender, Sexuality, and Sight in Medieval Text and Image* and *The Monstrous Middle Ages*. He contributed the chapter "Male-Male Love and Sex in the Middle Ages, 1000–1500" to *A Gay History of Britain: Love and Sex between Men Since the Middle Ages*.

Kevin Mummey is a doctoral candidate and graduate instructor at the University of Minnesota. He is currently working on his dissertation, a study of women slaveholders on the island of Mallorca in the late-fourteenth century.

Cory James Rushton is assistant professor of English at St. Francis Xavier University, Nova Scotia, Canada. His publications include *The Erotic in the Literature of Medieval Britain* and *A Companion to Medieval Popular Romance* (of both of which he was co-editor), and articles on various aspects of the Arthurian legend. He is currently editing a book on medieval disability and law for Cambridge Scholar's Press.

Sarah Salih is senior lecturer in the Department of English, King's College London. She has published widely on virginity, sexuality, and gender in the late Middle Ages. Her publications include *Versions of Virginity in Late Medieval England* and *A Companion to Middle English Hagiography* (as editor), and (as co-editor) *Medieval Virginities, Gender and Holiness: Men, Women and Saints in Late Medieval Europe* and *Julian of Norwich's Legacy: Medieval Mysticism and Postmedieval Reception*.

Jacqueline A. Tasioulas is fellow and senior lecturer in English at Clare College, Cambridge. She is the editor of *The Makars: The Poems of Henryson, Dunbar and Douglas*; and co-editor of *The Apocryphal Lives of Adam and Eve*. She is the author of various articles on medieval literature and science, including "Heaven and Earth in Little Space: The Foetal Existence of Christ in Medieval Literature and Thought."

INDEX